Essays in Russian Literature

THE CONSERVATIVE VIEW

ESSAYS
IN RUSSIAN
LITERATURE

The Conservative View:
Leontiev · Rozanov · Shestov

SELECTED, EDITED, TRANSLATED
AND WITH AN INTRODUCTION BY

Spencer E. Roberts

ATHENS

Ohio University Press

1968

ACKNOWLEDGMENTS

Grateful acknowledgment is made to the following publishers for permission to reprint excerpts from copyrighted materials:

George Allen and Unwin Ltd., London, and Russell and Russell, New York: Friedrich Nietzsche, *The Complete Works of Friedrich Nietzsche*, Edited by Dr. Oscar Levy, Eighteen vols., (1909–11).

Geoffrey Bles Ltd., London: Nicolas Berdyaev, *Leontiev*, Translated by George Reavey, (1940).

Hillary House Publishers, Ltd., New York: Renato Poggioli, *Rozanov*, (1962).

Alfred Knopf, Inc., (Random House), New York: D. S. Mirsky, *Contemporary Russian Literature, 1881–1925*, (1926).

CONTENTS

❦

INTRODUCTION

🌣

AT a time when the mainstream of Russian thought was
turned toward the common weal, Konstantin Leontiev,
Vasily Rozanov, and Lev Shestov devoted their efforts to the
individual personality. Their concern was not suffering humanity, but their own personal destiny, their own relation to
eternity. They tended, moreover, to ignore the moral precepts
so dear to the hearts of their contemporaries, either flaunting
them immorally or by-passing them altogether. As a result, their
Russian contemporaries largely ignored them, and the present-
day Soviets speak of them with contempt—if, indeed, they
speak of them at all. *The Great Soviet Encyclopedia* mentions
only Rozanov, and then merely to accuse him of having distorted Gogol. In the English-speaking world, their fate has been
little better: only a smattering of their writings has been translated. This is regrettable, since their philosophical views are
unquestionably interesting and original, and their criticism of
Russian literature is as perceptive as any.

Of the three, KONSTANTIN LEONTIEV (1831–1891) has
perhaps aroused the greatest antagonism. After all, in an age
of humanitarianism, what is one to think of someone who
regarded egalitarianism as one of the greatest evils; who insisted that social injustices are necessary for the development
of great and strong characters; who believed that despotism is
the basic prerequisite of a "flowering life," of truth and of
beauty; who opposed universal education on the grounds that

[vii]

it stifles national originality; who taught that happiness for everyone is unattainable on this earth; who loved and idealized war?

The Russian philosopher Berdyaev characterized him well when he called him "the precursor of Nietzsche" and listed the following mutual traits: "their aesthetic passion for destiny, their cult of force and aspiration for power, their aristocratism and vital tension, their way of basing the hierarchy of values on violence, their amoralism, their love for a flourishing culture, their fear of cultural decadence, their taste for cruelty placed at the service of the highest values, and their Renaissance attitude."

Leontiev's early life on the small family estate in the province of Kaluga was dominated by his mother, who instilled in him a love of conservatism and the monarchy. At the University of Moscow, where he studied medicine at her insistence, he held himself aloof from his fellow students, preferring to make friends outside the academic community—especially with young women. He was a very handsome man who could attract almost any woman he pleased, and one of his many affairs lasted five years. Marriage, however, terrified him, because of the loss of freedom he believed it entailed and because, he felt, it would destroy the poetry of life. In order to liberate himself completely, he broke off his five-year relationship with his Moscow girl friend, as well as a close friendship with a man, and thereafter confined himself to numerous short-term affairs.

Leontiev's interest in writing developed early, and at the age of twenty-one he completed his first full-length work, a comedy, which he submitted to Turgenev for appraisal. Turgenev recognized his talent and called his work "essentially morbid, but excellent." From then until the end of his life, except for a few brief intervals, Leontiev devoted most of his spare time to writing both fiction and nonfiction.

When the Crimean War broke out, he was granted his medical degree ahead of time and sent to the front as a military surgeon. This experience had a strong influence on his personality: he rid himself of the melancholy that had pursued him from childhood and became more virile. Here, also, he began to develop his theory of aesthetic immoralism.

After the war, he continued his medical practice for two years on the country estate of a chance acquaintance, the Baroness Rozen, but the quiet life proved deadening, so he went to Petersburg to devote himself completely to writing. With his limited financial means and his love of luxury, this was not easy; he soon had to supplement his income by giving lessons and by translating. Isolation continued to distinguish his life in the capital. The intelligentsia, who ordinarily would have been his closest friends, were for the most part fervently dedicated to liberal and democratic ideas, but to him, these ideas meant nothing; indeed they aroused his antagonism. He was interested only in his cult of beauty, and as a result he soon found himself alienated from the outstanding talents of the day.

In 1861, despite his earlier horror of personal enslavement, Leontiev suddenly left for Theodosia, where he married a Greek girl with whom he had had an affair during the war. (Illiterate and unintelligent, she had little in common with him, and their marriage was fated to become sheer torment for them both.) The extra financial burden forced him to give up his free-lance work and take a job that was offered him in the diplomatic service. His first assignment was in the Russian Consulate in Crete; appointments to various other posts in Greece and Turkey followed. These were the happiest years of his life—years of enchantment with the primitive and colorful life of the East, of numerous love affairs with native girls, and of productivity in his creative endeavors as he developed the philosophy of history and society which he was to defend vigorously almost to the end of his days.

According to his theory, civilizations, like human organisms, pass through three inevitable stages: 1) a primary simplicity; 2) a flowering complexity; and 3) final disintegration and death, preceded by a simplification of component parts, a decrease in the number of distinct parts, a weakening of central unity and vigor, and increased confusion. Everything is slowly lowered, mixed, and blended. Inwardly, the dying organism grows more uniform; outwardly, it begins to resemble its surrounding environment. In the human organism, Leontiev asserts, these stages correspond to the life of the embryo, to life itself, and to decomposition after death, when the body is again broken down into its constituent elements—nitrogen, hydrogen, oxygen, et cetera.

Everything in this process is predetermined, he believes, but in the case of civilizations man can slow it down, thus prolonging the period of flowering complexity. This period, a time when beauty rises to its greatest heights, is accompanied by a varied social structure, inequality of classes, and a strong aristocracy. It has great contrasts: poverty and richness, suffering and joy, injustice and justice—all united by a certain inner despotic unity. "Unity in variety," Leontiev says, "is the fundamental law of beauty." But when equality, brotherhood, and freedom are granted the people, the third stage sets in, and everything tends to become more alike and uniform. Although many consider this a period of progress, Leontiev says it is nothing more than the beginning of disintegration and decay. "Nothing truly great, lofty, and durable," he contends, "is achieved through epidemic liberty and equality, but only through a variety of situations, education, impressions, and rights, in a milieu unified by some higher and sacred authority." To him, that authority is the State and the Church, the latter being more powerful.

Values such as the Church, the State, and culture transcend personal values in his philosophy. They are completely incompatible with the idea of humanity. Bliss and absolute truth are not man's vocation on earth; therefore, as Leontiev puts it: "There is nothing terrible in the idea that millions of Russians have been obliged to live under the pressure of 'three atmospheres'—that of the bureaucracy, that of the landowners, and that of the Church—if only to enable Pushkin to write his *Eugene Onegin* and *Boris Godunov*, the Kremlin to be built, and Suvorov and Kutuzov to win their national victories. For glory, military glory . . . yes, the military glory of the Empire and the people, their art and poetry, are undeniable *facts, the real phenomena* of real nature. And as objectives, they are both lofty and attainable. But as to the godlessly righteous and vapidly blissful humanity to which you aspire in your tortuous 'modern' way, such a humanity would be eternally vile."

According to Leontiev, Europe had already experienced its period of flowering complexity—from the eleventh to the eighteenth century—and was now entering the stage of disintegration, the process having been hastened along by bourgeois liberals, who, by insisting on equality and liberty, had destroyed much of the variety of life. But the East, perhaps even Russia, still had a chance to prolong this period if it renounced the idea of universal happiness and relied on Byzantinism, which stands for autocracy in government and a Christianity quite different from that of the West with all its schisms and sects. He asks: "How can living poetry survive without mysticism and religious pomp, without the pageantry and the severities of the State, without a brilliant and firmly established nobility? Will it not become the poetry of *happiness for all, that of rational bourgeois contentment?*"

During his years in the diplomatic service, Leontiev wrote prolifically, the best work of the period being *A Husband's Confession* (1866). This was a rather daring book for the time: a middle-aged man, unable to satisfy his young wife, encourages her to have an affair with another man so that she can live a rich, full life. Leontiev later rejected it for its immorality.

During these years, too, his wife began to show early symptoms of madness, intensified, no doubt, by jealousy of her husband's many woman friends.

In 1871, Leontiev fell seriously ill, and at the same time

experienced a deep spiritual crisis. Death and damnation haunted him. He vowed that if cured, he would go to the monastery of Mt. Athos and learn how to become a true Christian. He was cured and made the journey. Indeed, except for a brief visit home, when he resigned from the Foreign Service and burned one of his unpublished novels as a sacrifice to the new life, he stayed there for a year, hoping to become a monk. His request was refused.

Reluctant to leave the East, Leontiev next took an apartment in Constantinople and set to writing *Byzantinism and Slavdom* (1875), a book in which he applies his philosophy of history to the Slavs and their world. However, he shows little sympathy in it for them. Their democratic tendencies repel him and lead him instead to place his hopes in the Greeks, the guardians of Byzantium, the defenders of autocracy. Especially obnoxious are the Western and Southern Slavs, for, in his eyes, they produced little more than an exceptionally disgusting bourgeoisie, and thus are unworthy of sympathy. As a matter of fact, he thinks it would be a good thing if the Germans and Turks would subject them to violence; perhaps it would prevent the Slavic world from becoming totally bourgeois. But he is not very optimistic about it, and by the end of his life he has finally decided that the Slavs are doomed to complete subservience to the Western bourgeoisie, and, moreover, that they will ultimately be beaten down by a Chinese invasion from the East.

In 1874, Leontiev returned to Moscow and then to his family estate, which was producing far too little income for him to meet his debts. That same year, he sought spiritual help in the Optina Monastery, fifty miles away, and later in another monastery near Moscow, where he became a novice; but the six months spent there gave him no peace. This is not surprising, as his desire for monastic life was constantly opposed by his desire to experience the joys of the world. There followed a period when he wandered from place to place, continued his love affairs, and pondered the meaning of death. He turned his pension, inadequate for the support of two people, over to his wife in Kozelsk; by now, she was completely insane.

The next few years were unpleasant ones. He took a job in Warsaw as an assistant editor of the *Warsaw Diary*, where his increasingly reactionary mood served him well, but he stayed only a few months and then returned home, more despondent than ever over his financial situation. In desperation, he accepted another post, this time as censor in Moscow, and even managed to stay with it for six years, but it gave him little pleasure. As far as his writing was concerned, these were his least productive years. During this time, his estate had to be sold to meet his ever-increasing debts.

Things took a turn for the better in 1887, when it became possible to retire on a small pension and rent a house near the Optina Monastery. Despite his worry over his personal salvation, the conflict of his elegant tastes with his poverty, and his feelings of guilt about his treatment of his wife (he thought God was punishing him for his infidelity), he managed to do a good deal of writing, the major work of the period being *Analysis, Style, and Atmosphere in the Novels of Count L. N. Tolstoy* (1890), which has been included in the present collection.

Although written in a nervous, choppy style that tends to irritate even the most patient reader, this old-fashioned critical work is filled with highly perceptive ideas that are still valid. Produced in an age that valued utilitarian principles in criticism and rejected the autonomous value of a literary work, it approached Tolstoy's work from the standpoint of formal analytical and aesthetic criticism for the first time. Respect for it has been almost unanimous on the part of those scholars who read Russian; for example, Prince Mirsky, in his excellent *Contemporary Russian Literature*, goes so far as to call it "the masterpiece of Russian criticism." Most of the essay is devoted to an examination of *War and Peace* and *Anna Karenina*, but there are also informative sections on nineteenth-century Russian realism in general. What bothers Leontiev most is its negative tendency, its vulgarity, its coarseness, its psychological analysis, and its preoccupation with petty detail, much of which, he feels, stems from Gogol. The fact that Tolstoy rejected all this in the stories he later wrote for the common people pleases Leontiev greatly. What he objects to most in *War and Peace* is its lack of historical verisimilitude—not regarding the actual events that Tolstoy depicts but the reaction of Tolstoy's characters to those events. To him, it is too much like that of the author, a man of a much later period. In this sense, he finds *Anna Karenina* much more reliable. To study it, he says, is to study life itself. Moreover, he feels, it has fewer of the defects of the Natural School which mar *War and Peace*.

Leontiev was happier now. Living near the Optina Monastery and constantly guided by the Elder Ambrose, he finally found peace. In 1891, he took monastic vows and entered the Troitsa Monastery near Moscow, where he died a few months later, having renounced his theory of history—but still insisting that it was right all the same.

VASILY ROZANOV (1856–1919), who carried on a lively correspondence with Leontiev during the final year of the latter's life, wrote a brilliant essay on him, the following excerpt of which admirably sums up Leontiev's philosophy:

A great aesthetician and politician, he saw in history the surging masses of peoples, loving and adoring them; but being only an aesthete and politician, he was altogether blind to the holy center of their general movement, which invisibly guides, preserves, and supports those who are advancing. He noticed only the wandering crowds, the naturalistic herds of "human cattle," but everything he noted in this sphere was true, exact, and scientific; but there is a holy image that, remaining unknown to him in its dark receptacle, has chosen these crowds, and guides them to the open temple awaiting them; and all that he so much loved in history, these blazing candles, waving banners, the smoke spiraling to heaven, all these exist not by virtue of their beauty, but by virtue of their service and their position in front of a small black icon. Out of this strange and almost pagan ecstasy emerges a third peculiarity of the writer we are studying: the excessive part played in his thought by negation at the expense of affirmation, by resentment at the expense of love, hope, and impulse. The aesthetic principle is essentially passive; it encourages contemplation, it holds us back, it turns us away from everything that contradicts it; but it can never inspire us to action or sacrifice. For the sake of the earthly Aphrodite, men will not embark on crusades, they will not start revolutions, they will not shed their blood. And Leontiev truly knew and loved her alone. The Heavenly Aphrodite, man's ethical principle, is what completely moves, inspires, and conquers man; for that he has shed and will never tire of shedding his blood. Leontiev had no hope of the future, and that was because, while worrying about men and fearing for them, he essentially failed to see in them the unique quality for which they could be respected, and he did not respect them. Blind to the sources of ethical impulses, with, as it were, an atrophied taste for them, he did not love man more than he might have loved his dress and the beauty of his movements. . . . That strange passiveness to reality, which has been called his "reactionary ethos," was the authentic product of it. His appeal to men was limited to a love of such remnants of beauty as survived in life, to an attempt to piece together and cement these fragments.

Rozanov, like Leontiev, was a solitary thinker who founded no schools and belonged to none himself. In reading him, as in reading Leontiev, we are often reminded of Nietzsche; in fact, he has often been called "the Russian Nietzsche." Born in Kostroma Province in a poor family where, according to him, no one ever smiled, Rozanov withdrew into himself and spent a good deal of time daydreaming. His early life (like that of Leontiev) was largely dominated by his mother, and because of this some obviously feminine traits remained in his psychosexual structure.

He graduated from the University of Moscow in 1881 and

for thirteen years reluctantly taught in provincial secondary schools. Shortly after leaving the university, he had married Apollinaria Suslova, a former mistress of Dostoevsky. This was the greatest error of his life. Cold and proud, she made him miserable, just as she had Dostoevsky, and when she left him a few years later, she refused to give him a divorce. This did not, however, prevent Rozanov from establishing a family. Another friend, Varvara Rudneva, moved in with him in 1891, took over the management of his household, and ultimately bore him five children. Although she was Rozanov's intellectual inferior, she proved to be an excellent companion. To the end of his days, he respected her as a moral genius and referred to her as "my friend."

Bored with teaching, Rozanov took a job in Petersburg in 1893, with the Office of State Control, and in 1899, joined the staff of the reactionary *New Times*. From then on, no matter what the government policy, Rozanov supported it in his writing, even if it meant calling for pogroms against the Jews, slandering the Protestants and Catholics, or praising the Synod for excommunicating Tolstoy. What he hated most in the radicals, as well as in the Populists, were their equalitarian tendencies, their enslavement to ideology, and their refusal to respect the peculiarities of the Self. Although he was certain that the revolution would fail, even if it managed to replace the monarchy, there are times in his writing when he seems to have welcomed its coming. But this is typical of Rozanov. He was in many ways an equivocal man. As a matter of fact, he did not even confine his writing to the conservative press; at the very same time he was expressing his highly reactionary views in it, he was contributing under a pen name to *The Russian Word*, the organ of the political left. Because of this duality in his thinking, one finds it difficult to determine just what his true social and political views were. He himself said his job was to write, and that it made no difference for whom he did it. Nevertheless, his more personal works, such as his diaries and letters, show that his reactionary views were the ones he really cherished.

As early as his teaching years, Rozanov had published not only numerous articles, but also the following long essays and books: *On Understanding* (1886), *The Place of Christianity in History* (1890), *The Theory of Historical Progress and Decline* (1892), and a highly perceptive study of Dostoevsky, *The Legend of the Grand Inquisitor* (1890). Most of the books he published during his days as a journalist were collections of his newspaper and magazine articles, primarily on sex or religion. What he published after 1912, however, was completely new and different in that for the most part it dealt with himself.

Much of Rozanov's religious philosophy centered around sex, which he believed existed before man, even before the world. To him, God was a sexual being. "The bond between sex and God," he said, "is stronger than the bond between intellect or even conscience and God." During copulation, man comes into contact with God, and as a result of this act souls are created or transferred from the highest world into this one. Rozanov found sex good even outside male-female sexual relations, and at times he defended the most extreme perversions. He himself imitated the Romans in their cult of the phallus; in fact, he said that during his research on Egyptian art the image of the phallus drove him to ecstasy. According to Renato Poggioli, Rozanov was a "Narcissus in love with his sex with which he identified and through which he also loved his soul." Morality was meaningless to him; he said he did not even know how to spell the word.

Poggioli says that Rozanov's attitude involves a new metaphysics: "Rozanov is on the one hand led to identify God with his creation, and to postulate a pantheistic and naturalistic faith, divinizing the biological element in man's existence and in God's universe. On the other hand, he tends to consider the divine presence as something physical, even corporeal—which man may perceive through his senses. Ultimately, Rozanov's

metaphysics spiritualizes, raising it to the level of a hypo-
stasis, sex itself."

A good deal of Rozanov's writing is directed against Christianity. He was greatly disturbed by the fact that Christ never
laughed or sang, that He seemed to be an advocate of asceticism and chastity, that He rejected earth for heaven. Christianity, Rozanov insisted, is too "otherworldly," too sexless and,
worst of all, rejects the family; under it, family life disintegrates, for Christianity does not need it. Equally repelling to
him was the New Testament's philosophy of death: "How
brief the rite of baptism, how boring the ceremony of wedding,
how quick the sacrament of confession and communion! But
man dies, and Christianity rises in all its power: what songs,
what words, what thoughts, what poetry!" The high point of
the New Testament, he contended, is not the resurrection of
Christ, but His crucifixion.

To Christianity, Rozanov opposed Hebraism and the figure
of God the Father (Whom he considered the only real God),
as well as most of the ancient primitive cults. These he compared to the bright sun; Christianity he compared to a dark
sky. They are earthly and worldly, and in them, sex is holy. For
Rozanov, the important thing is the immortality of *life*, not
the immortality of the *soul*.

Among the books he published after becoming a journalist
are: *In the World of the Obscure and the Uncertain* (1901);
When Authority Went Away (written after the Revolution of
1905, and one of the few places where, in a work under his
own name, he takes an almost radical position); *Around the
Walls of the Temple* (1906); *The Russian Church* (1906);
The Dark Face (1911); *Moonlight People* (1913); et cetera.
Most of these are attacks on Christianity and its Church. It is
generally admitted that *Solitaria, Fallen Leaves,* and *Fallen
Leaves, Another Basket,* all written after 1912, are the works
of his that will probably live. They are made up of small fragments—dreams, reminiscences, random thoughts, aphorisms—

which sound like the spoken word rather than the printed one. Rozanov described them as follows:

> The wind blows at midnight and carries away leaves. . . . So also life in fleeting time tears off from our soul exclamations, sighs, half-thoughts, half-feelings, which, being fragments of sounds, have the significance that they come straight from the soul, without elaboration, without purpose, without premeditation, without anything eternal. Simply, the soul is alive, that is, has lived, has breathed. . . . I have always somehow liked these sudden exclamations. Strictly speaking, they flow in continuously, but one can't succeed (there's no paper at hand) in putting them down, and they die. Afterward, one can't remember them for anything. Yet certain things I succeeded in jotting down on paper. The jottings went on piling up. And then I decided to gather together those fallen leaves.

From time to time, Rozanov also wrote on Russian literature, but his opinions, like those on numerous other subjects, are contradictory. This is not, however, the case with his work on Dostoevsky. What he said of him, the writer to whom he was closest and whom he understood best of all, is unquestionably a valuable contribution for all time. Equally valid are his views on Gogol, which were first expressed in *The Legend of the Grand Inquisitor* and later elaborated in the two essays included here. In these works, Rozanov was the first to demonstrate that Gogol was no realist, that his characters and situations came not from Russian life, but from his own troubled and confused mind, that the Russian literature that followed was no continuation, but a reaction against Gogol. This view, incidentally, is the one generally accepted by Western Slavic scholars; it is vigorously rejected by the Soviets.

After the revolution, Rozanov's life was miserable. Deprived of his livelihood, he moved his family to the monastery town of Sergiev Posad—today, Zagorsk—where he found refuge in a private home near the Trinity Monastery. For two years, he lived in extreme poverty, the thought of food constantly on his mind. Here he began his last book, *The Apocalypse of Our Times* (1918–1919), a bitter indictment against Christianity as well as the revolution. An iron curtain, he said (long before Churchill), had fallen on Russia; all was darkness, but somewhere in the darkness, there still glowed the soul.

If much of Rozanov's life was paradoxical, so was his death. For many years he had vigorously fought Christianity, but when he became ill in 1919, and realized that death was near, his attitude changed completely. His last days were a continuous acclamation and adoration of Christ. Near the end, he had priests from the monastery give him the Last Sacrament four times, Extreme Unction once, and read the prayers for the dying over him three times.

Soon afterward, his wife also died; his son froze to death; and one of his daughters hanged herself.

There are several points of similarity between Rozanov and LEV SHESTOV (1866–1938), the third writer represented in this book. Prince Mirsky compared the two as follows:

> Both value the human personality above all ideas and systems. Both found their first starting point in Dostoevsky, and later in a kindred spirit in the Old Testament. Both are mystics—but Rozanov is a biological mystic, a mystic of the flesh. Shestov is a pure spiritualist. Rozanov is an irrationalist in practice as well as in theory: he is no logician, and the only arguments he was capable of were emotional and "intuitive" arguments. Shestov fights reason with her own arms—in his confutation of logic, he has proved himself a consummate logician. Rozanov is deeply rooted in the Russian and Slavophile soil. Shestov has no roots in any soil: his thought is international, or rather supranational, and in this respect more akin to Tolstoy than to Dostoevsky.

Lev Shestov (originally Lev Isaakovich Schwarzmann) was born in Kiev in a family of rich Jewish merchants. They were a cultured group, and their house served as a gathering place for many intellectuals and artists. Shestov prepared for a legal career, but was denied his degree of doctor of laws when the censor rejected his dissertation on the grounds that it was too revolutionary. He then turned to writing articles on literature and philosophy for the local press, and also helped run his father's business. In 1896 he went to Rome, where he married a Russian Orthodox medical student, and later to Berne, to visit his sister, who was studying philosophy. Here he first became acquainted with Nietzsche's work, an acquaintanceship that was to have a profound influence on his later life. After a few unsuccessful literary attempts, he shifted his attention to the field of philosophy.

When Shestov returned to Russia in 1898, he brought with him two completed books: *Shakespeare and His Critic Brandes* and *The Good in the Teaching of Tolstoy and Nietzsche*. The first was published with great difficulty and was largely ignored by the public; but the second, which came out two years later, met with considerable success, largely due to the praise given it by the critic Mikhailovsky. In the book on Shakespeare, Shestov appears as an idealist, a position he was soon to abandon. The shift is already evident in the work on Tolstoy, where he contrasts Nietzsche's philosophy of cruelty with Tolstoy's moralizing and concludes with a theme that was to appear time and again in his works: namely, that goodness is not God, that man must search for what is beyond pity, beyond goodness—he must search for God.

Shestov next went to Petersburg, where he contributed to Diaghilev's magazine *The World of Art* and published the book included here, *Dostoevsky and Nietzsche: The Philosophy of Tragedy* (1903). It, too, was largely ignored. *The Apotheosis of Groundlessness* (1905), which followed, met with even less success. Undaunted, Shestov included its basic content—in a simplified form—in *Creation from Nothing* (1905), a highly illuminating essay, also included here, which the Nobel Prize winner Ivan Bunin and numerous other writers have called the best thing ever written on Chekhov.

For the next few years, Shestov lived mostly abroad, but by

1914 he realized the importance of native surroundings for his work and he returned to Russia, this time to Moscow. As his father's business was prospering and his wife was working in a hospital, he had no financial worries to distract him from his writing. All went well until the revolution. Unable to accept the ideas of the Bolsheviks, Shestov fled with his family to Kiev and later abroad—to Geneva and finally to Paris. An article on Dostoevsky, which he wrote for a special issue of *La Nouvelle Revue Française*, brought him to the attention of French intellectual circles, and from then on, his work was recognized both in France and in other western European countries. It was almost totally ignored in the English-speaking world. Much of what he had written before leaving Russia was now republished in France or Germany. Simultaneously, Shestov was writing new books, some of which appeared in their French edition before their Russian one—for example, his excellent study on Pascal, *The Night of Gethsemane* (1923). Other works of this period are: *In Job's Balances* (1929); *Kierkegaard and Existential Philosophy* (1936); and *Athens and Jerusalem* (1938). In addition to writing, Shestov lectured for many years on Russian philosophy at the *Institut des Études Slaves* of the University of Paris. When he died in 1938, he was engaged in a study of Hinduism.

Basically, his philosophy is that of a man beating his head against a stone wall—the wall being the universe governed by the laws of necessity, of logic, and of ethics. Most people have reconciled themselves to this wall and have found consolation in various philosophies that explain it away by reason. But Shestov refuses to participate in such delusion. He maintains that God exists; therefore, all things are possible for Him, even to the extent of causing that which has happened not to have happened. There is no question in Shestov's mind that this wall is hard and impenetrable, but he insists that if man keeps on butting his head against it, he might, in his helplessness, hopelessness, and despair, let out a cry that will carry him over to the other side, where God is, where all things are possible.

In Shestov's philosophy, reason is responsible for man's tragic fate. Its origin goes back to the time when man first ate of the fruit of the tree of knowledge. This resulted in the Fall, and, as a result, man was driven from paradise; he lost his freedom; he submitted to the laws of necessity. Thus, reason is the result of sin. But what Shestov wants is that man eat again from the tree of life—that he turn to the life *beyond* good and evil. However, this is not possible through rationalism, which binds man and prevents him from developing his own creative insights and getting to know real being. Under the tyranny of reason, man halts with the immutable and necessary. But when guided by faith, he finds all ways open to him. "Reason," Shestov says, "leads to necessity; faith leads to freedom."

This is what Shestov repeats in many of his works, but it is presented in such an interesting, erudite, and varied way that one always looks forward to more. The simplicity and clarity of his style, as opposed to the complexity and sometimes obscurity of that of Leontiev and Rozanov, delights. Many acquainted with Shestov's work in the original have pointed this out; some have even said that his is the finest polemical style ever used in Russia.

∴

THE essays included in this book were chosen because they are representative of the thinking of their authors, because they are important for a broad and clear understanding of Russian literature of the nineteenth century, and finally because, with the exception of *Creation from Nothing*, they have never before appeared in English. Indeed, in several instances, even their Russian edition is not readily available.

Spencer E. Roberts
New York City

1968

Essays in Russian Literature

THE CONSERVATIVE VIEW

DOSTOEVSKY AND NIETZSCHE:
THE PHILOSOPHY OF TRAGEDY

LEV SHESTOV

(1903)

Aimes-tu les damnés?
Dis–moi, connais-tu l'irrémissible?

CHARLES BAUDELAIRE

"I T would be exceedingly difficult for me to tell the story of the regeneration of my convictions, especially as it may not be so interesting,"[1] Dostoevsky says in his *Diary of a Writer* for 1873. Difficult, probably so. But hardly anyone would agree that it would not be interesting. The story of a regeneration of convictions—can any story in the entire field of literature be more filled with thrilling and all-absorbing interest? The story of a regeneration of convictions—why, that is first and foremost the story of their birth. Convictions are born for a second time in a man, before his very eyes, at an age when he has enough experience and keenness of observation to follow consciously this great and profound mystery of his soul. Dostoevsky would have been no psychologist if such a process had gone unnoticed by him. And he would have been no writer if he had failed to share his observations with other people. Evidently, the second half of the sentence quoted above was said for no particular reason, for propriety, which demands that a writer disdain, at least outwardly, his own person. As a matter of fact, Dostoevsky knew all too well how crucially important the question of the birth of convictions can be for us; he also knew

[1] F. M. Dostoevsky, *Polnoe sobranie sochinenij*, (St. Petersburg, 1894–1895), IX, 342.

that there is but one way to clear up this question, if only
slightly: by telling one's own story. Do you remember the
words of the hero of Notes from the Underground: "What can
a decent man talk about with the greatest of pleasure? Answer:
himself. So I shall speak about myself."[1] To a considerable
extent, Dostoevsky's works realize this program. With the
years, as his talent developed and matured, he spoke of himself
with ever greater daring and truth. But at the same time, he
always continued to the end of his life more or less to conceal
himself behind the fictitious names of the heroes of his novels.
True, this was no longer a matter of literary or social decorum.
Towards the end of his career, Dostoevsky would not have been
afraid to violate even more serious demands of social relations.
But he always felt obliged to say through his leading characters things that even in his consciousness would perhaps not
have been cast in such a sharp and definite form, had they not
appeared to him in the deceptive shape of judgments and
desires, not of his own ego, but of a nonexistent hero of a novel.
One is particularly aware of this in his footnote to Notes from
the Underground. There, Dostoevsky insists that "the author
of the notes and the notes themselves are, of course, invented,"
and that he merely set himself the task of portraying "one of the
representatives of a generation still alive." Methods of this
kind, of course, achieve directly opposite results. From the very
first pages, the reader is convinced that not the notes and their
author have been invented, but the annotation of them. And
if Dostoevsky had always adhered to this same system of
annotation in his subsequent writings, his work would not have
given rise to the most diverse interpretations. But annotation
was not a mere formality for him. He himself dreaded to think
that the "underground," which he had depicted so vividly, was
not something completely alien to him, but something kindred,
his very own. He himself was frightened by the horrors that
had been revealed to him, and he harnessed all the powers of

[1] Ibid., III (2), 74.

his soul to protect himself from them, with anything at all, with even the first ideals he came across. Thus were created the characters Prince Myshkin and Alyosha Karamazov. Thence also the frenzied sermons that fill his *Diary of a Writer* to overflowing. All this is merely to remind us that the Raskolnikovs, Ivan Karamazovs, Kirillovs, and other characters of Dostoevsky's novels speak for themselves and have nothing in common with their author. All this is merely a new method of annotation of *Notes from the Underground.*

Unfortunately, the annotation this time is so closely interwoven with the text that there is no longer any possibility of separating in a purely mechanical way Dostoevsky's actual experiences from the "ideas" that he invented. True, it is to a certain extent possible to indicate the direction in which the separation should be made. Thus, for example, none of the banalities or commonplaces tell us anything about Dostoevsky himself. They have all been borrowed. It is not even hard to guess the sources from which Dostoevsky took them—with, to tell the truth, a fairly unstinting hand. A second sign is the method of presentation. As soon as you detect hysteria, unusually high notes, and an unnatural cry in Dostoevsky's speech, you can conclude that an "annotation" is beginning. Dostoevsky does not believe his own words, and he is trying to replace a lack of faith with "feeling" and eloquence. Such desperate, breathless eloquence does perhaps have an irresistible effect on an untrained ear, but to a more experienced one, it suggests something totally different.

It goes without saying that the signs just pointed out by no means provide a mathematically correct way of solving the problem concerning us here. Even with them, there remains sufficient room for doubt and obscurity. Mistakes are, of course, possible in the interpretation of individual passages of Dostoevsky's works, even of whole novels. In that case, what are we to rely on? On critical instinct? But the reader will not be satisfied with such an answer. It reeks of mythology, antiquity, mustiness, falsehood—even of deliberate falsehood. Well, then, on what? One thing then remains: arbitrary action. Perhaps this word with its explicit candor will be more likely to win the favor of inordinately exacting people who distrust the rights of critical instinct, particularly if they suspect that, *après tout*, this arbitrary action will not be entirely arbitrary.

At any rate, our task is set. We must do the job that Dostoevsky himself planned, but failed to carry out: tell the story of the regeneration of his convictions. I shall merely note here that the regeneration was indeed an unusual one. Not a trace remained of Dostoevsky's earlier convictions, of what he believed as a youth when he first joined Belinsky's[1] Circle. Usually, people continue to regard dethroned idols as gods and abandoned temples as temples. But Dostoevsky not only burned all that he had formerly worshipped, he trampled it in the dirt. He not only hated his earlier faith, he despised it. There are few such instances in the history of literature. Modern times can name in addition to Dostoevsky, only Nietzsche. It was the very same thing with Nietzsche. His break with the ideals and teachers of his youth was no less sharp and tempestuous, and at the same time it was painfully agonizing. Dostoevsky speaks of the regeneration of his convictions; with Nietzsche, it is a question of a revaluation of all values. In effect, both expressions are but different words to denote one and the same process. If we take this circumstance into account, it will probably not seem strange that Nietzsche held such a high opinion of Dostoevsky. Here are his actual words: "Dostoevsky is the only psychologist from whom I was able to learn anything. I rank my acquaintance with him among the most splendid achievements of my life."[2] Nietzsche recognized Dostoevsky as a kindred spirit.

Indeed, if it is a similarity of inner experience rather than a

---

[1] Vissarion Belinsky (1811–1848), the father of Russian criticism, a leader of the Westerners. [Tr.]

[2] F. Nietzsche, *Nietzsche's Werke*, VIII (Leipzig, 1901), 158.

common origin, a common place of residence, and a similarity of character that binds people together and makes them kindred, then Nietzsche and Dostoevsky can without exaggeration be called brothers, even twins. I think that if they had lived together, they would have hated each other with the peculiar hatred that Kirillov and Shatov (*The Possessed*) felt for one another after their American trip, during which time they had to spend four months together, half-starving in a shed. But Nietzsche's acquaintance with Dostoevsky was only through the latter's books, and at a time when Dostoevsky was no longer alive. A dead man can be forgiven all—even the fact that he knows the secret that had been revealed to Kirillov and Shatov in the shed. He will betray nothing.

Nietzsche, however, was mistaken. No one can betray him to such an extent as Dostoevsky. And the reverse is also true: much that is obscure in Dostoevsky is clarified in Nietzsche's works. First of all, let us note one striking circumstance. As is well known, Dostoevsky liked to prophesy. And most of all, he liked to prophesy that Russia was destined to restore the idea of universal brotherhood to Europe, where it had been forgotten. One of the first Russians to gain an influence over the Europeans was Dostoevsky himself. But did his preaching attract many followers? People spoke of it a bit, they were even astonished by it—but they forgot it. The first gift that Europe gratefully accepted from Russia was Dostoevsky's "psychology," i.e., the underground man, with his various subspecies, the Raskolnikovs, Karamazovs, and Kirillovs. What a great irony of fate—don't you agree? But fate likes most of all to laugh at the ideals and prophecies of mortals—and this must be regarded as its way of revealing its great wisdom.

II

Dostoevsky's literary work can be divided into two periods. The first begins with *Poor Folk* [1845] and ends with *The*

House of the Dead [1861–1862]. The second begins with *Notes from the Underground* [1864] and ends with the Pushkin Speech [1880], that somber apotheosis of all Dostoevsky's creative work. From *Notes from the Underground,* which thus falls on the border between the two periods, the reader suddenly and quite unexpectedly learns that while the other novels and articles were being written, there was taking place in Dostoevsky one of the most horrible crises, that only the human soul is capable of preparing for itself and bearing. What was the cause of it? Penal servitude? Evidently not; at least, not directly. After his penal servitude, Dostoevsky wrote quite a number of articles in which he not only did not renounce his earlier convictions, but continued to proclaim them with a power of talent and genius such as he dared not even dream of in his younger years. After all, upon completing his penal servitude, he wrote *The House of the Dead,* a novel that everyone, even enemies of his new tendency, unanimously praises to this day as a "particularly" worthy work, or more precisely, as one that stands apart from all his subsequent novels. Here we still have *in toto* the very same Dostoevsky whose first novella had been read with such fervor in Belinsky's Circle. In "idea" and "conviction," *The House of the Dead* unquestionably belongs to a loyal disciple of the "furious" Vissarion, of George Sand, and of the French idealists of the first half of the nineteenth century.

Here we have almost the same thing as in *Poor Folk.* True, there is also a thing or two that is new here: there is a sense of reality, a readiness to see life as it really is. But who would think that a sense of reality could even partially threaten a man's convictions and ideals? Everyone, Dostoevsky himself included, would have considered such a hypothesis least likely. Reality is, of course, dismal and ugly, particularly the reality of penal servitude, whereas ideals are bright and clear. But, after all, this antithesis was the very soil on which his ideals had sprung up: not only did it not refute them, it vindicated them. All that remained was to urge and spur reality on until the distance between it and the ideals had become infinitely small or nonexistent. Accordingly, even the depiction of dismal reality was aimed at one thing only—to struggle against it and destroy it in the distant, but seemingly near, future.

In this sense, *Poor Folk* and *The House of the Dead* are of the same school and have one and the same purpose; the only difference is in the craftsmanship of the author, who in the course of fifteen years had managed to improve himself considerably in the art of writing. In *Poor Folk*, just as in *The Double* and "The Landlady," we are dealing with a still awkward, although talented, disciple, who is enthusiastically popularizing the great master Gogol as interpreted to him by Belinsky. In reading the stories just mentioned, you are, of course, reminded of "The Overcoat," "Memoirs of a Madman," and "The Terrible Vengeance," and probably think that popularization was unnecessary. Very likely, the reader would lose little if Dostoevsky's early stories had forever remained in their author's head. But the writer needed them. From early youth on, as if foreseeing his future task, Dostoevsky practiced the depiction of scenes that were somber and painful. For the present, he was imitating, but his time would come, and he would abandon his teacher and write on his own. It is, of course, strange to see youth showing a partiality for gray and for dark colors, but, after all, Dostoevsky never knew any others. Was it possible, you ask yourself, that he dared not face the light, not face joy? Was it possible that already in early youth he instinctively felt the need to sacrifice himself completely to his talent? But it is true: talent is a *privilegium odiosum*; rarely does it give its possessor earthly joys.

Until the age of forty, Dostoevsky patiently bore the burden of his talent. It seemed to him that this burden was light, that such a yoke was a blessing. With what delight he recalls his first literary attempts in *The Humiliated and Insulted*. According to him, he experienced his greatest happiness not when his

work was published, and not even when he first heard the
unusually flattering comments on it from the mouths of the
best writers and literary connoisseurs of the time. No, he considered the happiest hours of his life those when, as a still
unknown writer, he worked in silence over his manuscript,
shedding tears over his invention—over the fate of the downtrodden and oppressed government clerk Makar Devushkin.
I do not know if Dostoevsky was being completely frank here,
and if he actually did experience his greatest happiness while
shedding tears over his invention. Perhaps there is a certain
amount of exaggeration here. But even if this is so, if Dostoevsky, in making such an admission, was merely paying tribute
to the viewpoint that prevailed in his time—one that he himself shared—even so, the strangeness of his words can and
must arouse a feeling of alarm and suspicion in us. What sort
of man is it, what sort of people are they, who make it their
duty to rejoice so madly over the mishaps invented by them
for the unfortunate Makar Devushkin? And how is it possible
to combine "happiness" with the tears that they themselves
admit to shedding over their horrible invention? Note that
The Humiliated and Insulted is written in the same style as
Poor Folk. The fifteen-year interval had not in the least "re-
formed" Dostoevsky in this respect. Earlier he had shed tears
over Devushkin; now they are over Natasha. As for the delights
of creative activity, they, as is well known, never abandon a
writer.

At first glance, it would seem that nothing could be more
unnatural and, forgive me the word, more repulsive than all
these combinations of tears and delight. Whence the delight?
And why? The man had to tell that Makar Devushkin or
Natasha had been insulted, tormented, and crushed; apparently, there is nothing to rejoice at. But he spent whole months
and years over his stories, and then declared publicly, frankly,
and unashamedly—more than that, with obvious pride—that
these were the best moments of his life. The same frame of

mind is expected of the public reading works of this sort. It is expected to burst into tears and at the same time not to forget to rejoice. True, there are grounds for these demands. It is assumed that in this way, good feelings are aroused: "It deeply moves your heart to realize that the most downtrodden man, the lowest of the low, is also a human being and is called your brother."[1] And so in order to spread this idea among readers, a special class of people is needed, who spend their entire life mainly contemplating in their imagination all possible horrors and monstrosities that exist in such great variety on earth and then depicting them in their books. The pictures must be vivid, lively, gripping, and startling; they must strike the heart with a mysterious force. Otherwise, they will be condemned; otherwise, they will not produce the desired effect.

Let us put aside the readers with their hearts and good feelings. But what must be the situation of a writer who has assumed the dismal responsibility of arousing someone else's conscience by the depiction of various kinds of horrors? It is good if he manages, at least for a time, to bewitch his own conscience so that the scenes intended to have an effect on others pass without leaving a trace on it.

This would, of course, be unnatural, but, as we saw, it is psychologically possible. Even if Dostoevsky did exaggerate in reporting his first talks with his Muse, there is, at any rate, also undeniable truth in his story. Most likely, poor Makar Devushkin did give him many delightful hours. Youth, inexperience, the example of older and patently superior people—from such elements, almost any absurdity can result. Just recall the deeds that men have made up their minds to do when up ahead, even far off in the distance, an "idea" with its brilliant aureole would flash before them. Everything would be forgotten, everything would be sacrificed to it. Not only the fictitious Makar Devushkin, with whom it was necessary merely "to accustom himself as to an actual living relative," but real, living people, even

[1] Dostoevsky, *op. cit.*, IV, 29.

relatives, were forsaken as soon as the question of serving the idea arose. Is it surprising then that he was able to feel happy while having before him the imaginary face of a humiliated government clerk? However that may be, and whatever may have been involved here, the role of the inventor of dismal reality is all the more dangerous and terrible the more sincerely and completely people surrender themselves to it and the more talented the person who has taken it upon himself. Talent is, I repeat, a *privilegium odiosum*, and Dostoevsky, like Gogol, had sooner or later to realize how heavy was its burden.

III

"It deeply moves your heart to realize that the most down-trodden man, the lowest of the low, is also a human being, and is called your brother." These words fully express the idea for the sake of which Dostoevsky first embarked on his literary career. As you see, it is not striking for its originality. It was not striking for that quality even at the time when Dostoevsky began to write. He was not the first to proclaim it. In the fifties and for a long time afterward, it dominated the minds of all the better Russian people. At that time, its most outstanding spokesman was Belinsky, to whom it in turn had come from the West under the then fascinating name "humanity." Although Belinsky was a critic as far as his literary responsibilities were concerned, he can more readily be called a great preacher by mentality. Indeed, he viewed all the greatest works of literature in the light of a single moral idea. Three-fourths of his articles on Pushkin, Gogol, and Lermontov are an unbroken hymn to humanity. Belinsky aspired, at least in literature if it was impossible to do so in other spheres that were broader but inaccessible to his influence, to proclaim that solemn declaration of the rights of man, which in its time had caused such a vast upheaval in France, from where, as is well known, our new ideas mainly came. Along with the declara-

tion of the rights of man before society, there was brought to
us as its complement and, as was thought at the time, its
necessary presupposition the idea of the natural interpretability
of the world order.

Natural interpretability had indeed played its emancipatory
role in the West. In order to unbind their hands, reformers
had to declare that the entire social order of the past was the
result of a blind play of forces. Of course, we, too, had reckoned
on this. But at the time, we were unable to ascribe an auxiliary
meaning to truth. Truth is first and foremost truth. And natural
necessity had been established as dogma right along with
"humanity." The tragedy of uniting these two ideas was not
obvious to anyone at the time (with the partial exception of
Belinsky himself—but about that, below). No one yet sensed
that along with the declaration of the rights of man before
society (humanity), we had also been brought the declaration
of his lack of rights—before nature. And Dostoevsky least of
all suspected this. With all the ardor of a young and enthused
man, he pounced upon these new ideas. He had known Belinsky earlier from the latter's magazine articles. But personal
acquaintance with him fortified Dostoevsky's faith even more.
Many years later, in *The Diary of a Writer*, he said: "Belinsky
never took a liking to me; but at the time, I fervently accepted
his entire doctrine."[1] Dostoevsky does not explain in detail why
Belinsky did not take a liking to him. He limits himself to just
a few words of a general, but significant nature: "We separated
for various reasons—which, by the way, were most unimportant in every respect."[2] As far as we know, there had indeed
been no serious misunderstandings between them. But on the
other hand, it has been attested that Dostoevsky never felt
at ease in Belinsky's Circle. Every one in it, Belinsky included,
insulted him. And it must be assumed that those insults had
an unusually powerful effect on this already morbidly impres-

[1] *Ibid.*, IX, 175.
[2] *Ibid.*, 172.

sionable youth. They embedded themselves so deeply in his soul that later on, twenty-five years after Belinsky's death, he seized the first possible opportunity to get even for them. In the same issue of *The Citizen* from which we quoted Dostoevsky's words above, you find quite a number of unusually venomous remarks about Belinsky which Dostoevsky had long borne in his soul. Evidently the old wounds were exceedingly painful and the unavenged insults grievous to recall if it was necessary to pour out so much venom on his long-deceased teacher.

But Dostoevsky was right. There are things a person cannot forgive, and consequently, there are insults that cannot be forgotten. It is impossible to reconcile yourself to the fact that the teacher from whom you so joyfully, so wholeheartedly, and so impetuously received your faith has rebuffed and ridiculed you. But that is exactly what happened in the case of Dostoevsky and Belinsky. When the young and ardent disciple would visit his master to hear what he had to say on the subject of "the most downtrodden man, the lowest of the low," the master would be playing cards and talking about irrelevant matters. That was painful to bear for a person so gentle and trusting as Dostoevsky was at the time. But Belinsky's disciple was also irksome to him. Do you know that for some teachers there is no greater torment on earth than to have students who are too trusting and consistent? Belinsky was already approaching the end of his literary career when Dostoevsky was just beginning his. As a man enlightened by experience, he sensed all too deeply how much danger is concealed in every inordinately fervent enthusiasm for an idea. He already knew that an unsolvable contradiction lies concealed deep in the idea, and therefore he tried to confine himself to its surface. He understood that the natural order of things laughs at humanity, which in turn can merely bow its head submissively before the invincible foe. You, of course, recall Belinsky's celebrated letter, in which he demands that an account be rendered for "every blood brother." This means that the contradiction had already become crystal clear to him and that humanity no longer satisfied him. But Dostoevsky did not understand this, he could not understand it, and with all the ardor of a neophyte, he constantly returned in his conversation and writing to "the humblest man." You can imagine how distressing it was for Belinsky to listen to his young friend, especially as he himself could not openly confess his own thoughts and feelings!

As a result, the disciple, for "unimportant reasons," abandoned his master, who by now was bored even with *Poor Folk*, and who called Dostoevsky's next work "nervous twaddle." The story, as you see, is not a cheerful one. But the ball comes to the player. Both friends took with them painful memories of their short-lived acquaintance. Belinsky soon died, but Dostoevsky had for more than thirty years to bear within himself the memories of a teacher who had repudiated him and to contend with the agonizing contradiction that he had inherited along with humanity from the "furious Vissarion." I might note here that in his late works, Dostoevsky used the word "humanity" in an ironic sense only, and he always wrote it in quotation marks. Consequently, it had cost him dearly! Could he have believed this when he was rejoicing over his Devushkin and embracing Belinsky, Nekrasov,[1] and Grigorovich?[2]

The break with Belinsky was the first test that Dostoevsky had to stand. And he stood it with flying colors. He not only did not betray his faith, on the contrary, he seemed to give himself up to it even more passionately than before, although he was filled with so much fervor from the very beginning that the comparative degree is perhaps inappropriate here. The second test was his arrest in connection with the Petrashevsky affair. Dostoevsky was sentenced to death, but the sentence was later commuted to hard labor. But here, too, he remained

[1] N. A. Nekrasov (1821–1877), a Russian poet whose main theme was the Russian people, particularly the peasants and their suffering. [Tr.]
[2] D. V. Grigorovich (1822–1899), a sentimental realist whose novels describe the hard life of the peasant. [Tr.]

firm and unshaken—not only outwardly, but, as is evident
from his own reminiscences, even in the depths of his soul. His
testimony relates to 1873, i.e., to the time when he recalled his
past with disgust and indignation, when he was even ready to
slander it. Therefore, it is of particular value, and we shall
quote it here *in toto*: "The sentence of death by shooting,
which was read to each of us beforehand, had been read in all
seriousness; almost all the condemned were certain that it
would be carried out, and they suffered at least ten terrible,
inordinately horrible, minutes awaiting death. In those last
minutes, some of us (I know this for certain) instinctively
withdrew into ourselves and, while hastily examining the
whole of our still very young lives, we perhaps even repented
of some of our serious deeds (the kind that secretly remain on
everyone's conscience throughout his life); but the deed for
which we had been condemned, the thoughts, the ideas that
had possessed our minds, seemed to us not only something that
did not demand repentance, but even something that purified
us, a martyrdom for which much would be forgiven! And thus
it continued for a long time. Not the years of exile, not the
suffering broke us. On the contrary, nothing broke us, and our
convictions merely bolstered our spirits with an awareness of
an obligation fulfilled."[1] Thus the man recalls his past after a
quarter of a century. Consequently, the "humblest man" *was*
dear to his heart; consequently, his bond with Belinsky's ideas
was strong, and the recently disseminated opinion that Dostoevsky had been reckoned as a member of Belinsky's Circle
only through a misunderstanding, when in fact his heart belonged to a different world even in early youth, is completely
unfounded. And why, one might ask, was such a fabrication
necessary? To uphold Dostoevsky's honor? But where is the
honor in it? Is it really so necessary for a person still in diapers
to have his "convictions" completely formulated for the rest of
his life? In my opinion, it is not. A person lives and learns from

[1] Dostoevsky, *op. cit.*, IX, 342.

life. And he who has lived to old age without having seen anything new is more likely to astonish us for his lack of perceptiveness than to command our respect. However, I want least of all here to praise Dostoevsky for his perceptiveness. Generally speaking, this is no place to appraise his mental attributes. There is no question that this writer was an extraordinary man—at least in the eyes of someone who decides to study and speak about him so many years after his death. But precisely for this reason is it least of all necessary to ascribe to or invent for him special mental attributes. Here, more than anywhere else, one must bridle one's personal sympathies and antipathies and avoid overwhelming the reader with one's own convictions, however noble and lofty they may be. For us, Dostoevsky is a psychological enigma. The key to it can be found in one way only—by adhering as strictly as possible to truth and reality. And if he himself openly attested to a "regeneration of his convictions," then all efforts to pass silently over this exceedingly important event in his life for fear that it will impose unexpected and unusual conclusions on us deserve the severest possible censure. "Fear" is inappropriate here. Or, in other words, we must find the strength in ourselves to overcome it. A new truth, when first discovered, is always as disgusting and hideous as a newborn child. But in that case, we must turn our backs on Dostoevsky's entire life, on all his work, for his life was an involuntary and unbroken quest for that "ugliness" which is in question here. After all, the man had reason to spend dozens of years in the underground and at penal servitude; after all, he had reason from early youth on to associate solely with the Devushkins, Golyadkins, Natashas, Raskolnikovs, and Karamazovs, and not to see God's world. Evidently, there was no other path to the truth except through penal servitude, the dungeon, and the underground. But do all paths to the truth lie underground? And is every depth an underground? But about what else, if not about this, do Dostoevsky's works tell us?

IV

Upon his release from penal servitude, Dostoevsky immediately began to write feverishly. The first significant fruit of his new creative activity was the story *The Village of Stepanchikovo and Its Inhabitants.* In this work, the sharpest eye will not find even a hint that its author had been a convict. On the contrary, you sense in the narrator a good-natured, kind, and witty man. He is so good-natured that he allows the happiest possible outcome for the involved circumstances. The uncle, who has suffered a good deal of torment from Foma Opiskin and the General's wife, at the critical moment displays unprecedented energy and, by the way, even more unprecedented physical strength. From one blow by the uncle, Foma Opiskin is sent flying through the closed door, out to the porch, and from the porch into the yard, and the "tyrant" who had tormented everyone for so long is then and there deposed. But even this is too little for Dostoevsky. He does not even want to punish this tyrant too severely. Foma soon returns to the hospitable Stepanchikovo, but, of course, he does not behave so disgracefully as before; however, he is allowed somewhat to nag the people around him so that he will not feel too offended. Everyone is exceedingly pleased, and the uncle marries Nastenka. Dostoevsky had never before displayed such good humor in a single one of his works—either before or after his penal servitude. His heroes meet almost any fate imaginable; they kill or are killed, go mad, hang themselves, suffer *delirium tremens,* die from tuberculosis, are sentenced to hard labor— but what happened in *The Village of Stepanchikovo,* where there is even a chapter at the end entitled: "Foma Fomich Makes Everyone Happy," was never again to be repeated in his novels. And the ending—well, it is simply a pastoral idyll. You involuntarily ask yourself in amazement: can penal servitude have left no scars on this man? Can there be such incorrigible idealists that, no matter what one does to them, they continue to cherish their ideals and are able to turn every hell into a heaven? Just what didn't Dostoevsky see during penal servitude! But in his writing, he is so naïve that, exactly like a twenty-year-old youth, he arranges for the triumph of good over evil. How much longer must the man be beaten?

However strange that may be, Dostoevsky had but one feeling and one desire upon being released from penal servitude: a feeling of freedom and a desire to forget all the horrors he had suffered. What does it matter if someone else is now where he was? The burden has been removed from him, and he celebrates, rejoices, and again throws himself into the arms of the life that had once pushed him so sternly aside. You see that "invention" and "reality" are not one and the same thing. It was possible to shed tears over invention and make Makar Devushkin the subject of poetry; but it was necessary to flee penal servitude. It was possible to spend nights on end with the sad images of his imagination, in that blissful state called artistic inspiration. There, the greater the insult depicted, the more hopeless the grief described, the more dismal the past, the more hopeless the future—the greater the honor for the writer. After all, the highest praise an artist can be given is in the words: he captured and conveyed a genuinely tragic moment. But the conveyers of tragic moments fear real tragedy, tragedy in real life, no less than everyone else.

I am not saying this to reproach Dostoevsky. And, in general, I would be most grateful if the reader would remember once and for all that my objectives lie beyond the spheres of accusation and vindication. It would spare me unnecessary reservations, which are always annoying. Although the matter in question here is apropos Dostoevsky, it is not about him, at least not only about him. It is important for me merely to establish the following obvious principle: Dostoevsky, like everyone else, did not want tragedy in his own life, and he avoided it in every possible way; and if he did not escape it, it was through no fault of his, but because of outside circumstances over

which he had no control. He did everything possible to forget
his penal servitude, but his penal servitude did not forget him.
With all his heart, he wanted to reconcile himself with life, but
life did not want to reconcile itself with him. This is not only
evident from the story in question above—it is revealed in
everything else he wrote in the first years after his release from
penal servitude. From his new experience, he brought only an
awareness that there are dire horrors and monstrous tragedies
on this earth, and—for a writer this is not much—that everyone who can, must flee these horrors. Just as in the case of a
sinking ship: *sauve qui peut*. What was it in his solitary meditations, about which he speaks so eloquently in *The House of
the Dead*, that inspired him, that gave him faith, strength, and
courage? An awareness that he was not doomed to share the
fate of his fellow prisoners, that a new life awaited him. He
accepted what was happening to him, he submitted to fate,
for he was expecting something else. Here is what he said:
"What hopes made my heart thump in those days! I believed,
I resolved, I swore to myself that in my future life, there would
be none of the mistakes or lapses as before. I mapped out a
program for my entire future and firmly resolved to follow it.
There was revived in me a blind faith that I could and would
carry all this out. I looked forward to freedom, I prayed for it
to come as soon as possible, I wanted to test myself again in a
new struggle. At times, I was seized with feverish impatience."[1]

That is how Dostoevsky spoke of his penal servitude. He
wanted and was able to see it as merely a temporary ordeal,
and he valued it only in so far as it was connected with great
and new hope. And in the light of this new hope, he sees the
whole of his penal life. That is what gives *The House of the
Dead* a mellow tone, thanks to which it is held in particular
esteem by critics and is liked even by those readers who see
nothing in Dostoevsky's later works but intemperate, needless
cruelty. There is cruelty in *The House of the Dead*, but it is

[1] *Ibid.*, III (1), 288–289.

within reasonable bounds, just as much as is necessary—necessary, of course, for the readers. Here, too, of course, there are ghastly, staggering descriptions of both the unbridled behavior of the prisoners and the callousness of the prison authorities. But they are all of "moral significance." On the one hand, people are reminded that the prisoner is "also a human being and is called your brother." For this purpose, stories of the convicts' brutality are placed side by side with stirring scenes depicting the kind of feelings of the inmates of the House of the Dead. The Christmas Play, the purchase of the bay horse, the prison animals—the goat and the young eagle—all those idyllic moments, which Dostoevsky reproduced with such skill and sincerity, won him the well-deserved fame of an outstanding artist and a man of great heart. If his heart did not grow callous in prison, if in the midst of unbearable physical and moral torment he was able to preserve such sympathy in himself for all mankind, it meant that he had great strength concealed within him! And hence, people also came to the philosophical conclusion that no amount of penal servitude can prevail over genuine, deep-seated conviction. In all these raptures and conclusions, the "humblest man" was forgotten; he was left to live out his days in the "House of the Dead" or somewhere in another prison, in shackles, in chains, under the perpetual surveillance of soldiers—that "lifer," whom Dostoevsky had compared to a man buried alive. (A clever comparison, isn't it?) At the same time, people even forgot to ask exactly what it was that protected Dostoevsky's heart from rust. Was it really made of pure gold—or was some other reason involved here? The question is, of course, an interesting one. It never hurts to verify the legend of golden hearts, if only to have extra proof of its plausibility.

The passage quoted above arouses some doubt in the reader: the golden heart expects too much for itself! But the expectation of a new life always attended and consoled Dostoevsky during his period of penal servitude. In *The House of the*

Dead, "a new life" is recalled each time the person in whose name the story is being told is, for some reason or other, overcome by a particularly strong awareness of his difficult situation. Thus, for example, Goryanchikov happens to awake in the night after the first theatrical performance. "In terror," he says, "I raise my head and look about at my comrades sleeping in the flickering light of the cheap prison candle. I look at their pale faces, at their poor beds, at their utter poverty and misery, and it is as if I want to convince myself that all this is really true, and not the continuation of a hideous dream."[1] And how does Dostoevsky cope with this horrible sight? After all, it is an excellent opportunity to shed tears: no amount of invention can compare with what he saw. But in prison, one does not cry. We shall hear more about this in still greater detail from Dostoevsky. But for the time being, here is his ingenuous answer: " 'I won't be here forever, only for a few years,' I thought, and lay my head back on the pillow."[2] Do you hear? Only an answer like that fits the question just asked. I hope you noted the question. There is no reference to the theater, the goat, or the bay horse. There is no recollection of even the humane arguments that one meets elsewhere in the book. He can be reconciled by a single thought—that his penal servitude is not forever, but for a limited time only. Dostoevsky did not for a single minute forget this while he was a prisoner. He said: "I wanted to go on living after my release from prison."[3]

V

The Preface greatly hindered a correct understanding of *The House of the Dead.* Why was it necessary? Why did Dostoevsky have to tell an invented story according to which the notes

[1] *Ibid.,* III, 168.
[2] *Ibid.*
[3] *Ibid.,* 232

belong to Alexander Petrovich Goryanchikov, who had been exiled to hard labor for the murder of his wife? Because of the censor? But, as you know, he makes no effort in *The House of the Dead* to conceal the fact that Goryanchikov was sentenced to penal servitude for political reasons. Thus, when the latter takes it into his head to support the prisoners' grievances, the other political exiles remind him that his participation can only ruin the whole affair: "Remember," they tell him, "why we came here." And furthermore, there are very clear hints in other connections that the author of the notes has been jailed, not for criminal reasons, but political ones. In brief, the Preface could not deceive the censor. If it deceived anyone, it was the reader, by presenting Goryanchikov, the narrator of the story, in a false light. Judging by the Preface, we are dealing with a man who is irrevocably lost to life. He speaks with no one, reads nothing, and lives out his last days in a remote corner of Siberia, leaving his cubbyhole only to earn a few meager kopecks from lessons. And he dies alone, having forgotten everyone, and being forgotten by them as well. Of course, there are such people who are buried alive—not only in prison, but on the outside as well. But such people do not write their memoirs, and if they do, it is most certainly not in the tone of *The House of the Dead*. Where would they get the eyes to see convicts' fun and relaxation? Where would they get the vitality to be moved by the various manifestations of "good" that Dostoevsky found in prison. Goryanchikov could have described (if he had tried to describe—I repeat, such people seldom write) a hopeless, eternal hell. He has no hope. Doesn't that mean that there is no longer any hope for the whole world? I do not want to establish this as a principle—there is no need as yet for the reader to protest; for the time being, I am only speaking "psychologically." While Dostoevsky was compiling these notes and during his entire period of hard labor, he was the complete opposite of Goryanchikov. He was, above all, a man of hope—of great hope even; and therefore his way of understanding the world, his philosophy, was also a philosophy of hope. And this protected his heart from rust; this was also the reason why he brought back intact from penal servitude all tho "humanity" he had taken there with him. Would humanity have helped him if there had been an everlasting curse on his soul as there was on Goryanchikov's? Would his spirit have been sustained by "convictions" as he himself tells it, or, on the contrary, would the "convictions" themselves, despite all their loftiness, have needed support? This question is appropriate, precisely at this point. Goryanchikov would not have written *The House of the Dead*, but Dostoevsky did. And if a harsh note of dissonance can be heard from time to time in this novel, if at times one finds individual scenes and observations that unexpectedly destroy the general harmony of the "humane" mood, then this must be put down to the fickleness and inconstancy of hope. After all, she is a most capricious creature: she comes and goes at her own sweet will. Most likely, during Dostoevsky's stay in prison, she often forsook him, and for long periods at a time. And in those moments, when he felt himself doomed, indeed forever and ever, to comparison with the "humblest man," there appeared to him those new and terrible spiritual elements which were later on destined to develop into an entirely different philosophy, into a true philosophy of penal servitude, of hopelessness, into the philosophy of the underground man. We shall more than once, later on, have to deal with all this. But for the time being, it is still concealed; for the time being, "humanity" stands firm; for the time being, Dostoevsky wants but one thing: to return to his former life, to do his former work, only better, more carefully, without retreat, weakness, or concession. For the time being, there can be no question of a "regeneration" of convictions. The natural order of things has not yet raised its voice, and humanity triumphs.

In this respect, Dostoevsky's journalistic articles relating to the period in question are exceedingly important and interesting. There are only a few of them. They were published in the magazine *Time* in 1861. Despite their predominantly polemical nature, their quiet tone, their respectful attitude toward the adversary, together with a feeling of self-respect and a vigor of language and thought appropriate to it, they are truly unprecedented. Not that they were unprecedented for Dostoevsky, whose polemics (for example, his sharp remarks to Professor Gradovsky)[1] were sometimes simply disgraceful, but unprecedented for literature as a whole. Usually, as soon as polemics begin, even the very subject of the argument is immediately forgotten. The adversaries merely try to outdo one another in wit, resourcefulness, dialectics, and erudition. But in Dostoevsky's articles, there is none of this. He wants peace, not the sword. Peace, even with Dobrolyubov,[2] whom he values as a talented writer despite the extremity of his views; peace, even with the Slavophiles, whom he reproaches for their fanatic contempt for the merits of all non-Slavophile literature. Significant here also is the fact that Dostoevsky is seeking reconciliation—that same Dostoevsky, who many years later, after his Pushkin Speech, in which he called so fervently for the uniting of all parties, could not bear even the first objection and immediately threw off his "artfully donned" mask of universal humanity. But at the same time, his sharp remarks to the Slavophiles about the newspaper *Day*, which had just begun publication, must not be forgotten, especially by people who value his prophetic gift. Or perhaps it is just the reverse: such people should completely forget his polemic against *Day*, for it decidedly compromises Dostoevsky's prophetic abilities. What sort of prophet is he, if he cannot foresee his own almost immediate future—if in 1861, he so seriously and sincerely reproached the Slavophiles for their inability to appreciate the merits of the Westerners and so

[1] On the occasion of Dostoevsky's speech at the Pushkin Celebration in 1880. [Tr.]

[2] N. A. Dobrolyubov (1836–1861), an untraradical literary critic. [Tr.]

passionately defended the Westerners, in whom he himself was subsequently to see nothing but tittering liberals? It is permissible for a man, even a remarkable one, even a genius, to err; but, after all, a prophet is a prophet only because he always infallibly knows the future. The article in question here is little known. Therefore, it will not be redundant to quote two or three passages from it. They will convince the reader once and for all that Dostoevsky did not forget his faith while he was at penal servitude. Here is the first one (I have chosen it almost at random—the entire article is written in such a vein): "Let's come right out and say it: the Slavophile leaders are known to be honorable men. And if this is so, then how can they say that this entire body of literature [i.e., the literature of the Westerners] is 'indifferent to the misery of the common man?' How dare they say: 'The lie is in their censuring our nationality, not because of *indignant ardent love, but because of an inner dishonesty* [Dostoevsky's italics] that is instinctively hostile to all that honor and duty hold sacred?' What fanatic hostility! Who but a person in the last stages of raving madness could say a thing like that? Why, it reeks of the stake and the rack."[1] Dostoevsky had taken the underlined phrase from an article in *Day*. It filled him with indignation, and he could not forget it; later, when citing it again, he exclaimed: "How could you bring your hand to write it?" Subsequently, Dostoevsky was to bring his own hand to write sentences a good deal stronger than that. Who, in speaking of the Westerners and their fight against the pre-Reform system, doubted that behind their visible laughter lay invisible tears?! And perhaps the Slavophiles meant something else by "inner dishonesty?" But for the time being, Dostoevsky has no idea of the things he would end up saying. For the time being, he staunchly sides with the Westerners: "*As if the Westerners did not have the same feeling for the Russian spirit and nationality* as the Slavophiles did. [My italics.] They did, but the Westerners did not want to shut their eyes and ears like a fakir to

1 Dostoevsky, *op. cit.*, IX, 154.

certain phenomena that were incomprehensible to them; they did not want to leave them without an explanation or to regard them at all costs with hostility, as the Slavophiles did; they did not shut their eyes to the world, but wanted to reach the truth through intellect, analysis, and understanding. The Westerners turned to realism, whereas the Slavophiles are still clinging to their vague and undefined ideal."[1] And also: "The Westerners were following the path of relentless analysis, and after them went everything in our society that could possibly do so. The realists do not fear the results of their analysis. Suppose there is a lie in this mass, suppose it does contain a mishmash of all those lies that you read over and over again with such pleasure. We do not fear this gloating enumeration of our diseases. They may be lies, but we are guided by truth. We believe in this."[2] The entire article is written in such a vein. It is not particularly remarkable for its content. The magazines of the sixties were filled with such articles. Important here only is the fact that, at the time, Dostoevsky evidently did not yet suspect how far he would be obliged to deviate from all these ideas, despite the fact that he was already forty years old and had already experienced a good deal of unpleasantness—his quarrel with Belinsky, his penal servitude, and his soldiering. He dared not even think that his faith would soon abandon him. He fervently extolled realism, analysis, and Westernism. Yet, he was already on the eve of a great spiritual upheaval. This was the last tribute he would pay to humanity. A little while longer, and the old ideal would collapse, felled by an invisible foe. The period of the underground would begin.

VI

And when exactly did it begin? The fact is a remarkable one: at the very time when, apparently, the most cherished hopes of the generation of the fifties began to come true. Serfdom fell.

[1] *Ibid.*, 155–156.
[2] *Ibid.*

Quite a number of reforms—some proposed, some already under way—promised to realize the dream to which Belinsky
had devoted himself and over which Natasha (*The Humiliated
and Insulted*) had wept when Ivan Petrovich read her his first
story. Up to this point, the "humblest man" had been mentioned only in books; now his rights were recognized by everyone. Up to this point, "humanity" had been a mere abstraction;
now it was called upon to exercise its sway over life. The most
extreme idealists at the beginning of the sixties had to admit
that reality, usually so slow or even motionless, was not this
time lagging far behind their dreams. In literature, there was
a great celebration. Dostoevsky alone did not share in the
general rejoicing. He stood to the side, just as if nothing unusual had happened. More than that, he hid in the underground: Russia's hopes were not his hopes. They were of no
concern to him.

How are we to explain such indifference on the part of the
greatest Russian writer to events which were regarded in our
literature as marking the dawn of a new era in Russian history?
The stock explanation is simple: Dostoevsky was a great artist,
but a poor thinker. The value of stock explanations is well
known. This one is worth no more than the rest, but like every
platitude, it deserves attention. Not without reason did it come
into this world. People needed it, not to discover the way to
truth, but on the contrary, to block all paths to it, to stifle it,
to curb it. Incidentally, there is nothing surprising here if we
recall what sort of "truth" is in question here! How could it
help but be stifled when Dostoevsky himself was horrified by
it? I shall quote just one short passage here from the notes of
the underground man. This is what he says to the prostitute
who has come to him for "moral support": "Do you know what
I really want? That you all go to the devil, that's what. I need
peace. Why, I'd sell the whole world right now for a kopeck.
Is the world to go to pot, or am I to go without my tea? I say
that the world can go to pot, so long as I can always get my

tea."[1] Who is speaking in this way? Who took it into his head
to put such monstrously cynical words into his hero's mouth?
That same Dostoevsky, who a short time earlier had so fervently and sincerely said the words about the "humblest man,"
which I quoted several times already. Now do you understand
what an incredibly powerful blow was needed to drive him to
such great extremes? Now do you understand which truth it
was that must have been revealed to him? Oh, our publicists
were right a thousand times over when they sought a platitude
to replace such a truth!

Notes from the Underground is a heart-rending cry of terror
that has escaped from a man suddenly convinced that all his
life he had been lying and pretending when he assured himself
and others that the loftiest purpose in life is to serve the
"humblest man." Up to this point, he had considered himself
marked by fate to do a great work. But now he suddenly felt
that he was not a bit better than anyone else, that he cared as
little for all ideas as the most common mortal. Let ideas triumph
a thousand times over: let the peasants be freed, let just and
merciful courts be set up, let military conscription be abol-
ished—his heart would be no lighter, no happier because of it.
He was obliged to tell himself that if, instead of all those great
and fortunate events, misfortune were to befall Russia, he
would feel no worse—perhaps even better. What in the world
is a man to do who has discovered in himself such a hideous
and disgusting idea? And particularly a writer accustomed to
thinking that he is duty-bound to share with his readers all that
goes on in his soul? Is he to tell the truth? To go out to the
city square and openly admit to the public that his entire past
life, that all of his past words, had been nothing but lies,
pretense, and hypocrisy, that while he was crying over Makar
Devushkin he was not in the least thinking of the poor wretch,
but merely drawing pictures to console himself and the public?
And this at the age of forty, when it is impossible to begin a

[1] *Ibid.*, III (2), 171.

new life, when a break with the past is tantamount to burying oneself alive! Dostoevsky tried to go on speaking in the old way; almost simultaneously with *Notes from the Underground,* he was writing *The Humiliated and Insulted,* in which he forced himself to champion the idea of self-renunciation, despite the fact that he staggered beneath its weight. But where was he to get the strength for such systematic fraud and self-deception? He was already having difficulty sustaining the tone in *The Humiliated and Insulted.* Even it has pages in which the ominous light of the new revelation breaks through. True, they are few. The underground man is evident here only in the Prince's talk with Ivan Petrovich (at night in the restaurant), but it is enough for us to realize what a storm was gathering in Dostoevsky's soul. The Prince all the time ridicules "ideals" and "Schiller" in a most brazen way, while poor Ivan Petrovich sits there downcast, unable not only to defend himself, but even to behave with a semblance of dignity. When you let anyone, even in a novel, deride your holy of holies so caustically, it means you have taken the first step toward its denial. True, Dostoevsky lets the Prince triumph just once, and even then only for a moment. Later, in the pages that follow, all the characters seem to flaunt their nobility and selflessness before one another. But one rotten apple can spoil the whole barrel. Dostoevsky's pathos had dried up. Goodness and service to the idea no longer inspired him.

Notes from the Underground is a public, albeit a veiled, renunciation of his past. "I can't, I simply can't go on pretending. I can't go on living the lie of ideas, and yet I have no other truth. Come what may." That is what these notes say, however much Dostoevsky disclaims them in his comment. Never before had the "word" of a single Russian writer resounded with such hopelessness, with such despair. This accounts for the unprecedented boldness (Count Tolstoy would call it "effrontery"—after all, he spoke that way about Nietzsche) with which Dostoevsky let himself deride the dearest and most sacred human feelings. I have already pointed out that Dostoevsky tells his own story in *Notes from the Underground*. These words should not, however, be taken to mean that he himself had actually treated a chance female acquaintance so disgracefully; no, the story with Liza is, of course, fictitious. But the horrible thing about the *Notes* is that Dostoevsky felt the need—even in thought, even in his imagination—to do such a disgraceful thing. It was not Liza he drove away from himself at this point. I am certain there was always enough spontaneous pity in his soul for him to refrain from excessively harsh fits of anger and exasperation. He needed the character Liza merely to deride the "idea" and trample it in the dirt—that same idea that he had served throughout his life. The epigraph to the chapter in which this dreadful story is told is taken from the beginning of Nekrasov's celebrated poem: "When from the Darkness of Error." It was this poem and the holy of holies of those people from whom he had once "fervently accepted" his new doctrine that Dostoevsky was now so madly and blasphemously cursing. But this was the only way out for him. He could no longer remain silent. Something spontaneous, ugly, and horrible had awakened in his soul—and it was something beyond his power to control. As we saw, he did everything possible to preserve his old faith. He continued to pray to his former god even when there was almost no hope in his heart that the prayer would be heard. All the time, it seemed to him that his doubts would pass, that this was merely temptation. In these final moments, he continued, now with just his lips, to whisper his incantation: "It deeply moves the heart to realize that the humblest man is also a human being and is called your brother." But the words of this prayer not only did not console him, they were the venom that poisoned Dostoevsky, although people saw in them and still continue to see in them innocent and even soul-fortifying words. Lucky the person who senses nothing but the poetry of brotherhood in that sentence! But how is a person to cope with these works when the insignificance and absurdity of the humblest man's existence keeps pushing its way to the foreground? How can you tolerate it if you know from personal experience all the horrors of such a downtrodden existence? When the poetry of brotherhood is to be reserved for the new people just beginning life, and you must assume the role of Makar Devushkin, the object of sympathy of lofty souls? What will the great idea of humanity provide then? Hope for the future—very far off, of course—dreams of a different, a felicitous organization of mankind? But for the time being there is the unceasing, hateful, and hypocritical role of the priest of all that is "lofty and beautiful." It was not my idea to write the lofty and beautiful in quotation marks. I found it that way in *Notes from the Underground.* There, all "ideals" are presented in such a guise. There, Schiller, humanity, Nekrasov's poetry, the Crystal Palace, in brief, everything that had once filled Dostoevsky's soul with sympathy and delight— everything—is showered with sarcasms of a most venomous and personal nature. Ideals and sympathy for them arouse in him a feeling of revulsion and horror. Not that he was contesting the possibility of the realization of ideals. He did not even think of that; he did not want to. If the exalted dreams of his youth were destined to come true someday—all the worse. If the ideal of human happiness on earth were destined someday to be realized, Dostoevsky would curse it beforehand. I shall be frank: prior to Dostoevsky, no one dared to express such ideas, even with proper comment. Great despair was needed for such ideas to appear in the human mind; superhuman daring was needed for someone to appear with them in public.

That is why Dostoevsky never acknowledged them as his own, and always had a reserve supply of ideals for display; the more hysterically he cried out, the more they diverged from the nature of his cherished desires, or if you will, from the desires of his entire being. Every last one of his later works is filled with this duality. The question arises—what are we to look for in them, what are we to value? The demands of his soul, which break through to the surface despite "reason and

conscience," to use Tolstoy's favorite words, or the prescriptions for an elevated life, prepared more or less according to a
common stereotype? On which side is truth? Hitherto, "reason
and conscience" were regarded as the final judges. All that we
have in the way of ideals and hopes was created by them alone.
But now that a judge has been discovered over these judges,
what are we to do? Heed its voice, or remain true to tradition
and again reduce it to silence. I say "again," because people
heard that voice many times before, but they were seized with
terror and always stifled it with solemn cries in honor of the
old judges. And Dostoevsky did so himself, although, in this
sense, his works remind you of the sermons of those preachers,
who, under the pretext of fighting immorality, depict enticing
scenes of carnal joy. Whatever the traditionalists may say,
there can no longer be any doubt. We must let the man speak
in his own way. Forgive him all his sins beforehand—just let
him tell the truth. Perhaps—who knows—perhaps this truth,
which is so obnoxious at first sight, contains something far
better than the charm of the most ostentatious lie. Perhaps the
full force of sorrow and despair should not at all be directed
toward the preparation of doctrines and ideals suitable for
man's everyday life, as the teachers of mankind have hitherto
done, while always zealously concealing their own doubts and
misfortunes from the eyes of outsiders. Perhaps we should
abandon pride, the beauty of dying, and all external embellish-
ments and again try to catch sight of the much-slandered
truth? What if the old assumption that the tree of knowledge
is not the tree of life is false? It is worth examining this prejudice together with the theory of natural development, which
gives rise to it. The soul, insulted for all that it holds sacred,
will perhaps find the strength in itself for a new struggle.

VII

Such was the first stage in the birth of his convictions: hope
for the new life about which he had so often dreamed while

at penal servitude disappeared, and along with it went his
faith in a doctrine that previously seemed stable and eternally
true. There can be no doubt: hope had not been supported by
doctrine, but vice versa, doctrine, by hope. With this acknowledgment, there ends for man the thousand-year reign of "reason
and conscience"; a new era begins—that of "psychology,"
which Dostoevsky was the first in Russia to discover. Incidentally, few people have hitherto openly dared to acknowledge
the obvious antagonism between "reason and conscience" on
the one hand and "psychology" on the other. The majority
thinks it possible to retain the old hierarchy, in which psychology is obliged to occupy a subordinate position. Its job is
merely to report what goes on in man's soul, but the supreme
legislative rights are reserved, as before, for reason and conscience, who have the power to decide what should and what
should not be. Such an assumption is shared by even those
people who have done the most to further the progress of
psychology. Thus, for example, Count Tolstoy, who for dozens
of years in his books has been undermining our faith in the
legitimacy of claims of all kinds of absolutes, at least as much
as Dostoevsky has, still continues to praise "reason and conscience" above all else. He has a special art of saying these
words in such a tone that any doubt as to their sanctity and
inviolability begins to seem outrageous blasphemy. In this
respect, Dostoevsky could never compare with Count Tolstoy.
However, neither of them succeeded in combining the uncom-
binable. Their restless attempts to return to the "good old
words" merely attest to the fact that the business of destruction
not only is not less difficult, but much more so than the business
of creation. Only that person decides to destroy who can no
longer live otherwise. And if Dostoevsky went further in this
direction than Count Tolstoy, it was by no means because he
was more conscientious, honest, or sincere. No, in such matters,
the degree of determination is decided by completely different
laws. Man does his utmost to preserve his inherited faith, and

he renounces his rights only when it is utterly impossible to retain them. Dostoevsky, as is evident from the epilogue to *A Raw Youth*, dreamed of writing in the manner of Count Tolstoy. "Even Pushkin," he says "selected the subject for his future novels in 'Legends of Russian Family Life,'[1] and, believe me, everything that has thus far been beautiful in our life is contained therein. At least everything that has been brought to some degree of perfection." And later on, when discussing a novelist who would tackle a plot such as those selected by Pushkin, he continues: "Such a work, if created by a person of great talent, would belong not so much to Russian literature as to Russian history. The grandson of those heroes who have been depicted in a picture portraying three consecutive generations of a Russian family of the upper-middle cultivated class, side by side with and in connection with Russian history—this descendant of his ancestors could not be depicted in his present-day type other than in a somewhat misanthropic, solitary, and distinctly melancholy aspect. He would even have to appear as something of an eccentric." If we recall that, later on, Dostoevsky, in referring to *Anna Karenina*, called Count Tolstoy the historian of the upper-middle class, it will be quite clear that the quotations above refer to *War and Peace* and the types depicted in that novel. The beauty and perfection of Tolstoy's characters fascinated Dostoevsky. He, too, would have liked precision, clarity, and fullness of life; but he had to admit that such "happiness" had been swallowed once and for all by history, and that present-day man can only recall the past, which can never be returned. Resigned to fate, he turned to his solitary and misanthropic eccentrics. However, Dostoevsky is not entirely correct in these judgments of his. He himself, of course, has no place among the heroes of *War and Peace*. For him, these people are history, and only history. But their creator, Count Tolstoy, viewed them in an entirely different way and by no means wanted to turn them into a mirage of

[1] See *Eugene Onegin*, Chapter III, Verses XIII–XIV. [Tr.]

the past. On the contrary, he wanted to see in them what is eternally true and unchangeable. For him, Pierre Bezukhov, Natasha, Rostov, and Princess Marya were not people who had long since passed away, after having been compelled to yield their places to the new "solitary and misanthropic" man, i.e., the man from the underground; he insists that all his heroes are of the present day. True, his insistence is sometimes exaggerated and shrill, so that to a certain extent he betrays himself by it. *War and Peace* is the work of a man who needs not only to remember and tell a good deal, but also to forget a thing or two and ignore several others. Here we do not have that natural strength and stability that one senses in *The Captain's Daughter*. Unlike Pushkin, Count Tolstoy does not limit himself to the role of narrator and artist. He is constantly examining the sincerity and truth of almost every word his characters say. He needs to know whether they really believe in everything they do, whether they really know where they are going. Like Dostoevsky, he is a psychologist, i.e., he also seeks roots. And, as you know, all roots lie deep in the earth; consequently, Count Tolstoy, too, is familiar with the lonely work of the underground. He does not achieve that Homeric, patriarchal ingenuousness that is ascribed to him, although he strives for it with all his might. In these matters, "free will" betrays the man. He wants faith, but occupies himself with verification, and that kills every faith. It is only to his colossal creative talent that Count Tolstoy is indebted for the reading public's failure to sense how much art (I am almost ready to say artificiality) this great writer of the Russian land needed to produce his remarkable works. And not only Count Tolstoy's creative work, his whole life bears traces of an unceasing struggle with "psychology," with the underground. But it is still premature to judge his life. His writing, however, is one long attempt in some way or other—by force, cunning, or deceit—to vanquish the stubborn foe that is undermining the very foundations of a potentially happy and bright existence. And to a considerable extent he achieves this. He pays his tribute to the underground—proper and constant tribute—but always with a mien suggesting that it is not tribute, but a voluntary offering permitted by "reason and conscience." Dostoevsky's underground man, upon noting the falsehood of his life, becomes horrified and immediately severs himself from his entire past. But Count Tolstoy's heroes never cease to believe in "the lofty and beautiful." Even in those moments when the incompatibility of reality with ideals becomes crystal clear to them, they let reality come into its own; but never for a moment do they cease to revere ideals. Thus, the defeats of the Russian troops, the surrender of Moscow, et cetera, never have a too depressing effect on any of the heroes of *War and Peace* not directly participating in the military operations. Count Tolstoy mentions this fact repeatedly, so that, strictly speaking, the same effect should be produced as by the underground man's words to Liza: "I say that the world can go to pot, as long as I always get my tea." But such an effect is not produced. For example, Nikolay Rostov chats with Princess Marya, and, of course, their conversation touches on the latest news. But how do they react to the great tragedy being played out before their eyes? "The conversation was most ordinary and insignificant [!]. They spoke of the war, automatically, as everyone else, exaggerating their sorrow for this event." A bit later, Count Tolstoy explains further: "It was obvious that she [Princess Marya] could speak dissemblingly about Russia's misfortunes, but her brother was an object too close to her heart, and she was unwilling and unable to speak lightly of him." These remarks are unusually characteristic of *War and Peace*. Wherever Count Tolstoy can, he reminds us that Russia's misfortunes meant less to the upper classes of 1812 than their own personal afflictions. But while reminding us of this, he is able to preserve a semblance of unusual serenity of soul, as if nothing in particular had happened, indeed as if reason and conscience could watch with composure this display of such appalling egoism. And reason and conscience really do remain composed. Evidently they need only outward respect. One must be able merely to speak with them in a certain tone, as with capricious despots, and they grow quite tame. What an uproar they would have raised if Princess Marya, for example, instead of "dissembling" grief for Russia's misfortunes, had frankly declared in the manner of the underground man: "Is Russia to go to pot, or am I to go without my tea? I tell you, let Russia go to pot, as long as I can get my tea." Essentially, Count Tolstoy's characters Princess Marya and Nikolay Rostov are saying this very thing. And all the other characters in the novel (those of quality, of course—precisely those of quality—for the common ones do not permit themselves such frankness) scarcely surpass them in their patriotism. Ultimately, Count Tolstoy reduces everything in a roundabout way to a display of human egoism. Nevertheless, the lofty and beautiful do not end up in quotation marks, but retain their former position of respect. Count Tolstoy finds it possible, without any bitterness, to accept life as it is. Cautiously, unnoticed by the reader, he deprives reason and conscience of their sovereign rights and makes himself, or to put it more simply, everyman, the measure of all things. But he wants a complete theoretical victory ("the sanction of truth," as Dostoevsky says), and therefore does not openly overthrow all the former authorities; he merely deprives them virtually and gradually (Count Tolstoy does everything gradually) of all influence on life. And he knows what he is doing. In certain instances, he must still maintain the prestige and charm of the old authorities. Of course, he will no longer serve them, but they will still serve him. In all those instances when he is unable to wage the struggle with his own powers, he will turn to them for their miraculous assistance, and they will support him in difficult moments with their imperious voices.

VIII

In his analysis of *Anna Karenina*, Dostoevsky remarks in passing: "*Anna Karenina* is by no means an innocent thing." I quite agree! One must be exceptionally naïve to see nothing but poetry in Count Tolstoy's creative work. It is, however, curious that somewhat earlier, before the last part of *Anna Karenina* was published (it came out in a separate edition), this same Dostoevsky called Levin a man "of pure heart." Don't you agree that in certain cases, one should treat commonly accepted words with great care? A man of pure heart—after all, that is the same "innocence" mentioned above—yet Levin is the hero of *Anna Karenina*; the whole point of the novel is in him. But Dostoevsky, appearing in the role of literary critic, felt obliged *quand même* to support all sorts of ideals; therefore, he even applied so childishly tender an epithet to Levin. As a matter of fact, Dostoevsky was well aware of Levin's worth, and if at first he intended to keep his knowledge to himself, he had an important reason to do so. The publication of the last part of *Anna Karenina*, in which Count Tolstoy permits himself to ridicule the enthusiasm for the volunteer movement,[1] aroused Dostoevsky's indignation and made him say more than his literary position and the duties of a devout preacher would allow. Besides, Count Tolstoy had given too much leeway in *Anna Karenina* to the "underground man." Levin, for example, bluntly declares that "there is no immediate feeling for the oppression of the Slavs, nor can there be," and he finds strong support in the old Prince (a character whom the author finds most likeable, as becomes evident during the course of the novel). "And I, too," says the Prince, "was at a complete loss to understand why all the Russians had suddenly begun to love their Slavic brothers, while I feel no love for them whatsoever. But I calmed down when I arrived here and saw that there are people besides myself who are interested only in Russia, and not in our Slavic brothers. Konstantin, for instance." Such utterances from the mouths of positive characters in Tolstoy's novel Dostoevsky finds inappropriate. All this may be said, but with appropriate commentary, at least in the manner in which

[1] Russian volunteers fought on the side of the Serbs in the latter's war against Turkey in 1876. [Tr.]

it is said in *War and Peace*. There, even if people do feel indifferent to the fate of their country, they at least pretend to be passionately interested in the war, and thus seem to admit thcir "guilt." But here, Levin declares point-blank that he does not want to know a thing about the sufferings of the Slavs. He has only to add: as long as all goes well with me. But Count Tolstoy was not that bold, and therefore, Dostoevsky, in his own name, had to make Levin say a few words of this nature.[1]

This clash of the two great writers of the Russian land over the question of sympathy for the suffering of the Slavs is highly significant. How did it happen that "reason and conscience," such infallible judges, which Count Tolstoy praised to his dying day, prompted such diverse conclusions to these two equally remarkable men? Dostoevsky painfully sensed all the insult contained in the possibility of such a clash, and bitterly concluded his article: "People such as the author of *Anna Karenina* are teachers of society, our teachers, and we are but their students. What in the world are they teaching us?"

Nevertheless, the clash of these prophets was a matter of pure chance! Were it not for the Slavic affair, Dostoevsky could have found all the elements in *Anna Karenina* that had captivated him in *War and Peace*, and thus the readers would not have learned that "reason and conscience" do not always speak one and the same language. Evidently, Dostoevsky had become worked up over nothing. What if Levin did express his indifference to the fate of the Slavs somewhat more sharply than was necessary, what if he did blurt out the "poet's secret" —he makes up for it when the opportunity presents itself, and even when it does not, by extolling other exceedingly lofty ideals that are by no means alien to Dostoevsky. His renunciation of the Slavs does not at all indicate that he is ready to encroach on the sovereignty of "reason and conscience." On the contrary, it was Tolstoy's custom to attempt the unusual

[1] Dostoevsky, *op. cit.*, XI, 264.

only with their most gracious consent and authorization. Recall, for example, Levin's conversation with his wife in Part VI, Chapter 3, of the novel. Levin is "discontented with himself"; he feels "guilty" and "inferior" in comparison with others, even with Sergey Ivanovich Koznyshov (whom at heart he hates and tries his best to despise); in brief, his exceedingly demanding conscience and exceedingly strict reason must be gratified by his loyal feelings. The unusual tenderness and mellowness of Levin's heart in this scene almost borders on the absurd. His flirting with "good" reminds one of the way Gogol's clerk courts Solokha.[1] But Count Tolstoy is not speaking ironically of his hero. No, he is serious, although deep in his heart, it seems that he, too, senses the insolence in such an attitude toward ideals. The more his Levin withdraws into the narrow sphere of his personal interests the more "brazen" (this word was used in reference to Nietzsche and Dostoevsky, and justice demands that it be applied to Levin as well) he becomes in his praise of "good."

Oh, *Anna Karenina* is by no means an innocent thing! Levin despairs, Levin sees himself on the way to the eternal underground, to penal servitude while at liberty, to destruction—and he saves himself without even looking into the various means of salvation. "A man of pure heart!" Dostoevsky had good reason to praise him: the raven had smelled decay and could not conceal its joy! Look carefully into Levin's life, and you will be convinced that he was not only lying to "good" when he expressed his deep gratitude to it, but also deceiving "happiness," when he assured Kitty and himself that he was happy. It is all untrue, from the first word to the last. Levin was never happy—neither when he was engaged to Kitty, nor when he was married to her. He only feigned happiness. And as a matter of fact, is such a timid soul as Kitty (whoever wishes may omit the epithet) fit to be a lifelong companion for Levin? Could he really fall in love with her? And, generally

[1] In "The Night before Christmas." [Tr.]

speaking, is family life the proper atmosphere for Levin? The scenes in which this strange couple is depicted, despite the fact that they are written with unusual care and talent, show Levin as a man determined to do everything that happy and loving people do in certain situations. On the eve of his wedding, Levin, too, cannot sleep all night; in his confusion, as befits a bridegroom, he goes to extremes; he plans to embrace everyone, et cetera. When Kitty is pregnant, Levin watches over her every step, he is fidgety, he trembles. Finally, Vasenka Veselovsky pays them a visit, and this happy husband, as if he can hardly wait for the opportunity, makes for his wife a most absurd scene of jealousy accompanied by flashing eyes, clenched fists, and all that usually accompanies such occasions. The apotheosis of all this is Vasenka's banishment. Levin, a man of Christian meekness, who is unwilling to offend the Turks, literally throws his guest out of the house without a moment's hesitation. And moreover, he is not only not sorry, he is glad: not, however, because of his courage, which he does not even think of. He is glad that he, like everyone else, is capable of jealousy, and that his jealousy knows no bounds. Count Tolstoy, in one of his letters, says that he was filled with disgust as he worked on *Anna Karenina*. I think this is credible if we keep in mind the task that Levin had set him. What can be more disgusting than having at any cost to portray a man as happy and "good," when he is as alien to goodness as he is far-removed from happiness? Yet this is precisely what Count Tolstoy was trying to do. He had at any cost to adjust Levin to everyday life, i.e., to provide him with an occupation, a family, and so on. At the provincial elections, Levin has a conversation with a landowner acquaintance which is seemingly insignificant but worthy of attention:

" 'You're married, I hear,' asked the landowner.

'Yes,' Levin answered with proud satisfaction."

With proud satisfaction! What is there to be proud about? A man has married—hardly a great deed. But for Levin, marriage was not simply marriage, as for everyone else. For him, it was proof that he was no worse than anyone else. That is why, contrary to his custom, he does not so much verify his love for Kitty as he seeks appropriate outward ways to express it. That is why he forgives Kitty her past and agrees to follow *sur les brisées* (as Prince Andrey Bolkonsky put it in *War and Peace*) of Vronsky. For Levin to forego a family would mean dooming himself to *capitis diminutio maxima*; it would mean losing one of the universally acknowledged stays of life, and that would have been the most horrible thing of all for him. So he marries Kitty, as he would have married Dolly or any other woman of his circle who was not too disagreeable to him and who, at the same time, was sufficiently respectable to give his life an outwardly handsome appearance. But his love, solicitude, and jealousy—all this is merely nerves acting out a comedy for the eyes of himself and of others.

It goes without saying that such a marriage produces a feeling of pride in a man: "I, too," he says to himself, "have ground under my feet." And everything, absolutely everything, that Levin does, has one purpose: to convince himself and others that he has acquired sturdy roots so deep in the earth that no storm will ever topple him. Levin's task is at the same time Tolstoy's task as well. Yet, this great writer knows that there are both people who are falling and people who have *fallen*, people who are never to rise again. He frequently speaks of them; he concocts theories reconciling us to the fall. But is he himself to end up in the category of the fallen, to assume *capitis diminutio maxima*, to lose the right of protection by human and divine laws? He would not voluntarily consent to that for anything in the world. Anything would be better than that. Better to marry Kitty, better to farm, better to play the hypocrite before "good," better to deceive himself, better to be like everyone else—if only he is not cut off from other people, if only he does not end up being "buried alive." It was exactly the same with Dostoevsky. The only difference was that Count

Tolstoy still had the purely outward possibility of returning to people, whereas Dostoevsky had already lost it. It no longer mattered to Dostoevsky. ("The Dream of a Ridiculous Man") He knew that he would not escape his fate. But Count Tolstoy still had hope, and to his dying day he struggled against the horrible phantom of hopelessness, which never left him for long in peace.

IX

This struggle is characteristic of all of Count Tolstoy's creative work. In his person, we have the unique example of a genius striving at all costs to be compared with a mediocrity, to become a mediocrity himself. Of course, he fails to achieve this. However much he protects himself from the demands of his nature, it reveals its presence in him each time by stormy and impatient outbursts. In *War and Peace*, it seemed that he had summed up once and for all the conclusions and observations of his life. Everything he had seen is definitely and firmly secured in its place. And, above all, it is arranged so that, in general, it makes a reassuring and eye-appealing picture, despite the fact that none of the horrors of life which undermine man's confidence in his neighbor and Creator are forgotten in it. Prince Andrey dies an agonizing death after living an agonizing life; Petya Rostov is shot through the head by the French; the old Countess turns almost into an idiot before our eyes; Count Ilya Andreyevich, having ruined his children, retires inconspicuously into the background; Sonya becomes a parasite, et cetera. But all this is arranged in the picture so that instead of weakening the general bracing impression, it strengthens it even more. Dostoevsky could never grasp the secret of this aspect of Tolstoy's art. He imagined that a menacing cry, an imperious tone, a decisiveness of statement, and a few righteous and pious words can always cope with the anxiety in every human heart, his own

included. Thus, for example, in *The Idiot,* where Prince Myshkin plays the role of the conciliatory spirit, we find the following highly characteristic dialogue. After the nocturnal reading
in the garden, Ippolit, who is doomed to die, meets Prince
Myshkin and asks him a "question." "Tell me frankly," he says,
"what, in your opinion, is the best way for me to die? That
is, so that it turns out to be as virtuous as possible? Well, tell
me." How do you like a "question" like that? According to the
basic idea of the novel, Prince Myshkin is always supposed to
distinguish himself; he must be able to understand *everything*
and to emerge the victor from the most difficult situations.
But in that case, it must be thought that Dostoevsky, by
arranging a meeting for him with Ippolit, had simply decided
to ridicule his hero. Can there be any other reason for asking
questions, which, however hard you try, you will never be
able to answer sensibly or even in a remotely satisfactory way?
And note the form of the question: "So that it turns out to be
as virtuous as possible!" It seems as if Dostoevsky, in accordance with the old custom of the underground man, suddenly
felt the irrepressible urge to stick out his tongue at his own
wisdom. And indeed if Ippolit's question is impertinent, then
Prince Myshkin's answer is shocking. Here it is: " 'Pass us by,
and forgive us our happiness,' the Prince said in a quiet [!]
voice." Ippolit bursts out laughing right in his face. Dostoevsky
did not have the courage to make the poor boy submit to the
Prince's impudent sanctimony. And the quiet voice, always
particularly efficacious in such instances, had no effect whatsoever—nor did the magical words "forgive us." Oh, no, Dostoevsky did not know how, he did not have the slightest idea
how to use dark colors. He imagined that it was enough to
think up a pious-sounding name for the scene, and its subject
would be justified. Or, better put, he wanted to obtain the
true answer to Ippolit's question, and not just give the public
a work of art. With Count Tolstoy, it was quite a different
matter. He was deeply convinced that there is no answer, and

consequently that he must use artistic invention to insulate not only the readers, but himself as well from reality. In this respect, *War and Peace* is a masterpiece. Everything in it is carefully calculated; both the insignificant and the significant have their place in it. Daring questions are not forgotten, but they not only do not trouble the reader, they even seem to be answered as he reads along. No one comes to the dying Prince Andrey to report in a quiet voice that he has penetrated the mysteries of the world. On the contrary, the people around him are silent, and they remain silent, for they are frightened and devastated by the mystery and severity of the event. Prince Andrey is given all the honors a dying man could possibly wish, and no one further ventures to annoy him with his exacting demands. And, after all, that is the only correct and proper way to give a sound burial, for all eternity, to a man who is dying before his time. Count Tolstoy took it from the common practice of everyday life. As much grief, humility, weeping, and solemnity as possible—all this opens the way to the new life, all this will in the end reconcile one to any loss whatsoever. But this is not enough for Count Tolstoy. He dispatches his corpses to the next world in a way that they can no longer be of any importance whatsoever to the people who go on living. For this purpose, he is not even averse to using Schopenhauer's philosophy, after modifying it only slightly in accordance with the demands of art. In dying, Prince Andrey does not become "nothing"—no, he merely returns to the womb from which he came. Only his individuality is lost; but it is lost so completely that for some time before his death, all living things, even his own son, seem quite alien and unimportant to him. This purely Schopenhauerian "immortality of the soul," as depicted by Count Tolstoy, has an unusually soothing and reassuring effect on those who remain alive. Death is the awakening from life. "And as for the duration of life, it did not seem to him [Prince Andrey] any slower than the awakening from a dream as compared with its duration." These lines Count Tolstoy took almost verbatim from *The World as Will and Idea*, as he did his entire theory of death. This is strange. Generally speaking, Count Tolstoy dislikes borrowing, but this time he makes an exception. Schopenhauer's view seemed most appropriate to the needs of the moment. It does not, of course, promise true immortality; the immortality is not for the dying man, but for those who go on living. But who is going to think of the dead! Let them rest peacefully in the grave, and let the living enjoy life. Therefore, even death must be considered not from the standpoint of those departing, but from the standpoint of those remaining here on earth. In this sense, Count Tolstoy's portrayal is the height of perfection. It seems as if he has reached the limits of human knowledge; it seems that one step more, and the great mystery of life will be revealed to us. But this is an optical illusion. As a matter of fact, it is just the reverse: everything has been done here to see that the mystery remains eternally unrevealed. Death is presented as something totally different from life, and therefore completely incomprehensible to the living. In dying, Prince Andrey loses his human individuality, which, as it gradually dissolves and diffuses, finally disappears into something completely different from anything we can imagine. This different thing, this *Ding an sich* or "will" is in any case something that has its origin in Kant and Schopenhauer, and it is the "immortality" awaiting man. For the living, such a vast horizon seems an interesting spectacle. But the dying would not give two cents for such immortality. The late poems of Heine, who, by the way, was Count Tolstoy's favorite poet, can clarify a good deal on this score to anyone who is curious: The great German lyricist could be exceedingly sincere and truthful. But Count Tolstoy does not want to become involved with people who lack earthly hopes. The matter of Prince Andrey is not his personal matter. Prince Andrey must merely be dispatched from life in a decorous manner. He must be buried as deeply as possible in the earth and, in addition, must have a huge stone placed on his grave so that his corpse cannot rise and disturb the nocturnal slumber of the living—or better still, he must be turned into the *Ding an sich*. Herein lies the task of Tolstoy's art; herein lies the meaning of Kant's idealist philosophy: all the disturbing questions of life must in some way or other be transferred to the realm of the unknowable. Only then will there appear on earth that tranquillity which people who have once been frightened by a ghost value more than anything else in life. With Kant, this is not yet so evident; his anxiety was of a purely theoretical, abstract nature. His ghost was nothing but Hume's skepticism, which was threatening to undermine his faith in the apodictic nature of science. But Count Tolstoy had encountered a different kind of skepticism: an abyss had opened before him which threatened to swallow him; he saw the triumph of death on earth; he saw himself a living corpse. Terror-stricken, he cursed all the higher demands of his soul and turned for knowledge to mediocrity, averageness, to vulgarity, having correctly sensed that only from these elements can that wall be raised which will conceal the horrible "truth" from our eyes, if not forever at least for a long time. And he found his *Ding an sich* and his synthetic a priori judgments, that is, he learned how man rids himself of all that is problematical and creates fixed principles by which he can live. I suppose that no one will dispute the validity of "that is": after all, with a priori judgments, it is not their origin that is vital, but their apodictic nature, i.e., their universality and necessity. But we shall have more to say about the *Ding an sich* later on.

X

Nietzsche's Zarathustra says to his disciples: "So that no one could look into my inner depths and learn my ultimate will, I devised my long and bright silence. Many I found who were clever: they veiled their faces and muddied their waters so

that no one might see through them, deep down. But cleverer
mistrusters and diviners came to them and caught their most
carefully concealed fish. It is the clear, the bold, the transparent people who are the cleverest among those who are
silent: their ground is down so deep that even the clearest
water does not betray it."[1] Nietzsche himself was no such
clever man of silence: he muddied his water; but these words
can be fully applied to Count Tolstoy. He is clear, bold, and
transparent. Who would think it necessary to descend to the
bottom of his soul or believe that monsters live in its depths?
He himself likes to speak of his life as being "exceptionally
happy in the secular sense." And when as a youth you read his
works, how joyfully you view his bright, clear, and transparent
depths! It seems that Count Tolstoy knows and comprehends
all; it seems that the enigmatic and contradictory aspects of
life that trouble people are merely enticing bait for man, and
that the instability of all that exists is merely a deceptive
mirage. Instability—there is no such word for Count Tolstoy.
Recall, for example, the Epilogue to *War and Peace*. Are there
really any doubts that could not be resolved around the tea
table of Nikolay Rostov's cozy dining room by the content and
happy members of this large assembled family? True, Pierre
has brought a handful of ideas from Petersburg which seemingly threaten to destroy the peaceful well-being of these
inhabitants of Bald Hills. But, as you know, Count Tolstoy
refused to write *The Decembrists*, and wrote *War and Peace*
instead. The Decembrists, along with Andrey Bolkonsky, were
dispatched to the realm of the *Ding an sich*, where, according
to Kant's theory, all antinomies of the human mind are to be
sent. And life is left with a priori judgments, the chosen representative of which is the person best suited for such matters—
Nikolay Rostov. Would you like to hear the language of apriorism? Pierre Bezukhov, mumbling and lisping, begins to tell
something about his experiences in Petersburg: " 'In the courts,

[1] Nietzsche, *op. cit.*, "On the Mount of Olives."

bribery; in the army, nothing but the rod; military drill, depor-
tation—the people are harassed, education is stifled. Whatever
is young and honorable is crushed! Everyone sees this can't
go on much longer. Everything is too strained, and soon it will
break,' Pierre said (as people have always said since govern-
ments came into existence, and whenever people have examined the operations of any government whatever)." As you
well realize, these are the words of Hume's skepticism. Give
them free rein, and all the efforts expended on "war and peace"
will turn out to have been needlessly wasted. Therefore, it is
necessary to shift the trend of the conversation. And so Nikolay
Rostov is allowed to speak. As a man of the a priori, he dislikes
proof, and respects only universality and necessity. He comes
right out and says so to Pierre: "I can't prove it to you. You
say that everything in our country is rotten; I don't see it. If
Arakcheev were to order me to march against you [i.e., against
Pierre and his Petersburg friends] with a squadron and to
mow you down, I would do it without a moment's hesitation."
Splendidly said, isn't it? As a matter of fact, can anything be
proved to Pierre? And, furthermore, isn't Kant right—can we
really exist without a priori judgments, i.e., without those that
are supported not by scientific arguments, which are always
contradictory and unstable, but by a never-changing force, or
in other words, by necessity? Shortly before writing *War and
Peace*, Count Tolstoy performed a number of experiments with
"conscience"—not with the Kantian-Rostovian conscience,
which has principles, but with his own conscience of a man
of genius. And do you know what came of it? Not only the
a priori judgments, but almost all judgments disappeared. But
how can a man live without judgments, without convictions?
This great writer of Russia finally saw how convictions *are
born*, and understood what a great advantage the Rostovs
have over the Bolkonskys. Bolkonsky must not even be allowed
to go on living. Where would you end up with him? But
Rostov, even if you were to let him live a hundred years,

would never lead you down an unknown, false path (unknown and false are synonyms in the given instance). And see what deep respect Count Tolstoy has for Rostov. "For a long time after his [Nikolay's] death," he tells us, "the people retained a pious memory of his management." A pious memory! Retained it for a long time! Look back over everything that Count Tolstoy wrote: he never spoke of a single one of his heroes with such a feeling of gratitude and tender emotion. Why was that, you will ask? Why did this ordinary man deserve such gratitude? Precisely because of his commonplaceness: Rostov knew how to live, and, therefore, he was always stable. Throughout Count Tolstoy's career as a writer, he never valued anything so much as precise knowledge and stability, for he found neither the one nor the other in himself. He could only imitate Rostov, and it goes without saying that he was obliged to shower praise on his lofty model. This "pious memory," like the entire Epilogue to *War and Peace*, is an impertinent, deliberately impertinent, challenge hurled by Count Tolstoy at all educated men—if you will, at the entire conscience of our time. And it was precisely a deliberate challenge: Count Tolstoy understood, he understood only too well, what he was doing. "I bow before Rostov, but not before Pushkin or Shakespeare, and I declare this openly before everyone"—this is the import of the Epilogue to *War and Peace*. Note that during the period of his Yasnaya Polyana journals and his early literary-journalistic experiments, when he also repudiated Shakespeare and Pushkin, he at least opposed to them, not an educated landowner, but the entire Russian people. This did not as yet seem so strange. The Russian people, after all, is a great "idea," a magic carpet on which many a reader or writer has made his transcendental journey. But Rostov—why, there is nothing in him that even resembles an idea; he is sheer matter, stagnation, inertia. And to dare to apply the epithet "pious memory" to him! After that, how could anyone really believe that Count Tolstoy is naïve and innocent, or that his innermost depth is transparent and its bottom visible? Obviously Dostoevsky's "hunch" was better than that of Count Tolstoy's other readers: *"Anna Karenina* is by no means an innocent thing."

After Pierre's argument with Nikolay, Count Tolstoy takes us for several more minutes into the bedroom of his happy couple. In bedrooms, Count Tolstoy's conversations are carried on in a decidedly special way. In this case, the husband and wife are so accustomed to living with each other, so close, so inseparable that the one immediately catches the meaning of the other at the slightest hint. Here, you can detect nothing but the basic tune of family happiness: *Wir treiben jetzt Familienglück, was höher lockt, das ist vom Übel."* And Count Tolstoy once again depicts this entire idyll with what almost amounts to reverence. "Let the Shakespeares go on depicting tragedy; I, for my part, don't want to know about anything like that." Perhaps that was his thought as he accompanied his couples into the bedroom. But he did not openly say so. Openly, he prepared the solemn apotheosis of family happiness, which owns that all that is "higher" comes from the devil. However, there is a note of irony in this apotheosis—Count Tolstoy could not restrain himself. But, alas, the irony relates not to Rostov, but to Pierre, and not to his family and domestic affairs, but to his Petersburg plans. And even here, the irony is barely noticeable: the word "smugness" is flung at Pierre just twice, as if by chance.

But in the Rostov's bedroom, all is lovely. Countess Marya lets her husband read some pious literature of her own composition, and her husband, in reading this diary of his wife's, realizes his own insignificance before her loftiness of spirit. Moreover, Countess Marya offers, in regard to Pierre's dispute with Nikolay, a new argument in defense of apriorism, which Nikolay accepts with pleasure, despite the fact that, strictly speaking, he needs no argument whatsoever—herein precisely is his finest quality. Countess Marya says: "In my opinion, you are absolutely right. And I as much as told Natasha. Pierre says that everyone is suffering, is harassed, is becoming corrupt, and that it is our duty to help the poor. Of course [this "of course" is splendid!] he's right, but he forgets that we have other obligations which are closer, and which God Himself has marked out for us, and that we can risk our own necks, but not our children's." So that is how history is written! But that is not yet all. Having latched on to Countess Marya's argument, the a priori man immediately shifts the conversation from the children to business matters, the estate, the redemption of promissory notes, payment of debts, and to his wealth. To Countess Marya, such a transition seems unnaturally abrupt: "She felt like telling him [her husband] that one does not live by bread alone, that he attaches too much importance to *these matters* [Count Tolstoy's italics], but she knew that she must not say this, and that it would be useless. She merely took his hand and kissed it. He interpreted this gesture as a sign of approval and as sanction for his ideas." What wonderful impertinence! Show me one writer besides Count Tolstoy who would dare to play such a dangerous game so openly. Countess Marya, who "always yearned for the infinite, the eternal, and the perfect," assents, as if nothing had happened, to the most extreme hypocrisy as soon as instinct tells her that the stability of her "spiritual union" with her husband is threatened. One step more and this hypocrisy would be raised to law, a law—horrible to say—of conscience. If you will, no further step is needed; it has *already* been taken in Countess Marya's words. But strangest of all is the fact that Count Tolstoy does not give the slightest indication that he understands the abyss over which he has just leaped. As usual, he is clear, bright, and transparent.

What "psychology" Dostoevsky would have made of this! But Count Tolstoy is already experienced. He knows that each time an antinomy approaches, one must assume an air of piety, innocence, and childish naïveté—otherwise, goodbye forever to all a priori judgments, universality, necessity, stability, firm ground, and foundations! And he has no equal in this diplomatic art. Perhaps this is the result of origin and breed— a dozen generations of ancestors who served in an official capacity and who always needed a solemn countenance. In this way, Count Tolstoy achieves a dual goal: he has told the "truth," and the truth has not undermined life. Prior to Count Tolstoy, idealism did not know such subtle techniques. For its effects, it always needed a crude lie, fervent emotion, eloquence, tinsel, and even gaudy colors.

Had Dostoevsky recalled the Epilogue to *War and Peace*, he would have realized that it is an anachronism to be angry with Levin for his indifference to the Slavs' misfortunes. The time for anger was earlier—when he read *War and Peace*. And if he accepted *War and Peace*, then he must also accept *Anna Karenina*—completely, without any reservations, its last part included. As a matter of fact, the Slavic affair is also a great muddle! It contains one of the antimonies—to kill or not to kill. Therefore, why not make it a *Ding an sich*? Why not leave it, as Levin suggests, to the sole jurisdiction of the government, bearing in mind the example of our ancestors, who turned all matters of government over to foreign princes who were expressly invited for that purpose?

All Count Tolstoy's work, including his late philosophical-journalistic articles and even his novel *Resurrection* (one of his few works, almost the only one, that is relatively unsuccessful—in it, Count Tolstoy seems to be gathering up the crumbs from his own once-sumptuous table), remains within the bounds of the task I have indicated. He wants at any cost to tame those raging beasts bearing the foreign names skepticism and pessimism. He does not hide them from our eyes, but keeps them in what seem to be exceedingly sturdy and reliable cages, so that even the most distrustful person begins to regard them as tamed and safe once and for all. Count Tolstoy's final formula, which sums up his many years of tireless struggle,

and which he proclaims with particular solemnity in his book
What is Art, goes like this: "Goodness and brotherly love—
this is God." I am not going to speak about it here, as I had
occasion elsewhere to explain its meaning and signficance in
detail.[1] I want only to remind the reader that even this "conviction," which, according to Count Tolstoy's repeated assurance, has purest reason and truthful conscience as parents, is
by no means of such noble origin. It was begotten by that
same terror of the *Ding an sich,* by that same, almost spontaneous urge "back to Kant" (as representatives of the latest
school of German philosophy were shouting in chorus not so
long ago), by virtue of which Prince Andrey was dispatched,
Rostov extolled, Princess Marya poeticized, et cetera. That is
why, as we shall see below, the principle that Count Tolstoy
offered as the greatest and loftiest truth could seem a blas-
phemous, ugly, and disgusting lie to Dostoevsky.

XI

Thus, one way to struggle against pessimism and skepticism
is to create a priori judgments and the *Ding an sich*—in short,
idealism, which Count Tolstoy formulates in the words "Goodness is God." But simultaneously it follows from the foregoing
that idealism needs outward support. Levin had to marry
Kitty, to set up a household, to go hunting, et cetera, et cetera.
"Reason" alone proved insufficient to erect this ethereal structure. It needed a "material" foundation—an exceedingly material one. But the foundation goes deep in the earth; no one
sees it. This has always contributed a great deal to the triumph
of all that is "lofty" on earth. Recall, for example, the pro-
genitors of European idealism—Socrates and Plato—with their
doctrine of good. It seemed that it was spun from the purest
of ideas, which squeamishly avoid all contact with whatever

[1] L. Shestov, *Dobro v uchenii grafa Tolstogo i F. Nitshe* (Petersburg,
1900).

does not derive from reason. However, into the pure realm
of ideas, contraband was smuggled all the same—and what
contraband! It turns out that the doctrine of the superiority
of good over evil cannot (I am almost ready to say *does not
want to*) rest on dialectics alone, however "divine" they may
be. For support, it needs so crude and material a belief as the
belief in retribution. What more, strictly speaking, is necessary
after it has been proved that to experience injustice is better
than to do it to someone else? But as a matter of fact, this is
not enough. In Plato's dialogues ("Gorgias," "The Republic,"
and "Phaedo"), the most ordinary human expedient is called
upon to support good. There, it is stated that the wicked will
in due course (in the life to come) be punished, and the good
rewarded. If such certain victory belongs to good, then all
dialectics could probably be left in peace. The most backward
mind is capable of understanding the superiority of good,
which has behind it a protector who, although remote, has
been created according to an earthly model and who, moreover, is omnipotent. But strangely enough, you will find the
Socratic-Platonic idea of retribution in almost all idealistic
schools of ethics. All moralists have considered it necessary to
make God Himself the patron of good, or even, as in the case
of Count Tolstoy, to identify good with God (and in modern
times at that—the era of positivism, evolution, et cetera).
Evidently, the moralists' good did not seem very attractive in
itself, *an sich*, and people accepted it only for fear of incurring
the wrath of the omnipotent being. Idealism is by no means
so ideal as one might expect, considering the solemnity with
which its prophets spoke. In the final analysis, it lives by the
most earthly of hopes, and its a priori and *Ding an sich* are
merely high walls by which it defends itself from the more
difficult demands of real life. In this sense, idealism is like
an oriental despotic state: outside, all is resplendent, beautiful,
and eternal; but inside, there are horrors. Herein is also the
reason for that incomprehensible phenomenon whereby a doc-

trine which at first glance is so innocent has very often become the object of the bitterest hatred on the part of people who least of all deserve to be suspected of a "natural" tendency toward evil. But it can be safely said that every implacable enemy of idealism was at one time, like Dostoevsky and Nietzsche, an extreme idealist himself, and that "psychology," which has blossomed forth so luxuriously in recent times, is the work of apostates from idealism. And as a matter of fact, why would a man begin to pry into the innermost depths of his soul, why should he verify creeds that are unquestionably splendid, beautiful, and interesting? Descartes's *de omnibus dubitandum* is, of course, irrelevant here: for a methodological principle, man will never consent to lose the ground under his feet. More likely the reverse—lost soil gives rise to all doubt. Consequently, when it turns out that idealism could not withstand the pressure of reality, when a man, who by the will of the Fates has collided head-on with real life, suddenly sees to his horror that all the fine a priori judgments were false, then for the first time only is he seized by that irrepressible doubt that instantly destroys the seemingly very solid walls of the old air castles. Socrates, Plato, good, humanity, ideas—all the assembly of former angels and saints who were guarding the innocent human soul from attacks by the evil demons of skepticism and pessimism—vanish without a trace into thin air, and man, faced by his most horrible enemies, experiences for the first time in his life that fearful loneliness from which not even the most devoted and loving heart is able to deliver him. And precisely at this point begins the philosophy of tragedy. Hope is lost forever, but life remains, and there is much life ahead. You cannot die, even though you would like to. The ancient Russian prince was mistaken when he said that the dead have no shame.[1] Ask Dostoevsky. He will tell you differently through the mouth of Dmitry Karamazov: "I've

---

[1] Supposedly said by Grand Prince Svyatoslav, when faced by an overwhelming number of Greek troops in 970. [Tr.]

learned a lot this night. I've learned that it is impossible not only to live as a scoundrel, but also to die as one." Do you understand? All a priori judgments are lost, the philosophy of Kant and Count Tolstoy is ended, and there begins the realm of the *Ding an sich*. Would you like to follow Dostoevsky and Nietzsche there? No obligations are involved: whoever so desires has the right to go "back to Kant." You are not convinced that you will find here what you need—"beauty" of any kind whatsoever. Perhaps there is nothing here but ugliness. One thing only is certain: there is reality here—a new, unheard of, unwitnessed reality, or better put, a reality that has never before been displayed. And those who are obliged to call it their reality, those who do not have the possibility of returning to the simple life, where concern over Kitty's health, arguments with Koznyshov, the management of estates, the writing of books, et cetera, lead even such experienced men as Levin into the ordinary rut of human existence—such people will view everything with different eyes than we. We can renounce these people: of what concern are they to us? We have done so in the past, and we still do so today.

N. K. Mikhailovsky,[1] in his well-known and in many respects remarkable article, called Dostoevsky a "cruel talent." The characterization is most apt: I think it will always stick to Dostoevsky. Unfortunately, the critic wanted with these two words not only to give a characterization of the artist, but also to pronounce judgment on him and on all his work. Cruel—that means mutilated, deformed, and therefore also unfit. N. K. Mikhailovsky could only regret that it happened this way—that although Dostoevsky was a man of vast talent, he was not at the same time a priest of humanity. The critic's judgment in this case is based on the assumption that humanity is unquestionably better and more lofty than cruelty. Unques-

---

[1] N. K. Mikhailovsky (1842–1904), a leader of the Populists, a sociologist, and a literary critic. As a critic, he was mainly interested in the writer's message and his degree of public utility. [Tr.]

tionably? But where then is Descartes's principle which we just mentioned, where is *de omnibus dubitandum*? Mikhailovsky was, of course, acquainted with it. But as usual, it remained out of the picture, knowing all too well that it must always appear last if it wishes to be *bienvenu*.

In another of his articles, this same Mikhailovsky, when speaking of Proudhon, presents a number of facts intended to prove that the celebrated Frenchman, with whose name we in Russia associated the concept of the best fighter for lofty ideas, was something of a rogue in his personal life. He concludes his story with the following words: "It is not at all pleasant to single out these dark traits, because in doing so, one is obliged to tear something from the heart." And then immediately after this, in a strange association of ideas, he adds: "This is not just empty rhetoric." I do not know how the other readers took the words quoted above, but for my part, I indeed thought that they were empty rhetoric. Mikhailovsky was not obliged to tear anything from his heart. This does not mean that he was indifferent to Proudhon's ideas. And even less would I like to say that Mikhailovsky is inclined to talk for the mere sake of talking: on the contrary, you encounter "empty rhetoric" in his works just as seldom as you encounter serious thought in the majority of the other writers. But this time the insincerity was obvious, and that is why he needed his reservation. Obviously, even such an unexpected discovery as the fact that a creator of lofty ideas was not a completely honorable man in his personal life could not astonish Mikhailovsky. He was taken aback by his own placidity and, as he was unable to explain this strange phenomenon, or did not have time to think it over, he hastened to mask it with his trite phrase, which had lain for so long in his memory. A great deal is revealed in this apparently insignificant psychological fact. Evidently Proudhon himself meant nothing to Mikhailovsky (although he declares in his article that it was just the reverse). Proudhon was merely the incarnation of the great idea of humanity (permit me to use this word in its broadest sense); well, then, could a whole army of Proudhon-scoundrels, of even Proundhon-bandits and murderers, cast the slightest shadow of doubt on the sublimity of the idea? Humanity is not maintained by the authority of French writers; it is a part of Mikhailovsky's own soul, and its most stable part. He himself states this clearly in the Preface to the new edition of his collected works, where he sums up his many years of literary activity: "Every time the word 'truth' [*pravda*] comes to mind, I cannot help admiring its striking inner beauty. There is no such word, I believe, in any other European language. It appears that only in Russian are truth and justice [*istina i spravedlivost'*] called by one and the same word and thus seem to merge into one great whole. Truth—in this vast meaning of the word has always lain the object of my quests. I never could believe, and I do not now, that it is impossible to find a point of view wherein truth as verity and truth as justice go hand in hand, the one complementing the other." These words explain why Mikhailovsky remained calm when he made his discovery about Proudhon, although he knew that one should be deeply grieved in such cases. Of what importance is Proudhon, when a man's soul contains an idea as solid as granite, *aere perennius*, not made by human hands? It was this unwavering faith in the idea, in humanity, in truth, which took the discovery about Proudhon as a matter of secondary importance (Mikhailovsky had probably made more than one such discovery in his life and had wondered many a time at his soul's callousness and perhaps had even castigated himself for it) and which prevented the critic from pausing at the sight of this unusual case of a "cruel talent." After all, it was not a cruel mediocrity, but a cruel talent, i.e., a characteristic of man in connection with which even the most extreme positivists do not hesitate to recall the name of God. And suddenly talent proves to be in the service of cruelty! But Mikhailovsky is one of those fortunate chosen ones who have been given the possibility of serving ideas their whole life long. Such people are also served by ideas, which protect them from the most horrible of experiences. This was not the case with Dostoevsky. He failed to remain to the end of his life the priest of his early faith. He was doomed to the lot of deserter, betrayer, and traitor. Ideas avenge themselves on such people, and they do it mercilessly and inexorably. There is no form of inward and invisible disgrace, there is no form of humiliation that does not fall to their lot. Dostoevsky's penal servitude lasted not four years, but a lifetime. Mikhailovsky is, of course, right when he explains Dostoevsky's world view by the trials that he stood. But the question is, can such trials really prevent people from seeing the "truth"? Isn't it just the reverse? After all, it can be that an ordinary life among ordinary people gives one an ordinary philosophy! And who will guarantee that people need just such a philosophy as this? Perhaps in order to find truth it is necessary, above all, to free oneself from all commonplaceness. So that penal servitude not only does not vindicate "convictions," it refutes them; and the really true philosophy is the philosophy of penal servitude. If all this is so, then it means that the idea of humanity also, which was born among free people, has no right to pillory cruelty and reproach it for its dark, penal origin, but must instead yield to its humble opponent all the countless rights and advantages which it has thus far enjoyed in the world, and above all, its glittering retinue of poets, artists, philosophers, and preachers, who for thousands of years have tirelessly lavished it with great praise.

At any rate, justice demands that we at least listen impartially and attentively to the cruel underground man without being confused either by Count Tolstoy's fears or Mikhailovsky's firm belief in truth.

XII

Skepticism and pessimism arouse the same mystical horror in the underground man as in Count Tolstoy, but the former has

not been given the possibility of returning to commonplaceness, not even the possibility of decently pretending to himself
and others that he has returned there (he might just try that).
He knows that the past has long been forgotten, that granite,
aere perennius, things not made by human hands—in brief,
everything on which people have hitherto based their stability,
all their a prioris—have been irretrievably lost for him. And
with the boldness of a man bereft of hope, he suddenly decides
to cross the fatal boundary, to take that fearful step against
which he had been warned both by precepts of the past and
his own experience gained from forty years of life. It is impossible to overcome his unhappiness and doubts by means of
idealism. All attempts at struggle in this direction have come
to naught: "The 'lofty and beautiful' has weighed so heavily
on my neck these forty years," says Dostoevsky's underground
man. One thing remains: to abandon the fruitless struggle and
follow skepticism and pessimism in order to see where they
will lead. This means saying to himself: "Everything that has
been valued, everything that has been regarded as lofty and
beautiful, is forbidden fruit for me in this life. But I continue
to live, I shall go on living for a long time in new and terrible
circumstances. Therefore I shall create for myself my own
concept of the lofty and beautiful." In other words, there begins
a "revaluation of all values." Idealism, quite unexpectedly to
itself, turns from the innocent judge into the accused. Dostoevsky is ashamed to recall that he himself was once an idealist. He would like to renounce his past, and because it is impossible to deceive himself, he tries to imagine his recent life
in a different light; he invents extenuating circumstances for
himself. "Among us Russians, generally speaking, there have
never been any of those silly transcendental German and particularly French romantics on whom nothing has any effect,
even if the earth were to give way under their feet, even if all
France were to perish at the barricades—they are always the
same, even for decency's sake they do not change, and they

will go on singing their transcendental songs, so to say, to the grave, because they are fools. But with us here in Russia, there are no fools."[1] As if there are no "fools" in Russia! Who sang the praises of Makar Devushkin night after night? Who shed tears over Natasha, even at a time when the earth was already crumbling away under his feet? Alas, one cannot erase from the memory these pages from the past, no matter how much cunning one resorts to. Of all our romantics, Dostoevsky was the most fanciful, the most transcendental, the most sincere.

Now that Judgment Day had come, and he saw that the ways of its court differ from those promised by Socrates and Plato, and that, despite his virtues, he had been driven into outer darkness along with a multitude of people like him, he wanted to vindicate himself, at least a little. Perhaps he recalled—in such cases, as we know, memory is always tediously obliging—perhaps he recalled that, after all, people had warned him. They had told him that this court rejoices more over one repentant sinner than over a hundred righteous men. He must have understood that the righteous, all those "transcendental romantics," are considered ordinary, and that on Judgment Day, in their capacity as ordinary people, they cannot expect to be pardoned. Formerly, he had not heard or had not comprehended the warning voice, and now—now it is almost too late; now, remorse and self-torture are of no avail. He is doomed, and, of course, for all eternity. On Judgment Day, there are no other sentences. It is not the same as with Count Tolstoy and his dealings with conscience, which imposes humane, suspended sentences in which there is justice, mercy, and, above all, a promise of pardon. In this case, there is no pardon. But even worse is the fact that resignation, on which moralists always rely so heavily, does not help. Here is the testimony of the underground man, who is well versed in these matters: "Confronted by a wall, the direct people give up in all sincerity. For them, the wall is no evasion, as it is, for

[1] Dostoevsky, *op. cit.*, III (2), 106–107.

example, for us—no pretext to turn aside. No, they throw up their hands in all sincerity. For them, the wall has something soothing, morally assuaging, and final—perhaps even something mystical."[1] The language is, of course, different, but who would fail to recognize in this wall the Kantian a priori standing before the *Ding an sich*? They were a great satisfaction to philosophers, but Dostoevsky, who needed this "soothing, morally assuaging, and final" thing more than all else in the world, consciously preferred to dash his head against the wall rather than to reconcile himself to its impenetrability. "It is a fearful thing to fall into the hands of the living God!" You see that "eternal" truths were devised by the sages not so much for the people needing consolation as for the consolers, i.e., for themselves. This thought horrifies Dostoevsky. After all, his entire life, his entire past, had been the personification of the idea of the consoler. He was a novelist who taught people to believe that the horrible fate of the humiliated and insulted is expiated by the tears and good sentiments of the readers and writers. His happiness, his inspiration was nourished by the "humblest man," "our brother." Only when man sees for himself that for years on end he had been able to cherish such a hideous lie in his soul and revere it as a great and sacred truth, only then does he begin to understand that "ideas" must not be believed, to understand what splendid and alluring forms our basest impulses can assume if they need to gain ascendance over our souls. And indeed, what can be more terrible than a singer of "poor folk" watering his poetic flower garden with the tears of Makar Devushkin and Natasha?

Now it is clear why Dostoevsky cannot return to his former state of tranquillity, to the wall that contains so much that is morally assuaging and final for direct people. Better any truth at all than such a lie, he says to himself—and thence the valor with which he looks reality in the face. Do you remember the almost nonsensical, but brilliant, statement of Shakespeare's Lear: "Thou'dst shun a bear; but if thy flight lay toward the

[1] *Ibid.*, 77.

roaring sea, thou'dst meet the bear i' th' mouth."[1] Dostoevsky
fled reality, but he met idealism on the way and turned back:
all the horrors of life are not so terrible as the ideas invented
by reason and conscience. Rather than shedding tears over
Devushkin, it is better to tell the truth: let the world go to
pot, as long as I can have my tea. It was not easy for Dostoevsky to accept such a "truth." And what is a man to do
with it whose past included Makar Devushkin and penal servitude, and whose present includes epilepsy and all the delights
of the life of a struggling, middle-aged Petersburg writer who
is practically just beginning his career? At one time it was
thought that "truth" consoles and strengthens man and bolsters
his spirits. But the truth of the underground is of an entirely
different breed than its magnanimous predecessors. It does not
think of man at all, and if, metaphorically speaking, any intentions can be attributed it, they are not, at any rate, benevolent
ones. Its business is not to console. Perhaps to ridicule, to
offend—it is still capable of that. "More than anything else,
the laws of nature have constantly offended me throughout my
life," says the underground man. Is it any wonder then that
he can feel no tenderness either for truths or ideals, if both
of them, now in the form of the laws of nature, now in the
form of lofty doctrines of morality, do nothing but offend and
humiliate a childishly trusting and totally innocent being? How
is one to respond to such masters? What feeling other than
perpetual, implacable hatred can one have for the natural order
and for humanity? Spencer preached accommodation, the
moralists—submission to fate. But that is all very well if one
assumes that accommodation is still possible and that submission can at least bring peace. "If one assumes!" But psychology has already shown us that all assumptions are devised
solely for the assumers, and that even Count Tolstoy participated in the conspiracy against the humiliated and insulted.

　　Therein is the reason why Dostoevsky, to the surprise of his
contemporaries, refused with such strange obstinacy to venerate

[1] Act II, Scene 4. [Tr.]

the humane ideas that exercised complete sway over our literature in the sixties and seventies. Mikhailovsky was right in
seeing a "malevolent" man in him. (Scarcely had this epithet
crept into the pages of Mikhailovsky's works than we became
accustomed to meeting it in other places as well.) How, for
example, the underground man talks of "the future happiness
of mankind," i.e., of the cornerstone on which all the "convictions" of humanitarians have always rested and still rest today!
"Then," he says, "there will be new economic relations, completely ready-made, so that all possible questions will disappear in an instant, simply because all possible answers to
them will have been provided. Then the Crystal Palace will be
built. Well, in brief, then the bird Kagan[1] will come flying to
us."[2] Obviously, these are the words of a malevolent man
infringing on his neighbors' peace and happiness. But this is
nothing yet—for the time being, it is mere irony. Later, there
follows what almost amounts to a "call to action." "I, for example, won't in the least be surprised," he continued, "if suddenly,
for no rhyme nor reason, in the midst of the future universal
rationality, there appears a gentleman with a plebian, or perhaps I should say, a retrograde and sarcastic physiognomy,
who will stand with arms akimbo and say to us all: 'What about
it, gentlemen, how about giving this rationality a good kick
and overthrowing it once and for all for the sole purpose of
sending all these logarithms to the devil and living again
according to our own will?' "[3] Obviously, we are not dealing
here with a dialectician. Dostoevsky is not disposed to argue—
no, indeed! After all, he is destroying, not the hopes of others,
but of himself. "I most certainly didn't say that because I'm
so fond of sticking my tongue out," he admits later. "Perhaps
the only reason I became angry over it was because up to now
there hasn't been one building of all those you've built, at
which one can help sticking his tongue out." So the man with

---

[1] A bird from Russian folk literature. [Tr.]
[2] Dostoevsky, *op. cit.*, III (2), 89.
[3] *Ibid.*, 90.

the retrograde and sarcastic physiognomy has nothing to do with it. The question is whether Dostoevsky's Crystal Palace can be reconciled with his past, his present, and his everlasting penal servitude. And the answer to this is a sharp "no." If man's task is to find happiness on earth, then all is lost forever. This task is indeed impracticable, for how can future happiness atone for the unhappiness of the past and the present? Will the fate of Makar Devushkin, who was treated contemptuously in the nineteenth century, be improved because no one in the twenty-second century will be allowed to insult one's neighbor? Not only will it not be improved, it will become worse. No, if it has come to that, then let unhappiness dwell among men forever, let future Makars also be treated with contempt. At this point, Dostoevsky not only does not want to prepare the foundation for the future splendors of the Crystal Palace, he is filled with spite, with hate, and at the same time, with secret joy as he exults in advance over the thought that some gentleman will always be found to prevent the establishment of happiness on earth. This gentleman is, of course, purely imaginary; for a believer, he is, of course, no argument. But, after all, it is not a question here of arguments. The main point is that Dostoevsky does not want universal happiness in the future, he does not want the future to vindicate the present. He demands a different vindication and prefers to beat his head against the wall to the point of exhaustion rather than to find solace in the humane ideal. People chose a happy lot for themselves when they threw up their hands before the wall. But such a lot is not destined for everyone. The a priori exists only for people of a direct nature. What then remains for Dostoevsky?

XIII

In *Notes from the Underground*, Dostoevsky renounces his ideals—those ideals which, so it seemed to him, he had brought back from penal servitude intact. I say "seemed," for as a

matter of fact, what he took for ideals during his life in the
penal colony and in his first years of freedom was merely—
I hope this is now clear—a deceptive belief that upon serving
his sentence, he would become the free man he was before.
Like all people, he took his own hopes for the ideal and hastened to expel all memories of penal life from his mind, or at
least to adapt them to the conditions of his new life. But his
efforts led to nothing, or more precisely, to almost nothing.
The penal truths, however much he tried to polish and tidy
them up, retained too obvious traces of their origin. From
under their magnificent attire, sad branded faces stared out at
the readers; one could see shaved heads. In the loud, bombastic
words, one could hear the clanking of chains. Only *The House
of the Dead* was received by the public and critics as something kindred, ordinary, and free. And, indeed, in this work,
Dostoevsky displays—for the only time in his life—almost the
Tolstoyan art of reconciling reality with established ideals.
The reader laid down *The House of the Dead* enraptured,
elevated, filled with tender emotion, ready to struggle against
evil, et cetera—exactly as the aesthetics of the time demanded.
And, by the way, in his elevated mood and his readiness, he
considered Dostoevsky just as good and kind a person as himself. Yet, with a modicum of attention and a bit less enthusiasm, you can find pearls, even in *The House of the Dead*, such
as you will never find in the underground—for example, the
concluding words of the novel: "How much youth was needlessly buried within these walls, what mighty powers were
wasted there to no purpose! After all, the whole truth must be
told; those men were exceptional men. They were perhaps the
most talented, the strongest representatives of all our people.
But their mighty strength went to waste, it went to waste
abnormally, unjustly, and irretrievably." Is there a Russian who
does not know these lines by heart? And moreover, isn't it
partly due to them that the novel owes its fame? Consequently,
Dostoevsky did know how to embellish this hideous and disgusting idea. How? By saying that the best Russians were in

penal colonies! That the most talented, the most remarkable, the strongest people were murderers, thieves, arsonists, and bandits. And who said this? A man living at the time of Belinsky, Nekrasov, Turgenev, Grigorovich, at the time of all those people who have thus far been considered the pride and joy of Russia! And to prefer the stigmatized inhabitants of the House of the Dead to them! Why, that is downright madness. Yet two generations of readers have seen in this judgment an expression of Dostoevsky's great humanity. They thought that in his humility, in his love for his neighbor, he was singing praises in a new way to the humblest man. For propriety's sake, they did not even notice that, in his eagerness, the singer had indeed gone too far this time. Only recently did they notice (and, as a matter of fact, even this was fortuitous) the absurdity of such humility. But still, they did not venture to reproach Dostoevsky openly—so much had his reputation for sanctity grown because of the passage quoted above. They merely tried to reduce its importance by means of an appropriate interpretation. They began to point out that in Dostoevsky's time, convicts were not, strictly speaking, criminals in the true sense of the word, but merely objectors—for the most part, people who had rebelled against the outrageous practices of serfdom.

This explanation, although belated, was, of course, necessary. Unfortunately, it is completely without foundation. Dostoevsky was not particularly fond of the objectors in the penal colony; he merely tolerated them. Recall how he spoke of the political prisoners. His enthusiasm was for the real convicts, for those about whom his fellow prisoner, the Pole M . . . tsky, always said: "Je haïs ces brigands"—and it was only for them. In them, he found strength, talent, and singularity; he ranked them higher than Belinsky, Turgenev, and Nekrasov. Nothing is left to us but to be outraged by this judgment, to ridicule it, to curse it, to do whatever we please, but Dostoevsky meant precisely this and *only* this.

Unlike the Pole M . . . tsky, Dostoevsky saw in these brigands (if "all must be told," and I think it is high time it was) his "ideal," and just as he had done earlier in the case of Belinsky, he did now; he accepted their entire doctrine of life, which, although it had never been set down in books, was unquestionably most definite and clear. True, he accepted it, not joyfully and willingly, but because he could not do otherwise, and without considering what it might bring him: in such cases, a *beneficium inventarii* is not customary. He did not even want to admit to himself that his teachers were convicts. In defending his new views, he always referred to the common folk. "Something else changed our views, our convictions, and our hearts. That something else was our direct contact with the common people, brotherly union with them in our common misery, the realization that we ourselves had become the same as they, that we were on the same level as they and even on a level with their lowest representative."[1]

But what sort of people were they—those with whom Dostoevsky had lived? They were convicts; they were those elements that the people had rejected. To live with them means *not* to be on intimate terms with the people, *not* to be in contact with them, but to withdraw farther from them than have any of our Russian absentees who live permanently abroad. This must never for a single minute be forgotten. And if this is so, it also means that all Dostoevsky's veneration for the people, which had won him so many ardent and devoted followers, related to an entirely different deity, and that the Russians, the "trusting" readers, had been cruelly and unprecedentedly deceived by their teacher. True, Dostoevsky was not the first teacher to deceive his students. But few would have had the courage to make a substitution such as this. I suppose that Dostoevsky himself, despite his unusual acumen and sensitivity to everything pertaining to ideals and faith (he is the author of "The Grand Inquisitor"), did not, in the given instance, fully realize what he was doing. He did not want to

[1] Dostoevsky, *Grazhdanin*, No. 50, 1873.

believe in convicts, and if he placed them on such an impossibly high pedestal in the excerpt quoted from *The House of the Dead*, it was only in the vague hope that the convicts could still be subordinated to the higher idea. At least in his writing, Dostoevsky made open obeisance only once to his fellow convicts. And that was probably because the general tone of *The House of the Dead* removes all possibility of suspicion on the part of the reader. It contains as much sympathy for good as it does artistry. The reader had long since stopped scrutinizing the individual thoughts: say what you please, everything will be taken for the noble idea.

Yet, all the ordeals Dostoevsky underwent in Siberia were trivial in comparison with the horrible necessity of bowing down before convicts. Nietzsche asks: "My friend, do you know the word contempt? And the torment of your justice in trying to be fair to those who despise you?" And, indeed, there is no greater torment in life. But Dostoevsky was obliged to get to know it. The convicts *despised* him; this is attested to on almost every page of *The House of the Dead*; but reason, conscience, and "justice" did not permit him to revenge himself on them, to answer contempt with contempt. Like Nietzsche, he was still obliged to side with his inexorable foes, to acknowledge them—and, I repeat, not out of fear, not out of the greatness of his heart and its compassion for the humblest man, but out of conscience—as his teachers, as the best and most talented people, whose existence justifies all that is ugly, insignificant, and useless in life, i.e., the Dostoevskys, Turgenevs, Belinskys, et cetera.

Such was the terrible burden Dostoevsky brought with him from penal servitude. With the years, not only did it not grow lighter, it pressed down on him ever more and more. He was unable to cast it off until the very last days of his life. He had to bear it; he had to hide it from everyone's eyes, and at the same time to go on "teaching" people. How can one cope with such a task?

XIV

The answer to this question is in all Dostoevsky's subsequent literary work. From then on, he was to spend almost no time on the humiliated and insulted—only at odd moments, out of habit. His favorite subject is crime and the criminal. One question relentlessly pursues him: "What sort of people are convicts? How did it happen that they seemed to be right, that they still seem to be right for having despised me, and why do I involuntarily feel so insignificant, so weak and, horrible to say, so *ordinary* before them? Can this really be the truth? Is this what the people should be taught?" There can be no doubt that Dostoevsky asked himself such questions. Raskolnikov's article clearly attests to it. There, people are divided, not into good and evil, but into ordinary and extraordinary. All the "good" ones fall into the category of the ordinary, and, in their narrow-mindedness, obey the moral laws; but the extraordinary ones create their own laws, and to them, "all is permitted." Razumikhin correctly sums up the gist of this article when he tells Raskolnikov: "What is really *original* in all this [that is, in the article and in Raskolnikov's arguments explaining it] and what is exclusively your own, to my horror, is that you sanction bloodshed when one follows *the dictates of one's conscience*, and, excuse my saying so, you do it with such fanaticism. Consequently, that is the main idea of your article. But sanction of bloodshed *by conscience* is . . . why, in my opinion, that is more horrible than the official, legal sanction of bloodshed."[1] (The words "original," "the dictates of one's conscience," and "by conscience" were italicized by Dostoevsky.) Thus, "conscience" compels Raskolnikov to side with the criminal. Its sanction, its approval, its sympathy are not with good, but with evil. The very words "good" and "evil" no longer exist. They have been replaced by the expressions "ordinariness" and "extraordinariness." The former is connected with

[1] Dostoevsky, *Polnoe sobranie sochinenij* (1894–1895), V, 260.

the idea of vulgarity, worthlessness, uselessness, whereas the latter is a synonym for grandeur. In other words, Raskolnikov stands "beyond good and evil"—and this was thirty-five years ago, when Nietzsche was still a student dreaming of lofty ideals. Razumikhin told the truth—the idea was most original, and it belonged entirely to Dostoevsky. In the sixties, no one ever dreamed of such a thing, not only in Russia, but even in Europe. Even Shakespeare's *Macbeth* was regarded at the time as an edifying portrayal of the pangs of conscience in store for a sinner while still on earth. (Brandes[1] even now goes on interpreting *Macbeth* that way: *fabula docet.*)

Now the question arises: if Raskolnikov's idea is so original that it occurred to absolutely no one but its originator, why did Dostoevsky have to arm himself against it? What was the use in struggling against it? Against whom was Dostoevsky struggling? Answer: against himself, and only himself. He alone in the entire world envied the moral grandeur of the criminal, and, as he did not dare to express his true thoughts openly, he created various "situations" for them. First, in *The House of the Dead,* he expressed his admiration for convicts in such a way that he lured the kindest and most compassionate people to his side. Then he substituted convicts for the idea of the people. Then, for the remainder of his life he fought against the theoretical apostates from "good," although there was just one such theoretician in world literature—Dostoevsky himself. After all, if Dostoevsky's task really amounted to a struggle against evil, then he must have felt splendid. Who of his fellow writers did not have just such a task? But Dostoevsky had his own original, very original, idea. Struggling against evil, he offered in its defense arguments such as it never dared even dream of. Conscience itself intervened for evil! The idea on which Raskolnikov based his article was developed at great length and in a different form by Nietzsche in his *Toward a*

---

[1] Georg M. Brandes (1842–1927), a Danish author and literary critic. [Tr.]

Genealogy of Morals and still earlier in *Human, All-Too-Human.* I do not mean that Nietzsche borrowed it from Dostoevsky. When he was writing *Human, All-Too-Human,* no one in Europe had heard of Dostoevsky. But one can safely say that the German philosopher would never have been so bold and frank in expounding it in *Toward a Genealogy of Morals* if he had not felt Dostoevsky's support behind him.

At any rate, it is evident that, despite the novel's plot, Raskolnikov's real tragedy does not lie in his decision to break the law, but in the fact that he realized he was incapable of such a step. Raskolnikov is no murderer; he is guilty of no crime. The incident with the old pawnbroker and Lizaveta is invention, slander, and false accusation. And Ivan Karamazov, later on, was not involved in the Smerdyakov affair. He too was slandered by Dostoevsky. All these "heroes" are of Dostoevsky's own flesh and blood; they are transcendental thinkers, romanticists, designers of projects for a future ideal and felicitous social order, devoted friends of mankind, who have suddenly grown ashamed of their loftiness and transcendentalism and have realized that discussions about ideals are idle chatter that does not add one iota to the common treasury of human wealth. Their tragedy is in their inability to begin a new and different life. And so profound, so hopeless is this tragedy that it was not difficult for Dostoevsky to present it as the cause of the agonizing experiences of his heroes who murder. But there is not the slightest basis here on which to regard Dostoevsky as an expert on or an investigator of the criminal soul. Although he knew convicts, he saw them only in prison. Their earlier life, when they were free, and the history of their crimes remained just as much of a mystery to him as it does to all of us. The prisoners never spoke about all that. People will ask: what about poetic fantasy? In my opinion, it must not even be mentioned in connection with Dostoevsky. The ancient bards were endowed with fantasy. The Muses would indeed come flying to them at night and whisper in their ear

wonderful dreams, which these favorites of Apollo would jot
down in the morning. But to Dostoevsky, the underground
man, the convict, the Russian man of letters who used to carry
his wife's clothing off to the pawnshop, this sort of mythology
is most unbecoming. His idea wandered about the deserts of
his own soul. And from there, it brought the tragedy of the
underground man, of Raskolnikov, of Karamazov, et cetera.
These criminals without crime, these pangs of conscience without guilt form the content of Dostoevsky's numerous novels.
Herein is Dostoevsky himself, herein is reality, herein is real
life. All else is "doctrine." All else is a wretched hut hastily
knocked together from odds and ends of old buildings. Who
needs it? Dostoevsky himself, it must be noted, attached great
significance to his doctrine, just as Count Tolstoy and Nietzsche
did, just as almost all writers do. He thought that he could tell
people what to do and how to live. But of course, this ridiculous pretension always remained a pretension. People do not
live according to books; they never have.

At the end of *Crime and Punishment*, you read the following
promising lines: "But here begins a new story—the story of
the gradual renewal of a man, the story of his regeneration,
of his gradual crossing from one world into another, of his
acquaintance with a new, hitherto totally unknown reality.
This could constitute the subject of a new story, but our present
story is now ended." Don't these words sound like a solemn
promise? And didn't Dostoevsky, as a teacher, assume the
responsibility of showing us this new reality and these new
opportunities for Raskolnikov? But the teacher never went
beyond his promise. In the Foreword to *The Brothers Karamazov*, Dostoevsky's last work, we again come across this same
promise. One novel is too little for Dostoevsky. In order to
portray his true hero, he needs still another novel, although in
The Brothers Karamazov, which is spun out over a thousand
pages, there should have been room enough for the "new life"
as well. And, as you know, between *Crime and Punishment*

and *The Brothers Karamazov*, Dostoevsky wrote three whole novels, each of them massive: *The Idiot, A Raw Youth,* and *The Possessed*! But he never remembered his promise. *The Idiot*, with its Prince Myshkin, cannot, of course, be taken into consideration. If such a "new" reality is all that awaits man, if Prince Myshkin, that pitiful shadow, that cold, anemic specter, is to serve as our "ideal," then wouldn't it be better not to look into the future at all? The most unassuming and grievously insulted man, even Makar Devushkin, would renounce such "hopes" and return to his impoverished past. No, Prince Myshkin is nothing but idea, i.e., a void. And what a role he has! He stands between two women, and just like a Chinese roly-poly, leans now in one direction, now in the other. True, from time to time, Dostoevsky lets him have his say. But surely this is no great merit: it is the author himself speaking. Moreover, Prince Myshkin, like Alyosha Karamazov, is endowed with an unusual gift of foresight that practically verges on clairvoyance. But this, too, is no great virtue in the hero of a novel where the thoughts and deeds of all the characters are controlled by the author. And beyond these traits, Prince Myshkin is a complete nullity. Eternally grieving over those who grieve, he is unable to console anyone. He antagonizes Aglaya, and fails to soothe Nastasya Filippovna; he befriends Rogozhin, foresees his crime, but can do nothing about it. If only it were in his power to comprehend the tragic situation of the people around him! But he lacks even this. His grief is mere grief from a sense of duty. That is why he is so free with his words of hope and solace. He even offers his literary balm to Ippolit, but here he is met, or if you will, sent packing, as he well deserves. No, Prince Myshkin is a black sheep, even among Dostoevsky's eminent people, although they are all more or less unsuccessful. Dostoevsky understood and could portray only the rebellious, struggling, seeking soul. As soon as he tried to depict a man who had found himself, one who was composed and comprehending, he immediately fell into offensive banality.

Recall, for example, Father Zosima's visions of "the splendid unison of men in the future." Don't they reek of the tritest *Zukunftsmalerei*, which even the Socialists, who are so ridiculed in the underground, had long since repudiated? But in all such instances, Dostoevsky has no desire to think. With an indiscriminate hand, he takes from wherever it suits him: from the Slavophiles, from the Socialists, from the commonplaceness of bourgeois life. Evidently, he himself felt that this was not his task, and he performed it with astonishing negligence. But he was unable to renounce moralization and prophecy: they alone bound him to the rest of the people. This was the part of him that was best understood, that was esteemed, and for which he was elevated to prophet. However, one cannot live without people, entirely without people: "After all, every man must have at least somewhere to go. For there comes a time when he definitely must go somewhere," says Marmeladov. And for that occasion, one needs the customary uniform. After all, one must not appear in public with the words of the underground man, with deep respect for penal servitude, with all the "original" thoughts that filled Dostoevsky's head! People would not want to listen to such a neighbor; they would drive him away. People need idealism at any cost. And Dostoevsky throws this blessing to them by the handful, so that in the end, he himself at times thinks that such an occupation is indeed worth while. But only at times, so that afterward he can laugh at himself. Who is the person in question in the "Legend of the Grand Inquisitor"? Who is this cardinal, from whose hands the people get their daily bread? Isn't this legend a symbol of Dostoevsky's own prophetic work? Miracle, mystery, and authority—after all, his preaching consisted of these, and only of these elements. True, Dostoevsky intentionally refrained from saying the main thing. The Grand Inquisitor, who boldly undertook to correct Christ's work, is himself as weak and pitiful as the people whom he treats with such contempt. He made a dreadful miscalculation in appraising his role. He can tell but part of the truth—and not the most horrible part. The people accepted ideals from him indiscriminately, without examining them. But that was only because, for the people, ideals are nothing more than a pastime, a decoration, a formality. Their childish, naïve faith, which has not yet known doubt, demands nothing more for itself than a few words or other for its expression. That is why the people follow almost anyone who feels like leading them, and why they so readily change their idols: *le roi est mort, vive le roi*. But the old, wretched cardinal, exhausted by long hours of meditation, imagined that his feeble idea was capable of molding the confused, chaotic masses and giving them a fixed direction, that it was in its power to *play the benefactor* to hundreds of thousands, even millions of people. What a happy and dazzlingly splendid delusion! And, as you know, it is not only characteristic of the Grand Inquisitor in Dostoevsky's novel. In all ages, all teachers have thought that the world rested on their shoulders and that they were leading their students to happiness, to joy, to light! As a matter of fact, the flock needed the shepherds much less than the shepherds needed the flock. What would have become of the Grand Inquisitor if he had not held the proud belief that all mankind would perish without him? What would he have done with his life? And then this very old man, who with his keen mind can penetrate all the mysteries of our existence, cannot (perhaps he only pretends that he cannot) see one thing—the most important thing of all for him. He does not know that the people are not indebted to him for their faith, but he to the people—for the faith which at least partly justifies in his eyes his long, dismal, agonizing, and lonely life. He had deceived the people with his stories of miracles and mysteries; he had assumed the look of an omniscient and all-understanding authority; he had called himself God's deputy on earth. The people had trustingly accepted this lie, for they did not *need* the truth; they did not want to know it. But the old cardinal, with almost a century of experience behind him, with a mind sharpened by inquisitive and relentless thought, did not notice that he had fallen victim to his own deceit by imagining himself the benefactor of mankind. He *needed* this deceit, he had no other way to find faith in himself, and he accepted it from the hands of the contemptible, insignificant crowd.

x v

But Dostoevsky himself could not bear this deceit; he could not be satisfied with such "faith in himself." Despite his ability to talk so beautifully and seductively of the "proud loneliness" of his Grand Inquisitor, he understood that the whole magnificent masquerade of high-flown and noble words was needed, again, not for himself, but for others, for the people. Proud loneliness! Can present-day man really be proud when he is alone with himself? In public, in speeches, in books—that is a different matter. But when no one sees or hears him, when in the dead of night, in complete silence, he realizes what his life really is, how dare he use even one lofty word? Prometheus was lucky—he was never left alone. He was always heard by Zeus; he had an adversary, someone he could irritate and provoke to anger by his austere look and his proud words. He had a "cause." But modern man, Raskolnikov or Dostoevsky, does not believe in Zeus. When people abandon him, when he is left alone with himself, he automatically begins to tell himself the truth, and, my God, what a horrible truth it is! How few it contains of those fascinating and wonderful images which we, on the basis of poetic legends, have regarded as the constant companions of solitary people! Here, for example, is one of Dostoevsky's meditations (actually it is Raskolnikov's, but, as we know, it is one and the same thing):

"Therefore I'm definitely a louse," he added, grinding his teeth. "Because I myself am perhaps more vile and disgusting than the louse I killed, and *I felt beforehand* that I would tell myself so *after* killing her. Can anything really equal this horror? Oh, the vulgarity, Oh, the baseness! Oh, how well I understand the 'prophet,' with his sword in hand, mounted on his steed. Allah orders, and you must submit—you trembling creature! The prophet is right, he's right when he places an excellent battery of guns from one side of the street to the other and mows down both the innocent and the guilty without even deigning to explain. Submit, you trembling creature, and *wish not,* for that is not your business! Oh, I'll never forgive that old hag, not for anything in the world!"[1]

What humiliating, disgusting words and images! Isn't it true that Raskolnikov had to murder the old woman and Lizaveta "for poetry," in order to have a proper explanation for such moods? But as a matter of fact, no blood was shed here, no criminal act was committed. It is the usual "punishment" that is sooner or later in store for all "idealists." Sooner or later the hour will strike for each of them, and they will exclaim with horror and gnashing of teeth: "The prophet was right; submit, you trembling creature!" As early as three hundred years ago, the greatest of all poets pronounced a terrible judgment on the greatest of all idealists. Recall Hamlet's mad cry: "The time is out of joint!" Since then, writers and poets have never ceased to phrase these words in an infinite number of ways. But thus far, no one has wanted to come right out and say to himself that there is no use even trying to join the links once they have been broken, that there is no use trying to steer time back again into the channel from which it has gone. New attempts are ever being made to restore the illusion of former happiness. People tirelessly shout to us that pessimism and skepticism have destroyed everything, that we must again "believe," "turn back," become "direct," et cetera. And as binding cement, they invariably offer the old "ideas," while stubbornly refusing to understand that these ideas contained all

[1] Dostoevsky, *Polnoe sobranie sochinenij* (1894–1895), V, 272.

our unhappiness. What will you tell Dostoevsky when he declares to you: "It was as if I had taken scissors and severed myself from everyone and everything"?[1] Will you send him to play the benefactor to his neighbors? But he tried that path long ago, and then wrote "The Grand Inquisitor." Let whoever can continue to occupy himself with lofty truths and deceit, but Dostoevsky knows that if the bond of time lies in this, then it is severed for good. He speaks of this matter not as a dilettante who has read a lot of pamphlets, but as a man who has seen everything with his own eyes and felt everything with his own hands. Book V, Chapter 4 of *The Brothers Karamazov* is entitled "Rebellion." It means that Dostoevsky not only does not want to try to restore the former "bond," but is ready to do anything to show that there is no longer any hope here, that there cannot be any. Ivan Karamazov rebels against the most stable principles on which our contemporary world view is based. The chapter starts right off with the following words: " 'I must make a confession to you,' Ivan said. 'I could never understand how anyone could love his neighbors. It is precisely his neighbors, in my opinion, that he can't love; perhaps he could love those people at a distance.' "[2] Alyosha interrupts his brother with a remark intended to show us that Dostoevsky does not share Ivan's opinion. But we are already accustomed to this infant's importunate and monotonous babbling, and it bothers us very little, especially as we are reminded of another passage, this time, one from an entry dated 1876 in *The Diary of a Writer*. Dostoevsky says there: "I declare that love of mankind is totally inconceivable, incomprehensible, and utterly impossible without a concomitant belief in the immortality of the human soul." It is clear that there is no difference between Ivan Karamazov's words and those of Dostoevsky himself. Everything Ivan Karamazov says is based on the assumption that the soul is not immortal.

[1] *Ibid.*, 115.
[2] *Ibid.*, XII, 280.

True, he offers no evidence to support his "assumption," but, after all, Dostoevsky also makes his assertion "for the time being without substantiation." In any event, there is no doubt that neither the hero of the novel nor the author believes in the salutary power of the idea "love thy neighbor." If you will, Dostoevsky goes even further than Ivan Karamazov. He writes: "Moreover, I maintain that an awareness of one's utter inability to help or to be of the slightest benefit or relief to suffering mankind, while simultaneously being thoroughly convinced that mankind does suffer, *can even turn the love in one's heart into hatred for it*" (Dostoevsky's italics).[1] Isn't it unfortunate that Razumikhin did not happen to be present, and that there was no one to remind Dostoevsky that his idea was extraordinarily original? After all, this is the same thing as in Raskolnikov's article: *conscience* permits hatred for people! If you cannot help your neighbor, then you cannot love him either. But, as you know, precisely those neighbors who usually claim our love are, for the most part, people whom it is impossible to help—I am no longer speaking of all mankind. Formerly, it was enough to sing the praises of the suffering man, to shed tears over him, to call him brother. Now, this is not enough; people want to help him at any cost; they want the humblest man to cease being the humblest and to become the best! But if that is not feasible, they tell love to go to the devil, and place everlasting hatred on its vacant throne forever. Dostoevsky (I suppose that after the above quotations no one will again confuse him with Alyosha) no longer believed in the omnipotence of love or valued tears of compassion and tender emotion. The inability to help is the final and all-annihilating argument for him. He seeks strength and power. And you discover that the ultimate, the most sincere, the most cherished aim of his aspirations is the *Wille zur Macht*, and that it is as sharply and clearly expressed as it is with Nietzsche. He, too, could have followed Nietzsche's ex-

[1] *Ibid.*, X, 425.

ample and printed these words in huge, black letters at the end of any of his novels, for in them is the point of all his quests!

In *Crime and Punishment*, the chief task of all Dostoevsky's literary work is overshadowed by the idea of retribution, which has been cleverly fitted to the novel. To the unsuspecting reader, it seems that Dostoevsky is actually Raskolnikov's judge, and not the accused. But in *The Brothers Karamazov*, the question is posed with such clarity that it no longer leaves any doubt as to the author's intentions.

Raskolnikov is "guilty." By his own admission (forced from him by torment, and consequently unworthy of belief), he committed a crime: murder. People decline all responsibility for his suffering, however terrible it is. Ivan Karamazov knows this logic. He knows that if he were to propose his own fate for discussion, he would immediately be accused in some way or other of having "eaten the apple," as Dostoevsky puts it, i.e., of being guilty in thought, if not in deed. Therefore, he does not even try to speak of himself. He raises his famous question about the unavenged tears of a child. "Tell me," he says to his brother. "I ask you frankly. Answer me: suppose you were constructing the edifice of human destiny, with the aim of making men finally happy, of giving them peace and rest at last; but that in order to do it, you found it necessary and unavoidable to torture one single tiny creature—for example, that same little child who was beating its breast with its tiny fist [about which Ivan had told Alyosha earlier], and you had to erect this edifice on its unavenged tears—would you agree to be the architect under these conditions? Tell me, and don't lie." Alyosha answers this question, also in a quiet voice, as Prince Myshkin answered Ippolit, but the answer is, of course, different. No mention is made of "forgiveness," and Alyosha flatly rejects the proposed project. Dostoevsky has at last come to his final word. He now states openly what he had at first expressed with reservations and annotations in *Notes from the Underground*: absolutely no harmony, no ideas, no love or forgiveness, in brief, nothing that sages have devised from ancient to modern times can justify the nonsense and absurdity in the fate of an individual person. He speaks of a child, but this is merely for the "simplification" of an already complex question, or more probably in order to disarm his adversaries, who, in arguing, toy so cleverly with the word "guilty." And as a matter of fact, can that little child, beating its breast with its tiny fist, be any more horrible than Dostoevsky-Raskolnikov, when he suddenly realized that he had "severed himself as if with scissors from everyone and everything?" Recall what happened to Razumikhin when he followed Raskolnikov out of the room after that incredible, that horribly agonizing scene of the latter's leave-taking with his mother and sister: he suddenly divined the hell that was taking place in his unfortunate friend's soul. "'Do you understand?' Raskolnikov asked him with a painfully contorted face"—and the question makes one's hair stand on end. Yes, there are horrors on this earth that have never been dreamt of by the erudition of the most learned men. Compared to them, Karamazov's stories of Turkish brutality and of parents' torturing their children seem pale. And, of course, the "apple" explains nothing here. One must either "avenge" those tears or—but can there be an "or" for people like Dostoevsky, who themselves have shed them? What answer can there be here? "Back to Kant"? God be with you, the way is open? But Dostoevsky goes forward, no matter what may await him up ahead.

When Raskolnikov is convinced after the murder that he is forever cut off from his former life, when he sees that his own mother, who loves him more than anything in the world, has ceased being a mother to him (prior to Dostoevsky, who could have thought such horrors possible?), that his sister, who for the sake of his future had agreed to enslave herself forever to Luzhin, is no longer a sister to him, he instinctively runs to Sonya Marmeladov. Why? What can he find in that unfortunate, unschooled, and unknowledgeable girl? Why does he prefer that meek and humble person to his true and devoted friend, who can speak so admirably about lofty subjects? But he does not even think of Razumikhin! This friend, ready as he is to help, would not know what to do with Raskolnikov's secret. He would probably advise him to do good deeds and thus assuage his poor conscience. But Raskolnikov flies into a rage at the mere thought of good. In his deliberations, one already senses that agony of despair that later prompted Ivan Karamazov to ask his dreadful question: "Why must we get to know this *devilish* good and evil, when it costs so much." Devilish good and evil—do you understand what Dostoevsky is infringing on? Human daring can go no further than this. As you know, all our hopes—and not only those in books, but also those in men's hearts have thus far lived and been supported by the belief that no sacrifice is too terrible for the triumph of good over evil. And suddenly out of the blue, there appears a man who solemnly, openly, and almost fearlessly (almost, for Alyosha does babble something in objection to Ivan) sends to the devil everything before which all people of all ages have prostrated themselves! And people were so gullible that, because of Alyosha's pitiful chatter, they forgave Dostoevsky Ivan Karamazov's dreadful philosophy. In all Russian literature, there was but one writer, N.K. Mikhailovsky, who sensed in Dostoevsky a "cruel" man, an advocate of a dark power that everyone has considered hostile from time immemorial. But even he did not guess the full danger of this enemy. It seemed to him that one had but to expose Dostoevsky's "evil design," to call it by its real name, and it would be destroyed forever. He could not imagine twenty years ago that the ideas of the underground were destined soon to be revived and to lay claim to their rights, not timidly and fearfully, not under the cover of the usual conciliatory, stereotyped phrases, but boldly and freely, with a presentiment of certain victory. The

"devilish good and evil," which seemed to be a chance phrase
from the lips of a literary hero who was alien to the author,
is now decked out as the scholarly formula "beyond good
and evil," and in this guise it hurls a challenge at the millennial faith of all sages past and present. And before what did
Dostoevsky's "good" bow its proud head? Karamazov speaks
of the fate of a tormented child. But Raskolnikov demands an
answer for himself, and only for himself. And failing to find
the necessary answer with good, he rejects it. Recall his conversation with Sonya Marmeladov. Raskolnikov did not go to
her to repent. To the very end, he could not repent deep down
in his heart, for he felt that he was completely innocent; he
knew that Dostoevsky had burdened him with the accusation
of murder merely for appearance's sake. Here are his thoughts,
his very last while still in the penal colony: "Oh, how happy
he would be if he could consider himself guilty [i.e., of the
murder]. He could have endured anything, even the shame
and disgrace. He judged himself severely, but his embittered
conscience found no particularly terrible fault in his past,
except perhaps a *blunder* [Dostoevsky's italics], which could
have happened to anyone. But he felt no remorse for his
crime."[1] These words are a summary of Raskolnikov's entire
horrible story. He had been crushed for reasons unknown to
him. His task, all his aspirations now amount to justifying his
misfortune, to restoring *his* life—and nothing, neither the happiness of the entire world nor the triumph of any idea whatsoever can give meaning in his eyes to his personal tragedy.
That is why, as soon as he notices Sonya's Bible, he asks her
to read to him the "Resurrection of Lazarus." He is not interested in the "Sermon on the Mount," the "Parable of the Phari-
see and the Publican," or, in brief, in anything that had been
transferred from the Gospel to present-day ethics in accordance with Tolstoy's formula "Goodness and brotherly love—
this is God." He had examined and tried all that, and, like
Dostoevsky himself, was convinced that when taken separately,

[1] *Ibid.*, V, 539.

when torn from the general context of the Holy Scripture, it becomes not truth, but a lie. Although he does not yet dare to acknowledge the idea that truth lies not with science, but where these enigmatic and mysterious words are written: "He that endureth to the end shall be saved,"[1] he nevertheless tries to turn his gaze in the direction of those hopes that Sonya lives by. "After all," he thinks, "she's like me—also a humble person; she has learned by experience what it means to *live* such a life. Maybe I'll learn from her what our erudite Razumikhin cannot explain, what even an infinitely loving maternal heart, ready for any sacrifice, cannot guess." He tries again to revive in his memory that understanding of the Gospel that does not reject the prayers and hopes of a solitary, ruined man under the pretext that to think of one's personal grief means to be an egoist. He knows that his lamentations will be heard here, that he will no longer be strung up on the rack of ideas, that he will be permitted to tell the whole, terrible, hidden truth about himself, the truth with which he was born into God's world. But he can expect all this only from the Gospel that Sonya reads, which is as yet uncut and unaltered by science and Count Tolstoy, from the Gospel in which there is preserved, along with other teachings, the story of Lazarus's resurrection; where, what is more, Lazarus's resurrection—indicating the great power of the miracle worker—gives meaning also to the other words that are so puzzling and incomprehensible to the poor, Euclidean human mind. In the very same way that Raskolnikov seeks his hopes solely in Lazarus's resurrection, so Dostoevsky sees in the Gospel not the propagation of this or that moral philosophy, but the pledge of a new life. He said: "Without a sovereign idea, neither man nor nation can exist. And there is *but one* [Dostoevsky's italics] sovereign idea in this world: namely, the idea of the immortality of the human soul, for all the rest of life's 'sovereign' ideas that man can live by derive solely from it."[2]

[1] Matthew X, 22. [Tr.]
[2] Dostoevsky, *op. cit.*, X, 424.

XVI

All this, of course, is not "scientific"; moreover, it is all dia-
mctrically opposed to the basic premises of modern science.
And Dostoevsky knew better than anyone else how little support he could get from the latest acquisitions and achievements
of the human mind. That is why he never tried to make
science his ally, and, simultaneously, why he was equally wary
of going into battle against it with its own weapon. He
understood perfectly well that there are no longer any guarantees from Heaven. But the triumph of science, the certainty
and manifestness of its incontestability do not reduce Dostoevsky to submission. After all, he told us long ago that, for
him, a wall is not an insuperable obstacle, but merely an
evasion, a pretext. To all scientific arguments he has one
answer (Dmitry Karamazov): "How can I live underground
without God? A convict can't exist without God."[1] Raskolnikov
arouses violent, implacable feelings of hatred in his fellow
convicts because of his scientism, his adherence to indisputable
evidence, his lack of faith, which, in Dostoevsky's words, they
immediately sensed in him. " 'You're a pagan! You don't believe
in God,' they would shout at him. 'You ought to be killed!' "[2]
It goes without saying that all this is illogical. From the fact
that the convicts regard lack of faith as the most horrible of
crimes, it by no means follows that we must deny the incontestable conclusions of science. Even if all convicts and men
of the underground were to perish, we must not, because of
them, revise the axioms recently acquired from the work of
dozens of generations of men; we must not renounce a priori
judgments, which were vindicated only a hundred years ago,
thanks to the great genius of the Königsberg philosopher.[3]
Such is the clear logic of the people who live above ground

[1] *Ibid.*, XII, 700.
[2] *Ibid.*, V, 541.
[3] Kant. [Tr.]

as contrasted to the vague yearnings of those from the underground. It is impossible to reconcile the two inimical sides. They struggle to the point of complete exhaustion and, *à la guerre, comme à la guerre*, they are not fastidious about the means of struggle. Convicts have been slandered, cursed, and dragged through the mud since the world began. Dostoevsky tries to apply these same methods to free people as well. Why not, for example, make a vulgar lampoon of a scientist? Why not ridicule Claude Bernard?[1] Or slander and humiliate a journalist, an employee of a liberal publication, and along with him, all liberally inclined people? Dostoevsky did not stop at that. The things he fabricated about Rakitin! The most inveterate convict seems a noble knight in comparison to this future leader of the liberals, who for twenty-five rubles does not scruple to assume the role of pimp. All that is said of Rakitin is out-and-out slander of the liberals, and the slander is deliberate. Say what you will about them, there is no doubt that the best and most honest people joined their ranks. But hatred is not particular about its means. If they do not believe in God, they should be killed—this is Dostoevsky's inner impulse, this is what impels him to fabricate all sorts of cock-and-bull stories about his former liberal associates. The Pushkin Speech, in which all strata and parties of Russian society were apparently called on to unite, was in fact a declaration of unceasing struggle to the death. "Humble thyself, proud man; get to work, idle man." Surely Dostoevsky knew that these words would arouse a whole storm of indignation and resentment in the very people they were intended to reconcile. What do they mean? They summon the aboveground man to the underground, to penal servitude, to eternal darkness. Dared Dostoevsky hope for a single minute that anyone would follow him? He knew, he knew all too well, that those of his listeners who were unwilling to play the hypocrite would not accept his call. "We want to be happy here and now,"—that

---

[1] Claude Bernard (1813–1878), a French physiologist. [Tr.]

is what each aboveground man thinks. What does he care if
Dostoevsky has not yet completed his penal servitude? It is
said that everyone present at the Pushkin Celebration was
deeply moved by Dostoevsky's speech. Many even wept. But
what is surprising about that? After all, the speaker's words
were taken by the audience as literature, and only as literature.
Why not be moved, why not weep? It is a most common story.

But there also happened to be people who saw the matter
in a different light and who began to object. They answered
Dostoevsky by saying that they willingly accepted his noble
words about love, but that this in no way prevented—it must
not prevent—people from "concerning themselves with the
establishment of happiness here on earth," or in other words,
from having "social ideals." Had Dostoevsky allowed this, just
this one limitation, he could have reconciled himself for good
with the liberals. But he not only did not make concessions,
he attacked Professor Gradovsky (who had undertaken the
defense of the liberal cause) with such mad, with such unre-
strained fury that it seemed as if Gradovsky were robbing him
of his last possession. And the main thing is that Gradovsky
not only was not repudiating the noble doctrine of love for
man, to which Dostoevsky had devoted so many ardent pages
in his *Diary of a Writer*, in his novels, and in the Pushkin
Speech—on the contrary, he was basing all his plans for the
social order on it, and on it alone.

But this was precisely what Dostoevsky feared most of all.
In Renan's Preface to *The History of Israel*, there is a curious
appraisal of the significance of the Hebrew prophets: "Ils sont
fanatiques de justice sociale et proclament hautement que si
le monde n'est pas juste ou susceptible de le devinir, il vaut
mieux qu'il soit détruit: manière de voir très fausse, mais
très féconde; car comme toutes les doctrines désespérées, elle
produit l'héroisme et un grand éveil des forces humaines." In
this very same way, Professor Gradovsky regarded Dostoevsky's ideas. He found them "essentially" false, but admitted

their fruitfulness, i.e., their ability to arouse people and provide those heroes without which the progress of mankind is impossible. Actually, one could not have wished more. For a "teacher," at least, it should have sufficed. But Dostoevsky saw his condemnation in such an attitude toward himself. He had no need of "fruitfulness." He did not want to content himself with the handsome role of the old cardinal in "The Grand Inquisitor." He wanted one thing, and one thing only: to be convinced of the "truth" of his idea. And if necessary, he was ready to destroy the whole world, to doom mankind to eternal suffering—if only to guarantee victory to his idea, if only to rid it of all suspicion of being incongruous with reality. Worst of all was the fact that deep in his heart he obviously feared that right was not on his side and that his adversaries, although more superficial than he, were nearer the truth. That was what aroused such fury in him; that was what made him lose his self-control; and that is why he overstepped all the bounds of decency in his polemic against Professor Gradovsky. What if everything turns out exactly as scholars say, and his work, contrary to his will, ultimately plays into the hands of the liberals and proves to be fruitful, while the idea that guided him proves to be false, and if sooner or later, the "devilish good" actually does prevail on earth—an earth inhabited by content, joyful, and regenerated people beaming with happiness?

It goes without saying that the most sensible thing for a man with such views and sentiments to do would be to steer clear of journalism, where he would inevitably run into the practical question: what is to be done? In novels and philosophical discussions, one can, for example, assert that the Russian people like to suffer. But how can such an assertion be put into practice? By proposing the formation of a committee to protect the Russian people from happiness? Obviously, that will not do. Moreover, one cannot even express one's joy constantly over forthcoming occasions when mankind will have to suffer. One must not celebrate when sickness or famine befalls man; one must not rejoice over poverty or drunkenness. People are stoned for things like that. Mikhailovsky reports that the idea expressed in articles in *Notes of the Fatherland* for January, 1873, according to which "the people, after the Reform, and partly even in connection with it, are threatened with the misfortune of being mentally, morally, and economically fleeced," seemed "a new revelation" to Dostoevsky. Very likely, Dostoevsky understood, or, more accurately, interpreted, the articles in *Notes of the Fatherland* in exactly this way. The Reform, in which visionaries had placed so much hope, had not only not brought the "hateful happiness," it was threatening terrible misfortune. Evidently, the matter could get along even without the gentleman with the retrograde physiognomy on whom the underground dialectician had relied. It is still a long way to the Crystal Palace if the most lofty and noble undertakings bring only unhappiness instead of abundant fruit. True, as a publicist, Dostoevsky did not say such things openly. His "cruelty" did not yet risk such frankness. Even more than that, he never missed a chance to castigate (and how he castigated!) all possible manifestations of cruelty. For example, he rebelled at European progress on the grounds that "rivers of blood would be shed" before the class struggle would do our Western neighbors even the slightest good. This was one of his favorite arguments, which he tirelessly repeated dozens of times. But here one can be quite certain that all *argumenta* are *argumenta ad homines*. Dostoevsky afraid of blood and horror? But he knew how to produce an effect on people, and when necessary, he drew terrifying pictures. At almost one and the same time, he was reproaching the Europeans for their struggle, which was as yet relatively bloodless, and adjuring the Russians to declare war on the Turks, although, of course, the most modest war requires more bloodshed than dozens of revolutions. Or another more striking example of

his argumentation: Dostoevsky says that one of his "acquaintances" came out in favor of the retention of the flogging of
children, because corporal punishment hardens them and in-
ures them to combat. We are not, of course, interested in the
opinion of his "acquaintance" (in Dostoevsky's *Diary of a
Writer*, there is a multitude of "acquaintances" who express
"original" opinions), but it is curious that Dostoevsky himself
took an interest in this opinion and promised to think it over
at his leisure. Yet this same Dostoevsky, who was so willing
to deal out suffering to people, even to children, suddenly
grew sensitive and sentimental when the question arose of the
fate of Tatyana's husband.[1] Had Tatyana decided to leave him
and make him unhappy, all ideals would have been tarnished
forever! Well, now, I believe that many a person could be
found, and not only among advocates of "cruelty," who would
admit that a decent amount of "suffering" would by no means
be wasted on this gentleman, who held his nose and shoulders
so high. At any rate, wasted no more than it is on Russian
children, who, as we well know, are not forgotten by "suffering" even when out of school. One can find a great many such
examples in Dostoevsky. On one page, he demands renunciation of us in the name of delivering our neighbors from suffering, and on another, almost the very next, he sings the
praises of this same suffering.

From this, it follows that the underground man has nothing
to say when he appears in the role of teacher of man. In order
to keep up such a role, he must forever conceal his truth and
deceive people, as the old cardinal did. And if it is no longer
possible to remain silent, if the time has finally come to tell
the world the secret of the Grand Inquisitor, then people must
seek their priests not from among teachers as in the olden
days, but from among disciples, who always perform all sorts
of solemn duties willingly and in good faith. The teachers
have been deprived of their last consolation: they are no

[1] In Pushkin's *Eugene Onegin*. [Tr.]

longer acknowledged as the people's benefactors and healers. They have been told, and they will be told: physician, heal thyself. In other words: find your task, find your cause, not in the doctoring of our illnesses, but in looking after your own health. Look after yourself—only after yourself.

XVII

At first glance, the task seems simple. But look at it for a moment from the standpoint of Dostoevsky, the underground man, the Grand Inquisitor, and you will understand the torment that is concealed in this simplicity. To doctor oneself, to look after oneself, to think of oneself in the underground, when, apparently, no doctoring is any longer possible, when nothing is left to devise, when all is finished! But it is amazing: when man is threatened with inevitable death, when an abyss opens before him, when his last hope vanishes, he is suddenly relieved of all his burdensome obligations to the people, to mankind, to the future, to civilization, to progress, et cetera, and in place of all this, he is presented with the simplified problem of his lone, insignificant, and ordinary personality. All tragic heroes are "egoists." Each of them calls the whole universe to account for his unhappiness. Karamazov (Ivan, of course) declares bluntly: "I do not accept the world." What do these words mean? Why is it that Karamazov, instead of hiding from dreadful, insoluble problems as everyone else, goes straight at them, charges them just as a bear charges a huntsman's spear? After all, it is not because of ursine stupidity. Oh, how well he knows what insoluble problems are and how man must beat his already clipped wings against the walls of eternity! And nevertheless, he does not give up. No *Ding an sich*, no will, no *deus sive natura* tempts him to reconciliation. This man, forgotten by good, treats all philosophical systems with undisguised contempt and disgust. Karamazov says: "Some sniveling moralists call the thirst for life despicable." Not one of Dostoevsky's heroes who questions fate ends up a suicide, with the exception of Kirillov, who it is true does kill himself, but not to withdraw from life, but to test his strength. In this respect, they all share old Karamazov's point of view: they do not seek oblivion, no matter how difficult life may be for them. Ivan Karamazov's youthful daydreams, which he recalls in his conversation with the devil, can serve as an interesting illustration of this "point of view." A certain sinner was condemned to walk a quadrillion kilometers before the heavenly gates would be opened to him. But the sinner was stubborn. "I won't do it," he said. He lay down and refused to move from the spot. Thus he lay for a thousand years. Then he rose and started out. He walked a billion years. "And two seconds had not passed after the heavenly gates had opened to him when he exclaimed that for those two seconds, he would have walked, not only a quadrillion, but even a quadrillion quadrillion kilometers, even if it were raised to the quadrillionth power."[1] Such were the things Dostoevsky pondered over. Those staggering quadrillions of kilometers traversed, those billions of years of nonsense endured for the sake of two seconds of heavenly bliss for which the human tongue lacks the necessary words are merely an expression of the thirst for life about which we have been talking. Like his father, Ivan Karamazov is an egoist through and through. Not that he cannot, he does not want to try in some way or other to dissolve his personality in a noble idea, to fuse it with the "primordial," with nature, et cetera, as philosophers recommend. Although he received a very modern education, he is not afraid to make *his* demands in the face of the entire body of philosophical science. He is not even afraid that he will be confused (and at the same time rejected) with his father. He bluntly says so himself: "Fyodor Pavlovich, our dad, was a swine, but he thought correctly."[2] And Fyodor Pavlovich, the swine, who

[1] Dostoevsky, *op. cit.*, XII, 272.
[2] *Ibid.*, 702.

saw and knew perfectly well the opinion people had of him, "thought" that even though he had lived long enough, this life was too little for him. He also wanted immortality for himself. This is shown by the following conversation with his children:

"Ivan, tell me, is there a God or not?"
"No, there's no God."
"Alyosha, is there a God?"
"There is a God."
"Ivan, is there immortality, in some form or other—well, at least a little, a tiny bit?"
"There's no immortality either."
"None?"
"None."
"You mean, there's a complete blank? But maybe there is something or other. After all, there can't just be nothing."
"Absolutely nothing."
"Alyosha, is there immortality?"
"There is."
"Both God and immortality?"
"Both God and immortality . . ."
"Hmm. More than likely, Ivan is right."

As you see, like father, like son. Dostoevsky endows even Fyodor Pavlovich Karamazov with the ability to seek the "sovereign idea." After all, you must admit that the conversation is most characteristic. "More than likely, Ivan is right"— this is merely an objective conclusion which kept thrusting itself on Dostoevsky and which he feared so much. But the important thing here is the fact that Dostoevsky found it necessary to show Fyodor Pavlovich in a good light. It may seem to the reader that if there is immortality, it is not, at any rate, for such vermin as Fyodor Pavlovich, and that some law will certainly be found that will put an end to this disgusting being. But Dostoevsky cared little for the views of the readers. He keeps Rakitin at a mile's distance from his sovereign idea, but lets the old man Karamazov walk right up to it—he accepts him, if only partially, into the honorary society of convicts. Accordingly, all that is ugly, disgusting, difficult, and agonizing—in brief, all that is problematic in life—finds an ardent and exceptionally talented mouthpiece for itself in Dostoevsky. As if on purpose, he tramples before our eyes on talent, beauty, youth, and innocence. In his novels, there are more horrors than in reality. And how masterfully, how truthfully he describes these horrors! We haven't one artist who could describe the bitterness of insult and humiliation as Dostoevsky does. In the stories of Grushenka and Nastasya Filippovna, nothing strikes the reader so much as the disgrace these women must suffer. Nastasya Filippovna says of Totsky: "He would come here, disgrace me, insult me, infuriate me, seduce me, and then leave—I wanted a thousand times to throw myself into the pond."[1] And how much agony Grushenka suffered in recalling the wrong done her! She says: "Now that man who led me astray has arrived, and I've been sitting here waiting to hear from him. And do you know what that offender has been to me? Five years ago, when Kuz'ma first brought me here, I used to stay inside, hiding from people, so they wouldn't see or hear me. I was a thin, silly girl, and I'd sit here sobbing. For nights on end I wouldn't sleep. I'd keep thinking: 'Where is he now, the fellow who led me astray? Probably laughing at me with another girl. Oh, if only I could see him, if I could meet him sometime—I'd really get even with him. Oh, how I'd get even with him.' At night, in the darkness, I'd sob into my pillow and think back over all this. I'd torment myself on purpose and gloat over my anger. 'Oh, I'll get even with him, I really will get even with him!' That's what I'd cry out lying there in the dark. And then I'd suddenly think that I wouldn't do anything at all to him, and that he was laughing at me then, or maybe had completely forgotten me, and I'd throw myself from the bed to the floor, break into helpless tears, and shake— I'd lie there shaking until dawn. In the morning, I'd get up

[1] *Ibid.*, VI, 184.

madder than a dog, ready to tear the whole world to pieces. Then, what do you think? I began to save my money, I became merciless, I put on a lot of weight. I grew wiser—don't you think so? No, indeed, no one in the whole world sees or knows it, but when it gets dark, I sometimes lie there as I did five years ago, when I was a silly girl, clenching my teeth, crying all night long, and thinking: 'Oh, I'll get even with him, I really will get even with him!' Did you hear everything I said?"[1] That is how convictions "are born" in Dostoevsky's heroes and heroines, to say nothing of Raskolnikov, Karamazov, Kirillov, and Shatov. They were all subjected to unprecedented humiliation. How cleverly Dolgoruky (*A Raw Youth*) is thrown out of the gambling casino! How the underground man is humiliated! Dostoevsky assembled all the means at his disposal in order once again to strike a blow of unprecedented power at the reader's heart, but this time it was not to make the reader a better person or to have him magnanimously consent to call the humblest man his brother on Sundays and holidays. Now the task was different. Now it was necessary to force science, or "ethics," as Rakitin and Dmitry Karamazov call it, to admit that the chief problem of life cannot be solved by a felicitous arrangement of things for the majority, by the future happiness of mankind, by progress, by ideas, et cetera—in brief, by all that had previously been used to justify the disgrace and destruction of the individual man. And indeed, when faced with reality as depicted by Dostoevsky, the most inveterate and convinced positivist, the very best person would be ashamed to think of his ideals. When "egoism," which everyone slanders so much, leads to tragedy, when the struggle of a solitary human being turns into unceasing torment, no one would have the impudence to use lofty words. Even believing hearts grow silent. But here we encounter not the doctrine of the positivists or idealists, not philosophical theories or scientific systems. People can be brought to reason, philosophers

[1] *Ibid.*, XII, 420.

and moralists can be restrained in their pursuit of synthesis and the formation of systems, if they are shown the fate of tragic people. But what can be done with life? How can it be forced to reckon with the Raskolnikovs and Karamazovs? As you know, it has neither shame nor conscience. It looks indifferently on the human comedy and the human tragedy. This question leads us from the philosophy of Dostoevsky to the philosophy of his successor, Nietzsche, the first person openly to display on his banner the terrible words: the apotheosis of cruelty.

XVIII

We have traced the history of the regeneration of Dostoevsky's convictions. Basically, it amounts to an attempt to rehabilitate the rights of the underground man. If we now turn to Nietzsche's works, we shall find, above all, that although they bear little outward resemblance to what Dostoevsky wrote, they contain definite and clearly expressed traces of those moods and experiences that astonished us in the creative work of the latter. Nietzsche, too, was a romantic, a transcendental dreamer in youth. We learn this not only from his first book, *The Birth of Tragedy*, but also from his articles "Schopenhauer as Educator" and "Richard Wagner in Bayreuth," which immediately preceded *Human, All-Too-Human*, a work in which, for the first time in his life, he permits himself, still timidly and cautiously, to look at the world and its people with his own eyes. This experience cost him dearly. The majority of his friends, Wagner among them, turned from him. As is always the case, none of them were interested in the reason for the sudden change that had taken place in Nietzsche's soul. His friends merely raised the cry that he had "betrayed" his former convictions, and they found this quite sufficient to condemn the man. They all knew that Nietzsche was seriously and painfully ill. But even in this they saw no extenuating circumstances. Wagner, who a short time earlier had extolled Nietzsche's literary work, became so indignant upon reading *Human, All-Too-Human* that he did not even think it necessary to try to bring his young friend and student to reason. He simply grew silent and to his dying day did not resume his relations with Nietzsche. So that at the most difficult moment of Nietzsche's life, when, as is generally agreed, a person most of all needs moral support, Nietzsche was left completely alone. True, public opinion in this instance, as in many others, offers us an obvious error in the guise of an obvious truth. In the truly difficult moments of life, the support of friends usually does not and cannot provide a person with anything; it merely burdens him with the importunate demand for candor and confession. At such moments, it is best of all to be left alone. If you have the strength to bear your misfortune, you will emerge the victor. If you do not, no Wagner will help. I am, of course, speaking not of ordinary, everyday difficulties, when two minds are always better than one, but of those cases when, as Dostoevsky expressed it, the earth crumbles away beneath your feet. And, as you know, they occur much more frequently in life than in novels. On these occasions, friends can be of no help whatsoever. But Nietzsche's friends did not even think of helping him. They became his enemies, and as they did not wish to take the trouble to understand the man, they avenged themselves on him with contempt. In Nietzsche's own words— and this time they are particularly worthy of belief—the contempt of other people is much more difficult to bear than one's own contempt for oneself.[1] And indeed, no matter how much a man despises himself, he always has the hope deep in his heart that he will nevertheless find a way out of his difficult situation. But condemnation by other people is merciless, inexorable, and final. It is hurled at odd moments at the accused with the intention of never again being reconsidered.

Nietzsche avowedly wrote "Schopenhauer as Educator" and "Richard Wagner in Bayreuth" when he no longer believed

[1] Nietzsche, *op. cit.*, II, 376.

either in Schopenhauer's philosophy or Wagner's art. Yet both these articles are an out-and-out panegyric to them. Why then was such pretense necessary? Nietzsche explains that in taking leave of his teachers, he wanted to express his thanks and gratitude to them for the past. I suppose that the reader will not find such a way of expressing gratitude worthy of approval: one must be able to sacrifice one's friends and teachers for the sake of truth. Probably Nietzsche himself was of the same opinion; and if he nevertheless appears in the role of an undisguised partisan of Schopenhauer and Wagner, while knowing that the time had come to take leave of them, then he had other, perhaps less comely, but undoubtedly more profound and serious reasons to do so. Evidently, it was not a question of the teachers, but of the student: Nietzsche would probably have taken leave of the mentors of his youth with less ceremony, had he definitely known where to go after leaving them. We see that gratitude did not prevent him from subsequently writing a sharp article about Wagner, nor did it prevent him from calling Schopenhauer "an old counterfeiter." But that was near the end of his literary career, between 1886 and 1888. In 1875, he dared not yet think that it would be possible to oppose the thoughts and moods arising in his soul, vague and chaotic as they were, to Schopenhauer's harmonious and masterfully developed philosophy, which had already won recognition, and to Wagner's fame, which had resounded throughout Europe. At the time, it seemed to him that the most terrible thing that could befall a man was to suffer a break with his teachers and a betrayal of his former faith and convictions. He thought that a man receives his convictions once and for all from the hands of worthy teachers. Although he read a good deal, it never occurred to him that such convictions, when obtained ready-made from other people, are less valuable than his own view of life, which had been formed from his own ordeals, from his own suffering. Or, if you will, he knew that as well. He himself used to express such an opinion, for in the books he read (in Schopenhauer, for example), it was fre-

quently discussed in detail. But when the time came for a
"test," when uncertainty arose, Nietzsche, like everyone else in
his situation, failed to guess that this was what is spoken of
in books. He merely had a horrible feeling that something
unprecedentedly hideous and terrible had begun to stir in his
soul. In his torment, in his despair, he did not recognize the
celebrated "suffering," to which, following Schopenhauer's
example, he had given his blessing, and for which he had
called in his first book, *The Birth of Tragedy*. To himself, he
seemed so little like a hero, so little like one of the many
interesting sinners such as Tannhäuser, who pose so beautifully in Wagner's operas. In his situation, there was not even
a trace of the tragic beauty which he customarily admired in
the works of the classic writers. He had not stolen fire from
the heavens for the good of mankind. He had not guessed the
Sphinx's riddles, as Oedipus had. He had not even been in
Venus's grotto. On the contrary, when he surveyed his past, it
seemed to him an uninterrupted series of most shameful
humiliations. Here is the light in which he pictures his service
to art, i.e., the story of his relationship with Wagner: "In a
certain party," he says in an aphorism called "A Martyr in
Spite of Himself," "there was a man, who was too timid and
cowardly to contradict his comrades: they used him for all sorts
of purposes. They demanded anything at all from him, as he
feared the bad opinion of his companions more than death
itself. His was a pitifully weak soul. His comrades recognized
this, and used his characteristics mentioned above to turn him
into a hero, and finally even a martyr. Although this weak
man always said "No" inwardly, he would always say "Yes"
with his lips—even on the scaffold when the time came for
him to die for his party's convictions. Beside him stood one
of his old comrades, who had so tyrannized over him by words
and looks that he indeed suffered death with dignity, and
since then has been hailed as a martyr and a great character."[1]

[1] *Ibid.*, II, 86.

If these words sum up Nietzsche's "past," can anyone believe that upon taking leave of it, the man experienced a feeling of gratitude? Isn't it more likely that the articles "Richard Wagner in Bayreuth" and "Schopenhauer as Educator" were written only because Nietzsche still continued to feel Wagner's gaze directed at him (and perhaps not only Wagner's) and was unable to struggle against its hypnotic effect? And how could he struggle? To do that, it was first of all necessary to uproot all self-respect from his own being, to call his past by its real name, to admit that the newspaper critics, whom he customarily regarded as pitiful and unworthy rabble, were right when they called him "Wagner's literary lackey." In other words, it was necessary to doom himself to the life of the "humblest man." A person does not decide on such a horrible step immediately. Nietzsche still hoped that he might be of use to his party, if only by words that would support its principles and aspirations. At least his good name would be preserved; at least no one would know how shamefully and disgustingly unhappy he was. That is worth something. Nietzsche was a proud man. He did not want to display his wounds; he wanted to conceal them from the eyes of strangers. For this, it was, of course, necessary to pretend and to lie; for this, it was necessary to write fervent, laudatory articles in honor of both Schopenhauer and Wagner, whom he practically hated by then in his heart of hearts, for he considered them the main instigators of his terrible misfortunes. And indeed, who needed *his* truth? And what could he say if he wanted to speak the truth? Frankly admit his worthlessness? But aren't there a good many worthless people in the world? And could such a confession really surprise or interest anyone? As a matter of fact, nothing much had happened. Nietzsche thought that he was a worthy man destined to do a serious and important deed: it turned out that he was mistaken, that he was an insignificant and pitiful man. Such things frequently happen in life. No one even remembers them. Thus, for example, Nietzsche persuaded

himself that David Strauss,[1] whom the Germans considered a
great philosopher and an exemplary stylist, was really nothing
but an "educated Philistine" with a poor command of the customary literary language. Did this discovery really surprise or
shock anyone, Nietzsche included? Of course not. There were
enough noteworthy philosophers and exemplary stylists on
earth without David Strauss. If Nietzsche had reasoned objectively, he could easily have convinced himself that his own case
was of no particular importance. And, moreover, if he had also
recalled the fundamental principles of Schopenhauer's philosophy, he could have found perfect consolation in his misfortune.
After all, "will" remained unchanged; therefore, was it worth
thinking about the fact that an individual, i.e., one of billions
of instances of its objectification, had been crushed? But
usually "the basic principles of philosophy" instantly vanish
from the memory as soon as a person comes into conflict with
life. If Nietzsche did recall Schopenhauer, it was not to seek
consolation or support from him, but to curse him as his worst
enemy. "But this word I want to say to my enemies: What is
all murder compared to what you have done to me? What you
have done to me is worse than any murder; you have taken
the irretrievable from me: that is what I want to say to you,
my enemies. For you murdered the visions and dearest wonders
of my youth. You took my comrades from me, those blessed
spirits. In their memory, I lay down this wreath and this curse.
This curse is on you, my enemies."[2] These words of Zarathustra refer to Wagner and Schopenhauer. Nietzsche curses
his teachers because they ruined his youth.

XIX

But suppose we ask again: *Wozu solch Lärm?* What had happened? Was Nietzsche being destroyed? Was this reason

---

[1] David Strauss (1808–1874), a German theologian, biographer, and
idealist philosopher, who was influenced by the followers of Hegel.
[Tr.]
[2] Nietzsche, *op. cit.*, VI, 161.

enough to curse Schopenhauer's philosophy and Wagner's music? If we recall Nietzsche's early works, if we consider Zarathustra's "doctrine" of the superman, we see that, in effect, Nietzsche had no need whatsoever to be so upset. One life had been a failure—there is no great harm in that. Nature makes individuals by the millions, and her task lies not in preserving and developing individual specimens, but in perfecting the species. That is what Schopenhauer said. And that, or almost that, is what Zarathustra said. What does it matter if the youthful dreams of one professor were not fulfilled? Does this really threaten mankind with any danger?

Nietzsche understood perfectly well that the philosophical principles that he had accepted from Schopenhauer contained his condemnation. If only he had the right to consider himself a remarkable man! But in justification of himself, he could not even refer to his extraordinary talents. As is obvious from the aphorism "A Martyr in Spite of Himself," quoted in the preceding chapter, he saw in himself at that time a mere wretched servant of Wagner. Why then should such a nonentity continue to exist? Wouldn't it be better quietly and inconspicuously to withdraw into the background, to yield his place in life to a more worthy representative of the human species? At that precise time, the opportunity presented itself to Nietzsche to fulfill the lofty demands of generally accepted morality, which Schopenhauer's philosophy had taken under its protection, and to prove, not in words, but in deeds, that the idea of self-abnegation and self-sacrifice is not just a name, but a great force, capable of inspiring man and giving him the courage humbly to endure the most agonizing fate. But Nietzsche acted directly counter to the demands of his former "convictions," which he had received from his great teacher Schopenhauer. In his misfortune, instead of submitting and rejoicing over the past successes and new hopes of mankind—which, above all, would have been in keeping with the convictions expressed in *The Birth of Tragedy*—Nietzsche decided to verify by his own fate the justice and truth of

ideals bequeathed us by several millennia and brilliantly vindicated so many times by the best minds of mankind. As early
as *Human, All-Too-Human,* he raised the question of "the
values of nonselfish instincts, the instincts of pity, self-denial,
and self-sacrifice, which Schopenhauer had so persistently
painted in golden colors, idolized, and etherealized (*verjen-
seitigt*), until they finally became for him intrinsic values in
themselves (*an sich*)."[1] And in order to solve this problem,
he no longer turned, as before, when writing his first works,
to philosophers, poets, and preachers, in brief, to doctrines
that people have transmitted from generation to generation.
He felt that he would not find an answer for himself in all
this; it was as if all the teachers of mankind had conspired
to remain silent about what was most important for him.
And for a long time he did not venture to say a single word
about his own works, in which he had once spoken with the
pride and certainty of an omniscient and all-understanding
judge. Only later, many years later, did he make an attempt
in the Foreword, or more accurately the Afterword, to *The
Birth of Tragedy* to appraise his first literary attempts. How
strangely the human heart is constructed! Despite the fact
that this book seems to him to be poorly written in many
respects, despite the fact that he is perfectly aware of all its
defects ("but the book in which I had poured forth my youthful ardor and suspicion—what an *impossible* book had to grow
from a task so disagreeable to youth!"),[2] he cannot help feeling the tender affection of a father for it. Yet, strictly speaking,
he should have hated it just as much as he hated Schopenhauer's books and Wagner's music. It was, after all, a perfect expression of that alienation from life, of that fear of
reality, in brief, of that romanticism which, thanks to Nietzsche's typical hothouse-upbringing, had so completely possessed his trusting heart in very early youth. And not only

[1] *Ibid.,* VII, 292–293.
[2] *Ibid.,* I, 3.

The Birth of Tragedy, but all Nietzsche's early works down
to *Human, All-Too-Human* must have been odious to their
author for the same reason. All of them are romanticism of
the first water, i.e., a more or less graceful toying with ready-
made poetic images and philosophical concepts. For the
young Nietzsche, Schopenhauer's word was law. "I belong,"
he wrote in 1875, when he was already thirty years old and
when reality had already begun to make its first formidable
demands on him, "to the group of readers of Schopenhauer,
who know for certain after reading the first page of his works,
that they will read all that he wrote and, in general, listen
attentively to his every word. He immediately won my confidence, and it is no less intense now than it was nine years
ago. I understand him as if he were writing purposely for
me."[1] As you see, Nietzsche had made a poor choice of men
in which to place his confidence. And, in general, one must
handle "confidence" more carefully. Schopenhauer is least
suitable as a teacher of youth, if only because the questions
he deals with are usually of very little interest to a young
man, even a gifted one. And it was no better in the case of
music. Even Wagner, with his operas, is dangerous for immature people, for he obliges them to enter strange realms
that are beyond their comprehension. Later on, Nietzsche
himself realized this quite clearly. "I had a genuinely passionate love for art," he writes, "and finally saw nothing but
art in all that exists—in those years when other passions
usually excite a man's heart."[2]

But, strictly speaking, confidence in Schopenhauer's doctrine and love of Wagner are by no means always so fatally
destructive for a person. Had Nietzsche's life proceeded without chance complications, he would perhaps have preserved
in his heart his feelings of love and his devotion for his
teachers until ripe old age. Romanticism by no means always

[1] *Ibid.,* 398.
[2] *Ibid.,* XI, 130.

mutilates and spoils human destiny. On the contrary, it often successfully protects people from a clash with reality and helps for long years to preserve that beauty of spirit, that clarity and resplendence of views, that confidence in life, which we most of all esteem in philosophers. And to his dying day, Nietzsche could have gone on developing the ideas on which he had based *The Birth of Tragedy*. He could have taught people to reconcile themselves to the horrors of life; he could have done as his predecessors and glorified "the philosopher, the artist, and the saint." And he would probably have won the deep respect of his contemporaries and fame from posterity: after all, Professor Riehl[1] called *The Birth of Tragedy* a work of genius. True, it is perhaps possible to see a certain political cunning in the German professor's appraisal. Perhaps Professor Riehl did not find it convenient to condemn absolutely everything in Nietzsche, and, wishing to give the appearance of an impartial and fair judge, he perhaps preferred to exaggerate his praise of this book of Nietzsche, which most closely resembles the books that everyone else writes, in order to have a free hand later on to attack his other works. Nevertheless, there is no doubt that if Nietzsche had continued to write in the spirit of *The Birth of Tragedy*, he would have had to disassociate himself from commonly accepted opinions and convictions only in so far as this is allowed by the prevailing ideas on permissible and desirable originality. Of course, at the beginning of his literary career, he would also have had enemies, but in the end, he would have achieved that virtuosity of presentation which even subdues enemies and most of all guarantees a man the joyful respect of the people around him. Undoubtedly, Nietzsche would have written differently under different circumstances, and Professor Riehl could with a clear conscience have called his works brilliant.

But fate decided otherwise. Instead of letting Nietzsche

---

[1] Alois Riehl (1844–1924), a German positivist, neo-Kantian philosopher, logician, and critic. [Tr.]

calmly concern himself with the future of all mankind and even the whole universe, it asked him, as it did Dostoevsky, one short and simple question—about his own future. And this highly perceptive philosopher, who had intrepidly viewed the horrors of the whole world, became confused and flustered, like a child who has lost its way in a forest, before this simple and reputedly easy problem. In this matter, his past learning proved useless, even cumbersome, to him. "Everything solemn has become odious to me," he wrote. "What are we?"[1] Yet, what he called "solemn" was everything that he had formerly lived by, everything that he had regarded as the deepest wisdom, and in the dissemination of which he saw his predestined purpose. Now, all this had to be abandoned. But what would then remain? How could he look people in the face, what could he say to Wagner, how could he remain alone with himself? For a time, Nietzsche made attempts to reconcile his new life with his old "convictions." As was already pointed out, he wrote articles about Wagner and Schopenhauer, hoping that habit would prevail, and that he would again accommodate himself to a faith in ideals, which was so necessary to him now. But his calculation was false. Simulated dedication, even for a man in ordinary circumstances, is not an easy matter. And for Nietzsche, in his horrible situation, it became sheer torture. He saw that it was impossible to live as before. And knowing what awaited him, knowing that his friends, chiefly Wagner, would never forgive his treachery, he turned from the old gods and set out on a new path, although the new path as well promised nothing but danger, agonizing doubt, and perpetual loneliness.

XX

And with what did he set out on this new path? What did he have in place of his earlier convictions? The answer can be given in a word: nothing. Nothing but loathsome physical

---

[1] Nietzsche, *op. cit.*, XI, 153.

suffering in the present; shameful, humiliating memories of
the past; and a mad fear of the future. He could have no hope,
for what is a broken, sick man capable of when he has wasted
the best years of his life on futile, needless projects which had
brought him nothing? Until the age of thirty, like our Ilya
Muromets,[1] he sat in a corner, contemplating the ideals of
others. Now it was necessary to rise and walk, but his legs
refused to serve him. Kind old sages did not, and would not,
appear with a magic potion: nowadays, there are no miracles.
To top it all off, his illness assumed such proportions that he
had to give up his usual professorial duties, which had filled
his day, and remain idle from morning to night, alone with his
thoughts and memories. Even night did not bring him peace
and quiet, for he suffered from insomnia, the usual companion
of serious nervous disorders. And then such a man becomes a
writer and takes the liberty of turning to the public with his
word. What can he tell us? That he suffers, that he has suffered? But we have already heard enough complaints from
poets; the young Lermontov long ago openly expressed that
idea, which others had kept to themselves. What business is
it of ours if Nietzsche suffered or not? And, moreover, it is
a different matter with poets. They do not just complain. Who
would listen to them if they "just" complained? They express
their complaints in beautiful, resonant poems, and from their
tears, flowers grow. We admire the flowers and forget the
tears; the divine harmony of the poetry makes us rejoice at
even the most plaintive tune. But Nietzsche is a philosopher:
he cannot and must not sing. He must speak. Is it possible that
he would decide to offer the public the dull and monotonous
story of the horrors he had to experience? Or does philosophy
also have its flowers and poetry, which also constitute its
raison d'être? And is this science of sciences also an art—the
art of passing off various interesting and entertaining things
as truth? Let us listen to Nietzsche's explanations. In these

[1] A legendary hero in the early Russian folk epic. [Tr.]

matters, few people can compare with him in range and variety of experience. He will tell us in detail how he wrote his books. "Whoever can even slightly imagine," he writes, "the consequences involved in every deep suspicion; whoever knows the horror and chills of loneliness to which every uncompromising difference of outlook condemns us, will also understand how often I had to seek shelter in some sort of veneration or hostility, in scientism or flippancy or stupidity, in order to recover from myself, and to find temporary self-forgetfulness; and why, in those instances when it was impossible to find ready-made what I needed, I had to make it myself, to falsify it, and to invent it (what else have poets ever done?). And for what purpose does art in general exist?"[1] Not a bad confession, is it? Art is understood to be the deliberate falsification of reality, and philosophy is recommended to use the same method. Otherwise, it will be impossible to bear the horror and chill of loneliness. But can falsification, particularly if deliberate, really help in such cases? Does one's own view of life really become less dismal when the mind and conscience resort to such tricks? And furthermore, is it really in our power to change our "view" arbitrarily? We see what we see, whatever lies before us, and no efforts of the will can make black seem white to us, or vice versa. Evidently, Nietzsche thought otherwise. In the Preface to the third volume of his collected work, he says: "It was then [i.e., during his illness] that I learned the hermitic habit of speech that is known only to those who are lonely and who have suffered much. I spoke without witnesses, or more accurately, without thinking of witnesses. And I always spoke of things that did not at all concern me, but I gave the impression that they were important to me. Then I also learned the art of appearing cheerful, objective, curious, and, most of all, healthy and derisive: in a sick man, I dare say, this is a sign of good taste. Nevertheless, a keener

<hr />

[1] Nietzsche, *op. cit.*, II, 3–4.

and a more sympathetic eye will not miss what perhaps gives a particular charm to these writings [*Human, All-Too-Human*]: the fact that a sick and unfortunate man is speaking here *as if* he were not sick and unfortunate. A man is striving here at all costs to maintain equipoise, composure, and even gratitude to life; here reigns a stern, proud, ever cheerful, ever excited will, which has set itself the task of defending life against suffering and warding off all conclusions which usually grow like poisonous fungi in all kinds of marshy soil—from suffering, disappointment, satiety, and isolation."[1]

Now we know how Nietzsche wrote his books. Evidently, he had not been given the possibility to escape the power of ideas. Formerly, in defending Wagner and Schopenhauer, he spoke of things that did not concern him, but he did it with a look that made them seem important to him; now, upon entering a new career as an "advocate of life," he again, evidently, suppresses in himself all protest, all that is personal, all that is essentially his own, in order to glorify his new client. Again he plays the hypocrite, again he plays a role, but this time it is no longer unintentional, no longer with a clear conscience as in youth: now he is fully aware of his conduct. Now he knows he cannot do otherwise, and not only is he not horrified when he must say "Yes" aloud when his entire being says "No," he even prides himself on this art and finds a particular charm in it. He rejects all conclusions growing on the soil of disappointment, suffering, isolation, et cetera —the only conclusions that could appear to a man in his situation. Then who, or what, was it that dwelt in him and had been given such sovereign rights over his soul? Was it perhaps his old reason, which had once played such a dirty trick on Nietzsche and therefore had been deprived of all its former rights, that had again occupied its former predominant position by force or by cunning? Or were his conscience and shame before the public again enticing Nietzsche to an alien

[1] *Ibid.*, III, 5–6.

faith and persuading him, sick and miserable as he was, to feign health and happiness? A fact of unusual importance! At this point, we must note that in all of his work, down to the very last, in which Nietzsche speaks as an unequivocal immoralist and atheist, in which he takes as his slogan the fearful words that had served in the Middle Ages as the secret password of a Mohammedan sect that had clashed with the Crusaders in the Holy Land: "Nothing is true, everything is permitted"—in all of his works, Nietzsche always, unfailingly, appeals to some higher court (at one time, it is simply called "life," at another, "the totality of life"), and does not venture to speak in his own name. An impression is produced which is best summed up by Dostoevsky's derisive words: "Everything is permitted, and that's that! And if you want to swindle, what further need is there of the sanction of truth?"[1] For partisans of the categorical imperative, Nietzsche's passion for the sanction of truth could serve as the best refutation of his entire doctrine, and I am most surprised that no one has as yet challenged him with this seemingly irrefutable argument. Especially as the contradictions that one encounters in Nietzsche's judgments—a shortcoming for which he was so often reproached—mainly derive from this veneration of the new "Moloch of abstraction," which has now replaced numerous old ones. I do not, however, mean by this that the sanction of truth or, perhaps I should say, every last sanction in general is on the side of those who proclaim that *not* all is permitted and who refrain from swindling—in the sense, of course, in which Dostoevsky used the word (after all, even such reservations are still necessary). Moreover, I have already pointed out that, in Dostoevsky's admiration of penal servitude, there are clear indications of an awareness that precisely this sanction, which the idealists have hitherto boasted as their inalienable and undivided prerogative, had been illegitimately appropriated by the latter.

[1] Dostoevsky, *op. cit.*, XII, 769.

Schiller once, without any hesitation, without even thinking that any hesitation was possible, put the following words into the mouth of Phillip the Second:

Gern mag ich hören,
Dass Karlos meine Räte hasst, doch mit
Verdruss entdeck ich, dass er sie verachtet.

In this sentence, the relations of those types of which Phillip II and Don Carlos are representatives, are, as it were, defined and fixed once and for all. Don Carlos despises Phillip II, but Phillip would feel flattered if he could see at least hatred for himself on the part of his son. And no one had any doubt that between good and evil, to use more general terms, such relations would continue for all eternity: evil is not in a position to get the better of good's scorn, and therefore it secretly scorns itself. That is, the sanction of truth is on the side of Don Carlos and his beauty of soul. As for Phillip, if he wants to "swindle," then let him abandon hope of any sanction. That is the way it was in Schiller's time. But now the situation has changed. Now the Don Carloses look to the Phillips for hatred just as they would for charity, but, other than contempt, they get nothing. Example: Dostoevsky and penal servitude, or Nietzsche, who expressd this idea with such frightful clarity in the words of Zarathustra quoted above: "My friend, do you know the word contempt? And the torment of your justice in trying to be fair to those who despise you?" Translate these words into concrete language —and such translations must be made by anyone who wants to find more than just aesthetic pleasure in books—and you will get a new formula for the mutual relations of Phillip and Don Carlos. It is no longer Phillip who knows the word contempt, it is no longer he who is tormented by the need to admit that justice (the sanction of truth) is not with him, but with his enemies—on the contrary, all these pleasures now fall to the lot of Don Carlos.

XXI

But let us put aside the argument about sanction and what it is people actually strive for when they try so ardently, maliciously, and mercilessly to prove the incontestability and exclusiveness of their rights to it. Something else interests us now. What are we to do with the work of a writer who, by his own repeated admission, has said in his books that he is not the sort of person he actually is? To the Russian reader, Nietzsche's manner is really not unusual. We have Dostoevsky, who speaks as if he were not the underground man, not Raskolnikov, not Karamazov, and who simulates faith, love, humility, and what have you. We have Count Tolstoy, who wrote out of "vanity, ambition, and pride," as he himself says in an outburst of belated remorse in *A Confession*. So that we cannot straightaway reject Nietzsche even if we want to, for it would be necessary right after him to reject Dostoevsky and Count Tolstoy as well. So we must raise the following question: what is the use of such pretense, and furthermore, is it necessary? At this point, suppose we again let Nietzsche speak for himself. In the Preface to *Human, All-Too-Human*, from which we already quoted in the preceding chapter, there is a remark which, as it were, completely clarifies and justifies such strange methods: "It was then," says Nietzsche, "that I came upon the aphorism: 'a sick man has as yet *no right* to pessimism,' and it was then that I began a patient, persistent campaign against the unscientific basic tendency of all romantic pessimism, which tries to magnify and interpret individual personal experiences into general judgments, even universal condemnations—in brief, it was then that I forced myself to change direction. Optimism for the sake of restoring my strength, in order later to again have the right to be a pessimist—do you understand that? Just as a physician transfers his patient to a completely different environment, I, as physician and patient in

one, forced myself into a totally different and untried zone
of the soul."[1] But are these reasons adequate justification of
the author's pretense? Let us assume that a sick man indeed
has no right to be a pessimist (an enviable right!) and that
optimism, as a change of mental climate, can really be help-
ful to a student of Schopenhauer and Wagner. But how could
the readers who happened upon the first edition of both volumes of *Human, All-Too-Human*, which had not yet been
supplied with the explanatory prefaces (they were not written until eight years later)—how could they guess that they
were dealing not merely with books, that is, with the author's
convictions, but with an artificially created atmosphere, suitable only for certain kinds of diseases? Neither the titles of
these works nor the ideas expounded in them revealed anything of the sort. And if Nietzsche's literary activity had been
confined to just the first four volumes of his works, the keen-
est and most sympathetic eye would never discern the
author's purposes in them. Even now, when we have the
long prefaces, when we are acquainted with the last four
volumes of his works, and when we know Nietzsche's biography, critics remain stubbornly convinced that in *Human,
All-Too-Human* and *Dawn*, Nietzsche is a consistent positivist. Therefore, these books evidently failed to achieve their
goal. Nietzsche should have taken these experimental cures
not in public, but at home, without informing anyone of
them. Could Nietzsche not have known this elementary truth?
Thus, the given explanation can be only of biographical significance to us, and can least of all shed light on the methods
Nietzsche used to seek truth in this period of his life. Yet in
Human, All-Too-Human, he already quite explicitly, if not
boldly, expresses the moral judgments to which he adhered
until the end of his life: he himself points this out in the
Preface to *Toward a Genealogy of Morals*. And if we wish to
go to the source of Nietzsche's world view, if we wish to

[1] Nietzsche, *op. cit.*, III, 9.

learn how his new convictions "were born" (and, after all, that is the whole point of our investigation), we have no right to view his "positivist" works merely as experiments in autotherapy. We must seek in them everything that later led Nietzsche to the formula "beyond good and evil," to the apotheosis of cruelty, to the glorification of egoism, to the doctrine of eternal renewal, to the *Wille zur Macht*, and even to the ideal of the superman—and they do contain all this. A careful study of them convinces us that they sometimes tell more about their author than do the impassioned words of Zarathustra and the unrestraint of overtaxed creative power which manifested itself in *Antichrist*. So that the story of autotherapy must be taken with great reservations and, for the time being, even completely rejected.

Much more important and therefore worthy of closer scrutiny is another explanation, to which we have already called the reader's attention in passing. Nietzsche says that in *Human, All-Too-Human* he set himself the task of "defending life against suffering and warding off all conclusions which usually grow like poisonous fungi in all kinds of marshy soil— from suffering, disappointment, satiety, and isolation." This is undoubtedly a way of seeking truth, although it is, of course, a negative one. It remains for us only to test its efficacy. Does it really lead, indeed can it lead, to "truth," or on the contrary, does it lead away from it? Let us again turn to Nietzsche's experiment. In discussing Socrates and his teachings, he says: "Philosophers and moralists deceive themselves in supposing that they are extricating themselves from decadence when they merely wage war on it. Extricating lies beyond their strength: what they choose as a means, as salvation, is itself but another expression of decadence; they change its expression, but they do not get rid of decadence itself. Socrates was a misunderstanding. The most blinding daylight, rationality at any price, life made clear, cold, cautious, conscious, without instinct, opposed to the instincts—

all this was only a disease, another kind of disease, and by no means a return to 'virtue,' to 'health,' to 'happiness.' To *have* to fight the instincts—that is the formula of decadence: as long as life is ascending, happiness equals instinct."[1] All this is in reference to Socrates and his preaching of a struggle with oneself or the "improvement theory," as Nietzsche expresses it. To conquer *decadence* in oneself is considered absolutely impossible. Socrates was a decadent, and his efforts to save himself were merely a new expression of decadence, of decay. He is unsuitable as a teacher, and his doctrine must be totally rejected. But what about Nietzsche? Besides the fact that his literary remains contain notes in which he himself admits that he is spiritually close to Socrates ("Socrates, I must admit, is so close to me that I am always struggling against him"),[2] we find the following words in the introduction to an article on Wagner in Volume VIII, the same one in which he condemns the morality of improvement as a hopeless way of saving hopelessly lost people: "I am just as much a child of my age as Wagner, i.e., I am a decadent. The only difference is that I recognized the fact and struggled against it. The philosopher in me struggled against it."[3] But, after all, the very struggle, as we just saw, is but an "illness," a new expression of decadence. Thus, all Nietzsche's work came to naught, and despite his attempts at autotherapy, he remained the same decadent as, in his words, Socrates and Wagner were. How can this fundamental contradiction be resolved? By admitting that Nietzsche unjustly condemned the present, and Wagner and Socrates along with it, or on the contrary, by agreeing that a struggle against decadence is also decadence and assigning Nietzsche himself to the category of hopeless, useless people? As you see, the question is a vital and huge one—but because of the hugeness of a question,

[1] *Ibid.*, VIII, 74.
[2] *Ibid.*, X, 452.
[3] *Ibid.*, VIII, 1.

one should not forget to note its characteristic psychological feature. As for Socrates, Nietzsche was unusually vigorous in his criticism of the fruitlessness of all sorts of attempts to struggle against "decadence." Even the sage's millennial fame, previously contested by no one, did not cause Nietzsche to mitigate his condemnation of the illustrious Greek. But when the matter touched him personally, it was as if the theory had never existed. It turns out that not only is it possible to struggle against decadence, but that victory is guaranteed such a struggle—providing there is sufficient courage, persistence, and energy. "Life itself," Nietzsche says in another place, "rewards us for our persistent will to life, for such a long struggle as the one I waged with myself at the time against the pessimistic weariness of life. In the end, we receive life's great gift, the greatest it can bestow—we regain *our* task."[1] Hadn't Socrates displayed courage and energy? Yet it did him no good! But Nietzsche had saved himself, and he considers himself justified in again assuming the great mission of teacher of mankind, for which Socrates had proved unsuited. I have compared two of Nietzsche's contradictory judgments here, but not, of course, to accuse him of inconsistency. Important here only is the fact that, although he had all the "objective" data to include himself among the lost people, the decadents, and the men such as Socrates, he not only did not include himself in this category, but, on the contrary, solemnly and confidently disassociated himself from it. Herein is revealed a characteristic not only of Nietzsche, but of all mankind. None of us, despite all outward evidence, would sign a moral condemnation of ourselves. This is an inherent characteristic of human nature about which the majority of people have never heard, thanks to various lofty doctrines. Nor had Nietzsche heard of it when he was studying with Wagner and Schopenhauer. But in *Human, All-Too-Human*, he realizes it clearly: "Whether man has a serpent's

---

[1] *Ibid.*, III, 10.

sting or not can only be learned by stepping on it with your
heel. A woman or a mother would say: by someone's stepping
on a loved one or her child. Our character is determined
much more by the absence of certain experiences than by
what we have undergone."[1] And so it was with Nietzsche
himself. As long as the circumstances were favorable, how
could anyone (himself included) have suspected a "serpent's
sting" in this meek, gentle man, who was capable of such
deep and unselfish devotion, or, metaphors aside, how could
anyone have suspected the extreme degree of egoism which
had presented the underground man with the dilemma:
should the world continue to exist or should he, the underground hero, have his tea? How could anyone, I repeat, in
observing Nietzsche, a man who, with such selflessness and
such intelligent persistence, had devoted his entire soul to
the service of art and science, imagine that it was not art,
not science, not the world, and not humanity that was his
chief purpose? And that at the moment when, by the will
of the fates, Nietzsche would be confronted with the question of whether to preserve the marvels of human culture,
whose praises he had sung, or his solitary, insignificant life,
he would be obliged to renounce his most cherished ideals
and admit that all culture, that the whole world, is worthless
if a single individual such as Nietzsche cannot be saved?
This thought seemed insane to him; to his dying day, he
could not completely accept it, and the more stubbornly it
pursued him, the more passionately he tried to escape it, or
at least to subject it to some ideal. It frightened him by the
havoc it caused people; it seemed monstrous to him because
of its fruitlessness, for other than destruction and denial,
other than nihilism, it evidently could bring nothing. But it
was not so easy to repudiate it. Nietzsche was neither the
first nor the last to struggle against it. We saw the incredible
efforts Count Tolstoy made to tear egoism up by the roots,

[1] *Ibid.,* 33.

to extirpate all remnants of it from his soul. The same with Dostoevsky. But the egoism not only did not diminish, it continued to grow and to assert its rights in ever-new forms. It was the same with Dostoevsky as with the legendary serpent—each time its head was cut off, two new ones would appear. And so it was with Nietzsche. He solemnly declared: "Above all, you must be convinced with your own eyes that injustice manifests itself most of all where a shallow, narrow, impoverished, rudimentary life cannot refrain, for the sake of self-preservation, from undermining quietly and untiringly, and from calling into question all that is higher, greater, richer."[1] These words are not, as it would seem at first glance, an expression of Nietzsche's personal judgment. The only thing original here is the form; the idea is as old as the hills. Show me the philosopher or the moralist who does not consider it his duty to extol a rich and lofty life to the detriment of a poor and narrow one? Only the Gospel says: "Blessed are the poor in spirit"—but modern science, following the precedent of science in every past age, has understood these words most conditionally, or frankly speaking, it has not understood them at all, and has ignored them with customary respect, just as people at large gatherings ignore old, distinguished guests who are of no use to anyone and who have been invited only for propriety's sake. Everyone knew that the rich in spirit are blessed, and that the poor are wretched now and forevermore. Nietzsche's judgment is merely a rehashing of this axiom, which has long been familiar to everyone. Having rebelled against everything, he not only did not venture to contest it, but unconditionally accepted it as dogma, as a *noli me tangere*. But if he paid tribute in words to a prejudice so deeply ingrained in us, he put into practice in every aspect of his life a principle that is its direct opposite. After all, he himself was poor in spirit. After all, he, too, had undermined; he, too, had subjected all that is higher, greater, and richer

[1] *Ibid.*, II, 11.

to doubt, and he did it solely to justify his own poor and wretched life—although this motive is always concealed by him with extraordinary care and consistency. In his diary for 1888, he explains the meaning of *Human, All-Too-Human*: "It was a war, but a war without gunpowder and smoke, without military procedures, without pathos, without mutilated limbs—all this might still be called idealism. A number of errors, one after the other, are calmly placed on ice: the ideal is not repudiated, it is frozen. For example, 'genius' is frozen here: a little farther on, the 'saint'; still farther, the hero is turned into a big icicle; at the end, 'faith' and so-called 'conviction' are frozen; even compassion is considerably chilled; the *Ding an sich* is frozen almost everywhere."[1] This is a surprisingly accurate description of *Human, All-Too-Human*: two lengthy books are fully summarized in a few words. But at the same time, it is merely a variation on the theme that we are now discussing—a "poor, rudimentary life" that dares to subject to doubt the legitimacy of the rights of all that is higher, richer, et cetera. Nietzsche "freezes" all that man has respected from time immemorial; he ridicules the hero, the genius, the saint. And when? In 1876–1878, when the last remnants of life were barely smoldering in him, when, by his own admission, he had completely dissipated his strength without benefit to himself and to others. As you see, "conviction," or, if you will, theory, is one thing and practice another. One remembers that Count Tolstoy became horribly indignant over such separation of theory from practice. He used to say that there must be an awfully large number of stupid theories if such an opinion can exist. I should say there are! Might I ask if there is even one "intelligent" theory? And could Count Tolstoy be what he is if he had adhered to his theoretical views in his personal life? If he had really "repudiated himself," and, in some secluded spot, far from everyone's eyes, unseen, unheard, had spent his days behind the plow or in devout conversation

---

[1] Förster-Nietzsche, *Das Leben Friedrich Nietzsche's*, II, 296.

with his peasant neighbors? Or what would have happened to Nietzsche if he had conscientiously submitted to the conclusions of his intellect? But, fortunately, few people yield to conclusions. Deep in man's soul, there is another mighty, irrepressible force. It possesses us and ridicules "free will," which, in the meaning usually given it, would lead us to the worst possible acts of folly. This "will" tempted Nietzsche to condemn Socrates. And whom did Nietzsche (and Count Tolstoy) not condemn? What would happen to the human race if all such condemnations did not remain mere words, but had power over real life? But free will is free only with respect to the man to whom it belongs. And the one time its condemnations could be meaningful, it sensibly renounces its rights, as if instinctively sensing that it can bring nothing but misfortune.

This solves the contradiction in Nietzsche's judgment of Socrates and of himself. His words about Socrates were theory. Of what concern are they to us? But in his works, he tells us of his life, of that poor life which undermined everything that is lofty and great, and which for its own preservation subjected everything to doubt that mankind reveres. That is another matter. Here, free will became silent; here, the hubbub that always accompanies discussions about a "rich life" is barely audible. Perhaps in this silence, new words will reach our ears, perhaps there will be revealed the truth about man, and not human truth, which has become so disgusting and which has worried the life out of us all.

XXII

Thus, we must least of all seek in Nietzsche's works those conclusions to which he came in rejecting the longings that naturally arose in his soul. On the contrary, for our part, we must systematically and consistently reject and eliminate all such judgments, just as one eliminates all illegitimate claims.

Let a sick and suffering man speak as a sick and suffering man, and only about subjects that are of importance to him. Nietzsche says that an *unbedingte Verschiedenheit des Blicks* leads to the horror and chill of loneliness, and that deep distrust of life threatens even more horrible results. We know all that, and nevertheless we demand from Nietzsche only the truth about his life. And the main thing, after all, is that he himself wants with all his might to speak out, to reveal his agonizing secret to the reader, as Dostoevsky does in his "Grand Inquisitor." Otherwise, what was the purpose of the prefaces? Why not leave us with the belief that the two volumes of *Human, All-Too-Human* are ordinary books in which a healthy man is reasoning as a healthy man about subjects of equal interest to everyone? If Nietzsche did not express himself frankly and openly to his dying day, it was only because he dared not risk such a step, or more probably, because the time had not yet come to speak frankly with people about everything. In their minds, there is already a glimmer of the new truth, but for the time being it seems to be not truth, but a scarecrow, a horrible phantom from another world that is alien to us. People dare not call it by its real name; they speak of it in semihints, conventional signs, and symbols. We saw the cunning to which Dostoevsky resorted: his thinking is almost impossible to pin down; it is even difficult to follow; it slips and writhes like an eel, and finally, as if on purpose, disappears in a thick fog of irreconcilable contradictions. The same is true of Nietzsche. You must pay the closest attention, you must have that "sympathetic eye" about which he speaks, in order to understand his works and not become lost in the confusion of unfounded hypotheses, arbitrary psychological conjectures, lyrical digressions, and enigmatic images. He knows this himself: "It is not for nothing," he says, "that I was and perhaps still am a philologist, i.e., a teacher of slow reading. It trains one, finally, also to write slowly. At present, it is not only my habit, but even my taste to write nothing but what will drive to despair everyone who is in a hurry. Philology is that esteemed art, which demands one thing above all from its followers—to step aside to give themselves time to think things over, to quiet down, to decelerate their movements."[1] But perhaps patience and good will alone are insufficient. Schopenhauer was right when he remarked that "personal experience is a necessary condition for understanding both poetry and history: for it serves as a sort of dictionary of the language which they speak." Such a dictionary is to a certain extent also required when one reads Nietzsche's works. For despite all his theoretical deliberations, he was nevertheless obliged to use his own experience as his sole source of knowledge: "In whatever situation you may be," he says, "let yourself serve as the source of your experience."[2] And it is, of course, impossible to do otherwise. This system of pretense can at best give a handsome outward appearance to a writer's works, but by no means will it ever provide him with their necessary content. Thus, in Dostoevsky, the thinking of the underground man is concealed behind the façade of an accusatory narrative: "Look," it seems to say, "what bad, selfish people there are, and how these poor bipeds are sometimes possessed by egoism." However, Nietzsche was no novelist; he could not speak through the "mouths" of supposedly outside heroes; he needed scientific theory. But are there really no theories that could fit his new experience?

Provided there is a desire to look for it, a theory will be found. Nietzsche decided on positivism, which bases its utilitarian point of view on morality merely because, when so desired, morality gives fullest scope to the underground idea. Like Dostoevsky, he could have become an extreme idealist and played the role of accuser. He could have chastised all manifestations of egoism, i.e., he could have spoken of his own "base" thoughts and raged at his readers as Count Tolstoy

[1] Nietzsche, *op. cit.*, IV, 10.
[2] *Ibid.*, II, 266.

does. The choice of form was decided partly by chance and partly by the peculiar cast of Nietzsche's character and the mental depression he had experienced in the early years of his illness. He lacked sufficient strength to thunder and curse, so he joined up with cold cognition. Then, in his later works, he began to feel at home in his role and armed himself with menacing bolts of lightning. But in *Human, All-Too-Human* and *Dawn*, we are faced with a positivist, a utilitarian, and a rationalist, who is coldly and calmly reducing all the loftiest and noblest manifestations of the human soul to their basest and most rudimentary form, supposedly for purposes of theoretical knowledge. "*Human, All-Too-Human*," Nietzsche writes in his diary for 1888, "is a monument to a crisis. It is a book for free minds [*ein Buch für freie Geister*]: almost every sentence in it expresses a victory; I have liberated myself in it from all that is alien to my nature. All idealism is alien to me; the name of the book says: where you see a manifestation of idealism, I, alas, see merely that which is human, all-too-human. I know people better."[1] As you see, in 1888, Nietzsche was much bolder and more confident than in 1876, when he wrote *Human, All-Too-Human*. But, nevertheless, he relies even here on the fact that he knows "people," i.e., not himself, but others! Yet the entire content of *Human, All-Too-Human* was taken solely from his own experience: Nietzsche had only the possibility of convincing himself that idealism was alien to *him*, that in his soul the seat of ideal aspirations was occupied by human, all-too-human impulses. And in 1876, this discovery not only did not gladden him, it destroyed him. After all, he was still completely imbued at the time with Schopenhauer's doctrine. After all, at almost this very time, while praising his teacher, he exclaimed: "Schopenhauer teaches us to sacrifice the ego, to subordinate it to the noblest goals—especially those of justice and mercy."[2] Can one believe

[1] Förster-Nietzsche, *op. cit.*, II, 296.
[2] Nietzsche, *op. cit.*, I, 410.

that he immediately renounced the "noblest" goals and acknowledged his own human needs as the sole legitimate and
just ones? Alas, he did not go that far, nor could he do so even
at the end of his life—but at the moment of his split with
Schopenhauer and Wagner, he, of course, regarded his inca-
pacity for self-sacrifice as a monstrous anomaly of psychological make-up, characteristic of him alone. Before deciding to
speak of himself gradually and unobtrusively under the cover
of a universally recognized scientific theory, he spent many a
sleepless night trying to return his dissolute soul to the lofty
doctrine of self-sacrifice. But all attempts proved fruitless. The
more he tried to convince himself of the necessity of renounc-
ing his ego and the brighter he painted for himself the picture
of the future prosperity of mankind, the more bitter, insulting,
and painful it was for him to think that he would not be
present at the triumph of life, that he was even deprived of
the possibility of actively assisting in the coming victory of
mankind. "People will reach their highest goals; there will
not be one humiliated, wretched being on this earth; truth
will shine forth to each and everyone. Is that too little to
console your poor heart with, can't that atone for your disgrace? Forget yourself, renounce yourself, look at others, admire and rejoice at the future hopes of mankind, as the sages
have taught us to do since time immemorial. Otherwise, you
are twice a nonentity. Otherwise, you are not only a broken
man, but also a morally doomed one." Such words, and even
more dreadful ones, which are used by a man only when
alone with himself, and which were never before brought out
into the open by a single one of the boldest psychologists, not
even by Dostoevsky, were whispered to Nietzsche by his conscience, which had been reared on idealist doctrines. After
all, he came from a family of Lutheran pastors: his father
and grandfather were preachers, his mother and grandmother
were daughters of preachers. Have you ever had occasion to
hear or read German Protestant sermons? If so, you will under-

stand what was taking place in Nietzsche's soul. He was not asked if he could meet the demands made on him. No one wanted to strengthen, guide, or encourage him. Day and night, he heard only a stern voice thundering over him and pronouncing the terrible adjuration: *ossa arida, audite verbum Dei.* Nietzsche understood then that it was useless for him to expect anything more from people. For the first time in his life, he knew what it meant to be completely alone. The whole world was against him, and, therefore, he was against the whole world. Compromise, concession, and agreement were impossible. For it was one of two things: either Nietzsche was right, or his tragedy was indeed so profound, so unprecedently horrible that all people must forget their usual joys and sorrows, their daily cares and interests and go with him into eternal mourning for a young life that had been unjustly ruined, or he must renounce himself and fulfill—not hypocritically, but with all his heart and soul—the demands being made on him in the name of eternal wisdom. But if it was impossible to force the entire human race to share the grief of one German professor, then, vice versa, it was equally *impossible,* by using all sorts of threats and torments, to extort from this German professor a voluntary renunciation of his rights to life. The whole world and one man had collided, and it turned out that these two forces were of equal magnitude; more than that, on the "world's" side were all the traditions of the past, all human wisdom from past ages, Nietzsche's own conscience, and finally, evidence itself. And on Nietzsche's side—well, what did he have on his side but despair?

Then what was it that supported Nietzsche in this mad and unequal struggle? Why did he not retreat before his infinitely powerful adversary? Where did he get the courage not only to fight, but even for one minute to look such an enemy straight in the face? True, the struggle was horrible and unprecedented. But, because of this, it astonishes us all the more. Doesn't it have concealed within it that truth about man, which we were discussing at the end of the preceding chapter? And doesn't this mean that human truth, by rising along with the world against Nietzsche, was a lie?

XXIII

Herein is the essence of what Nietzsche called the *"unbedingte Verschiedenheit des Blicks."* Herein is what distinguishes his view of life from all other philosophical world views that have thus far existed. Human reason, human wisdom, and human morality, having conferred on themselves the right of definitive and final judgment, said to him: you are crushed, you are ruined, there is no salvation for you, there is no hope for you. Wherever he looked, he heard these cold, ruthless words. The loftiest ultrametaphysical doctrines did not at all differ in this case from the judgments of common, ordinary men who have never glanced into a book. Schopenhauer, Kant, Spinoza, the materialists, and the positivists, in observing Nietzsche and his fate, could tell him nothing more than is contained in the famous statement of a phlegmatic Byelo-Russian to his drowning comrade: "Don't ruin your health, Foma; go to the bottom!" The only difference is that the "scholars" were not as frank as the Byelo-Russian peasant, and, moreover, they demanded an attitude of respect, compassion, reverence, and even gratitude toward themselves: after all, they provide metaphysical or moral consolation! After all, they are not of this world—they are of pure reason, of *conceptio immaculata*! And all that is not with them, all that is against them, belongs entirely to the contemptible, wretched, earthly human ego, from which philosophers, thanks to the loftiness and genius of their nature, had fortunately liberated themselves long ago.

But Nietzsche felt that all metaphysical and moral ideas had completely ceased to exist for him, whereas the greatly slandered ego had grown to unprecedented, colossal proportions and had blotted out the entire world before him. Another person in his place would have submitted, perhaps for good; another person would even have died with the conviction that his was the misfortune to appear in this world without those lofty virtues that adorn other people, particularly those eloquent and pathetic teachers of good. But, fortunately, even before his illness, Nietzsche himself had managed several times to appear in the role of teacher, and consequently he already had in his own past a certain amount of material for "psychology." Looking back over his early literary works, which had won such enthusiastic praise from Wagner and other celebrities of the time, he naturally had to ask himself the question: "After all, my appearance was no less noble and ideal than that of all other writers. I preached goodness ardently and well, I invoked truth, I sang hymns to beauty— probably no worse than Schopenhauer himself in his youthful works. Yet, one heavy blow of fate—a simple, ordinary, stupid event, a misfortune that could have happened to anyone, to the great and the small of this world—and I suddenly became convinced that egoism, which I never suspected in me, is just as characteristic of me as it is of any ordinary mortal. Doesn't this mean that all other teachers also are hypocritical, that they, too, when they preach truth, goodness, love, and mercy, are merely playing a solemn role—some of them sincerely and unwittingly, as I once did, others perhaps dishonestly and deliberately? Doesn't this mean that all great and saintly men, if they were put in my place, would find as little solace in their truths as I did? And that when they spoke of love, self-sacrifice, and renunciation, there was concealed in all their pretty phrases, like a serpent among flowers, that same devilish egoism which I so unexpectedly discovered in myself, and which I am so desperately and fruitlessly fighting?" This still vague idea—perhaps it is not even idea, but instinct— determined the nature of Nietzsche's immediate quests. He had by no means been so confident in freezing ideals, as he says in his diary for 1888. In his writings, we have scores of indications as to how much wavering and doubt he had to experience in the early days of his independent creative work. In his literary legacy, there is a remark relating to 1876, i.e., to the period when he was writing *Human, All-Too-Human*: "How is it possible," he asks himself, "to find pleasure in the *trivial* thought that the motives of all our actions boil down to egoism?"[1] As you see, there is as yet no certainty: the thought seems trivial to him, but some force, which is still incomprehensible to him himself, attracts him to it. Later, in 1886, when casting a retrospective glance at the genesis of *Dawn*, he said: "In this book, you see the underground man at work—digging, mining, undermining. You can see him— always provided that you have eyes for such deep work—making his way slowly, cautiously, gently but surely, without showing signs of the weariness that usually accompanies a long privation of light and air. It might even be said that he is content with his work in the dark. It even begins to seem as if some faith is leading him on, as if he finds solace in his work. Perhaps he needs a long period of darkness, he needs an unintelligible, hidden, enigmatic something, for he knows what awaits him: his own morning, his own redemption, his own rosy dawn."[2] But he was still a long way from faith, from dawn. His favorite thought, from which he never parted at the time, and which he varied in the most diverse ways, is expressed in the following aphorism: "Do you think that all good things have at all times had conscience on their side? Science—unquestionably a good thing—has got along for a considerable time without conscience, and it has always made its way into life without any pathos, clandestinely, by round-about ways, hiding behind a veil or a mask, like a criminal, or at best, with the feeling a smuggler must experience. Good conscience has bad conscience for its stepping-stone, not for its opposite. For all that is good has at one time been new

[1] *Ibid.*, XI, 133.
[2] *Ibid.*, IV, 3.

and consequently strange, antimoral, immoral, and has gnawed
like a worm at the heart of its fortunate discoverer."[1] This
explains well enough how much struggle, wavering, and doubt
Nietzsche had to bear on his "new" path. It was terrifying
for him everywhere to see the "human," only the human, but at
the same time, it was necessary. It was not out of mere curiosity, not even out of scientific inquisitiveness that he began
his underground work: he needed a long period of darkness,
he needed the incomprehensible, the mysterious, the enigmatic. Oh, how he was tempted to go "back"—to that simple,
easy, well-organized world in which he had lived in youth!
How he wanted to reconcile himself with "conscience," to
acquire again the right to speak solemnly and in concert with
all teachers about lofty subjects! But all paths "back" were
forbidden him. "Up to now," he says, "we have meditated
least profoundly on good and evil: this was always too dangerous a subject. Conscience, a good reputation, hell, and at
times even the police, have not permitted and do not permit
frankness; in the presence of morality, as before all authority,
we are not permitted to think, much less to speak: here we
must *obey*! Since the beginning of the world, no authority has
voluntarily agreed to become the subject of criticism; and to
criticize morals—to regard morality as a problem, as problematic—did that not mean becoming immoral oneself? But
morality has at its disposal not only every means of intimida-
tion wherewith to frighten away ruthless criticism; its strength
and security lie rather in a certain art of enchantment, in which
it is a past master—it knows how to inspire. It can often
paralyze the critical will with a single look, or even lure it to
its side, yes, even turn the critical will against itself, so that
the critic, like a scorpion, thrusts the sting into its own body.
Morality has since time immemorial possessed all the resources
of the art of convincing: there is no orator who would not
turn to it for assistance. Morality has shown herself to be

[1] *Ibid.*, III, 49.

the greatest mistress of seduction ever since men began to discourse and persuade on earth—and, as for us philosophers, she has been a veritable Circe for us."[1]

And so everything in life is merely *"human, all-too-human"*—and in this is salvation, hope, and a new dawn? Could one think up a more paradoxical statement? As long as we only had Nietzsche's early works, in which he assured us that objective truth alone is important for him, we could explain to ourselves such strange thinking by regarding Nietzsche as a member of that fairly widespread group of scholars who sit in their ivory tower and forget the world, people, and life while engaged in their theoretical work. But now it is obvious that Nietzsche *never* was a positivist. For what has positivism in common with a new dawn? Positivism has its own dawn, its own hopes, its own justification; its faith is in utilitarian morals, those same morals that Nietzsche had so stubbornly and for so long undermined. Utilitarianism, realizing that it can in no way help the inhabitants of the underground, deliberately ignores them. True, it sets man's happiness as its task, and, in principle, does not wish to deny anyone the right to life. But in those instances when a person has been denied it by so-called circumstances beyond his control, utilitarian morals are helpless, and not wishing openly to admit their impotence, they throw themselves into the arms of idealism. Imperceptibly to the untrained eye, they replace the words "man's happiness" with other words that are quite similar at first sight—"the majority's happiness." But the similarity here is only superficial. "The majority's happiness" does not mean the same as "man's happiness"—it means the direct opposite. For in the latter case, it is assumed that everyone will benefit, whereas in the former, the minority is sacrificed to the majority. But does positivism have the right to call for sacrifice, can it justify sacrifice? After all, it promised happiness and only happiness; after all, over and above happiness it sees no

[1] *Ibid.*, IV, 5.

meaning in life, and then suddenly—sacrifice! It is clear that
in a difficult moment, it cannot get along without the aid of
idealism; it is less clear, but just as certain, that utilitarianism
never even wanted to break away from ideals. It was merely
flaunting its scientific nature, but deep down in its soul (utilitarianism had a "soul"—who would have thought it!), it believed in justice, goodness, truth, spontaneous intuition, in all
the lofty and sacred words. And, as was already pointed out,
Dostoevsky, in depicting Rakitin as "greasy," was slandering
the creed of positivism.

But Nietzsche had long since taken leave of ideals. "The
majority's happiness" did not attract him. Sacrifice? Perhaps
he was still capable of being inspired by this pretty word, but,
alas, he no longer had anything to sacrifice. What could he
offer? His life? That would not be sacrifice, but suicide. He
would have been glad to die in order to rid himself of this
hateful life. But rich gifts only are brought to the altar; and
a wretched, exhausted, and mutilated being is not to the taste
of good, which, like pagan idols, demands young, fresh, beautiful, and happy lives that are untouched by suffering.

XXIV

Consequently, under the cover of positivism, Nietzsche pursued entirely different goals. He used positivism and scientism
for secondary purposes: at one time, he needed to "seem"
cheerful, inquisitive, derisive, et cetera; at another, he needed
a theory to which a sick and suffering man could turn when
rejecting the judgments that were naturally springing up inside
him. For us, all this can be only of a purely psychological
interest, especially as Nietzsche always shaped his own course
and merely waited for the opportunity to liberate himself from
the theory that was hampering him and to speak boldly in his
own way. But daring needs talent and strength; it needs a
weapon for the fight, and several years passed before Nietzsche

decided to proclaim his "underground" ideas openly. Incidentally, I suppose that true positivists would prefer not to
have *Human, All-Too-Human* and *Dawn* in their libraries.
Despite the fact that in these books Nietzsche wages unceasing war on metaphysics, he reveals in his scientific endeavors
an anxiety that verges on tactlessness. The strength of positivism lies in its ability to pass in silence over all problems
regarded by it as fundamentally unsolvable, and to direct
our attention only to those aspects of life in which there are
no irreconcilable contradictions: after all, the limits of our
knowledge end at precisely the point where irreconcilable
contradictions begin. In this sense, Kantian idealism is, as we
know, a most reliable ally of positivism, and the celebrated
argument between Whewell [1] and Mill, if it was not, strictly
speaking, an argument over words and scientific terminology,
was, at any rate, of very limited theoretical significance. Albert
Lange, [2] in condemning Mill and assuming the defense of
Whewell and Kant, merely displayed for us one more example
of human bias. I would go further: in my opinion, it was not
Mill, as Lange states, but more probably Whewell who displayed a certain amount of bad faith. Why did they have to
drive Mill to foolish admissions? Anyone else in the latter's
place would have found it possible in some way or other to
dodge them and avoid assuming the responsibility for extreme
conclusions, which, as we know, always compromise all kinds
of theories. Doesn't the Kantian theory of the a priori lead to
absurdity—to what in philosophical language is called theoretical egoism, i.e., to the necessity of each person's thinking
that apart from himself, there is no one else in the entire
universe? Even the most conscientious Kantians do not conceal
this. Schopenhauer, for example, frankly states that theoretical

---

[1] William Whewell (1794–1866), an English philosopher, remembered
for his work on the theory of induction and for his interest in the physical
sciences. [Tr.]
[2] Friedrich Albert Lange (1828–1875), a German philosopher, a neo-
Kantian, one of the leaders of the "Back-to-Kant" movement. [Tr.]

egoism cannot be refuted. But this does not in the least prevent him from developing his philosophical theses, which proceed from Kantian principles. When an unexpected obstacle arises, he laughs it off. Theoretical egoism, he says, is indeed an impregnable fortress, but the garrison stationed in it is so weak that one can, without even capturing it, boldly advance and not fear attack from the rear. And that is about the only way to save idealism from the *reductio ad absurdum* that threatens it. Another more widespread and reliable method is simply to forget about theoretical egoism, to ignore it. If Mill had wanted to resort to such methods, he could have concluded his polemic a good deal more successfully. But Mill was an honest man. Mill was honesty personified, even when compared with the Germans, who claim this virtue solely for themselves. And yet his honesty is depicted as bad faith! I do not know if Mill had occasion to read Lange's book, but, if he did, it probably once again confirmed in his eyes the hackneyed truth according to which there is no justice among men.

And in what did they see Mill's bad faith? Unlike Kant, he did not want to acknowledge nonempirical knowledge, and in the causal connection of phenomena, he saw only their factual, true, but not necessary, relation. It goes without saying that it never occurred to Mill to attack the immutability of the laws of nature. But isn't the experience of several millennia adequate proof of immutability? Why then resort to a dangerous metaphysical method of proof, when, as a matter of fact, no one in our time any longer seriously doubts the regularity of natural phenomena? Metaphysics frightened the positive thinker. Today, people proclaim the apriority of the law of causality, the ideality of space and time, and tomorrow, on the very same basis, they will justify clairvoyance, dancing tables, witchcraft, or what have you. To Mill, acceptance of apriorism seemed a most hazardous step for philosophy. And, after all, his anxiety was not without basis: the very near future showed that he was right. Schopenhauer had already used Kant's theory of the ideality of time to explain the phenomenon of clairvoyance. And his conclusion is logically irreproachable. If time is a form of our knowledge, if, consequently, we only know as the present, past, and future that which actually occurs outside time, i.e., synchronously (it is all the same), then it means we cannot see the past or the future, not because it is altogether impossible, but merely because our cognitive abilities are fashioned in a certain way. But our cognitive abilities, like the whole of our mental organization, are not immutable. Among the billions of normal people being born, it is possible from time to time to have deviations from the norm. Perhaps a brain will sometime be formed in such a way that its possessor will not perceive phenomena in time, and consequently, for him, the future and the past will merge with the present, and he will be able to predict events that have not yet happened and to see those that for others have already been swallowed by history. As you see, the consistency in this deduction is purely "mathematical." Mill, with his conscientiousness, would have been reluctantly obliged to believe in clairvoyance if he acknowledged the apriority of time. Worse still, he probably would not even have avoided theoretical egoism, and would have been obliged to declare that he alone existed in the whole universe! So that he had serious grounds to dread Kantian idealism. But this does not at all mean that the cause of science was any less dear to his heart than it was to Kant's, or that he was not trying to prove once and for all the truth of the regularity of natural phenomena: he was merely avoiding dangerous hypotheses and risky methods of proof.

And then his opponents, for their part, presented him with the following objection: if the regularity of natural phenomena can be proved only by experience, i.e., by the events of history, then it must be assumed that, in principle—theoretically at least—it, too, can sometime come to an end. At present, regularity still prevails, but one fine day, the reign of arbitrariness will begin. Or: here on earth, there is causality, but somewhere on a distant planet, there is not. You cannot provide any evidence to the contrary, for historical observation can be only of limited and relative significance. Anyone else in Mill's place would have in some way or other extricated himself, but Mill could not help being honest, and he admitted that we indeed have no evidence as far as the future and as far as distant planets are concerned. This means, to put it more simply, that objects that until now have been at rest have not moved of their own accord without an outside cause, but that tomorrow everything might take a different turn: stones might fly into the air, mountains might move from their places, and rivers might flow backwards.[1]

That is, once again, none of this will actually happen: the history of a thousand years attests to this convincingly enough, but in principle, such a possibility cannot be denied. This, or almost this, is what Mill said, or more accurately, what he was obliged to say. It is clear that a positivist accepts such conclusions reluctantly, and only in those cases where the unusually well-developed conscience of a scholar impels him

[1] I think it necessary to explain that I am presenting Mill's views in "my own words." Mill, of course, does not speak of "tomorrow" (*he reserves tomorrow for positivism*), nor does he mention mountains that move or rivers that flow backwards: I have added all these specific examples in my own name, for the sake of clarity, of course. But to avoid criticism, I shall quote the appropriate passage from his *Logic*: "I am convinced that anyone accustomed to abstraction and analysis, who will fairly exert his faculties for the purpose will, when his imagination has once learnt to entertain the notion, find no difficulty in conceiving that in some one, for instance, of the many firmaments into which sidereal astronomy now divides the universe, events may succeed one another at random without any fixed law; nor can anything in our experience or in our mental nature constitute a sufficient, or indeed any reason for believing that this is nowhere the case.

"Were we to suppose (what it is perfectly possible to imagine) that the present order of the universe were brought to an end, and that a chaos succeeded in which there was no fixed succession of events and the past gave no assurance of the future; if a human body were miraculously kept alive to witness this change, he surely would soon cease to believe in any uniformity, the uniformity itself no longer existing." (*A System of Logic*, Book III, Chapter 21 § 1.)

to do so. It is also clear why Mill looked so pained and crushed when he made these admissions. Lange, having correctly noted that Mill's customary serene and equable frame of mind had betrayed him, hastened to inform his readers that the reason for it was a guilty conscience: Mill felt that he was driven to the wall, and, as he was unwilling to admit his error, he allowed conclusions that were patently absurd to him. As a matter of fact, it was just the reverse: Mill had sacrificed to his conscience not "truth," but his peace of mind. The idea of the possibility of effect without cause was odious to him to the very depths of his soul; it tormented him, and if there had been the slightest possibility, he would have repudiated it. But what had he been offered by the idealists? A priori concepts, with the prospect of dancing tables and a belief in clairvoyance? In that case, it would be better to have effect without cause somewhere off in the far distance and after many thousands of years (almost a priori causality). First of all, you do not deceive yourself here, and secondly, when all is said and done, no one will ever use this thesis, as it *cannot be put into practice* and as no one needs it—even Kant himself did not strive for more. So there was just one unpleasant moment, but, on the other hand, the empirical basis for the reliability of our knowledge is a bulwark against skepticism with which no metaphysical theories of knowledge, not even Kantian, bear comparison.

The reader sees that Mill's opponents were not conscientious. I do not think that they failed to sense the vulnerability of idealism. Anyone even slightly versed in philosophical problems knows very well that no system has as yet been devised that is entirely free of contradictions. Perhaps we should not say that too loudly, but, as you know, even Schopenhauer declared that every philosophy that does not acknowledge premises is a fraud. Only the uninitiated do not know this secret. And if this is so, it means that common literary decency demanded that Whewell and Lange leave

Mill alone, that they not touch his premises, and that they not go beyond a certain point in the argument. They had both theoretical egoism and clairvoyance on their conscience—great and grievous sins, no matter how cleverly Schopenhauer joked about the matter. They should have forgiven the positivists effect without cause in the sense that Mill allowed it. One can rid oneself of such conclusions only by means of premises—why then should proof be demanded from Mill? And, above all, to what do such demands lead? They can only undermine confidence in science in general—i.e., in all attempts to simplify, pacify, smooth out, and tame reality. They only open the way to skepticism, which, like a vulture after prey, pursues all sorts of dogmas that have been carried to absurdity; consequently, because of completely unwarranted theoretical claims, they *betray* the common cause to the most dangerous enemy that can possibly exist. For the chief task of science as well as morality consists in providing people with a firm foundation in life, in teaching them to know what is and what is not, what one may do, and what one may not. However, the means to achieve this are a secondary matter; at any rate, they are not so important as to forget the main goal because of them. How poorly the Kantians understand this, yet how well Kant himself knew it! Despite the fact that he could not help rejoicing and thinking highly of his new point of view in philosophy, he saw in Hume not his enemy, but an ally and precursor, and he esteemed Hume's argumentation highly. And, after all, Mill is probably as important to science as Hume. Just note the patience and knowledge of his field that he displays in his *System of Logic* or in his treatise on utilitarianism as he avoids all reefs encountered on his way; how steadily and devotedly, and with what a firm and reliable hand he guides his scholarly ship to the shore inhabited by positivism, i.e., certainty, evidence, and finally, the crowning virtue, Kantian-Tolstoyan stability. Isn't that a colossal merit? And do a priori judgments really lead to greater stability and clarity than Mill's method?

But, as was already stated, the argument between idealism and positivism and even materialism is, in the final analysis a mere argument over words. However much the opposing sides taunt each other, it is clear to an outside observer that they are essentially in agreement, and that it is the same old story: one friend does not recognize another. As for Nietzsche, only his early works can be connected with one of the existing schools of philosophy. But beginning with *Human, All-Too-Human*, i.e., from the moment he viewed the world with his own eyes, he immediately withdrew to a point equidistant from all systems. From positivism and materialism, he took a weapon with which to fight idealism, and vice versa, as he wanted nothing more sincerely and profoundly than the destruction of all world views that had been devised by man. The "stability," which was considered the supreme and ultimate goal of philosophical systems, and which all founders of such schools had laid claim to, not only did not attract him, it frightened him. Kant, the materialists, and Mill had needed it, because it guaranteed them the immutability of that position in life that was dear to them. But Nietzsche strove above all to *change* his position: what could stability promise him? The "savoir pour prévoir" or the regularity with which positivism had tried to lure us sounded to him like insulting mockery. What could he foresee? That one cannot return the past? That he would never be cured and would finally lose his mind? He knew this without either positivism or science. But did Kantian idealism, with its crowning virtue—the morality of the categorical imperative—tell him anything else? Nietzsche was and always remained sympathetic only to the language of skepticism—and not, of course, the skepticism of the drawing room or the study, which amounts to witty remarks or theorizing, but the skepticism that permeates a man's entire soul and unsettles his life forever. Zarathustra says: "The shore has disappeared from my sight, the waves of the infinite have engulfed me." What could be done here by the positivists or idealists, who think that their entire task is to convince man of the proximity of the shore, to conceal infinity from him, and to restrict him to the limited sphere of phenomena that are the same for all people, that yield to precise definition, that are customary and comprehensible? For Mill, the necessity of acknowledging the possibility of effect without cause, even on a distant planet, was most distressing. Lange, following in Kant's footsteps, accepted apriorism merely not to see himself forced to acknowledge randomness in nature. But all their worries were alien to Nietzsche; on the contrary, their apprehensions were his hopes. His life had meaning, it could only have meaning, if all scientific systems were merely voluntary self-restraint of the timorous human mind. His life's task amounted precisely to going beyond the limits of those spheres into which he had been driven by the traditions of science and morality. Thence his hatred for science, which found expression in his fight against philosophical systems and in his aversion to morality, which inspired the formula "beyond good and evil." There was just one question for Nietzsche: "Lord, why hast Thou forsaken me?"[1] Do you know those simple words, which are filled with such infinite grief and bitterness? Such a question can have but one answer: both human science, which has accommodated itself to the average, everyday life, and human morality, which justifies, extols, sanctifies, and raises norms to laws (the pious memory of Rostov's administration, "goodness is God"), are false. Or to use Nietzsche's words: nothing is true, everything is permitted—or a revaluation of all values.

XXV

Hence that strange, alien nature of Nietzsche's philosophy. There is no stability in it, no balance. It does not even seek them: as in the case of Dostoevsky's world view, it lives by contradictions. Nietzsche never misses an opportunity to

[1] Nietzsche, *op. cit.*, IV, 113.

ridicule so-called strength of conviction. Premises, which Schopenhauer considered so essential for philosophy and which he not only justified, but did not even consider necessary to conceal, as is usually done, find in Nietzsche their most caustic and vicious critic. "There is a point in every philosophy," he says, "when the 'convictions' of the philosopher appear on the scene; or, to put it in the words of an ancient mystery play: *Adventavit asinus, Pulcher et fortissimus.*"[1] But along with such statements, you also find others that seem to be diametrically opposed to them: "The falseness of a given judgment does not constitute an objection to it, so far as we are concerned. It is perhaps in this respect that our new language sounds strangest. The real question is how far a judgment furthers and maintains life, preserves a given type, possibly cultivates and trains a given type. We are, in fact, fundamentally inclined to maintain that the falsest judgments (to which belong the synthetic a priori judgments) are the most indispensable to us; that man cannot live without accepting the logical fictions as valid, without measuring reality against the purely invented world of the absolute, the immutable, without constantly falsifying the world by means of numeration. That getting along without false judgments would amount to getting along without life, negating life. To admit untruth as the fundamental condition of life: this implies, to be sure, a perilous resistance against customary value-feelings. A philosophy that risks it nonetheless, if it did nothing else, would by this alone have taken its stand beyond good and evil."[2] But the question naturally arises: if untruth and false judgments are the basic conditions of human existence, if they help to preserve, or even to develop life, then weren't those sages right who, like Dostoevsky's Grand Inquisitor, passed off this untruth as *truth*? And wouldn't the most sensible thing be to remain with tradition, i.e., to refrain

[1] *Ibid.*, VII, 16.
[2] *Ibid.*, 12–13.

completely, as before, from seeking truth and, in this regard,
to hold to opinions that have been formed unconsciously, i.e.,
to have those premises, those "convictions," in connection
with which Nietzsche recalled the disrespectful words of the
ancient mystery play? If synthetic a priori judgments are so
necessary to man that life is impossible without them, that to
repudiate them would mean to deny life, then they might as
well retain their former respectable name, "true judgments,"
in which guise they can, of course, best fulfill their noble
purpose. Why expose their falseness? Why not follow the example of Kant and Count Tolstoy and place their roots in
another world, so that people will not only believe in their
truth, but will even be convinced that they have a celestial, a
metaphysical, basis? If a lie is so essential to life, then it is
no less essential that people think that this lie is not a lie, but
the truth. But, evidently, Nietzsche is interested not in "life,"
over which he makes such a fuss, but in something else—
at least not in a life such as the one thus far defended by
positivists, by synthetic a priori judgments, and by their
priests, the teachers of wisdom. Otherwise, he would not have
begun to shout out, almost on the public square, philosophy's
professional secret; on the contrary, he would have tried to
conceal it as carefully as possible. Schopenhauer had made
a tactical error in proclaiming that philosophy is impossible
without premises, but Nietzsche goes even further. So in the
final analysis, he is not in the least interested in the question
of preserving and sustaining what he calls by the abstract
word "life." Although he speaks of such a "life," as many
others do, he does not care about it or even think about it.
He knows that "life" has existed thus far without the tutelage
of philosophers and that it will continue to get along on its
own strength in the future as well. By justifying synthetic
a priori judgments in such a risky way, Nietzsche was merely
trying to *compromise* them, in order to open the way for himself to complete freedom of investigation, in order to win for

himself the right to speak of things about which other people remain silent.

Zarathustra says: "Down there [among people] all speech is useless! There, the best wisdom is to forget and pass by: *That* have I learned now! He who would understand everything in man must grapple with everything."[1] In his youth, Nietzsche himself was no different in this respect from other philosophers. It was not of his own free will that he fell to stopping at places where others pass by and to remembering what others forget. "Suffering asks about the cause, but pleasure is inclined to keep within itself and not look backward."[2] But not all suffering teaches us to question. Man is born a positivist, and by no means must he first go through a theological and metaphysical stage in order to acquire a taste for the limitation of knowledge, as is recommended by positivist philosophy. On the contrary, he avoids too great wisdom and, above all, even tries to escape suffering, to rid himself of it. And only when all efforts in this positive direction prove fruitless, when he is convinced that it is impossible to "adjust himself," that it is impossible to find a situation in which "suffering" ceases to make itself felt, does he leave the bounds of positivist truth and begin to question, without giving any further thought as to whether or not his questions are permitted by contemporary methodology and epistemology. "At the present time," Nietzsche says, "we all live, relatively speaking, in a security that is much too great to make us true psychologists: some survey their fellow men as a hobby, others out of boredom, and others again merely from habit; but never to the extent they would do so if they were told by an authoritative voice: 'Discern or perish!' As long as truths do not cut us to the quick, we assume an attitude of contempt towards them: they still appear to us too much like 'winged dreams,' as if we could or could not have them

[1] *Ibid.*, VI, 271.
[2] *Ibid.*, V, 50–51.

at our discretion, as if we could be aroused from these truths as from a dream!"[1] You see how the boundaries of the cognizable world are extended: all that is needed is an authoritative voice to say "discern or perish," a categorical imperative, which Kant did not think of. Finally, it is necessary for truths to cut us to the quick—but none of this is mentioned either in epistemology or in logic. There, the process of seeking truth is portrayed in an entirely different way; there, to think means to proceed calmly, consistently, and painlessly (although with effort) from conclusion to conclusion until what is sought is found. But with Nietzsche, to think is to worry, to be tormented, to writhe in convulsions. If you recall, it is the same in Dostoevsky's novels; none of the leading characters ever thinks according to the rules of logic. Everywhere in his books, there is nothing but frenzy, anguish, tears, and the gnashing of teeth. The theoretical philosopher sees needless, even harmful, excess in all this. Spinoza says: "*Non ridere, non lugere, neque detestari, sed intelligere.*" He thinks that it is possible "to understand" by means of abstract or—as people are inclined to call it—objective thinking. But what has philosophy "understood" up to now? Nietzsche had legitimate doubts as to whether the methods recommended by Spinoza and hitherto always practiced by teachers of wisdom actually do provide the most reliable or even the only reliable way to the truth. "Yes, perhaps in our struggling interior, there is a good deal of concealed *heroism*, but certainly nothing divine, or eternally reposing in itself, as Spinoza supposed. *Conscious* thinking, and especially that of the philosopher, is the weakest, and on that account also relatively mildest and quietest way of thinking: thus it is precisely the philosopher who is most easily misled concerning the nature of our knowledge."[2]

Not only the "philosopher," but all of us, we people of modern upbringing, precisely because of the circumstances of

[1] *Ibid.*, IV, 311.
[2] *Ibid.*, V, 253.

our development, are hardly capable of making correct judgments about nature, about the limits of our knowledge, and about "truth." True, superstition has always existed among men; you cannot name a period when some error or other was not regarded as truth, and a great truth at that. But never before have people been so deeply convinced of the infallibility of their methodology as in our time. Our century, as you know, is called the century of skepticism *par excellence*; in other words, people think that once something is presented as truth, it is done so only after the most careful and thorough investigation possible, when there can no longer be any doubt about it. But we are utterly incapable of "believing," even if we wanted to. Yet, from childhood on, we are trained to "believe" and, above all, to believe the most implausible things! A peasant boy or a young savage, of course, also believes what his elders tell him. But usually he is told nothing that is implausible or that constrains his thinking. He is told, for example, that there are sorcerers, wood goblins, and witches. All this is untrue—none of it exists, but, as you know, it is all conceivable and comprehensible. From these stories, the young mind merely concludes that there are extremely horrible and interesting things that it has not yet seen, but that it will perhaps some day see with its own eyes. It is another matter with a child of our society: its mind is unencumbered by fairy tales; it knows that demons and sorcerers do not exist, and it trains its mind not to believe such lies, even if its heart is inclined toward the miraculous. But on the other hand, from very early age on, it is given reliable information, the implausibility of which surpasses absolutely every fib ever told by the most imaginative writers of fairy tales. For example, it is told—and in an authoritative tone before which all doubt subsides—it must subside—that the earth is not motionless, as the evidence indicates, that the sun does not revolve around the earth, that the sky is not a solid, that the horizon is only an optical illusion, and so on endlessly. All this is learned in early, very early, childhood and usually without even those considerations and proofs that are provided in elementary geography textbooks. And all this is accepted as the absolute truth, and not even subject to verification, for it comes from the child's elders, for it is so written in books. Now tell me, which fairy tale (and it doesn't even have to be from those that educated people recommend for the common folk, but from those that illiterate writers manufacture for profit) contains a lie more obvious to a child than the truths that we teach it? A sorcerer, a witch, a demon—they are merely something new, but they are comprehensible and do not contradict the evidence. But the revolving earth, the motionless sun, and so on—all this is, of course, absolute nonsense to a child. And yet it is the truth; the child knows it for certain, and he lives for years on end with this implausible truth. But doesn't this coercion of the child's mind impair its cognition? Doesn't a belief in the import of nonsense become its second nature? And finally, isn't the tendency of each of us to accept as truth only what seems to our entire being to be false certain to remain in our minds forever? Or, if this conclusion seems too paradoxical or exaggerated, must we not, at any rate, be ready to believe in what to us is an obvious absurdity (*intelligere* in other words), as long as it is provided with a certain argumentation and comes from learned people or from their books? For example, Schopenhauer's will, Kant's *Ding an sich*, or Spinoza's *deus sive natura*? Our mind, having assimilated so much nonsense in childhood, has lost the ability to defend itself and accepts everything except what it was warned against from early childhood on, i.e., the miraculous, or in other words, effect without cause. Here, it is always on guard; here, it cannot be enticed by anything—neither by eloquence, inspiration, nor logic. But if the miraculous is not involved, then everything goes. What, for example, does contemporary man "understand" by the words "the natural development of the world"? Forget for a moment, for just a moment—provided that is possible—your schooling, and you will immediately be convinced that the development of the world is frightfully unnatural: *it would be natural if there were nothing at all*—neither the world nor its development. And yet there is almost no one today who does not believe as firmly in the theory of naturalism as a devout Catholic believes in the infallibility of the Pope. More than that even: the Catholic may in some way or other be dissuaded, but contemporary modern man will under no circumstances seriously accept the idea that the world evolved unnaturally, and, consequently, that randomness in nature, effect without cause, about which Mill speaks, has any other use than to indicate the limits of our knowledge. For him, as for Mill and Kant, this is a truth, beyond which there can be neither thought nor life. Those who deny it suffer what is commonly believed to be the most horrible of all punishments: everlasting sterility. Such is the dragon that guards positivism and idealism! Who has the courage to engage in a struggle against it? And how can an ordinary man, a mere man, hazard such a fearful deed and openly proclaim: nothing is true, everything is permissible? For this, must he not first of all cease to be a person? For this, must he not first of all find in himself some other still unknown and untried forces that we have thus far scorned, that we have feared? Listen to Nietzsche's prayer, and you will understand, at least in part, how convictions are born in our soul, and what it means to go one's own way and have one's own view of life: "Oh, heavenly powers, grant me madness! Madness, that I at length may believe in myself! Grant me delirium and convulsions, sudden flashes of light and periods of darkness; induce in me such shivering and feverishness as no mortal ever experienced before; frighten me with mysterious noises and ghosts; force me to howl, whine, and creep about like a beast, if only I can come to believe in myself! I am devoured by doubt. I have slain the law, and I now dread the law as a living person dreads a corpse. If I am not *above* the law, I am the most outcast of people. From whence comes this new spirit that dwells in me, if not from you? Prove to me that I am one of you—nothing but madness will prove it to me."[1]

XXVI

Nietzsche's prayer was heard: the denizens of Heaven sent him madness. On one of his solitary walks in the Engadine Mountains of Switzerland, he was suddenly struck, as if by lightning, by the thought of "eternal recurrence," and from that moment on, the nature of his work changed completely. Now we are no longer confronted by the underground man, timidly and carefully undermining commonly accepted convictions under the cover of theories that are alien to him. We are addressed by Zarathustra, who believes in his prophetic mission and who dares to oppose his opinion to that of everyone else. But, strangely enough, despite the fact that Nietzsche saw the origin and primary source of his new world view in the idea of eternal recurrence, he nowhere develops this idea clearly or in detail. Several times in *Thus Spoke Zarathustra*, he begins to speak of it, but each time he breaks off almost in the middle of a word. So that one involuntarily suspects that "eternal recurrence" was, in the final analysis, merely an incomplete and inadequate expression of the sudden rapture that Nietzsche had experienced. This seems probable, especially as the idea itself is old and does not belong to Nietzsche. The Pythagoreans had spoken of it, and Nietzsche, a classical philologist, could not, of course, help knowing it. Obviously, it had a different meaning for him than for the ancients, and, accordingly, he could link other hopes with it. And, indeed, what new meaning could the promise of eternal recurrence give his life? What could he derive from the conviction that his life, such as it was, with all its horrors, had already been

[1] *Ibid.*, IV, 23.

repeated countless times, and furthermore, that it must again be repeated an equal number of countless times without the slightest change? If Nietzsche saw in "eternal recurrence" only what the Pythagoreans had spoken of, it must have given him very few new hopes! And vice versa, if "eternal recurrence" gave him new strength, it was because it promised him something other than a mere repetition of what he in fact already had. Therefore, one can safely say that for Nietzsche, this idea was first and foremost a symbolic protest against the now prevalent theory of knowledge and its practical conclusions concerning the role and the significance of the individual in the world. It did not express all that Nietzsche thought it did. That is why, although he calls himself the teacher of eternal recurrence, he teaches anything he feels like except recurrence, and refuses to come right out and tell his "final idea." Evidently, in the presence of mankind's millennial prejudices and convictions, even "madness" does not have the courage to be completely candid. Here is the passage from Zarathustra's conversation with life that attests to this: "Life thoughtfully looked back and said quietly: 'Oh, Zarathustra, you are not faithful enough to me! You love me not nearly so much as you say; I know you are thinking of leaving me soon. There is an old, extremely heavy droning bell; at night, its ringing can be heard as far as your cave. When you hear this bell strike the hour at midnight, then you think between one and twelve—you think, Oh, Zarathustra, I know it, of how you want to leave me soon.'

" 'Yes,' I answered hesitantly, 'but you also know—and I whispered something into her ear, right through her tangled, yellow, foolish tresses. 'You *know* that, Oh, Zarathustra? Nobody knows that.' And we again looked at each other and at the green meadow over which the cool evening was running just then, and we wept together. But then life was dearer to me than all my wisdom ever was."[1] What did Zarathustra whisper

[1] *Also sprach Zarathustra*, "Das andere Tanzlied."

to life? What is the secret that no one knows but Zarathustra? Evidently, it is directly related to "eternal recurrence," but, at any rate, it is less abstract and empty. Life has tormented Zarathustra, and he wants to part from it, but the secret known only to him reconciles him to his suffering and teaches him to love reality more than wisdom. Immediately following the conversation with life, there is inserted as the third part of the same song ("The Other Dance Song") a strange, but extremely interesting poem, evidently intended to explain, at least in part, the meaning of the "secret." It consists of twelve lines, corresponding to the twelve strokes of the midnight bell:

ONE!

Oh, man! Take heed!

TWO!

What does the deep voice of midnight say?

THREE!

I was sleeping, I was sleeping.

FOUR!

I awakened from a deep sleep.

FIVE!

The world is deep.

SIX!

And deeper than day had thought.

SEVEN!

Deep is its sorrow.

EIGHT!

Joy—deeper yet than suffering.

NINE!

Sorrow says: Go!

TEN!

But all joy wants eternity.

ELEVEN!

—Wants deep, deep eternity.

TWELVE!

You see that the important thing in "eternal recurrence" is not the word being defined, but the word doing the defining, i.e., not recurrence, but eternity. However deep sorrow may be, it must pass and yield its place to everlasting joy. And day (i.e., Mill and Kant) cannot judge the profundity of the world. Isn't this the secret that Zarathustra whispered to life? And wasn't this what was revealed to him when he was first struck by the idea of eternal recurrence "at six hundred feet above sea level, and even higher above all human thoughts?" But let us lay aside our conjectures about Nietzsche's unrevealed secrets: if he remained silent, he had reason to do so; there are things about which one may think, but about which one must not speak except in symbols and hints. At least, one must not speak of them now, as long as Mill's hypothesis of effect without cause is accepted by us as valid only for distant planets or for the even more distant future, as long as day judges the world. In *Thus Spoke Zarathustra*, we find quite a number of attempts by mental effort alone to break away from the authority of modern theories. I might, for example, point to Zarathustra's speech which concludes the second part of the book ("The Stillest Hour"), or "The Convalescent," "The Seven Seals," et cetera, from the third part. Nietzsche had by no means accustomed himself as yet to his new midnight reality. As the heir of his ancestors, he could abandon the customary atmosphere of positivism only for a few moments at a time; for him, life beyond the boundaries of what is called the cognizable world, however much it attracted him, was not yet the "normal" life. Each time the ground gave way under his feet, he was seized with mystical horror; he himself did not know what was happening to him: whether he was seeing a new reality or merely dreaming terrible dreams. Before him, therefore, was a perpetual tragic alternative: on the one hand, reality—positive, but spiritually bankrupt and empty; on the other, a new life—alluring and promising, but frightening as a ghost. It is not surprising that he constantly hesitated in choosing his path, and that at one time he would call forth his "final idea" with horrible incantations, while at another, he would lapse into complete apathy, almost torpor, to rest from extreme mental strain. You will not find a single writer in modern literature who experienced such rapidly changing moods as those you observe in Nietzsche: at almost one and the same moment, you can find him at two diametrically opposite poles of human thought.

Professor Riehl was correct in noting that Nietzsche is not fit to be a teacher. His works do not and cannot provide hard-and-fast rules for the guidance of students. He is always experimenting, subjecting himself to tests. Sometimes it seems to him that our life is merely an "experiment in cognition." But does philosophy exist only for "students"? Of course, youth, or "the younger generation," as our people used to say in the old days, needs guidance; it needs an answer to the question: what are we to do? But there is no need to turn with this question to Nietzsche, Dostoevsky, or Count Tolstoy, i.e., to men who are unsettled themselves. If we had no other grounds, it would suffice to mention the instability of their own convictions to disqualify them as teachers. How can we entrust a young soul to them if they themselves cannot vouch for the future? Count Tolstoy, for example, after having arranged for such a solemn apotheosis of Levin's family life, wrote, just a few years after *Anna Karenina*, *The Death of Ivan Ilyich* and then even *The Kreutzer Sonata*. The story of Levin's marriage and his family life on the one hand, and that of Ivan Ilyich and Pozdnyshov on the other, are, in the final analysis, one and the same story, but told in a different way and elucidated, or if you prefer, evaluated differently. In order to convince oneself of this, it is enough to read *Anna Karenina* and *The Kreutzer Sonata* in succession. The relationship between Levin and Kitty is exactly the same as that between Pozdnyshov and his wife: there can be no doubt about it. However, Levin's family life is recommended to us as exemplary, while Pozdnyshov says of his life: "We lived like swine." Why did Count Tolstoy omit from Levin's story what he emphasized in Pozdnyshov's? What can a student learn from a teacher like Count Tolstoy? Generally speaking, once a person has betrayed his convictions, he is no longer fit to be a teacher, because convictions for a limited time only are worthless. Surely their chief merit lies in the fact that they promise a foundation for life. Convictions are not proved, but accepted—if not wholly, at least in part—on faith; one can believe only in what is stable, in what has not been subject to vacillation, at least not before one's eyes. And a real teacher, a person whom one can with a clear conscience recommend as a leader of youth, must, above all, be able to provide his students with the greatest possible number of "eternal" principles, which are valid for all ages and for all situations. Such teachers never completely die out; there are many of them— the younger generation usually turns to them for edification and guidance, and from them it obtains all that it needs. Even more than that—these teachers know how to protect their students from dangerous contact with writers such as Dostoevsky, Nietzsche, and Count Tolstoy. Take a look at the textbooks on literary history and see what the Germans have made of their Goethe! With the existing commentaries, it is no longer such a terrible thing to put *Faust* even into the hands of an adolescent. Yet, from the "teacher's" viewpoint, can there be a more harmful and immoral work? Count Tolstoy had reason to repudiate Goethe in *What is Art!* And as a matter of fact, what does Faust need? He has lived a long, honest, and industrious life; he enjoys the respect and esteem of the public, and he is able to inspire his students, who flock to him from all over, with ideas of good and to impart to them knowledge—of a limited, but useful nature—which he managed to acquire through long years of persistent study. It would seem that he would rejoice in his old age, but, no, he is discontent; he becomes involved with the devil, and sells his soul to the enemy of mankind in exchange for Gretchen. What does it all mean? Of course, in simple language, it means that the later love comes, the more it burns. The only thing that surprises me here is that Count Tolstoy did not recall this wonderful Russian proverb in connection with *Faust*. The people he liked best to talk with, those "clever peasants," would surely have reasoned thus. From their point of view, Wagner[1] is much more moral and lofty than Faust, and yet in Goethe, he is presented as the caricature of a fool, and only because, as Mill and Kant teach, he remained within the bounds of the cognizable world and had no dealings with demons. Try to apply Kant's moral principle to Faust: what would happen if all people did as Faust—abandoned their respectable and useful scholarly work and in old age fell in love with a Gretchen? But Wagner is true to the Kantian principle to the end! And, according to Mill's utilitarian point of view, he would be right, and Spinoza would be obliged to praise him. Kant and Goethe wrote almost simultaneously. But Kant strictly forbade all sorts of thoughts of eternal recurrence, demons, and Gretchens to disturb his philosophical peace of mind: their place is in the intelligible (or, as is usually said, the unintelligible) world. But Goethe had summoned them to him and left it to the Wagners to live according to Kant's system of morality. Evidently, Raskolnikov was right, and there really are two standards, one for the ordinary people, the other for the extraordinary. The Fausts do not lose our respect, despite the fact that they ignore all sage proverbs and philosophical doctrines and permit themselves to disparage commonly accepted morality; they turn their backs on the ideal blessings provided by the scholar's library and his teaching and seek life for themselves. Was Faust an "egoist"? Are the greatest men egoists, and is the morality of self-denial left to the mediocre Wagners?

But, I repeat once again, moral ideas, much more so than all other systems, have thus far rested on premises obtained entirely from observations of outward human relations. The moralists were guided by the same instinctive desire to limit

[1] The character in *Faust*, of course. [Tr.]

the field of observation as were the scholars when they formulated their theories of natural development. Kant's categorical imperative and Mill's utilitarian principles had one purpose only—to bind man to the average, customary norms of life, which were assumed to be equally valid for absolutely all men. Both Kant and Mill firmly believed that the moral law is just as binding, comprehensible, and dear to the heart of every man as is the law of causation. Even if there is a possibility of its losing its binding nature, it probably can only be somewhere on another planet or in the infinitely distant future (with Kant, in the intelligible world), but here on earth it must be acknowledged by all mortals without exception. But if there are those who are unwilling to repudiate "effect without cause," and who, rather than seek traces of randomness in spheres inaccessible to and of no concern to us, try to discover the absence of regularity right here on earth, in their immediate environment, then how can we count on their readiness to subject their will, which they know is free, to universal norms, solely for the triumph of the scientific order, which they detest more than anything else? Isn't it natural that they would behave quite differently, and like the gentleman with the retrograde physiognomy in *Notes from the Underground,* would violate the rules merely to destroy every law? Neither the profundity of Kant's thought, nor the clarity and persuasiveness of Mill's arguments would make any impression on them. The insight of these people will not surprise you, and as for dialectics, even Hegel himself would throw up his hands before Dostoevsky's underground philosopher. It is not by chance or even by virtue of their restless nature that they seek chaos and randomness on our earth, where science has found so much strict harmony and order: harmony and order stifle them; they choke in an atmosphere of naturalism and regularity. And no science, no preaching will attach them to that reality, which in the judgment of recognized sages has hitherto been acknowledged as the only

real one. For the time being, they have made a relative reconciliation with "cause and effect": they were forced to do so
by outward necessity. But if it had been in their power, they
would long ago have moved mountains and turned back rivers,
without the slightest concern that such action on their part
would threaten international trade, navigation, and sessions
of parliament with the worst possible disruption. But that is
not in their power. They can only exult over the fact that
the law of causation is not a priori (Mill's priceless admission!—if the men of the underground had made it, no one
would have believed them; they would not even have believed
themselves), and that even the serene and lucid Mill must
at least have had moments when he felt uneasy about the
disorder prevailing on another planet. They secretly hope that
future Mills will, in this regard, have to experience even
greater misery. But in the field of moral relations, where their
freedom is in no way restricted except by the abstract prescriptions of moralists—here only is it possible for them to
celebrate their victory. Despite all efforts on the part of Kant
and Mill, their kingdom is *here*, (the underground people no
longer doubt this). It is a kingdom of whim, uncertainty, and
an infinite number of completely new and untried possibilities.
Here, miracles happen right before your eyes; here, what was
strength yesterday, becomes weakness today; here, mountains
move; here, "saints" bow down before convicts; here, genius
yields to mediocrity; here, Mill and Kant would have lost their
scholarly-oriented heads if they had even for a moment decided to leave their little world, which is fortified with a priori
judgments, and glance into the realm of the underworld.
Spinoza maintained that constancy is the predicate of perfection, and he made this "axiom" the foundation of his mathematically constructed system of ethics. The underground men
think differently: for them, constancy is the predicate of the
greatest possible imperfection, and accordingly, in their "revaluation of all values," they by no means assign the chief

places to the representatives of idealism, positivism, and materialism—in brief, to all those systems which, under the guise of philosophy, proclaim to mankind that in the old world, all is well.

XXVII

Now it is time once again to raise Nietzsche's question: "How is it possible to find comfort in the trivial *thought* that the motives of all our actions can be reduced to egoism?" Only now, when we have behind us the idea of "eternal recurrence" and all the tempestuous longings of Faust, does the word "comfort" prove to be out of place. It must be replaced by another word more appropriate to the occasion. Apparently, we are dealing here with an *imperative*, and, what is more, with a categorical imperative, against which man is unable to defend himself. Nietzsche had unconsciously, and without even foreseeing where he would end up, started down the path of doubt. More than that even—he was almost certain that he would not arrive at any results whatsoever, and he adhered to his "positivism," mainly because it demanded less pretense and freed him from that solemn language which, with his awareness of his personal insignificance, was most disgusting of all. But isn't it amazing! People are constantly being warned against skepticism and pessimism, they are constantly being persuaded of the necessity of preserving their faith in their ideals at all costs, but neither the warnings nor the persuasion has any effect: we are all being drawn forward by a fatal force to the *unknown*. Are we not right in seeing in the spontaneity of this attraction a pledge of future success, and should we not, on the strength of this, now seek in pessimism and skepticism not enemies, but unrecognized friends? And wasn't Raskolnikov right in his reasoning: there are indeed two moralities, one for the ordinary people, and the other for the extraordinary, or, to use Nietzsche's blunter but more expressive terminology—a morality of masters and a morality of slaves? And at this point, the most important question of all arises: what is the source of both these moralities? At first glance, it probably seems that the decisive factor here is the cast of a person's character; the slaves, or ordinary people, submit, whereas the masters, or extraordinary people, command. Accordingly, Nietzsche, Dostoevsky, and also Faust must be assigned to the second category. However, Faust lived to a ripe old age before he took it into his head to protest against his "dog's" life, and, if it had not been for Mephistopheles' fortunate intervention, he would have died in a halo of virtue. The same can be said of Dostoevsky and Nietzsche: they were driven by chance from the Wagnerian path of commonplaceness. If it had not been for the penal servitude of the one and the terrible illness of the other, they would never have guessed, as most people never do, that they are bound hand and foot with chains. They would have written well-intentioned books, in which they would have sung the beauty of the world and the loftiness of souls that are submissive to necessity: their early works all too convincingly attest to this. More than that—the reader recalls how horrified Nietzsche became, as he himself admits, each time circumstances compelled him to accept new "knowledge." He wanted to go on living as before, and only when the new knowledge cut him to the quick, when he heard a stern voice above him say: "discern or perish"—only then did he decide to open his eyes. And Dostoevsky? How much the mere tone of *Notes from the Underground* is worth! How much torment, how much agony can be heard behind the desperate words he addresses to Liza. Faust also suffered a great deal before he summoned the devil. In short, all these "extraordinary" men who revolted against the fetters of the coercive laws of nature and human morality did not rebel of their own free will: like serfs grown old in their master's service, they were forced to choose freedom. This was no "revolt of slaves of morality," as Nietzsche teaches, but something for which the human tongue lacks words. Therefore, "character" is irrelevant here, and if there are two moralities, it is not a morality of ordinary and extraordinary people, but a morality of *commonplaceness and a morality of tragedy*—this correction must be made in Dostoevsky and Nietzsche's terminology. This circumstance, by the way, explains Dostoevsky and Nietzsche's astounding knowledge of the most intricate workings of the "slave's" soul—what people praise as their psychological insight. Nietzsche himself once remarked that he considered himself particularly fortunate for having to side for a time with his future adversaries.[1] In doing so, he learned all their "secrets" and later had a powerful weapon for his struggle against them. Dostoevsky does not say this, but, of course, he could have said it. Indeed, the psychology of "good" had never before been revealed with such ruthlessness as in the works of these two writers. And Nietzsche must be given his due: in this matter, he sometimes outdoes his illustrious Russian colleague. For Nietzsche, "good" was a synonym of weakness; the "good" are weak but cunning enviers, who have decided that they will retreat before nothing to avenge themselves on their opponents, the "evil," for the unhappiness of their own poor and wretched lives. As an illustration, here is a small sample of Nietzsche's attitude toward the "good": "They are all men of resentment, men physiologically maimed and riddled with worms; it is a whole quivering kingdom of burrowing revenge, indefatigable and insatiable in its attacks on the happy, and also in the art of disguising revenge, of seeking pretexts for it. But when will they really reach their final, fondest, most sublime triumph? Undoubtedly when they succeed in pushing their own misery, in fact, all misery, *into the consciousness of the happy*; so that the latter begin one day to be ashamed of their happiness and to say to themselves: 'It is a shame to be happy! There is too much misery on earth.' "[2]

---

[1] Nietzsche, *Werke*, V, 245.
[2] *Ibid.*, VII, 435.

In these few words, you immediately sense that you are dealing with an expert on the "slave soul." See how the question is put: are the happy, the successful, the strong in body and spirit responsible for the fact that so much unhappiness exists in the world? And must they assume responsibility for the world's grief? There can be no doubt that attempts were and are being made to foist the responsibility on them. Let each person re-examine the history of his dealings with conscience—won't he say that the best moments of his life were poisoned by the realization that it is shameful to be happy when so many of his neighbors are perishing all around him? As for Nietzsche himself—evidently, he can boast a particularly interesting past in this respect: "To my charity," says Zarathustra, "you always sent the most impudent beggars; around my pity you have always crowded the incurably shameless. Thus you wounded the faith of my virtue."[1] But this, too, is not the point. When Nietzsche was writing *Thus Spoke Zarathustra* and *Toward a Genealogy of Morals*, the question of insolent beggars and incurably shameless people, as well as all very distant memories, had receded into the background and had long since ceased to bother him. Very likely, the happiness of the happy people also interested him in a theoretical way only, as an argument: the moralists weary us to death with pictures of human grief—why, then, not contrast other pictures with them, why not show the moralists how their "unhappy" neighbors, like an infection, are poisoning the existence of those who have still retained their physical and mental strength? I am sorry that space does not permit me to quote one or two chapters here from Nietzsche's *Toward a Genealogy of Morals*. It would do the Russian reader, who has been brought up on the preaching of Dostoevsky and Count Tolstoy, no harm to be convinced at least once of the fact that the power of eloquence, a fervent tone, and sincerity can be directed not only toward the defense of what in our country is traditionally called "truth," but that one can be just as pro-

[1] *Ibid.*, VI, 162–163.

phetically inspired by the cause of "evil" as by the cause of "good." If you compare Tolstoy's provocative article on the Moscow census with the work in question here, you will have to admit that there is no less persuasiveness, pathos, and finally, legitimate and righteous indignation in Nietzsche than in Count Tolstoy. But if it is possible to be equally "indignant" in defense of the strong against the weak and the weak against the strong, then where, finally, is the truth? Who is "right," Count Tolstoy or Nietzsche? Or is it that indignation, pathos, and passion are meaningless in themselves and do not in the least guarantee the righteousness of the cause for which they stand? Or is it perhaps that strong or weak, good or evil, right or wrong are but a pretext, and that the pathetic preachers have totally different goals and cares? We have been so plagued with sermons that it is high time such a question were raised. And, indeed, why should preachers turn to us with their indignation? Why does Count Tolstoy or Dostoevsky tell us of the tribulations of mankind? Isn't it natural, finally, that we, for our part, should address all these questions to them? Let Count Tolstoy, who up to now has been trying to prove that it is shameful to be happy when there is so much misery in the world, explain to us the source of his own peace of mind, and why he is not ashamed to lead a quiet and joyful (a favorite word of his) life when there is so much grief around him! We could turn to Nietzsche with the same question, after having worded it somewhat differently. We might tell him that before reproaching the unhappy people for their existence, he should be happy himself, and that before demanding that only the healthy in body and the strong in spirit be preserved, he, too, should be strong in body and spirit. And with these questions, it would become clear how important it is when reading books to acquaint oneself with the biography of their authors, i.e., to learn how convictions "are born." Nietzsche, until the age of thirty, played the pitiful role of Wagner's servant (it is difficult to repeat, but I should have said—of Wagner's literary lackey). From thirty to forty-four, he suffered painful and loathsome attacks of an incurable disease; and from forty-four until his death, i.e., for almost eleven years, during which he was in a semiconscious state, he preached against the unhappy and sick, i.e., the physiologically maimed! And at the same time, against their defenders, "the good and the just!" This psychological enigma, after all, is well worth thinking about! I would remind you, by the way, that in this regard, as in many others, Nietzsche's "convictions" are surprisingly like Dostoevsky's. Dostoevsky also despised "the good and the just," as was already pointed out in its place: they were embodied for him in liberals and progressives of every hue. Dostoevsky let himself call Nekrasov's heartfelt and poetic poem "On the Volga," which in the seventies was read not only by representatives of the "thinking proletariat," but by almost the entire Russian intelligentsia, "buffoonery." "Buffoonery," Dostoevsky said, yet Nekrasov's readers wept pure and sincere tears over his poetry in general and over the poem "On the Volga" in particular! But Dostoevsky and Nietzsche hated those tears of sympathy and that compassion-inspiring poem more than anything in the world. This is the view, or if you will, the "taste" of true convicts, of people of the underground, of people of tragedy. For a long time, they had known no tears; they were aware that tears do not help, and that pity is futile. But, after all, there are many other things besides tears and pity that do not help—why then such hatred for pity? After all, the "evil" are also powerless to change the lot of the hopelessly condemned—why then such aversion to "the good and the just?" Isn't it only because "the good and the just" were poor teachers when they taught Dostoevsky and Nietzsche the theory of self-denial? One can forgive an error, especially an honest error, even if it had to be dearly paid for. Belinsky sincerely regarded his doctrine as the only true one, and he himself suffered a good deal because of it. And Nietzsche's teachers also had no intention of deceiving their students.

But Nietzsche and Dostoevsky had long since reconciled themselves to the past. They were now fighting for the future.

But pity for "the good and the just" was depriving them of their last hope. You recall that Dostoevsky, when he was a prisoner, accepted alms from a young girl, and for a long time afterward he guarded with loving care the mite she had given him. Perhaps Nietzsche also had occasion during his wanderings to accept gratefully a word of love and sympathy from a child or one of the common folk whose understanding of good and evil differed greatly from ours. He rejected both love for his neighbor and pity, which had been elevated to the position of a final principle, and which had become a theory that claimed divine rights. He knew that intelligent people of today would give him not just one mite, but hundreds, even thousands, that they would clothe, warm, feed, and shelter him, that they would look after him as one of their own when he fell ill. But he knew that their care would not be lavished on him free of charge, not unselfishly, and that ultimately they would demand of him, not gratitude—we have now risen above gratitude—but an admission that in return for all the attention and love shown him, he was obligated to feel perfectly content in his heart of hearts, however difficult his situation might be. In his neighbors' love for him, he must have seen the realization of the supreme ideal, i.e., the first and last demand that a person can make on life. This pity, which had been raised to the level of an ideal, and also its priests aroused in Nietzsche all the indignation of which he was capable. He saw that they wanted to buy his rights of primogeniture with a mess of pottage. And although he himself had almost ceased to believe in these rights, he refused to strike a bargain with them. With contempt and horror, he rejected the gifts offered him, lest he be obliged to renounce a possible struggle.

XXVIII

This all explains why Nietzsche needed his underground work, and the kind of hope it was that gave him the strength to bear for so long the absence of light and air. He instinctively felt

that the contemporary world view and the commonly accepted
morality, although they are based on so-called solid scientific
facts, are powerful only because of human gullibility and
human weakness. He himself was "unhappy," and saw that
pity, the only remedy that morality has at its disposal, is more
horrible than complete indifference. "Isn't pity," Zarathustra
asks, "the cross on which he is crucified who loves people?"[1]
To pity a person means to admit that he can no longer be
helped by other means. But why not say this openly, why
not repeat after Nietzsche: a hopelessly sick man must not
wish to be a physician. For what purposes is the truth concealed? To Nietzsche, it is clear that the "good" pity the unfortunate merely to avoid thinking of their own fate, to avoid
searching, to avoid struggling: "Now I understand clearly what
people once sought above all else when they sought teachers
of virtue. They sought sleep for themselves and soporific virtues to promote it. For all these highly praised sages who were
teachers of virtue, wisdom was sleep without dreams: they
knew no better meaning of life."[2] And, of course, Nietzsche
would pass calmly by the slumbering people and their soporific virtues if only they would leave him in peace. But we
remember the dreadful anguish to which he had been subjected
by morality. At the time when, to use Dostoevsky's words, the
laws of nature, i.e., sickness, had deprived Nietzsche of sleep
and rest, the laws of mankind, as if in mockery, were demanding composure and sleep of him and, as is their custom, threatening anathema in case their demand was not met. "Wisdom"
offered him its soporific virtues and was offended when they
proved to be devoid of any salutary power. Instead of helping
the suffering man, it demanded that encomia and hymns be
offered to itself. That is its usual way. That is why in Dostoevsky, as we have already seen, Ivan Karamazov revolts against
"the devilish good and evil," which had so impudently dared

---

[1] *Ibid.,* 15.
[2] *Ibid.,* "Von den Lehrstühlen der Tugend."

to demand human sacrifices to itself. After Dostoevsky, Nietzsche repeated almost the same thing that Ivan Karamazov said: "Oh, my brothers," Zarathustra says, "who represents the greatest danger for all man's future? Is it not 'the good and the just,' who say and feel in their hearts, 'We already know what is good and just, we possess it also; woe unto those who still seek here.' And whatever harm the 'evil' may do, the harm done by 'the good' is the most harmful harm! Oh, my brothers, one man once looked into the hearts of 'the good and the just,' and said: 'They are pharisees.' But He was not understood. 'The good and the just' themselves were not free to understand Him; their spirit is imprisoned in their good conscience. The stupidity of 'the good' is unfathomably shrewd. This, however, is the truth: that 'the good' *must* be pharisees—they have no choice. 'The good' *must* crucify him who invents his own virtue! That is the truth!"[1] The poor "good and the just!" Could they possibly think, after believing so deeply in the infallibility of their truth, that such a horrible accusation awaited them? And yet it is already two thousand years old. Two thousand years ago, one man looked into their hearts and said: "They are pharisees." True, they did not understand Him. They do not understand Him even now, and who knows, perhaps "all" will never understand Him, for, in His words, they know not what they do. Perhaps those who do not understand are not supposed to understand. Why do they only say: woe unto those who still seek here? Why do they direct their brutal strength against the Dostoevskys and Nietzsches? Or is this also "necessary"? But Dostoevsky and Nietzsche no longer take into account the needs of "the good and the just" (the Mills and the Kants). They have understood that man's future, if man really has a future, rests not on those who now rejoice in the belief that they already possess both goodness and justice, but on those who know neither sleep, rest, nor joy, and who continue to struggle and search. Abandoning their old ideals, they go

[1] *Ibid.,* "Von alten und neuen Tafeln."

to meet a new reality, however terrible and disgusting it may be. It must be noted here that, on the whole, Nietzsche's doctrine was misinterpreted. Accustomed to moralistic outlooks, the modern mind sought in all that Nietzsche said nothing but traces of a new moral doctrine. Nietzsche himself was partly responsible for this. Like almost every writer, i.e., a person who speaks to people, he involuntarily accommodated himself to a certain extent to his audience and gave it not only an advisory, but sometimes even a decisive voice in his opinions. The same thing was done by Dostoevsky, who, as we saw, felt himself bound even more so than Nietzsche by the "spirit of the times." His audience, however, listened keenly and eagerly and then fished from the master's words all that was "its own," all that was familiar, and comprehensible—and they did not in the least concern themselves about the rest. In Dostoevsky and Nietzsche, they found a system of morality—some, a new one, others, an old. Perhaps future generations will read them just as calmly as they now read Goethe. Little by little, expository criticism will adapt Zarathustra and Raskolnikov to the needs of "the good and the just," after having convinced them that Dostoevsky and Nietzsche were struggling against abstract or extinct pharisees, and not against that ever existing commonplaceness (positivism and idealism), which is the most dangerous and inexorable enemy that people of tragedy can possibly have. Nietzsche used to say that when he was with people, he thought as everyone else, and that he sought solitude mainly because it was only when he was alone with himself that he felt his thinking to be free. Commonplaceness is terrible in that it hypnotizes the solitary thinker with its millions of eyes and imperiously subjugates him to its will. But to live in solitude is also difficult! Nietzsche remarks with bitter derision: "In solitude, you devour yourself; in company, you are devoured by the many: now, choose!"[1] But, after all is said and done, you must choose solitude: in spite of everything, it is

[1] *Ibid.*, III (2), 168.

better than "forsakenness," i.e., the realization that in the midst of a vast number of people, you are alien to everyone else. "Oh, solitude," says Zarathustra, "oh, my *home*, solitude! Too long have I lived wildly in wild, strange places, not to return home to you in tears! Now threaten me with your finger, as mothers threaten; now smile at me, as mothers smile; now say to me: 'And who was it that, like a tempest, once stormed away from me? Who shouted in parting: "Too long have I sat with solitude; I have forgotten how to be silent!" That, I suppose, you have learned again now? Oh, Zarathustra, I know everything. Also that you were more forsaken among the many, being one, than ever with me! To be forsaken is one thing, to be lonely, another: that you have learned now.' "[1] The reader now sees what Nietzsche's task was: he assumed the cause of the man who had been abandoned and forgotten by good, by science, and by philosophy. I hope it is now clear why "altruism" did not attract Nietzsche: among the forsaken, the old argument between altruism and egoism does not exist. More than that, both of them are amazed that they could have once been at loggerheads. They hardly believe that it was reality, and that even to this day it continues to be reality. And how could they believe it, when both of them, both altruism and egoism, were compelled to wallow in the dust and, while gnawing the earth, foolishly to cry out to the modern god-monster of necessity or "natural development": "Not ours, not ours, but thine be the praise." Praise to natural development! Praise to necessity! In the face of these impotent gods, does altruism really mean more than egoism, more even than crime? Here, all distinctions made by man are smoothed over, effaced, and destroyed forever. If egoism means nothing, if it is necessary to renounce oneself, then it is necessary at one and the same time to renounce both one's neighbor and all that people hold dear. And conversely, if we can look fearlessly in the face of naturalism, then the individual person must be guarded against

[1] *Ibid.*, VI, "Die Heimkehr."

"necessity" to the same extent that the whole world is. There is no choice, nor can there be one, although "commonplaceness," which has accepted the morality of accommodation and refused a struggle, in principle sanctions and puts into practice the opposite view and tries with all its might to force all people to accept its principles; these principles it elevates through the mouths of "the good and the just" on the one hand, and of their regular patrons the unfortunate and the unhappy of all kinds on the other, to supreme laws of morality and calls them ideals. Therefore, the men of tragedy, the "forsaken," must wage a double struggle: against both "necessity" and their neighbors, who can still adjust themselves, and who, because they are unaware of what they are doing, side with mankind's most horrible enemy. Hence Nietzsche's binomial formula: "Nothing is true, everything is permitted." Its first part is directed against necessity and natural development; its second, against those who, consciously or unconsciously, rise to the defense of the "laws of nature," which had so offended Dostoevsky. But Nietzsche not only does not strive to rid life of all that is enigmatic, mysterious, difficult, and agonizing—he goes in quest of all this. In the laws of nature, in order, in science, in positivism and idealism, there is a guarantee of unhappiness; in the horrors of life, a guarantee of the future. This is the basis of the philosophy of tragedy: to this lead skepticism and pessimism, which Kant had at one time so greatly feared, and which people try with all their might to avoid as they would exceedingly dangerous monsters.

Nietzsche was reproached for his hatred of the weak and the unfortunate and for his aristocratic morality. I have already remarked that moralities of every kind, both aristocratic and democratic, were alien to Nietzsche. His task lay "beyond good and evil." Like Karamazov, he did not accept a moral interpretation or justification of life. But he is guilty of hating "the weak." They were as obnoxious to him as their constant protectors, "the good and the just." Not because of their unhappiness, not because of their failures, but because of their readiness to accept the "pity" offered them as consolation. They entered into a conspiracy against life in order to forget their misfortunes—and this, Nietzsche considers the most horrible crime of all, a betrayal of the great cause; this, he never forgave anyone. His entire doctrine, his entire life's task amounted to a struggle. Wasn't it natural for him to hate those who, by their tractability and cowardice, not only strengthen the ranks of their already countless adversaries, but also confuse the few fighters who have not yet lost courage? It is curious that Nietzsche's teacher, Schopenhauer, set little store on courage; he did not even understand what purpose it could have in life. "Courage," he wrote, "is, as a matter of fact, quite a secondary virtue, a virtue merely for noncommissioned officers—one in which we are even outdone by animals; that is why, for example, we say 'brave as a lion.'" And, of course, Schopenhauer had his reasons to think like that: in order to write books with a pessimistic tendency, but with an optimistic faith, it is not necessary to have courage. In such matters, wit, a dialectical resourcefulness of mind, the ability to find a pretty comparison or a pointed epithet, seem incomparably loftier qualities. How strange the words of Schopenhauer quoted above must have sounded to Nietzsche, providing he had occasion to recall them. "Art for art's sake," whether in philosophy or in poetry, had long since stopped attracting him. "The struggle against purpose in art," he wrote, "has always been merely a fight against a moralizing tendency, against the subordination of art to morality. *L'art pour l'art* means: to the devil with morality! When the purpose of preaching morality and of improving mankind has been excluded from art, it still by no means follows that art is altogether purposeless, aimless, senseless—in short, *l'art pour l'art*, a worm biting its own tail. What does the tragic artist communicate of himself? Isn't it precisely his fearless attitude toward that which is terrible and questionable? Before tragedy, what is warlike in our soul celebrates its

Saturnalia; whoever is used to suffering, whoever seeks out suffering, the heroic man, extols his own existence by means of tragedy—to him alone does the tragic artist offer this drink of sweetest cruelty."[1] Obviously, not just noncommissioned officers need courage; man, too, must at times envy the qualities of wild animals! "Do you have courage, oh, my brothers?" asks Zarathustra. "Are you stouthearted? *Not* the courage before witnesses, but anchorite and eagle courage, which not even the gods behold? Whoever looks into the abyss, but with the eyes of an eagle, whoever *grasps* the abyss with the talons of an eagle—that man has courage."[2] Zarathustra's constant companions were the eagle and the serpent: from them, he learned to soar in the clouds and to crawl on the earth, to look boldly into the sun and not lose touch with the earth. How many times he was within a hair's breadth of destruction, how often he was seized with despair by an awareness that the task he had assumed was impracticable, that tragedy must ultimately yield to commonplaceness! Zarathustra's words bear clear traces of this struggle of hope against hopelessness. But in the end, Nietzsche achieved his goal nevertheless. He ventured not only to raise the question of the underground man, but also to provide an answer to it. "The great epochs of our life," he says, "come when we gain the courage to rebaptize what we regard as evil in us, and call it goodness."[3] This means that Nietzsche decided to regard his "egoism," which he formerly called "the serpent's sting," and which he feared so much, not a disgraceful quality, but an ennobling one. The same idea is expressed even more sharply and fully in another aphorism: "At the risk of offending innocent ears, I submit the following: egoism belongs to the nature of an aristocratic soul—I mean the unalterable belief that other beings must by the nature of things be subordinate to a being such as 'us,' that they must be sacrificed to us. The aristocrat accepts the fact of his egoism

---

[1] *Ibid.*, VIII, 135.
[2] *Ibid.*, VI, 419–420.
[3] *Ibid.*, VII, 101.

without question, and also without seeing harshness, con-
straint, or arbitrariness therein, but rather as something that
may have its basis in the primary law of things; if he had to
find a designation for it, he would say: 'it is justice itself.' "[1]

In so far as these words relate to Nietzsche himself (i.e., in
so far as they can be of interest), there is a slight inaccuracy
here. He did not regard his egoism as a fact that demanded no
explanation. And, in general, "egoism," as we recall, troubled
Nietzsche very, very much—it seemed trivial and disgusting
to him. So that in view of this, the word "aristocrat" should be
replaced by another, less pretty word—"the underground
man"—especially as everything that Nietzsche said about the
aristocracy had little to do with him personally. He himself
was only an "underground man," as the reader has probably
long since concluded. He joined the aristocrats, the happy ones,
the lucky ones, the victors, only for outside reasons, which are
fully explained by his following admission: "The great advantage of an aristocratic origin is that it gives one strength better
to endure poverty."[2] It seemed to Nietzsche that his *poverty*
would be less noticeable behind aristocratic manners.

There is some truth to this. But poverty remains poverty
regardless of any manners. And the egoism about which Nietzsche speaks was the egoism not of an aristocrat, serenely and
confidently accepting sacrifices, but the egoism of a poor man,
a beggar, indignant and outraged over the fact that even his
sacrifices are disdained. Nietzsche's great merit lies in his ability
to defend before the eyes of the whole world the "egoism" of
poverty—not the poverty that is fought by social reform, but
the kind for which, even in the best organized state of the
future, there will be found nothing but pity, virtues, and
ideals. After all, in the state of the future, as in the states of
today, there is no place for tragic people; in it, the so-called
bourgeois morality will be changed only in so far as it is necessary for the "happiness of the majority." But for people such as

[1] *Ibid.*, 265–266.
[2] *Ibid.*, IV, 193.

Dostoevsky and Nietzsche, it will be preserved in its entirety; as in the past, it will be their lot to have those celebrated ascetic ideals and that "beautiful and lofty," which for thirty years weighed so heavily on the neck of the underground man. But Nietzsche did not want virtues and asceticism, and he did not believe in the morality of abnegation. He had reason to spend so much time tracking down the "psychology" of preachers of morality. He already knew that all the pompous words of abnegation in the mouths of moralists and philosophers were sham. "What," he asked, "do such people have in common with virtue?" By virtue, they usually understand those principles of life that guarantee them the greatest success in their cause. "What then," Nietzsche asks, "does the ascetic ideal betoken in a philosopher? Asceticism provides him with the condition most favorable to the exercise of his intelligence. Far from denying 'existence,' he affirms *his* existence, and his alone, perhaps even to the point of *hubris: pereat mundus, fiat philosophia, fiat philosophus, fiam!*"[1] The last words are an almost literal translation of the famous statement of the poor hero from the underground: "Is the world to go to pot, or am I to have my tea? I say that the world can go to pot, as long as I get my tea." Could he ever believe that the phrase he had hurled in a fit of blindness and anger at the unhappy prostitute would be translated by a famous philosopher into the language of Cicero and Horace and offered as a formula defining the essence of the *highest* of human aspirations? If Dostoevsky could have foreseen that such great glory awaited his little hero, he would probably have omitted his comment to *Notes from the Underground.*

XXIX

So, *pereat mundus, fiam,* let the whole world perish, the underground man will not renounce his rights or exchange them for

[1] *Ibid.,* VII, 413.

the "ideals" of pity and all other such blessings that have been specially prepared for him by present-day philosophy and morality. For Dostoevsky, this was a dreadful truth, which he ventured with horror and shame to express through the mouths of the heroes of his novels. With Nietzsche, it was a new and very great "declaration of rights," for the sake of which he had undertaken all his underground work. This also accounts for Nietzsche's cruelty. He does not strive *to deliver* himself and others from "suffering." In this respect, as in many others, he differs markedly from Schopenhauer, his teacher in youth. The latter, as we know, taught people to seek peace in life. He wrote that one must never buy pleasure at the price of suffering, not even at the risk of suffering, for in so doing, one pays a positive, real price for something negative—that is, for something illusory. On the contrary, whoever sacrifices pleasure in order to escape suffering always comes out ahead. These words are highly characteristic of Schopenhauer's philosophy and of all philosophy in general. The wisdom of the official sages has always regarded suffering as something that, by its very nature, is absurd, senseless, and needless, something that is to be avoided at all costs. And so-called worldly wisdom, in so far as it has found expression in words, has always regarded suffering in exactly this same way. The majority of folk sayings advise moderation and order as the supreme virtues that best guarantee man a happy and peaceful existence. A bird in the hand is worth two in the bush. Yet human life, not when it is guided by proverbs and dicta of the sages, but such as it has been in all ages and with all peoples, seems to be just such an everlasting, relentless pursuit of elusive happiness, of the two birds in the hand, against which moralists have always cautioned us. People flee in disgust from the bird in the hand, although it is almost forcibly thrust upon them. Henry IV dreamed of providing every peasant with chicken for Sunday dinner. If the peasants had seen the chicken as their ideal and had aspired only to a quiet and peaceful life, while sacrificing

their "pleasure" so as not to suffer, as Schopenhauer and
proverbs teach us, perhaps the history of mankind would have
been less horrible. But the peasants, like their rulers, had a
different view of life and never chose a painless existence as
their ideal. On the contrary, man, such as nature created him,
is willing to accept long years of suffering and great misfortune for one moment of happiness, for the illusion of happiness. In such instances, he forgets all considerations, all calculations, and pushes ahead toward the unknown, often to certain destruction. Where is the truth—in popular wisdom or
in reality? Must one really be so afraid of the unknown, of
suffering, and of destruction, as we educated people are accustomed to think—we, who draw our judgments from books that
have accumulated over the centuries—or is it that the common
man, who had never lost the habit of trusting his spontaneous
impulses, knows more than the most learned philosophers?
From the viewpoint of modern positivist science, there cannot,
of course, be even a question here. But Dostoevsky, who had
been in a penal colony, had learned a different truth from his
fellow prisoners, i.e., from men whose fearlessness in the face
of suffering had brought them to the House of the Dead. From
penal servitude, he brought with him the "conviction" that
man's task consists, not in crying over Makar Devushkin and
dreaming of a future in which no one will offend anyone else,
and where everyone will spend his days in peace, joy, and
pleasure, but in being able to accept reality with all its horrors.
He was reluctant—oh, how he was reluctant—to accept this
penal truth! At first, he thought that he could rid himself of it
by platonic respect and begin to live as before! But it is not
man who pursues truth, as Schopenhauer thought, but truth,
man. Penal wisdom caught up with Dostoevsky after many
years, when he was living a long way from Siberia—in Petersburg in the midst of positivists—and forced him to acknowledge it, to serve it. "The Russian people love to suffer"—this
was no paradox, as Dostoevsky's adversaries thought, it was

a truth, but a truth from a different world, which writers had forgotten, which they would remember only to say with eyes flashing with indignation: it must not be. It must not be, but it is! Dostoevsky would answer this as follows: love not the people you imagine to be happy, but those who are unhappy, ugly, and disgusting. Let their life be yours. Can you do that, do you want to? But your help, all your projects for reform are the worst possible solution. In this, too, people saw a paradox—those people from "the good and the just," who were prophetically inspired by social ideals and the future happiness of mankind.

Then, after Dostoevsky, came Nietzsche. He, too, had come from penal servitude—from the underworld, from the realm of tragedy, from which there is no return to the world of the commonplace. Listen to him—he will finish telling you what Dostoevsky did not have time to explain (or perhaps did not even know how to). "But I rejoice," says Zarathustra, "in great sin as my great *consolation*. Such things, however, are not for long ears. Not every mouth has the right to these words. These are fine, far-away things. And the sheep's hooves must not touch them. Higher men, do you think I came here to put right what you have spoiled? Or to make more comfortable beds for you sufferers? Or show you who have erred and lost the way an easier road? No! No! Thrice no! Ever more and more frequently the better ones of your kind will perish; for you, it will be ever more and more difficult."[1] It was necessary to make the reservation: "Not every mouth has the right to these words." The "aboveground" people think differently, they must do so, (for them, the morality of "must" and "must not" is also obligatory). But Dostoevsky and Nietzsche spoke, and they had a right to speak, in the name of the underground people—no one, of course, will contest this, not even those who are unwilling to reckon with their views. However, if they do contest it, no great harm will be done. The philosophy of

[1] *Ibid.*, VI, 420–421.

tragedy by no means seeks popularity or success. It struggles, but not against public opinion; its real enemy is the "laws of nature," whereas human judgments are frightening to it only in so far as they confirm by their existence the permanency and immutability of laws. However brave the solitary thinker may be, he is involuntarily seized from time to time with horror at the thought that the majority, "everyone," whom he learns to despise, is perhaps right after all. But if his speaking and writing colleagues are against him, then he has for him the silent people, who live a special, unexplored, and mysterious life. It is not the "clever peasants," from whom Count Tolstoy seeks confirmation of his doctrine, but the unintelligent, crude, common people who must be retaught, transformed, and enlightened, in brief, adjusted to our ideals. Even when the people know their proverbs, they, in any case, live according to a different wisdom, which we cannot discredit in their eyes by temperance societies, tearooms, schools, edifying literature, or progress. They do not take exception to us; they even agree with us; they occasionally drink our tea; they read and are moved by stories written for them by Count Tolstoy; but they go on living in their own way, seeking their own joys, and intrepidly going to meet their suffering. And it is not only the Russian people who do this, as Dostoevsky wrote, but all people. In France, Italy, and Germany, you will find the same thing as in Russia. Ideals of chicken for Sunday dinner and of universal happiness have always been devised by teachers and scholars. That is probably why these ideals will never be realized, although optimists believe that their kingdom is near. The very fact that it is now possible to have teachers such as Dostoevsky and Nietzsche, who preach love of suffering and proclaim that the best people must perish, in as much as things will become ever worse and worse for them, shows that the rosy hopes of the positivists, materialists, and idealists were mere childish dreams. No social changes whatsoever will banish tragedy from life; therefore, the time has evidently come, not to deny suffering as a kind of fictitious reality from which a person can deliver himself by the magic words "it must not be," as he delivers himself from the devil by the sign of the cross, but by accepting it, by acknowledging it, and perhaps, finally, by understanding it. Hitherto, our science has only been able to turn away from all that is horrible in life, as if it were completely nonexistent, and to oppose it with ideals, as if ideals were the true reality. A difficult time has come for the "intelligentsia." Formerly, it would weep over the suffering people, call for justice, demand new procedures, promise (although, by the way, it had no right to do so) different procedures, and rejoice at its readiness to dissemble and lie, as well as at its skill in these matters; in this, it saw its outstanding moral quality. Then a new demand was made on it. Not, of course, by science—after all, science was created by scientists and demanded only what was easiest for scientists to perform. Then life appeared before us with its demands. It does not even think of ideals. With enigmatic severity, it tells us with its mute tongue things the like of which we never heard before, which we never even suspected. Dostoevsky and Nietzsche were merely interpreting its incomprehensible language when they said that things will become ever worse and worse for us. Our calculations have proved wrong. The peasants will not have chicken for Sunday dinner, and we shall be deprived of all the material and spiritual blessings with which science has provided us. And only when there is no longer any real or imaginary hope of finding salvation under the hospitable roof of positivist or idealist doctrine will people abandon their everlasting dreaming and emerge from the semidarkness of their limited horizons, which has hitherto gone by the celebrated name "truth," although it has merely signified the unconscious fear of conservative human nature before that mysterious unknown called tragedy. Then, perhaps, they will understand why Dostoevsky and Nietzsche abandoned humanism for cruelty and inscribed on their banner the strange words: *Wille zur Macht.* Philosophy's task is not to teach us humility, submission, or renunciation. All these words were devised by philosophers not for themselves, but for others. When Count Tolstoy says: Do the will of him who sent you here, and he writes the word "him" with a small letter, we immediately understand that he is following the example of other preachers who had preceded him and is demanding that we do his own will. Without realizing it, he is repeating, in a way that is familiar and therefore inoffensive to the ear, the words of Nietzsche and the underground man: *pereat mundus, fiam.* For all people, there exists, in the final analysis, just this one law (in Dostoevsky, it is "the supreme idea"). "The great" more or less boldly voice it, but the "nongreat" keep it to themselves. However, the law is the same for everyone. Are we not right in seeing in its universality a sign of its strength, and therefore in admitting that the "sanction of truth" is for the hero of the underground? And that the declaration of rights proclaimed by Nietzsche and his *Wille zur Macht* are something greater than the ideals and *pia desideria* that have hitherto filled our scholarly books? Perhaps the underground man was unjust to the "laws of nature" when he said that they offended him more than anything else! After all, those laws gave him—an insignificant, despised creature whom everyone had rejected—a proud sense of his human dignity and led him to the conviction that the entire world is worth no more than one underground man!

In any event, the philosophy of tragedy is, in principle, hostile to the philosophy of commonplaceness. In those instances when commonplaceness says "the end" and turns away, Dostoevsky and Nietzsche see the beginning and start to seek. In *Thus Spoke Zarathustra*, there is the story of "the ugliest man," which symbolically depicts Nietzsche's own terrible life. It is too long for me to quote more than a few excerpts here, and I advise those readers who are interested in Nietzsche's philosophy to read it all, if possible in the original. "Suddenly the landscape changed, and Zarathustra entered a realm of death. Black and red cliffs rose rigidly; there was no grass, no tree, no bird's voice. For it was a valley that all animals avoided, even beasts of prey; only a species of ugly, fat green snakes came here to die when they grew old. Therefore the shepherds called this valley 'Snakes' Death.' Zarathustra, however, sank into gloomy reminiscence, for he felt as if he had stood in this valley once before. And much that was grave weighed on his mind; he walked slowly, and still more slowly, and finally stood still. But when he opened his eyes, he saw something sitting by the wayside, shaped like a human being, yet scarcely like a human being—something inexpressible."[1] It is the "ugliest man," who has withdrawn from people and come to the gloomy valley of "Snakes' Death." Why has he withdrawn from people? "They [people] persecute me," says the ugly man to Zarathustra. "Now *you* are my last refuge. They persecute me, *not* with their hatred, *not* with their soldiers: I would mock such persecution and be proud and glad of it!

"Has not all success hitherto been with the well-persecuted? And whoever persecutes well, learns readily how to *follow*; for he is used to going after somebody else. But it is their *pity* —it is their pity that I flee, fleeing to you. Oh, Zarathustra, protect me, you my last refuge, the only one who has understood me."[2] Such people, inhabitants of "Snakes' Death," come seeking hope from Zarathustra. And what do they want? Listen further. The ugliest man says: "Everyone else would have thrown me his alms, his pity, in look and speech. But for that, I am not beggar enough, as you guessed; for that, I am too *rich*, rich in what is great, in what is terrible, in what is ugliest, in what is most inexpressible. Your shame, Zarathustra, honored me! With difficulty, I escaped the throng of the pitying, to find the only one today who teaches, 'Pity is obtrusive'—you, Oh,

[1] *Ibid.*, 382–383.
[2] *Ibid.*, 384.

Zarathustra. Whether it be a god's pity or man's—pity offends the sense of shame. And to be unwilling to help can be nobler than that virtue that jumps to help. But today, pity is called virtue by all the little people: they have no respect for great misfortune, great ugliness, for great failure."[1] *They have no respect for great misfortune, great ugliness, for great failure!* This is the final word of the philosophy of tragedy. Not to transfer all the horrors of life into the realm of the *Ding an sich*, outside the bounds of synthetic a priori judgments, but to respect them! Can idealism or positivism respond in this way to "ugliness"? When Gogol burned the manuscript of the second volume of *Dead Souls*, he was declared insane—otherwise, it would have been impossible to rescue ideals. But Gogol was more correct when he burned his precious manuscript (which could have provided immortality on earth to a whole score of "sane" critics) than he was when he wrote it. This is something idealists will never tolerate; they need "Gogol's works," but they are unconcerned with Gogol himself, with his "great misfortune, great ugliness, and great failure." So let them abandon the realm of philosophy forever! And why do they need it? Are their services insufficiently justified if one refers to railroads, telegraphs, telephones, co-operative societies, and even the first volume of *Dead Souls*, in so far as it contributes to progress? But philosophy is a *philosophy of tragedy*. Dostoevsky's novels and Nietzsche's books speak only of the "ugliest" people and their problems. Dostoevsky, Nietzsche, and also Gogol were extremely ugly people themselves, and they had none of the commonplace hopes. They tried to find their refuge where no one ever seeks, where, as is generally believed, there is not, and cannot be, anything but eternal chaos and darkness, where even Mill admits the possibility of effect without cause. There, perhaps, every underground man means as much as the whole world; there, perhaps, people of tragedy will indeed find what they have been seek-

[1] *Ibid.*, 385.

ing. People of commonplaceness will not wish to cross the fatal boundary in pursuit of such an incredible "perhaps." But, after all, no one asks them to. Hence, the poet's question: "Aimes-tu les damnés? Dis-moi, connais-tu l'irrémissible?"

CREATION FROM NOTHING
LEV SHESTOV
(1905)

Résigne-toi, mon cœur, dors ton sommeil de brute.

(BAUDELAIRE)

CHEKHOV is dead; now it is possible to speak freely about him. For to speak of an artist means to uncover and display the "tendency" concealed in his works—and it is by no means always permissible to perform such an operation on a living person. After all, there was a reason for Chekhov's concealing himself, and, of course, the reason was a serious and an important one.

It seems to me that many people sensed it, and that partly for this reason we have not yet had a real appraisal of Chekhov. In analyzing his works, critics have thus far limited themselves to platitudes and clichés. They have, of course, known that they were wrong: but anything is better than to force the truth from a living man. Only N. K. Mikhailovsky tried to draw closer to the sources of Chekhov's creative work, and, as we well know, he recoiled in fright, even in disgust. Here, by the way, the late critic could have convinced himself once again of the fantastic nature of the so-called theory of art for art's sake. Every artist has his specific task, his life's work, to which he devotes all his energies. A tendency is ridiculous when it expects to replace talent, to conceal weakness and lack of content, or when it borrows from the stock of ideas popular at the given moment. "I am defending ideals; consequently everyone must sympathize with me." Claims of this sort are frequently made in literature, and the famous

[184]

controversy over free art was evidently maintained only by
the double meaning given the word "tendency" by its opponents. Some wanted to think that nobility of tendency can
save a writer; others were afraid that a tendency would bind
them to undertake tasks that are alien. Evidently both sides
were upset over nothing: ready-made ideas will never supply
mediocrity with talent; on the contrary, an original writer will
at all costs set himself his own task.

Chekhov had his own cause, although some critics said that
he was a servant of art for art's sake and even compared him
to a bird fluttering lightheartedly through the air. To define
his tendency briefly, I would say that Chekhov was the poet
of hopelessness. Stubbornly, despondently, monotonously, during his entire period of literary activity, for almost twenty-five
years, Chekhov did one thing only: in one way or another he
killed human hopes. In my opinion, this is the essence of his
creative activity. Little has been said about it up to now—and
for completely understandable reasons. After all, what Chekhov did is called crime in ordinary language, and it is subject
to the severest possible punishment. But how is a talented man
to be punished? Even Mikhailovsky, who more than once in
his time set an example of ruthless severity, did not raise his
hand against Chekhov. He warned his readers and pointed out
the "evil fire" which he had noticed in Chekhov's eyes. But
he went no further. Chekhov's great talent had won the
rigorously strict critic over to his side.

It may be, however, that Mikhailovsky's own position in
literature played more than a little role in the relative mild-
ness of his sentence. For thirty years in succession, the younger
generation had listened to him, and his word had been law.
But then everyone became sick and tired of eternally repeating: "Aristides is just, Aristides is right." The younger generation felt the desire to live and to speak in its own way, and it
finally ostracized the old teacher. In literature, the same custom prevails as in Tierra del Fuego: the young, growing men

kill and eat the old. Mikhailovsky struggled as best he could, but he no longer felt the strength of conviction that grows from a sense of being right. Inwardly, it was as if he sensed that the young were right—not, of course, because they knew the truth (what truth did the economic materialists know?), but because they were young and had their lives before them. A rising star always shines brighter than a setting one, and the old must voluntarily give themselves up to be eaten by the young. Mikhailovsky, I repeat, sensed this; and perhaps this is what destroyed his former confidence and the firmness of his opinions. In truth, he was like Gretchen's mother in Goethe, and he would not accept rich gifts that happened to come his way without first seeking the advice of his confessor. He took Chekhov's talent also to his pastor, who evidently rejected it as suspect. But Mikhailovsky no longer had the courage to oppose public opinion. The younger generation esteemed Chekhov for his talent, his great talent, and obviously was not going to repudiate him. What remained for Mikhailovsky? He tried, as I said before, to warn them. But no one listened to him, and Chekhov became one of the most beloved Russian writers.

Yet the impartial Aristides was right this time as well, just as he was right when he warned against Dostoevsky. Now that Chekhov is gone, we may speak of this matter. Take Chekhov's stories—each one separately, or even better, all of them together: watch him at work. It is as if he were constantly in ambush, spying on and waylaying human hopes. Don't worry: he will not overlook a single one of them; not one of them will escape its fate. Art, science, love, inspiration, ideals, the future—run through all the words with which mankind has been, and still is, accustomed to be consoled or entertained—Chekhov has only to touch them, and they instantly fade, wither, and die. And Chekhov himself faded, withered, and died before our eyes. The only thing about him that did not die was his amazing art of killing by a single touch, by even a breath or a glance, everything by which men live and of which they are proud. Moreover, he was always perfecting himself in this art, and he attained a virtuosity superior to that of any of his rivals in European literature. I would not hesitate to put him far ahead of Maupassant. Maupassant often had to make strenuous efforts to overcome his victim. Very often the victim, crushed and broken, but still alive, would escape from Maupassant. In Chekhov's hands, everything died.

II

I must remind you, although it is common knowledge, that in his early works, Chekhov is much different from the Chekhov to whom we have become accustomed in recent years. The young Chekhov is cheerful, carefree, and perhaps even like a soaring bird. He published his work in humorous magazines. But as early as 1888 and 1889, when he was only twenty-seven and twenty-eight years old, two of his works appeared ("A Dreary Story" and the play *Ivanov*) which laid the foundations of a new creative art. Evidently a sharp and sudden change had taken place in him, and it was completely reflected in his works. We do not as yet have a thorough biography of Chekhov, and we probably never shall have, because there is no such thing as a thorough biography; at least, I cannot name a single one. Usually biographies tell us everything except what is important to know. Perhaps it will sometime be revealed to us in the minutest detail who Chekhov's tailor was, but we shall probably never find out what happened to Chekhov in the time that elapsed between the completion of his story "The Steppe" and the appearance of his first drama. If we want to know, we must rely on his works and our own acumen.

Ivanov and "A Dreary Story" seem to me the most autobiographical of his works. In them, almost every line sobs. It is difficult to imagine that a person could sob so much while merely looking at someone else's sorrow. And it is evident that this sorrow is a new and unexpected one, just as if it had fallen from the sky. It exists, it will always exist, but he does not know what to do about it.

In *Ivanov*, the main hero compares himself to a worker who has overstrained himself. I think we shall not be wrong if we apply this comparison to the author of the drama as well. Chekhov overstrained himself—there can be almost no doubt about it. And he did not overstrain himself from heavy and hard work. It was not a feat beyond his strength that broke him, but a simple, insignificant event: he stumbled, slipped, and fell. Along comes this senseless, stupid, practically invisible incident, and the earlier Chekhov, merry and joyful, is no more; there are no more humorous stories for *The Alarm Clock*. Instead, there is a morose and sullen man, a "criminal," whose words frighten even experienced and sophisticated people.

If you want to, you can easily get rid of both Chekhov and his work. There are two magic words in our language: "pathological" and its brother "abnormal." If Chekhov overstrained himself, we have a perfectly legitimate right, sanctified by science and all traditions, to ignore him, particularly if he is already dead, and consequently cannot be offended by our disregard. That is, if you wish to get rid of Chekhov. But if, for some reason or other, you have no such desire, the words "abnormal" and "pathological" will have no effect upon you. Perhaps you will go further and try to find in Chekhov's experiences a criterion of the stablest truths and premises of our knowledge. There is no third way: you must either reject Chekhov or become his accomplice.

In "A Dreary Story," the hero is an old professor; in *Ivanov*, the hero is a young landowner. However, the theme of both works is the same. The professor overstrained himself, and thus cut himself off from his past life and from the possibility of taking an active part in human affairs. Ivanov also overstrained himself and became a superfluous, useless man. If life were so arranged that death would occur simultaneously with the loss of health, strength, and capability, the old professor and young Ivanov could not have existed for a single hour. It is clear even to a blind man: both of them are broken and unfit for life. But, for reasons unknown to us, wise nature has not provided for a coincidence of this kind: very often a man goes on living after he has lost the ability to take from life that in which we are accustomed to see its essence and meaning. And even more striking: a broken man is usually deprived of everything except the ability to be aware of and to feel his situation. Or if you prefer, the ability to apprehend is refined, sharpened, and increased to colossal proportions. Often an average, mediocre, and banal man who falls into the unusual situation of Ivanov or the old professor is changed beyond recognition. There appear in him signs of a gift, of talent, even of genius. Nietzsche once asked the following question: "Can an ass be tragic?" He left it unanswered, but Count Tolstoy answered for him in *The Death of Ivan Ilyich*. As is evident from Tolstoy's description of his life, Ivan Ilyich is a man of an average, mediocre nature—one of those who go through life avoiding all that is difficult and problematical, caring solely for the tranquillity and pleasantness of earthly existence. As soon as the cold wind of tragedy blew on him, he was completely changed. Ivan Ilyich and the last days of his life interest us no less than the story of Socrates or Pascal.

I would like to point out in passing—and I consider this extremely important—that in his work, Chekhov was influenced by Tolstoy, and particularly by Tolstoy's later writings. This is important, because part of Chekhov's "guilt" consequently falls on the great writer of the Russian land. It seems to me that if there had been no *Death of Ivan Ilyich*, there would have been no "Dreary Story," no *Ivanov*, nor many other remarkable works of Chekhov. This most certainly does not mean, however, that Chekhov borrowed a single word from his great predecessor. Chekhov had enough material of his own—in this respect, he needed no help. But a young writer would hardly venture to present himself to the public at his own risk with the thoughts that make up the content of "A Dreary Story." When Tolstoy wrote *The Death of Ivan Ilyich*, he had behind him *War and Peace*, *Anna Karenina*, and the firmly established reputation of a first-rate artist. Everything was permitted him. But Chekhov was a young man whose entire literary baggage amounted to several dozen stories hidden in the pages of little-known and uninfluential periodicals.

If Tolstoy had not paved the way, if Tolstoy had not shown by his example that it is permitted to tell the truth in literature, to say whatever one pleases, Chekhov would perhaps have had to struggle with himself for a long time before venturing to make a public confession, even in the form of short stories. And even though he came after Tolstoy, what a terrible struggle Chekhov had to wage against public opinion! "Why does he write his ghastly stories and dramas?" everyone asked himself. "Why does this writer systematically choose for his heroes situations from which there is not, and cannot possibly be, any way out?" "What can be said to the old professor and to Katya, his ward, in answer to their endless complaints?" As a matter of fact, there is something that can be said. Down through the ages, literature has amassed a large and diverse supply of all sorts of general ideas and world views, both metaphysical and positivist, which teachers recall every time overexacting and overrestless human voices begin to be heard. And this is precisely the point: Chekhov himself, a writer and an educated man, rejected beforehand all possible consolations, both metaphysical and positivist. Even in Tolstoy, who also had no great respect for philosophical systems, you do not find such sharply expressed aversion to all sorts of world views and ideas as in Chekhov. He knows very well that world views are to be esteemed and respected, and he considers his inability to genuflect before that which educated people hold sacred a shortcoming against which he must struggle with all his might. And he does struggle against it with all his might, but to no avail. The struggle leads to nothing—on the contrary, the longer Chekhov lives, the weaker becomes the power of lofty words over him, despite his own reason and conscious will. In the end, he is completely freed from all kinds of ideas, and loses even the notion of a connection between the events of life. In this is the most significant and original feature of his creative work.

Jumping a bit ahead, I shall refer here to his comedy *The Sea Gull*, in which, contrary to all literary principles, the basis of the action is not the logical development of passions or the inevitable connection between cause and effect, but naked chance, ostentatiously naked. In reading this play, you think at times that you have before you a copy of a newspaper with an endless series of news items, piled one on the other without order or a well-thought-out plan. Sovereign accident reigns everywhere and in everything, this time boldly challenging all world views. In this, as I said before, is Chekhov's greatest originality, and oddly enough, it is the source of his most agonizing experiences. He had no desire to be original; he made superhuman efforts to be like everyone else—but you cannot escape your destiny! How many people, particularly among writers, bend over backwards to be different, and, nevertheless, they cannot rid themselves of clichés—yet Chekhov was original against his will! Apparently, originality does not depend upon the readiness to express unpleasant opinions at any cost. The newest and boldest idea can and often does seem vulgar and boring. In order to become original, one must not think up an idea, but do a difficult and painful deed. And in as much as people avoid toil and suffering, whatever is really new is usually born in man against his will.

III

"It is impossible to reconcile yourself to a *fait accompli*; nor can you refuse to reconcile yourself: and there is no middle course." Under such circumstances, "action" is impossible; consequently, you can only "fall down, wail, and beat your head against the floor." Chekhov says this of one of his heroes, but he could say it of them all, without exception. The author takes care to put them into such a situation that only one thing remains for them: to fall to the floor or to beat their heads against the wall. With strange, enigmatic stubbornness, they reject all the customary means of salvation. Nikolay Stepanovich,[1] the old professor, could have tried to forget himself or to console himself by recalling his past. But memories only annoy him. He was an eminent scholar—now he is unable to produce. He was able to lecture and hold the attention of his audience for two whole hours—now he cannot do it for even a quarter of an hour. He had friends and comrades, he loved his students and assistants, his wife, and children—now he has no interest in anyone at all. If people do arouse any feelings in him, they are only feelings of hatred and spite. He must admit this to himself with the truthfulness that came to him, from heaven only knows where, to replace the former diplomatic art, inherent in all intelligent and normal people, whereby they see and say only what is conducive to decent human relations and healthy states of mind. Everything that he now thinks, everything that he sees only poisons in himself and others those small joys that adorn human life. He feels with a certainty that he never achieved in the best hours and days of his earlier theoretical researches that he has become a criminal without having committed a crime. Everything he formerly did was good, necessary, and useful. He tells of his past, and you can see that he was always right, that he could have let the severest judge come to him at any hour of the day or night to examine not only his deeds, but his thoughts as well. But now, not only would a stranger condemn him, he condemns himself. He frankly admits that he is filled through and through with envy and hate:

> The best and most sacred right of kings is the right to pardon. And I have always felt myself a king. I was compassionate and

[1] The leading character in "A Dreary Story." [Tr.]

readily pardoned everyone right and left. But now I'm no longer a king. Something is going on inside me which belongs only to slaves. Evil thoughts wander around in my head day and night, and feelings that I never knew before have built a nest in my soul. I hate and despise; I'm exasperated, indignant, and afraid. I've become much too strict, exacting, irritable, unfriendly, and suspicious. What does it all mean? If these new thoughts and new feelings have come from a change of my convictions, then where could such a change have come from? Has the world become worse and I better, or was I blind and indifferent before? But if this change has come about because of a general decline in my physical and mental powers—after all, I'm sick and losing weight every day—then I'm in a sorry state: it means that my new thoughts are abnormal, unhealthy, and that I must be ashamed of them and consider them worthless.

This question is asked by the old professor, who is on the point of dying, and at the same time by Chekhov himself. Which is better: to be a king, or an envious, spiteful, old "toad," as he calls himself in another place? It goes without saying that the question is original. In the words quoted above, you feel how much Chekhov had to pay for his originality, and with what great joy he would have exchanged all his original thoughts (at the moment when his "new" point of view became clear to him) for the most ordinary, banal capacity for good will. There is no doubt in his mind that his way of thinking is pitiful, shameful, and obnoxious. His moods are as disgusting to him as his appearance, which he describes as follows: "I'm a man of sixty-two, with a bald head, false teeth, and an incurable tic. My name is as brilliant and beautiful as I myself am dull and ugly. My head and hands tremble from weakness; my neck, like that of a Turgenevian heroine, looks like the neck of a double bass; my chest is sunken, my back narrow. When I speak or read, my mouth twists to the side, and when I smile, my whole face is covered with senile, deathlike wrinkles."

A pleasant figure? Pleasant moods? If the kindest and most compassionate person were to give even a side glance at such

a freak, a cruel thought would automatically awaken in his
heart: that at the earliest possible moment he should kill, completely destroy, this pitiful and loathsome creature, or if the
laws prevented one from taking such a drastic step, at least
hide him as far as possible from human eyes, somewhere in
a prison, a hospital, or an insane asylum—methods of struggle
permitted not only by legislation, but also, if I am not mistaken, by everlasting morality. But here you run up against a
peculiar kind of resistance. The old professor does not have
the physical strength to struggle against prison guards, executioners, hospital attendants, or moralists: even a small child
could knock him down. Persuasion and petition—he knows
very well—will not help. Therefore, he resorts to desperate
means: he begins to shout to the whole world in a wild, horrible, heart-rending voice about some rights of his: "I feel like
crying out in a voice other than my own that fate has doomed
me, an eminent man, to death; that in a half-year or so, there
will be another person in charge here in the lecture hall. I
want to cry out that I am poisoned; that new ideas which I
did not know before have poisoned the last days of my life
and keep stinging my brain like mosquitoes. And at the same
time, my situation seems so horrible to me that I want all my
students to be terrified, to jump from their places, and rush
panic-stricken to the exit, shrieking in despair."

The professor's arguments will hardly move anyone. Indeed
I do not know if there are any arguments in the words just
quoted. But that horrible, inhuman moan! Imagine the picture: an ugly, bald old man with trembling hands, a distorted
mouth, a shriveled neck, eyes mad with fear, rolling about
on the ground like a wild animal and wailing, wailing, wailing!
What does he want? He has lived a long and interesting life;
now he has only to bring it nicely to a close and take leave of
his earthly existence as calmly, quietly, and solemnly as possible. But he bellows and throws himself about, calls practically
the whole universe to judgment, and grasps convulsively at the

few days that are left for him. And Chekhov? What does
Chekhov do? Instead of passing indifferently by, he sides with
the prodigious monster; he devotes page after page to the
"experiences of his soul," and little by little brings the reader
to a point where, instead of a natural and legitimate feeling
of indignation, there are awakened in his heart needless and
dangerous sympathies for this disintegrating, decaying creature. But the professor cannot be helped—everyone knows
that. And if he cannot be helped, it means we must forget
him: that is a truism. What good or what sense can there be
in the endless picturing—or, as Count Tolstoy would say,
daubing—of the unbearable torment of the agony that inevitably leads to death?

If the "new" thoughts and feelings of the professor were
radiant with beauty, nobility, or self-denial, it would be a
different matter: the reader could learn a thing or two from
them. But, as is evident from Chekhov's story, all these qualities belong to his hero's old thoughts. Now that his sickness
has begun, there has arisen in him an indomitable disgust for
everything that is even slightly reminiscent of lofty feelings.
When his ward Katya turns to him for advice as to what she
should do, this famous scholar, the friend of Pirogov,[1] Kavelin,[2] and Nekrasov, who had taught so many generations of
young people, does not know what to tell her. He absurdly
runs over in his mind a number of pleasant words, but they
have lost all meaning for him. He asks himself what he should
answer her. "It is easy to say: 'Work, or distribute your prop-
erty among the poor, or know yourself,' and because it is easy,
I don't know what to answer."

Katya, who is still a young, healthy, and beautiful woman,
has by Chekhov's efforts fallen like the professor into a trap
from which no human power can set her free. And from the
moment she experiences hopelessness, she wins all the author's

[1] N. I. Pirogov (1810–1881), a noted surgeon. [Tr.]
[2] K. D. Kavelin (1818–1885), a liberal publicist and historian. [Tr.]

sympathy. As long as a person is settled in some job, as long as he has something ahead of him, Chekhov is completely indifferent to him. If he does describe him, he usually does it quickly and in a tone of scornful irony. But when a person becomes entangled, and so entangled that he can in no way be disentangled, Chekhov begins to come to life. Then color, energy, an upsurge of creative force, and inspiration appear in him.

Perhaps the secret of his political indifference lies in this. Despite all his distrust of projects for the future, Chekhov, like Dostoevsky, was evidently not entirely convinced that social reforms and social science are ineffective. No matter how difficult the social problem may be, it can still be solved. Perhaps people are destined at some time to arrange things well enough on earth so they will live and die without suffering; humanity cannot go beyond this ideal. Perhaps the authors of thick treatises on progress do guess and foresee something. But that is precisely why their work is alien to Chekhov. At first instinctively, and then consciously, he was drawn to problems that are essentially unsolvable, like the one depicted in "A Dreary Story." In it, there is helplessness, sickness, and the prospect of inevitable death, and no hope at all of changing the situation one iota.

Such an inclination, whether it be instinctive or conscious, clearly contradicts the demands of common sense and normal will. But nothing else could be expected from Chekhov, an overstrained man. Each of us knows or has heard of hopelessness. Everywhere before our eyes horrible and unbearable tragedies are being played out, and if each doomed person were to raise such a terrible alarm about his ruin as Nikolay Stepanovich, life would become hell. It is Nikolay Stepanovich's duty not to shout his suffering to the whole world, but to see to it that he disturbs people as little as possible. And it was Chekhov's duty to assist him in every possible way in this creditable endeavor. There are a great many dreary stories

in the world—you cannot even count them all! And it is especially the stories of the kind that Chekhov tells that should be
hidden as far as possible from human eyes. After all, we are
dealing here with the decomposition of a living organism.
What would we say to a man who opposed the burying of
corpses, who began to dig decaying bodies from the grave,
even though he did it on the grounds, or rather on the pretext,
that they were the bodies of his close friends, even outstanding
men of renown and genius? Such an occupation could arouse
nothing but fear in a normal and healthy mind. In olden times,
sorcerers, soothsayers, and wizards, according to folk superstition, consorted with the dead, and in this strange occupation
found a certain pleasure or even a genuine satisfaction. But
they usually hid from other people in forests and caves, or
withdrew to deserts or mountains, to give themselves up in
isolation to their unnatural tendencies. And if, by chance, their
actions were found out, normal men responded with the stake,
the gallows, or the rack. What is called evil, the worst kind
of evil, usually has had as its source and origin an interest in
and a taste for carrion. Man would forgive any crime—cruelty,
violence, murder—but he would never forgive the unmotived
love of death and the search for its secret. In this regard, our
present day, although it is free from superstitions, has pro-
gressed very little since the Middle Ages. Perhaps the only
difference is that we, busy with practical matters, have lost
the natural sense of good and evil. Theoretically, we are even
convinced that nowadays there are not and cannot be wizards
and sorcerers. Our confidence in and indifference to this matter
reached such a point that everybody saw even in Dostoevsky
only the artist and publicist, and seriously argued with him
as to whether the Russian folk should be flogged and whether
we ought to take Constantinople.

No one but Mikhailovsky vaguely guessed what it was all
about when he called the author of *The Brothers Karamazov*
a "treasure-digger." I say he "vaguely guessed," for I think that

the late critic made the remark partly in an allegorical tone—
even in one of jest. Yet not one of Dostoevsky's other critics
made a truer slip of the tongue, even accidentally. Chekhov,
too, was a "treasure-digger," a sorcerer, a soothsayer, and a
conjurer; this explains his unusual passion for hopelessness,
decomposition, decay, and death.

Chekhov was not, of course, the only one to choose death
as the subject of his works. But it is not a question here of
subject matter, but of how the subject matter is treated.
Chekhov understood that: "In all the thoughts, feelings, and
ideas that I form about anything," he says, "there is something
lacking that is universal and that could bind them all together
into one whole. Each emotion and each thought lives apart in
me, and in all my opinions about science, literature, my students, and all the pictures that my imagination draws, not
even the most skillful analyst will find what is known as a
general idea, the god of the living man. And if this is lacking,
it means there is nothing. In poverty like this, a serious illness,
the fear of death, the influence of circumstances and people
would have sufficed for me to overthrow and smash to bits
all that I earlier regarded as my world view, and all in which
I saw the meaning and joy of my life."

In the words just quoted, there is expressed one of the
newest of Chekhov's ideas, and it defines all of his subsequent
creation. It is expressed in a modest, apologetic form: a man
admits that he is unable to subject his thoughts to a higher
idea, and in such an inability, he sees his weakness. This was
enough to avert from him to a certain extent the thunder of
criticism and public opinion. We willingly forgive repentant
sinners! But it is a completely useless indulgence: to declare
oneself guilty in order to atone for one's guilt is not enough.
What was the sense in Chekhov's sprinkling his head with
ashes and publicly admitting his guilt, if inwardly he remained
unchanged? If, at the time when he was verbally acknowledging the general idea as god (written to be sure with a small

letter) he did absolutely nothing for it? In words, he sings the praises of this "god," while in deeds, he curses it. Earlier, before his sickness, his "world view" brought him joy; now it had been smashed to bits! Isn't it natural to ask the following question: did this "world view" ever bring him joy? Perhaps his joy had its own independent source, and the world view was invited only as a general to a wedding, for outward show, and never played any important role?

Chekhov relates in detail the joys the professor derived from his scholarly research, his classes, his family, a good dinner, et cetera. In all this, the world view and the idea were also present, but they not only did not interfere with life, as it were, they embellished it; so that it seemed he was working for the sake of the idea as well as creating a family and having dinner. But now, when for the sake of the idea, he has to remain inactive, to worry, to lie awake at night, to swallow disgusting food—the world view is torn to shreds. Consequently, it turns out that a world view with a dinner is good, and a dinner without one is good too (this needs no proof), but a world view "in and of itself" is completely worthless.

This is the essence of Chekhov's words quoted above. With horror, he admits the presence in him of this "new" idea. It seems to him that he alone is such a weak and unimportant person, that everyone else should be fed on ideas and world views instead of bread. And that is the way it actually is, if we are to believe what people tell in books. Chekhov castigates, torments, and worries himself in every possible way, but he cannot change things. Worse than that—world views and ideas, which a great many people treat quite indifferently (actually these innocent things do not deserve any other attitude) become for Chekhov objects of bitter, inexorable, and merciless hatred. He is unable to liberate himself straight away from the power of ideas, and therefore he begins a long, slow, and stubborn war (I would call it a guerrilla war) against the tyrants who had enslaved him. His struggle, in general as well

as in its separate episodes, is of great absorbing interest, precisely because the most distinguished representatives of literature have thus far been convinced that ideas have a miraculous
power. What are most writers doing? They are constructing
world views—and at the same time, they believe that they are
doing an unusally important and sacred job! Chekhov insulted
a great many literary men. If they let him off rather easily, it
was first of all because he was very careful and fought with
the appearance of a man bringing tribute to the enemy, and
secondly, because in the case of talent much is forgiven.

IV

The contents of "A Dreary Story" thus boils down to the fact
that the professor, in telling of his "new" thoughts, is, in
essence, declaring that he does not find it possible to acknowledge the power of the "idea" over himself and to fulfill conscientiously what people call the supreme purpose, in the
service of which they customarily see their mission, the sacred
mission of man. "Let God judge me, I haven't the courage to
act according to my conscience"—this is the one and only
answer Chekhov finds in his heart to all demands for a "world
view." And such an attitude toward a world view becomes
second nature with Chekhov. A world view makes demands, a
man acknowledges the justice of the demands and systematically fails to fulfill a single one of them. Moreover, he acknowledges less and less frequently the justice of the demands.
In "A Dreary Story," the idea still judges the man and torments
him with the mercilessness characteristic of all that is inanimate. Just like a splinter piercing a living body, the idea, alien
and hostile to the organism, ruthlessly carries out its lofty
mission until the man resolutely decides to remove the splinter,
no matter how painful this difficult operation may be. As early
as in *Ivanov*, the role of the idea began to change. The idea
no longer persecutes Chekhov, but Chekhov the idea, and with

the grossest scorn and mockery. The voice of living nature gains the upper hand over artificial habits of culture. True, the struggle still goes on; if you like, it even alternates with happiness. But the former submission is gone. More and more Chekhov emancipates himself from all former prejudices and goes—where does he go? He himself could hardly answer that question. But he prefers to remain without an answer rather than accept any of the traditional ones. "I know very well that I'll live no more than half a year. It would seem that I should now be chiefly occupied with questions of the darkness beyond the grave, and those visions that will visit my sleep underground. But for some reason or other, my soul does not want to know about these questions, although my mind acknowledges their full importance."

In contrast to what had occurred before, reason is again respectfully pushed out of the door, and its rights are transferred to the "soul," to the dark, vague aspiration which Chekhov, now that he stands before the fatal boundary separating man from the eternal mystery, instinctively trusts more than the bright, clear consciousness which beforehand determines even views of the beyond. Will scientific philosophy be outraged? Is Chekhov undermining its firmest foundations? But, as you know, Chekhov is an overstrained, abnormal man. You are not obliged to listen to him, but once you have decided to hear him out, you must be ready for anything. A normal man, even if he is a metaphysician of the most extreme transcendental doctrine, always adjusts his theories to the needs of the moment; he destroys only to build later from the old material. For this reason, he is never short of material. Obedient to the basic law of human nature, long ago noted and formulated by the sages, he limits himself to and is content with the modest role of a seeker of forms. From iron, which he finds ready in nature, he forges a sword or a plow, a spear or a sickle. The thought of creating from nothing hardly occurs to him. But Chekhov's heroes, for the most part abnormal people, are confronted with this unnatural and therefore horrible necessity of creating from nothing. Before them always lies hopelessness, helplessness, and the sheer impossibility of any action whatsoever. Yet they continue to live; they do not die.

At this point, a curious question of extraordinary importance presents itself. I said that it is contrary to human nature to create from nothing. But nature often takes ready material from man, and, at the same time, she imperiously demands that he should create. Does this mean that nature contradicts herself? That she perverts her creatures? Isn't it more accurate to admit that the idea of perversion is purely of human origin? Perhaps nature is far more economical and wise than our sages, and perhaps we would learn much more if, instead of dividing people into necessary and superfluous, useful and harmful, good and bad, we temporarily suppressed in ourselves the tendency to subjective evaluation and tried to treat her creations with greater confidence? Otherwise, we immediately arrive at an evil gleam, a treasure-digger, a sorcerer, a magician; and a barrier that cannot be broken down either by logical arguments or by cannons is erected between men. I have little hope that this idea will seem convincing to those who are accustomed to maintaining the norm. And it is probably unnecessary that the notion of the fundamental opposition of good and bad which exists among men should disappear, just as it is unnecessary that babies should be born with the experience of adults, or that rosy cheeks and black, curly hair should disappear from the face of the earth. At any rate, it is impossible. The world has many centuries behind it; many nations have lived and died on the earth, yet as far as we know from the books and traditions that have come down to us, the argument between good and bad has never ceased. And it always happened that good did not fear the daylight, and that good people lived the life of the community, while the evil ones were always alone. It cannot be otherwise.

All Chekhov's heroes fear the light. Chekhov's heroes are

lonely. They are ashamed of their hopelessness, and they know that people cannot help them. They go somewhere, perhaps even forward, but they call on no one to follow. Everything is taken from them; they must create everything for themselves. Probably from this comes the undisguised contempt with which they respond to the most precious products of ordinary human creativity. No matter what you start to talk about with a Chekhovian hero, he has but one reply to everything: *no one can teach me anything.* You offer him a new world view, but on hearing your first words, he already feels that all it amounts to is an attempt to lay the old bricks and stones in a new way, and he turns away from you, impatiently, often rudely. Chekhov is an extremely cautious writer. He is afraid of public opinion, and he takes it into consideration. And nevertheless, what undisguised disgust he displays before accepted ideas and world views. In "A Dreary Story," he at any rate preserves an outwardly respectful tone and attitude. Later on, he dispenses with all precautions, and instead of reproaching himself for his inability to submit to the general idea, he openly revolts against it and even ridicules it. In *Ivanov*, it is already adequately expressed; there was reason for the storm of indignation this play aroused in its day.

As I said earlier, Ivanov is a dead man. The only thing the artist can do with him is to give him a decent burial, that is, to praise his past, to pity his present, and then, in order to temper the dismal impression made by death, to invite the general idea to the funeral. He could recall the universal problems of mankind in any of countless stereotyped forms, and the difficult case which seemed insoluble would be eliminated. In addition to the dying Ivanov, he should have portrayed the bright life of a young person full of promise, and the impression of death and destruction would lose all its poignancy and bitterness. But Chekhov does the exact opposite: instead of providing youth and the idea with power over destruction and death, as is done in all philosophical systems

and many works of art, he demonstratively makes the worthless wreck Ivanov the center of all events. Along with Ivanov,
there are young lives, and the idea is also given its representative. But the young Sasha, a charming and fascinating girl, who
falls heart and soul in love with the broken hero, not only fails
to save her loved one, she herself perishes under the burden of
a task that is beyond her strength.

And the idea? It is enough merely to recall the figure of
Doctor Lvov, whom Chekhov entrusted with the responsible
role of a representative of the all-powerful idea, and you will
immediately understand that he considers himself not as its
subject and vassal, but as its worst enemy. Doctor Lvov has
only to open his mouth, and all the characters, as if by prior
agreement, vie with each other in their haste to cut him off in
the most insulting way with gibes, threats, and almost with
blows on the head. Yet the young doctor attends to his duties
as a representative of the great power no less capably and
conscientiously than his predecessors—Starodum[1] and the other
venerable heroes of our early drama. He takes the part of the
offended, wants to restore rights that have been violated, is
outraged by injustice, et cetera. Can he have exceeded the
limits of his plenipotentiary powers? Of course not. But where
Ivanovs and hopelessness reign, there is not and cannot be a
place for the idea.

It is impossible for them to live together. And before the
eyes of the astounded reader, who is accustomed to think that
all kingdoms can fall and perish and that only the might of the
idea's kingdom remains inviolable for all time, there occurs a
spectacle: the idea is dethroned by a helpless, broken man.
And the things Ivanov says! In the very first act, he fires off
the following tirade, and not at a chance stranger, but at the
incarnate idea—Starodum-Lvov:

> I have the right to give you advice. Don't marry a Jewess, a
> crank, or a pedant: choose something ordinary, grayish, without

[1] A *raisonneur* in Fonvizin's eighteenth-century comedy *The Minor* [Tr.]

any bright colors, without superfluous shades. In general, construct your entire life from clichés. The more gray and monotonous the background, the better. My dear fellow, don't fight thousands of people single-handed, don't fight windmills, don't beat your head against the wall. And God save you from all sorts of rationalized methods of farming, unusual schools, fiery speeches. Shut yourself up in your shell, and do the small job God has given you. It's pleasanter, honester, and healthier.

Doctor Lvov, the representative of the all-powerful, sovereign idea, feels that his ruler's rights have been infringed on, that to tolerate such insults means in fact to surrender one's sovereignty. After all, Ivanov was, and must remain, a vassal. How does he have the heart to give advice, how dare he raise his voice when it is his duty to listen reverently and to obey silently and submissively? Why this is rebellion! Lvov tries to draw himself up to his full height and answer the insolent rebel with dignity, but nothing comes out. In a weak, trembling voice, he mutters the usual words, which only a short time earlier had an invincible power. But they do not have their usual effect. Their strength has departed. Where? Lvov does not even dare admit it to himself: to Ivanov. And it is no longer a secret to anyone. Whatever vile, dirty tricks Ivan may have played—and Chekhov does not stint in this regard: his hero's service record contains all sorts of offenses, almost to the deliberate murder of a woman devoted to him—it is to him and not to Lvov that public opinion is disposed. Ivanov is the spirit of destruction—rude, brusque, ruthless, stopping at nothing. But the word "scoundrel," which the doctor tears out of himself with agonizing effort and throws at him, does not stick. Somehow, he is right, with his own special right, which everyone finds incomprehensible, but incontrovertible, if we are to believe Chekhov. Sasha, a young, sensitive and talented creature, passes indifferently by the honest Starodum-Lvov on her way to adore him. The entire drama is constructed on this. True, Ivanov finally shoots himself, and this may, if you will, give formal grounds to think that the final victory remains with Lvov. And Chekhov did well to end the play thus, and not to drag it out endlessly. It would have been no easy matter to tell Ivanov's entire history. Chekhov continued to write for fifteen years, all the time telling the unfinished story, and nevertheless he had to break it off without reaching the end.

Anyone who would take it into his head to interpret Ivanov's words to Lvov as meaning that Chekhov, like Tolstoy of the *War and Peace* period, saw his "ideal" in the everyday arrangement of life, would have a poor understanding of the author. Chekhov was only defending himself against the "idea," and he said the most insulting thing to it that occurred to him. For what can be more insulting to the idea than to listen to the praise of everyday life? But on occasion, Chekhov could just as venomously depict everyday life. Take as an example the story "The Literature Teacher." The teacher lives entirely according to Ivanov's prescription. He has his work, and his wife Manyusya—neither a Jewess, nor a crank, nor a pedant—and a home that serves as his shell, but all this does not keep Chekhov from driving the poor teacher gently and slowly into the customary trap and bringing him to a state where he can do nothing but "fall down, wail, and beat his head against the floor." Chekhov had no "ideal," not even the ideal of everyday life, which Count Tolstoy lauded with such inimitable and incomparable skill in his early works. An ideal presupposes submission, the voluntary renunciation of one's right to independence, freedom, and power—and such demands, even hints of such demands, aroused in Chekhov all the force of aversion and disgust of which he alone was capable.

v

So Chekhov's real hero, his only one, is the hopeless man. Such a person has absolutely nothing "to do" in life except perhaps to beat his head against the stones. No wonder he is unbearable to the people around him. He brings death and destruction with him everywhere. He himself knows it, but he is powerless to avoid people. With all his heart, he longs to tear himself away from his terrible situation. Most of all, he is attracted to fresh, young, untouched beings; with their help, he hopes to recover his lost right to life. A futile hope! The beginning of destruction always proves invincible, and in the end, the Chekhovian hero is left alone with himself. He has nothing, he must create everything himself. And it is this "creation from nothing," or more accurately, the possibility of creation from nothing, which is the sole problem that can interest and inspire Chekhov. When he has stripped his hero of everything, when nothing is left for his hero but to beat his head against the wall, Chekhov begins to feel something like satisfaction: a strange fire lights up in his dimmed eyes. It was not without reason that Mikhailovsky called it evil. Creation from nothing! Doesn't this task exceed the limits of human strength, of human rights? For Mikhailovsky, there evidently was but one answer to this question. As for Chekhov himself, if this question were put to him in such a deliberately sharp form, he would probably be unable to answer it, even though he continually had to do with this activity, or better, *because* he continually had to do with it. One can say without fear of error that the people who without hesitation answer the question in either sense have never come close to it, or in general to any of the so-called ultimate questions of life. Wavering is a necessary component part in the judgment of a man whom fate has brought face to face with fateful problems. How Chekhov's hand trembled as he was writing the closing lines of "A Dreary Story!" The professor's ward—the person nearest and dearest to him, but like himself overstrained and bereft of hope, despite her youth—has come to Kharkov for his advice. The following conversation takes place between them:

"Nikolay Stepanovich," she says, turning pale and pressing her hands to her breast. "Nikolay Stepanovich! I can't go on living like this any longer. I can't! For God's sake, tell me quickly, this very minute, what I'm to do. Tell me what am I to do?"

"But what can I say? I'm at a loss. I can't tell you anything."

"Tell me, I beg you," she continues, gasping for breath and trembling all over. "I swear to you. I can't go on living like this any longer. I haven't the strength."

She falls to a chair and begins to sob. She throws her head back, wrings her hands, stamps her feet. Her hat falls from her head and dangles by its elastic band; her hair is disheveled.

"Help me, help me," she implores. "I can't stand it any longer."

"I can't tell you anything, Katya," I say.

"Help me," she sobs, grasping me by the hand and kissing it. "After all, you're my father, my one and only friend. You're intelligent and well educated, and you've lived a long time. You were a teacher! So tell me what I'm to do."

"Honestly, Katya, I don't know."

I am puzzled, confused, and moved by Katya's sobbing, and I can hardly remain standing.

"Let's have breakfast, Katya," I say with a forced smile. "Don't cry any more."

But instantly I add in a despondent voice: "I haven't long to live."

"Just one word, just one word," she cries, stretching out her hands to me.

But the professor does not have this word to give. He shifts the conversation to the weather, to Kharkov, and to other insignificant things. Katya rises and, without looking at him, stretches out her hand.

"I feel like asking her," he finishes his story, "does this mean you won't be at my funeral?"

But she does not look at me. Her hand is cold, like that of a stranger . . . Silently, I see her to the door. Now she has left me and is walking down the long corridor without looking back. She knows that I'm following her with my eyes, and probably she will look back on the landing. No, she did not look back. Her black dress has showed for the last time, her steps have died away. . . . Goodbye, my treasure!"

The only words the intelligent, educated, and long-lived
Nikolay Stepanovich, a teacher his whole life long, can give
in answer to Katya's question are: "I don't know." In all the
vast experience of his earlier years, there is not a single pro-
cedure, rule, or suggestion that might in the slightest fit the
wild absurdity of the new conditions of his own life and
Katya's. Katya cannot go on living in this way, and he himself
cannot continue to put up with his loathsome and shameful
helplessness. The both of them—he old, she young—would
like with all their heart to support one another, but neither
of them can think of a way to do it. To her question: "What
am I to do?" he answers, "I haven't long to live." To his "I
haven't long to live," she replies with a frenzied sobbing, a
wringing of the hands, and the absurd repetition of the same
words over and over. It would have been better if she had
asked nothing, if she had not started a frank, heart-to-heart
conversation. But they do not as yet realize this. In their
earlier life, conversation would ease their minds, and frank
confession would draw them closer together. But now it is
just the reverse. After such a meeting, they can no longer
stand each other. Katya leaves the old professor, her foster
father, her dear father and friend, with the realization that he
has become a stranger to her. As she is leaving, she does not
even turn around to him. She feels that nothing is left for
them except to beat their heads against the wall. In doing that,
everyone acts at his own risk, and there can indeed be no
hope of a comforting union of souls.

VI

Chekhov knew what conclusions he had come to in "A Dreary
Story" and *Ivanov*. Some critics also knew, and reproached
him for it. I shall not venture to say just what the reason
was—fear of public opinion, or horror at his own discoveries,
or both of them together, but evidently there came a moment

when Chekhov decided at all costs to abandon the position he had taken and turn back. The fruit of this decision was "Ward No. 6." In this story, the hero is the same familiar Chekhovian character, a doctor. And the setting is pretty much the usual one, although somewhat changed. Nothing in particular has happened in the doctor's life. He ends up in a godforsaken provincial hole, and gradually, by always shutting himself off from people and life, he reaches a state of total will-lessness, which, to his way of thinking, is the ideal of human existence. He is indifferent to everything, starting with his hospital, which he hardly ever visits, and where his coarse drunken assistant holds sway over the patients, who are fleeced as they are treated.

In the mental ward reigns a guard who is a retired soldier; he uses his fists to manage the unruly patients. The doctor does not care, just as if he were living far away in another world, and he does not understand what is going on before his very eyes. By chance, he comes to the mental ward and starts a conversation with one of the patients. The patient complains to him of the abominable disorder in the ward. The doctor listens quietly to what he says, but responds in words rather than deeds. He tries to show this insane man that external conditions can have no influence whatsoever on us. The insane man does not agree, becomes insolent, makes objections, in which, as in the thoughts of many insane people, absurd statements are intermingled with very profound remarks. Actually, there is so little nonsense that from the conversation you would never guess that you were dealing with someone who is insane. The doctor is delighted with his new acquaintance, but doesn't lift a finger to make life easier for him. Just as before, the poor fellow is at the mercy of the guard, who beats him up on the slightest infraction of the rules. The patient, the doctor, the people around them, the entire setting of the hospital and the doctor's apartment are described with amazing talent. Everything arouses in the reader a mood of complete nonresistance and incredible indifference: let them get drunk, fight, steal, resort to violence—it makes no difference, because it is evidently so preordained by the supreme council of nature! It is just as if the doctor's professed philosophy of inactivity has been prompted and whispered by the immutable laws of human existence. It seems that one is powerless to break away from its hold. Up to now, everything is more or less in the Chekhovian style. But the end is entirely different. Thanks to the intrigues of his colleague, the doctor himself ends up in the mental ward as a patient. He is deprived of freedom, locked up in a wing of the hospital, and even beaten—beaten by the same guard with whose help he had taught submission to his insane acquaintance. The doctor instantly awakens as if from a dream. A desire to struggle and protest appears in him. True, at this point he dies, but nevertheless the idea is victorious. The critics could consider themselves completely satisfied: Chekhov had openly repented and renounced the theory of nonresistance. And apparently "Ward No. 6" was warmly received at the time. By the way, we might add that the doctor has a very beautiful death: in his final moments, he sees a herd of deer, et cetera.

And indeed, the story's construction leaves no doubt in our minds. Chekhov wanted to yield, and he yielded. He had begun to realize how intolerable it is to be hopeless, how impossible to create from nothing. To beat one's head against the stones, perpetually to beat one's head against the stones, is so terrible that it would be better to return to idealism. The wonderful Russian saying proved to be true: "No one is immune to poverty or prison." Chekhov joined the host of Russian writers, and began to glorify the idea. But not for long! His very next story, "The Duel," is already of a different nature. Its conclusion is also seemingly idealistic, but only seemingly. The main hero Layevsky is a parasite, like all Chekhov's heroes. He does nothing, can do nothing, does not even want to do anything, lives partly at the expense of others, goes into debt, seduces women, et cetera. His situation is intolerable. He is living with another man's wife, of whom he is sick to death, just as he is sick to death of himself, but he is unable to get rid of her. He is always short of money, and everywhere he turns, he is in debt. His former friends dislike and despise him. He always feels that he is ready to run away, anywhere at all, without looking back, if only he can get away from the place where he is now living. His common-law wife is in approximately the same, if not an even more terrible state. Without knowing why, without love, without even feeling any attraction, she gives herself to the first vulgar man who comes along. Then it seems to her that she has been covered from head to foot with filth, and that the filth has stuck so close to her that a whole ocean could not wash it off. This couple lives in a desolate backwater in the Caucasus, and naturally attracts Chekhov's attention. Needless to say, the subject is an interesting one: two people are covered with filth, and they cannot stand either themselves or others.

For contrast, Chekhov makes Layevsky clash with the zo-ologist, Von Koren, who has come to the seaside town on busi-ness, the importance of which everyone recognizes—to study the embryology of the jellyfish. Von Koren, as is obvious from his name, is of German origin, and consequently is inten-tionally portrayed as a healthy, normal, pure man—a descend-ant of Goncharov's Stolz,[1] the direct opposite of Layevsky, who, for his part, is closely related to our old friend Oblomov. But in Goncharov, the contrast between Stolz and Oblomov is of quite a different nature and significance than in Chekhov. The novelist of the forties hoped that a *rapprochement* with Western culture would renew and revive Russia. And Oblo-mov himself is depicted as a man who is not yet completely hopeless. He is merely lazy, inactive, and unenterprising. It

[1] In the novel *Oblomov*. [Tr.]

seems that if he were to awaken, he would outdo a dozen men like Stolz. But Layevsky is a different matter. He has already awakened, he awakened a long time ago, but his awakening did him no good. "He does not like nature. He has no God. Either he or his friends had ruined every trustful girl he had known. His whole life long he had not planted a single tree or grown a blade of grass in his garden. And while he lived among the living, he had not saved the life of a single fly, but had only ruined and destroyed, and lied and lied."

The good-natured lout Oblomov degenerated into a revolting and horrible animal, whereas the pure Stolz lived and remained pure even in his posterity! But he speaks differently to the new Oblomovs. Von Koren calls Layevsky a scoundrel and a villain and demands that the severest possible punishment be meted out to him. It is impossible to reconcile Von Koren and Layevsky. The oftener they encounter each other the deeper, the more inexorable and merciless is their hatred of each other. They cannot live together on the earth. It must be one or the other: either the normal Von Koren, or the degenerate, decadent Layevsky. Moreover, all the external, material force is on Von Koren's side. He is always right, always victorious, always triumphant, both in his deeds and in his theories.

It is a curious thing: Chekhov is the implacable enemy of all kinds of philosophy. Not one of the characters in his works philosophizes—or if he does philosophize, it is usually unsuccessful, ludicrous, weak, or unconvincing. But Von Koren, a typical representative of the positive, materialist school, is an exception. His words breathe strength and conviction; they even contain pathos and a maximum of logical sequence. There are many materialist heroes in Chekhov's stories, but these people have in them a trace of veiled idealism, according to the stereotype developed in the sixties. Such heroes Chekhov keeps in the background and derides. Idealism of all kinds, both open and concealed, arouses in him a feeling of intolerable bitterness. It was easier for him to listen to the merciless threats of straightforward materialism than to accept the cachectic consolations of humanizing idealism. An unescapable force exists in the world, crushing and crippling man—this is clear to the point of palpability. The slightest imprudence, and the greatest as well as the most insignificant people fall victim to it. You can deceive yourself about it only so long as you know of it solely by hearsay. But whoever has once been in the iron clutches of necessity loses his taste for idealistic self-delusion forever. He no longer diminishes the enemy's strength—he is more inclined to exaggerate it. And the pure, logical materialism that Von Koren preaches shows as fully as possible our dependence upon the elemental forces of nature. When Von Koren speaks, it sounds like the pounding of a hammer, and each blow hits not Layevsky but Chekhov himself on his most painful spots. He gives Von Koren more and more strength, and he places himself under his blows. For what reason? Why? How strange it is! Perhaps Chekhov cherished a secret hope that self-inflicted torment might be the one way to a new life. He hasn't told us so. Perhaps he did not know why himself, or perhaps he was afraid to offend positive idealism, which exercises such complete sway over contemporary literature. He dared not as yet oppose European public opinion—after all, our philosophical views were not thought up by us; they were brought in from Europe! And in order not to quarrel with people, he thought up a stereotyped, happy ending for his ghastly story. Layevsky turns over a new leaf: he marries his mistress, abandons his life of dissipation, and spends his time assiduously copying documents to pay his debts. Normal people can be completely satisfied, for normal people read only the concluding lines of a fable—the moral; and the moral of "The Duel" is a most wholesome one: Layevsky reforms and begins to copy documents. True, it may seem that such an ending is more like a mockery of morality; but normal people are not very astute psychologists. They fear double meanings and, with the "sincerity" characteristic of themselves, they take all the writer's words at face value. Good luck to them!

VII

The only philosophy that Chekhov took seriously, and therefore struggled against seriously, was positivist materialism—precisely, positivist materialism, which is limited and which never pretends to theoretical completeness. Chekhov felt with all his heart the terrible dependence of a living man upon the invisible but all-powerful and patently callous laws of nature. After all, materialism—and particularly scientific ma-terialism, which is reserved and does not seek the final word or logical completeness—amounts to a description of the external conditions of our existence. The experience of each day, each hour, each minute, convinces us that a lonely, weak man, coming up against the laws of nature, must always adapt himself and yield, yield, yield. The old professor cannot restore his youth; the overstrained Ivanov cannot regain his strength; Layevsky cannot wash off the filth covering him—an endless series of inexorable, purely materialistic impossibilities against which human genius can set nothing but submission or oblivion. *Résigne-toi, mon cœur, dors ton sommeil de brute*—we shall find no other words to accompany the pictures that are unrolled in Chekhov's works. The submission is external, but under it is hidden a deep, malicious hatred of the unknown enemy. Sleep and oblivion are only seeming, because surely a man does not sleep, does not forget, if he calls his sleep, *sommeil de brute*.

But how can he do otherwise? The stormy protests which fill "A Dreary Story," the need to let off pent-up indignation, soon begin to seem useless, and even insulting to human dignity.

The last play in which Chekhov protests is *Uncle Vanya*. Like the old professor and Ivanov, Uncle Vanya sounds the alarm and raises an unheard-of fuss over his ruined life. In an uncharacteristic voice, he, too, fills the stage with his wailing: "My whole life has been wasted, my whole life has been wasted." As if any of the people around him, anyone in the whole world, could be responsible for his misfortune! But shouting and wailing are not enough for him. He heaps insults on his own mother. Needlessly and aimlessly, like a madman, he starts to shoot his revolver at his imaginary enemy, the pitiful, unhappy father of the unattractive Sonya. His voice is not enough, so he resorts to his gun. He is ready to shoot off all the cannons on earth, to beat on every drum, to ring every bell. It seems to him that the whole world is asleep, that he must awaken the people around him. He is ready for any absurdity, for he has no rational way out. No man can admit right off that there is no way out.

Then begins a Chekhovian story: he is unable to accept the situation, and at the same time, he cannot refuse to accept it; all he can do is beat his head against the wall! Uncle Vanya does it openly, in front of other people, but how painful it is for him later on to recall his intemperate bluntness! When everyone is leaving after this agonizing and absurd scene, Uncle Vanya realizes that he should have kept silent, that certain things should not be admitted to anyone, not even to one's closest friend. *A stranger's eye cannot stand the sight of hopelessness.* "Your life has slipped by—blame yourself for it. You are no longer a person; everything human is alien to you. Your friends are no longer friends, but strangers. You have no right either to help others or to expect help from them. Your lot is absolute loneliness." Gradually, Chekhov becomes convinced of this "truth": *Uncle Vanya* is his last experiment with a noisy public protest, with a defiant "declaration of rights." And even in this play, Uncle Vanya is the only one who rages, although the characters include both

Doctor Astrov and poor Sonya, who would also have been justified in raising an uproar and even in firing the cannon. But they keep silent. They even repeat some pleasant, angelic words on the subject of mankind's joyous future—or to put it differently, their silence is doubly deep, for "pleasant words" coming from the mouths of such people indicate their final estrangement from life. They have withdrawn from everyone, and they let no one come near them. With pleasant words, they have shut themselves off, as with the Great Wall of China, from the curiosity and prying of their neighbors. Outwardly, they are like everyone else, and therefore no one dares to touch their inner life.

What is the meaning, what is the significance of this intense inner labor in people whose lives are finished? Chekhov would probably have answered this question with the same words that Nikolay Stepanovich answered Katya: "I don't know." He would have added nothing more. But this life is more like death than life; it alone attracted and interested him. That is why his speech became quieter and slower year after year. Of all our writers, Chekhov is the quietest. All the energy of the heroes of his works is directed inward instead of outward. They create nothing visible; worse, they destroy everything visible by their outward passivity and inertia. A "positive thinker" such as Von Koren does not hesitate to denounce them with horrible words, and the more satisfied he is with himself and his justice the more energy he puts into epithets: "Villains, scoundrels, degenerates, monkeys," et cetera. The things Von Koren thought up to call the Layevskys! This patently positive thinker wants to force Layevsky to copy documents. The secretive positive thinkers, that is, the idealists and metaphysicians, do not use invective. On the other hand, they bury Chekhov's heroes alive in their idealist graveyards, otherwise known as world views. Chekhov himself refrains from a "solution of the problem" with a persistency to which the majority of the critics very likely wished a better lot, and he continues his long stories about people and the life of people who have nothing to lose, just as if the only interesting thing in the world were this nightmarish suspension between life and death.

What does it tell us? Something about life or death? Again it is necessary to answer: "I don't know"—those same words which arouse the greatest disgust in positive thinkers, but which in some enigmatic way are the invariable elements in the opinions of Chekhov's people. That is why the philosophy of materialism, although hostile, is still so dear to them. It holds no answer that can force us to joyful submission. It beats and destroys man, but it does not call itself rational or demand gratitude. It needs nothing, for it is soulless and speechless. You can acknowledge and simultaneously hate it. If you manage to cope with it—you are right; if you fail—*vae victis*. How comforting sounds the voice of the explicit mercilessness, of inanimate, impersonal, indifferent nature, as compared with the hypocritical and saccharine melodies of idealist, humanist world views! Yet—and this is the main thing—a struggle against nature is possible. And in the struggle against nature, no holds are barred. In the struggle against nature, man always remains man, and, consequently, right, no matter what he undertakes for his salvation, even if he were to refuse to accept the basic principle of the universe—the indestructibility of matter and energy, the law of inertia, and so on; for the most colossal dead force must serve man. Who will dispute this?

A world view is a different matter! Before uttering a word, it makes an incontestable demand: man must serve the idea. And moreover, this demand is regarded as self-evident and extraordinarily sublime. Is it surprising that in the choice between idealism and materialism, Chekhov inclines toward the side of the latter—the strong but honest opponent? It is possible to struggle against idealism only with scorn, and in this respect, Chekhov's works leave nothing to be desired. But how is it possible to struggle against materialism? And can

it be vanquished? Perhaps Chekhov's methods seem strange
to the reader, but apparently he came to the conclusion that
there is only one method of struggle, to which the ancient
prophets had resorted: to beat one's head against the wall.
Without thunder, without cannon fire, without alarm, in loneliness, in silence, far from their friends and their friends'
friends, to gather all the forces of despair for an attempt long
ago condemned by science and common sense. But do you
really have the right to expect from Chekhov sanction of the
scientific method? Science took everything from him: he was
condemned to create from nothing—that is, to an activity of
which a normal person, using normal means only, is utterly
incapable. In order to do the impossible, it is first of all necessary to renounce routine methods. No matter how stubbornly
we may continue our scientific research, it will not provide us
with the elixir of life. After all, science began by ridding itself
of the yearning for human omnipotence as unattainable in
principle; here, methods are such that success in certain fields
even precludes a search in others. In other words, the scientific method is defined by the nature of the tasks that science
undertakes. And indeed, not one of her tasks can be carried
out by beating one's head against a wall. Although this
method is not new (I repeat, it was known to and used by
the prophets), it promised more to Chekhov and his heroes
than all inductions and deductions (which, by the way, were
not invented by science, but have existed since the world
began). It is suggested to man by a mysterious instinct, and
it appears on the scene every time it is needed. The fact that
science condemns it is not strange. It, in turn, condemns
science.

VIII

Now perhaps the subsequent development and trend of Chekhov's creative work will be understandable, as well as that
peculiar and unique combination in him of "sober" materialism

and extraordinary stubbornness in seeking new paths, which are always devious and risky. Like Hamlet, he wants to dig a mine one yard deeper under his opponent so that he can simultaneously blow up both the engineer and the thing the engineer is building. His patience and endurance in this difficult underground work are really amazing and to many people intolerable. Everywhere there is darkness, not a single ray, not a single spark; but Chekhov goes slowly forward, barely, barely moving. An inexperienced or impatient eye will perhaps observe no movement whatsoever, and very likely Chekhov himself does not know for sure whether he is moving forward or marking time. To calculate beforehand is impossible. It is even impossible to hope. Man has entered that stage of his existence in which the mind, cheerful and foreseeing, refuses its services. There is no possibility of his getting a clear and distinct idea of what is going on. Everything takes on a tinge of fantastic foolishness. You believe and yet disbelieve everything.

In "The Black Monk," Chekhov tells of a new reality, and in a tone which sounds as if he himself is puzzled as to where reality ends and phantasmagoria begins. The black monk lures a young scholar off into some mysterious remoteness, where mankind's best dreams are to come true. The people around the scholar call the monk a hallucination and fight him with medicines—bromides and a nourishing diet including milk. Kovrin himself does not know who is right. When he talks with the monk, he thinks the monk is right; when he sees before him his sobbing wife and the serious, worried faces of the doctors, he admits that he is under the influence of fixed ideas, which are leading him directly to insanity. In the end, the black monk triumphs. Kovrin lacks the strength to put up with the banality surrounding him; he breaks with his wife and her relatives, who seem to be executioners, and goes off somewhere, but as far as we can see, he gets nowhere. He finally dies in order to give the author the right to end his story.

It always happens this way: when the writer does not know what to do with his hero, he kills him off. Sooner or later this device will probably be abandoned. In the future, writers will probably convince themselves and the public that all kinds of artificial endings are quite needless. If the material is exhausted, break the story off, even in the middle of a word. Chekhov sometimes did that, but only sometimes. For the most part, he preferred to satisfy the traditional demands and to provide his readers with an ending. This device is not so unimportant as it may seem at first sight, for it can be misleading. Take, for example, "The Black Monk." The hero's death is, as it were, an indication that every abnormality must, in Chekhov's opinion, definitely lead through an absurd life to an absurd death. Yet, this was hardly Chekhov's firm conviction. Evidently he expected something from abnormality, and therefore paid so much attention to people who are unsettled. He was convinced that there is no exit from the intricate labyrinth, that the labyrinth with its vague wanderings, its never-ending hesitations and vaccillations, its unmotived grief, its unmotived joys—in a word, everything that normal men so fear and avoid—had become the essence of his life. Of this and only this should a writer tell. A normal life was not invented by us, nor was an abnormal one. Why then is only the first one regarded as the true reality?

Chekhov's play *The Sea Gull* must be regarded as one of his most typical, and therefore one of his most remarkable works. In it, the artist's true attitude toward life found its fullest expression. Here all the characters are either blind and afraid to move from their places for fear of losing their way home, or they are half mad, rushing and tossing about without rhyme or reason! It is just as if the celebrated actress Arkadina clings with her teeth to her seventy thousand rubles, her fame, and her last lover. Trigorin, the writer—also famous—works unceasingly, day after day; he writes, writes, and writes, without knowing the why or the wherefore. People read and praise his works, but he is not in control of himself; like Marko, the

ferryman in the story, he works like a fiend, taking passengers
back and forth from one shore to the other. The river, the
boats, and the passengers are deadly boring—but how can he
rid himself of them? He could turn the oars over to the first
person who came along—such a solution is so very simple, but
after it, as in the story, he would have to go to heaven.

Not only Trigorin, all the more mature characters in Chekhov's works remind us of Marko, the ferryman. It is evident
that they do not like their work, but, as if they were hypno-
tized, they cannot escape the influence of an alien power. The
monotonous, regular, and mournful rhythm of life has lulled
to sleep their consciousness and their will. Chekhov everywhere stresses this strange and enigmatic characteristic of
human life. His people always speak, always think, always do
one and the same thing. One of them builds houses according
to a plan made once and for all ("My Life"); another makes
his round of visits from morning to night, collecting rubles
("Ionich"); still another buys up houses ("Three Years"). Even
his characters' speech is intentionally monotonous. One of them
invariably says: "Not bad"—both when the occasion warrants
it and when it does not; another says "boorishness," et cetera.
They are all monotonous to the point of stupidity, and they
are all afraid to break this stupefying monotony, just as if it
were the source of exceptional joys. Read Trigorin's mono-
logue:

> Lets talk . . . Let's talk about my splendid life . . . Well,
> now, where shall I begin? (Thinking a bit.) There are such things
> as obsessions, when a person thinks day and night, for example
> of nothing but the moon. And I, too, have my moon. Day and
> night I'm obsessed with one persistent idea: "I must write, I
> must write, I must." I've barely finished one story than, for some
> reason or other, I must write a second, then a third, and after
> the third, a fourth. I write unceasingly, as fast as possible. I
> can't do otherwise. But what, I ask you, is so bright and splendid
> about that? Oh, what a preposterous life it is! I'm with you now,

I'm excited, and yet every moment I'm aware that an unfinished story is waiting for me. I see a cloud shaped like a grand piano. It smells of heliotrope. I quickly make a mental note: a cloying smell, the color of mourning—I must remember to use these words when describing a summer evening. I note my every word, my every phrase—yours too—and hurry as quickly as possible to lock all these words and phrases into my literary storehouse; maybe they will come in handy. When I finish work, I rush off to the theatre or go fishing; at last I'll have a rest and forget myself—but no! A new plot for a story is already rolling around in my head like a heavy ball of iron; it is already drawing me to my desk; I must hurry to write and write again.

And so it goes forever, forever; I have no rest from myself, and I feel that I'm devouring my own life, that in order to obtain the honey I give to someone else I use the pollen of my best flowers, that I pick these very flowers and trample them down to the roots. Surely I must be insane. Do my friends and neighbors treat me as if I were sane? "What are you writing? What are you going to please us with next?" One and the same thing, always one and the same thing, and I think that the attention, the praise, and the delight of my friends is nothing but deceit. They are robbing me as they would a sick man, and sometimes I'm afraid that they will sneak up at any minute, seize me, and haul me off into an insane asylum, as they did with Poprishchin.[1]

What is the reason for all this? Throw in the sponge and begin a new life? That is impossible. Until an answer comes from heaven, Trigorin will not throw in the sponge, he will not begin a new life. In Chekhov, only the young, the very young and inexperienced, speak of a new life. They are always daydreaming of happiness, regeneration, light, joy. They fly headlong into the flame, and burn to death, just like foolish butterflies. In *The Sea Gull*, it is Nina Zaryechanaya and Treplev; in other works, other heroes, both men and women. They are all searching for something, longing for something, but not a single one of them does what he wants. They all live

---

[1] In Gogol's *Diary of a Madman*. [Tr.]

apart; each one is totally absorbed in his own life and indifferent to the lives of others. And the strange fate of Chekhov's
heroes is that they strain their inner powers to the utmost, but
there are no visible results. They are all pitiful. One of the
women takes snuff, dresses carelessly, pays no attention to her
hair, is uninteresting. One of the men is irritable, grumbles,
drinks vodka, bores everyone around him. What they say and
what they do is irrelevant. They cannot adapt the outer world
to themselves; I would even say they do not want to. Matter
and energy unite according to their own laws—these people
live according to their own, as if matter and energy did not
exist at all.

In this respect, Chekhov's intellectuals do not at all differ
from the illiterate peasants and the semiliterate bourgeoisie.
Life on the manorial estate is the same as in the small town
in the hollow, the same as in the country village. No one
believes that by changing his outward conditions he can
change his fate as well. Everywhere reigns an unconscious
but deep and ineradicable conviction that the will must be
directed towards ends having nothing in common with the
organized life of mankind. Even worse, the organization seems
to be the enemy of the will, the enemy of man. It is necessary
to gnaw away, to spoil, to destroy, to ruin. To think things
over quietly, to foresee the future—that cannot be! One must
beat his head, endlessly beat his head, against the wall. What
does this lead to? Does it really lead to anything at all? Is it
a beginning or an end? Is it possible to see in it the pledge
of a new and inhuman creation, a creation from nothing? "I
don't know," answered the old professor to sobbing Katya.
"I don't know," answered Chekhov to all sobbing and tormented people. With these words, and only with these, can
we end this article on Chekhov. *Résigne-toi, mon cœur, dors
ton sommeil de brute.*

THE NOVELS OF COUNT L. N. TOLSTOY:
ANALYSIS, STYLE, AND ATMOSPHERE—
A CRITICAL STUDY
KONSTANTIN LEONTIEV
(1890)

❧

I [1]

ABOUT a year ago, in the daily *Citizen*, I began to publish under the title "Two Counts: Alexey Vronsky[2] and Lev Tolstoy" my thoughts on the question of which of these men should be the more valuable to Russia—the creator himself or the so real and plausible creation of his genius? The great novelist or the resolute, energetic, and well-educated soldier, who, at the same time, was obviously capable of bearing the heavy burden of public service?

I myself broke off this discussion at the halfway point, and left it unfinished (why, I shall explain below). But to those who read my article, I hope it was clear at the very beginning that from a patriotic standpoint I prefer Vronsky not only to Levin,[3] but even to Count Tolstoy himself.

In our troubled times, which are both irascible and faint-hearted, the Vronskys are much more useful to us than the

---

[1] This chapter of the article was published in issues 157 and 158 of *The Citizen* (1890), accompanied by the following letter from the author: "Dear Sir: My article entitled 'Analysis, Style, and Atmosphere' is now being published in *The Russian Herald*. The editors of that magazine very kindly accepted my work, but asked that I eliminate its first chapter. That chapter, however, is important to me as a necessary introduction, and for me to see my article without an explanatory introduction would be awkward. Therefore, I am turning to you with a most humble request —to publish it in *The Citizen* simultaneously with the appearance of my aforementioned article in *R. H.* [signed] K. Leontiev."

[2] In *Anna Karenina*. [Tr.]

[3] *Ibid.* [Tr.]

great novelists, and all the more so than those eternal "seekers" such as Levin, who, for all that, never find anything that is clear and stable.

Concerning novelists, I said there bluntly: "Without these Tolstoys, that is without the great artist-writers, it is possible even for a great people to live for a long time, but without the Vronskys we could not even live half a century. Without them, there would also be no national writers, for the nation itself would soon perish."

Although we know Vronsky's character mainly from his private life (as is almost always the case in novels), and the author presents him to us while in those youthful years when a man's public-service career is still limited—even in the case of a man placed high in society—nevertheless, even in these circumstances, the young Count's spiritual and intellectual make-up is clear enough for us to say: May God send Russia as many *such* illustrious men as possible—men who are bold and cautious, stable and moderately passionate, not physically delicate; men who are outwardly glittering, but inwardly, in their heart of hearts, serious. That is what I wanted to say about Vronsky when speaking of Russian "heroes" in general.

At the time, I had a long and detailed discussion in mind. I wanted from precisely this aspect—*everyday life*, not art— to examine anew all the main "heroes" of our literature, beginning with its first live protagonist (i.e., Onegin) *down to its last in time* (Troyekurov in Markevich's *The Turning Point*): Pechorin,[1] Beltov,[2] both Aduyevs (*A Common Story*),[3] Rudin,[4] Lavretsky,[5] Bazarov[6] and other of Turgenev's heroes, Oblomov,[7] Raisky (*The Precipice*),[8] Kalinovich[9] and the "Men of the Forties,"[10] and finally Count Tolstoy's main heroes. I

[1] *A Hero of Our Times*, Lermontov. [Tr.]
[2] *Whose Fault?*, Hertzen. [Tr.]
[3] Goncharov. [Tr.]
[4] *Rudin*, Turgenev. [Tr.]
[5] *A Nest of Gentlefolk*, Turgenev. [Tr.]
[6] *Fathers and Sons*, Turgenev. [Tr.]
[7] *Oblomov*, Goncharov. [Tr.]
[8] Goncharov. [Tr.]
[9] *A Thousand Souls*, Pisemsky. [Tr.]
[10] From Pisemsky's novel of the same name. [Tr.]

wanted to set three of them above all the rest as *real, living people*: Andrey Bolkonsky,[1] Vronsky, and Troyekurov. And, it seems, not without sufficient grounds. For if we really do not want to see the Bazarovs, Volokovs, [2] Solomins,[3] and Nezhdanovs[4] triumph in all spheres of our Russian life, we must set against them as the ideal, not the Levins, who change their opinions and views almost daily, not the Karenins, who are afraid to take a gun into their hands and who are accustomed to judge life only as it is reflected in official documents and scholarly books, but such bold, convinced, resolute, and even *physically* strong men such as Troyekurov and Vronsky.

That is clear. But in all fairness, I intended to praise a third person as well—Andrey Bolkonsky!

And it was at this point that my idea met with a completely unexpected obstacle. . . .

I was obliged to ask myself: do I have the right, when considering the nature, upbringing, character, and degree of social value and personal charm of the persons mentioned above, *to compare the authenticity of the portrayal* of my contemporaries—Rudin, Lavretsky, Bazarov, Levin, Vronsky, and Troyekurov—*with the authenticity of the portrayal* of the heroes of 1812 in the novel *War and Peace?*

Perhaps yes, and perhaps no!

The conditions of artistic creation are not always the same. In the contemporary novels all the authors had observed life at first hand, but when Count Tolstoy reproduced the life of the people of 1812, he was obliged for two-thirds of his artistic work to make do with only the resources of his imagination. That is a great difference. The honor due the author is perhaps also much greater because of this circumstance; but when it is a question not of the strength of the creative work, but of an appraisal of the characters as *real people*, then it is permissible to doubt as I doubted.

---

[1] *War and Peace*, Tolstoy. [Tr.]
[2] *The Precipice*, Goncharov. [Tr.]
[3] *Virgin Soil*, Turgenev. [Tr.]
[4] *Ibid*. [Tr.]

The strength of the brilliant creative work in two of Gogol's great stories—"Viy" and "Notes of a Madman"—is equal; however, from the standpoint of real authenticity, we cannot compare Viy himself with the Petersburg clerk Poprishchin. Much more creative energy was, of course, expended by Pushkin on his creation of Tsar Boris[1] than on his portrayal of Onegin,[2] into whom—this is clear to everyone—he put much that was personally his own; however, his Onegin is *more authentic* than his Godunov.

That is what I am speaking about.

These vacillations in my thinking apropos the heroes of 1812 in the novel *War and Peace* led me, to my own surprise, to an entirely new path. I decided to leave unfinished my discussion of the social value and the personal psychological significance of various nineteenth-century Russian heroes and devote myself to a general, purely aesthetic problem: *Style, analysis, and the conveyance (or nonconveyance) of a certain spirit of the time and milieu.*

Count Tolstoy's heroes unexpectedly gave me occasion to make a detailed comparison of the merits and demerits of his two chief and great works. And the analysis of *Anna Karenina* and *War and Peace* also *made me* almost automatically express certain of my basic views, both on literary aesthetics in general and on the weak sides of the entire Russian school of realism from the time of Gogol to the present.

I know that both these words and opinions of mine in the field of "pure" criticism will seem strange to many, and because of their unusualness will even make an extremely unfavorable impression on some. Perhaps someone will call them "psychopathic paradoxes," just as people recently called other views of mine relating to history.

Not only am I not very deeply grieved over this, I myself am even ready to say that if people are going to look some-

[1] *Boris Godunov.* [Tr.]
[2] *Eugene Onegin.* [Tr.]

where for "psychopathy," they should more than likely do it in the critical attempt offered here. I myself must admit that it is highly subjective, perhaps even to the point of idiosyncracy or whimsey.

It is difficult to judge for oneself, especially where sentiment does not come from reasoning, but where reasoning develops from *invincible* sentiment. It can happen that our entire train of thought—however clear and correct it may be in its final outcome—is based on a feeling, on a choice of personal taste that to everyone else will seem not only strange or "alien" (as this same Count L. N. Tolstoy likes to put it), but even downright ugly.

So be it! I am used to intellectual isolation and to the fact that even those people who sympathize with me in a thing or two find it right on occasion to reproach me for a love of paradox and for "useless originality." What can one do? As people think, so they write; as they feel, so they speak!

Moreover, in such cases having to do with human weakness, I always recall an opinion of John Stuart Mill that is highly beneficial to me. He says that even *the mistakes of people who dared to think in their own way have done more good than great truths repeated by untalented lips.*

Besides, I think that aesthetic criticism, like sincere religious debate, must inevitably proceed from keen *personal* feeling, and must try only to justify and affirm this feeling logically. In the case of religion, *personal faith* first—general affirmation later; in this case, *subjective taste* first—elucidation, later.

Raw scientific evidence and cold scientific impartiality are impossible in either case.

In aesthetic questions there are but two kinds of impartiality that will do: either that which is *frankly personal*, toward the writer himself as to a person, or that which is more abstract, in the sense of *independence of* his political, religious, and moral tendency. Impartiality or, let us even say, impassivity of these two kinds is the direct responsibility of the conscientious critic; it is the ideal of critical thought.

A person who would try to persuade both himself and others that Saltykov's[1] *Mon Repos* is a worthless thing, merely because Saltykov was a revolutionary—such a person would not deserve the name of good critic. As you know, it is possible in the end, after crowning the talent of a "harmful citizen" with laurels, not only to subject him to "civil anathema," but also to punish him severely if it is beyond one's powers to cope with him. For the State is more precious than one or two extra literary stars. But in criticism, one must not fail to pay proper tribute to a great talent. Or another example, just the reverse. As far back as the sixties, I knew people (not many, though) who, while they fervently sympathized with the then revolutionary movement among intellectuals and found both Nekrasov and Dobrolyubov exceedingly useful because of their ideological tendency, *could not, however, bring themselves to prefer* the poetry of this same Nekrasov to the poetry of Fet[2] or Polonsky.[3] And in reading Turgenev, these same people, these "revolutionaries and democrats," these friends of *The Contemporary*,[4] admired his story "First Love" but aesthetically despised his *On the Eve*. And, indeed, either one must think not at all of the beautiful, both in art and *life itself*, or have the tastes of a triumphant lackey not to see that the story "First Love" has both poetry and truth gushing from every line, whereas the whole of *On the Eve* is "daubed" almost on the order of the progressive-democratic cads. *Mon Repos* is sincere and powerful, because of Saltykov's inner physiological spite and his truly brilliant cantankerousness.

---

[1] M. E. Saltykov (1826–1889), a satirist, who wrote under the pseudonym N. Shchedrin. [Tr.]

[2] A. A. Fet (1820–1892), an impressionist poet whose work consists mainly of small etchings of his native land and of love poems. Politically, he was a conservative. [Tr.]

[3] Ya. P. Polonsky (1819–1898), another of the nontendentious poets. [Tr.]

[4] The organ of the liberal Westerners and radicals. Nekrasov was its editor from 1846 to 1866. [Tr.]

And "First Love" is written sincerely, elegantly, and power-fully as a result of the natural elegance of Turgenev's entire nature. As for *On the Eve*, which breathes coldness and false-hood, I think that in it Turgenev describes the love of his tedious Yelena for his wooden Insarov with the same sincerity with which Saltykov might say "God, Save the Tsar!" It is not surprising that I, for example, thought as much even twenty-five or thirty years ago; even then, I could not stand either the bloodthirsty "devil's sabbath" of *The Contemporary* or the false humanity of Nekrasov. I could even be prejudiced against a civic tendency, because of an early hatred of democ-racy. But I recall those old St. Petersburg acquaintances of mine with pleasure, because the so erroneous and harmful mood of their political thinking of the time could not kill either their superior taste or their critical honesty. The per-version of their civic feelings did not blind their critical clairvoyance.

Such infatuation, prejudice, or tendentious sham, of course, spoils and discredits all criticism, especially that which is purely aesthetic.

But there are prejudices of a different kind: invincible in-clinations of taste and sympathy, of disgust and disinterested vexation. A person is *sickened* by much of what pleases the majority; a person finds unpleasant what *almost* everyone (if not everyone) is accustomed to; he almost automatically pays *particular* attention to what others do not even mention.

Must he definitely remain silent, only because it seems to him that he alone feels this way? And what if he is by no means *alone*?

What if among readers and connoisseurs there happen to be those who think and feel something similar, and who are only waiting for a more decisive or experienced voice that can justify in their eyes their own artistic instinct, that can answer their confused, but strong, aesthetic tendency with a more detailed argument?

What if one can permit oneself to call aesthetics in its true form a science (or more accurately, something that, although immature, is nevertheless pseudoscientific and which aspires some day to become a science)? After all, the very etymology of the term "aesthetics" tells us that it is the study of a *sense* of the beautiful, of the laws governing this *sense*.

(*Aisthanomai* in Greek means "I feel," "I sense"; *uisthēsis* — "feeling," et cetera.)

Moreover, in our time, feeling (I would remind the reader also of this) has been given certain *philosophical* rights. For information on this question one can, by the way, consult Grot's recent article "The Significance of Feeling in Man's Cognition and Activity" (*Moscow Gazette*, January, 1889) and also the works of Astaf'yev: "The Psychological World of Woman," "Feeling as a Moral Principle," et cetera.

Feeling frequently foresees a future intellectual truth, no matter what its category: religious, political, scientific, et cetera. And if feeling is to be given rights that are not only psychological but also *practically* logical, then where is there a better basis for granting these rights than in aesthetics, the study of precisely *a sense* of the beautiful?

The whole point here is whether a somewhat original, say, feeling of some critic or connoisseur or other is normal or abnormal. Is this taste, which in due course may also be acknowledged by many others as normal and even superior, physiological? Is this clairvoyance somewhat of a critical nature and inculcated by some fortunate individual peculiarities, or is it actually a fortuitous and completely exceptional *idiosyncracy* verging perhaps on psychopathy?

What rights are to be given this feeling? *Psychological* ones only, i.e., the kind we acknowledge for a great many of those stupid things that people, even very intelligent ones, constantly do? Or are we to see in it a *presentiment* of clearer and more precise future *truths and logical definitions*?

These problems must not be worked on by anyone with a more or less exceptional feeling just like this one.

He must leave these solutions to others.

Therefore, well aware of the extreme subjectivity of my appraisal, I do not even try carefully to conceal my "I" behind supposedly general views.

I avoid such expressions as "we," "it seems to us," "it is clear to everyone," et cetera.

Who would be deceived by those expedients and "proprieties"?

It seems to me, in such cases, that it is much more modest and proper if one speaks directly in one's own name and for oneself alone.

Let all this even be taken as something in the nature of a personal confession, aesthetic in content.

I am guilty of having offended many in my criticism, perhaps even *the whole Russian literary school of recent times*, for I cannot set it as an everlasting and definitive example. But I *am unable* to feel and think otherwise about it, and I am probably too old to change!

Two more reservations.

In the article offered here, I speak primarily of the two major and longer works of Count Leo Tolstoy (*War and Peace* and *Anna Karenina*); our other well-known and eminent writers I mention everywhere only in passing, *in connection with* the novels of Count Tolstoy, although, for the most part, always with this same purpose of denouncing our predominant *style*.

It was impossible to write about all of them here in detail. That is the way the plan of my work turned out. But I think that my wishes are clear enough so that it will not be difficult to verify my view (by referring to the *style* of other of our writers) and to determine its proper place—in the ranks of truly foolish whims and paradoxes or in those of useful and rather new truths.

My second reservation is as follows: I beg both the editors of *The Russian Herald* and my readers to forgive me for including herewith the chapters that were published more than a year ago in *The Citizen*.

When I saw that my work was growing beyond the dimensions of a daily newspaper, I decided to finish it for a large magazine; but I could not change these introductory chapters. I am unable to write any better about this same subject a second time. There are exceptional cases when one must willy-nilly violate custom.

II

Several years ago one of our eminent writer-scholars, during a friendly chat in which he was discussing the merits of *Anna Karenina*, noted in passing: "He who studies *Anna Karenina* studies life itself."

I think this connoisseur was right, and that this novel is in its way an accomplishment unequaled both in extraordinary truthfulness and in depth of poetry by any other European literature of the nineteenth century. In some respects, it surpasses *War and Peace*.

To study these two great works of Russian literature is extremely interesting and instructive.

Moreover, it is a pleasure.

My literary shortcoming, as I said before, lies in the fact that I am by no means an unconditional admirer of our contemporary Russian school, which has recently won such great world fame. It is new to foreigners and impresses them, primarily by the way in which it differs from the Western literatures with which they have long been acquainted.

Its very content, Russian life itself, with which they are so little acquainted, must be of great interest to them, not to mention the many peculiarities of our artistic style.

As a Russian, I am, of course, glad that we are finally being given our just due in at least one thing. And in order to understand clearly how high we have risen intellectually in the past thirty years, I have only to recall what Turgenev said in the fifties.

As a youth, I was an inordinate admirer of *A Huntsman's Sketches*, and I once asked him why he did not translate them into French himself and publish them in Paris.

He answered: "How can *we* aspire to world significance? It's enough if we are read in Russia."

Now the times have changed. The Russian literary school of a realistic tendency has fulfilled its purpose. From Gogol to Tolstoy inclusive—from the merry *Evenings on a Farm Near Dikan'ka* to the touching *Stories for the People*—our literature has given us many excellent, and several great, works.

And in this same period, between the fantastic idealism of Gogol's early tales and the semireligious spirit of Tolstoy's late stories, it has experienced a great many fluctuations within the bounds of realism—from the very elegant and fragrant works of Turgenev ("Faust," "Spring Freshets," "First Love") to the absurdly coarse sketches of Reshetnikov[1] and Uspensky.[2]

It goes without saying that this contemporary Russian school (from Gogol to Tolstoy) is rich within the bounds of its realism; it is original: its content can even give foreigners a very clear understanding of Russian reality.

For all this, it fully deserves its recent world fame, and we can only wonder at the fact that Western critics and connoisseurs were so late in realizing their error and discovering this literary America.

All this is true; nevertheless, while I am sincerely glad that Europeans have finally had their eyes opened and have begun to esteem and understand what we have long known and esteemed (without even asking their permission), I find that

---

[1] F. M. Reshetnikov (1841–1871), a rather mediocre writer, mainly remembered for his novel about peasant life *The People of Podlipoye*. [Tr.]

[2] G. I. Uspensky (1840–1902), one of the leading Populist writers. [Tr.]

in some respects our school is simply intolerable, even in the person of its greatest representatives.

It is especially intolerable from the standpoint of what can in some instances be directly called language, and in others by a more general term: outward manner or style.

But this dissatisfaction with the general spirit and general style of almost this entire school must not stand in the way of critical fairness or even of certain intellectual biases within the bounds of this not entirely approved school. It is possible (and sometimes even very useful) when one is impelled by a natural aesthetic reaction to prefer indiscriminately to this Russian school of the past half century (from the forties to the nineties) everything that differs from it: Zhukovsky's[1] "Childe Harold" and "Ondine"; *The Lives of the Saints* (in Old Church Slavic) and Voltaire's philosophical novels; Tyutchev's[2] ethereal poems and Barbier's frenzied, revolutionary iambs; Victor Hugo and Goethe; Corneille and Calderon; Eugenia Tur's[3] *Niece* and Marko Vovchok's[4] early stories; George Sand's *Lucrezia Floriani* and the monk Parfeny's[5] *Stories About the Holy Land*; Horace's odes in Fet's translation and *Manon Lescaut*; Sophocles' tragedies and the modern Greek epic songs for children. . . . No matter what the basic content of all the works listed above, no matter what the trend of thoughts, feelings, convictions, and predilections of any of the authors just mentioned, no matter how diverse the manner of these styles and literary schools, they all, nevertheless, contain a certain salutary force for one who grew up on the predominant Russian school of recent years.

[1] V. A. Zhukovsky (1783–1852), a poet, a superb translator, and the first representative of Russian pre-Romanticism. [Tr.]

[2] F. I. Tyutchev (1803–1873), a metaphysical poet. [Tr.]

[3] Pseudonym of Yelizaveta Vasil'yevna Salias de Turnemir (1815–1892), a liberal writer whose early works were admired by Turgenev. [Tr.]

[4] Pseudonym of Marya Vilinskaya-Markovich (1834–1907), a novelist whose books tell mostly of the hard lot of the peasant. [Tr.]

[5] Parfeny (1808?–1878), Abbot of Spaso-Preobrazhensky Monastery. His stories influenced Dostoevsky when the latter was working on *The Brothers Karamazov* and *The Possessed*. [Tr.]

Neither in *The Lives of the Saints*, "Childe Harold," *Lucrezia Floriani*, Voltaire, Goethe, Corneille, nor even in Marko Vovchok or the elder Aksakov[1] is there anyone who incessantly cuts his chops "with his elbows raised high," nor one who is forever looking for "vanity and vanity," or "spinelessness and spinelessness." Nowhere in all the above-named works is an exacting connoisseur jarred by statements such as: "Deep in thought, Manya *began to pace* the room"; or " 'Whoa!' said the coachman, *with the air of an expert examining the hind quarters of a horse whose legs were spread wide apart.*" Nor anything such as: "Potugin *looked down*—then, *grinning, he stepped forward* and answered her silently with a *nod* of the head." After so many years of "pacing," "snorting," "sniffing," "sobbing," "nervous pouring of vodka," and "sputtering in anger" (Dostoevsky's characters, for example, sputter too often—more so than people do in real life), one can rest equally well on all the works mentioned above, whether they be Russian or foreign, old or new.

I, at least, have been finding rest in all these works for a very long time now (since the sixties)—both in those that are Russian, but not of *today*, and in those that are not in the least Russian.

Even if we assume that all this indicates nothing but an aesthetic whim in me, or a surfeit of literary "gastronomy" (and I dare say I would agree with this), still, I am not yet deprived by this whim of the ability to distinguish, *even within the bounds of this Russian school which has bored me so much as a reader and connoisseur*, one author from another, one work from another, true genius from popularity and fame, et cetera. . . .

Although I am not too fond of the general spirit and general style of our school, still, as a contemporary of it and as one who grew up on it, I cannot help testing on myself the strength of its merits in its best and most profound works.

---

[1] S. T. Aksakov (1791–1859), a prose writer mainly remembered for his beautifully written memoirs of life on an estate in Eastern Russia. [Tr.]

And Count Tolstoy not only is no stranger to the common defects of our predominant school, he has even paid generous tribute to these defects during his long literary career.

In some cases, he has been even worse in this regard than many poor writers; he has been more uneven and more unbearable than they in the use of its trivial details. He has been so much more ponderous in these cases that we have been entitled to make strict demands of taste on him.

But from the day of the conception of *War and Peace* and since the time of its creation, he has so immeasurably outgrown (although on this same soil of the uneven and the unnecessary) all his contemporaries in all other good respects that nothing more can be added to the path of truthful and, so to say, perfected realism.

In this field, he cannot be surpassed, for every school of art, like everything in nature, has its limits and saturation point beyond which it cannot go.

This is true to such an extent that upon completing *Anna Karenina* Count Tolstoy himself felt the need to take a different path—that of his stories for the people and his moral sermons.

He probably suspected that he would not write anything better than *War and Peace* or *Anna Karenina* in his old manner, in his old style, and he did not want to write anything worse. I am, of course, not saying here that his new tendency was beneficial or harmful; I am merely saying that he abandoned his earlier style—probably on a brilliant "hunch."

He, too, had become satiated with this almost-fifty-year-old, universal Russian style—finally! Thank heaven!

Moreover, even in Count Tolstoy's recent work, we are justified in distinguishing his moral sermons from his new little stories, in distinguishing his unfortunate attempt to "reform" Christianity and replace the requirements of personal faith with the duties of practical ethics from his fortunate idea of making a complete change in the manner of his narratives.

The first matter—that of his preaching—lies beyond the scope of literary criticism, and when it is a question of style and atmosphere, as it primarily is with me, we can put this preaching completely aside for the time being.

But the matter of such stories as "The Little Candle," "The Three Hermits," "What Men Live By," et cetera, on the contrary, touches directly on the question of outer devices (which, by the way, are of great inner significance), about which I intend to speak in more detail in the chapters that follow. I think that the final change in Count Tolstoy's "manner" came about quite independently of the moralizing tendency of these little stories, or of any specific purpose. The spirit of their content and the plots themselves could have been different. For example, the religious element could have been expressed much more strongly in them than it now is, considering the author's strange inclination toward pure ethics. (I might add in passing that this inclination is strange, precisely in a mind of genius and in our time, after a whole century of fruitless hopes for pure ethics!) Or, on the contrary, given some other mood of the author, the content of these stories, which are exemplary in language and poetic "atmosphere," could have been completely immoral, pagan, sinful, sensual, et cetera.

Here, it is not a question of that; it is not a question of *what* was told, but merely of *how* it was told.

Pushkin's "Stone Guest" is elegant in its simplicity and the great extent of its conciseness. And just as elegant and simple is his handling of Pimen's nocturnal conversation with Grigory in Chudovo Monastery. In the first work, glittering immorality has been consciously raised to the life ideal. But the scene in *Boris Godunov* has an air of austere and, at the same time, fragrant sanctity about it.

Leskov's[1] well-known and splendid little story "The Sealed Angel" is simple, elegant, pure, and free of all "natural" eccen-

[1] N. S. Leskov (1831–1895), a novelist with an unusually broad knowledge of the Russian people and their life. [Tr.]

tricities. At the same time, it is not only completely moral, but also somewhat more *religious* than Count Tolstoy's stories.

Also very elegant and irreproachable in the purity and simplicity of their form are a great many works of earlier French literature which are not in the least didactic in content and tendency (for example, "Frederick and Bernadette" and other stories of Alfred de Musset; they are exceedingly pure and simple in form, but sensuous in content).

That is what I am speaking about.

For me, I repeat, the important thing here is not *what* Count Tolstoy writes about, but *how* he writes it.

What is important is the fact that our most brilliant realist, while still at the height of his creative powers, became bored and disgusted with many of the customary devices of the very school of which he had for so long been the chief representative.

That is a significant sign of the times!

This tendency is noticeable not only in Count Tolstoy, but in many other people as well. It is even very noticeable in our younger writers: in Gnedich,[1] Orlovsky,[2] et cetera.

In these younger men we find ever less and less of those intolerable eccentricities, those turns of expression, and those tricks that our Russian literary school inculcated in all of us from the forties to the eighties.

With Tolstoy, this tendency, this special type of reaction, appeared much earlier than with all the rest (it could already be felt in the Yasnaya Polyana fragments and tiny stories); it appeared earlier and expressed itself more vividly, sharply, and successfully than with all the rest.

III

Count Tolstoy's two chief works, *Anna Karenina* and *War and Peace* not only can but should be compared. In compar-

[1] P. Gnedich (1855–1925), a writer, translator, and art historian. [Tr.]
[2] Pseudonym of V. Vorovsky (1871–1923), a literary critic, revolutionary, and later a Soviet diplomat. [Tr.]

ing their particularities and giving preference in such a detailed examination, first to one and then to the other, we must
admit that the sum of their merits is equal.

In *War and Peace* the task is more noble and the choice
more gratifying; but, for the very reason that in *Anna Karenina* the author was to a greater extent left to his own resources
and no longer aided by the historic grandeur of events provided from without, and so had to choose something for himself from the motley of events flashing by in the contemporary
stream and "fix" what he had chosen with a "lasting idea,"
one wants to give preference to the author of *Karenina* instead
of the author of the national epic.

It goes without saying that *War and Peace* contains more
tragedy and more stunning scenes. Moreover, the very nature
of the tragedy is better. In the epic, people are fighting for
their native land (this is true on both sides, for the French
are waging offensive wars for the predominance of France,
for the benefit of their native land). In the contemporary
novel, the warfare of the Russian "volunteers" on the side of
Serbia takes place only in the distance and is unconditionally
condemned by the author. There are two attempts at suicide
(successful and unsuccessful), and there are thoughts of suicide on the part of Levin. It is incomparably more somber,
and even more vulgar; however, Count Tolstoy is not to blame
here, but contemporary life. This, too, was provided from
without, just as the conflagration of Moscow and the Battle
of Borodino were provided from without in *War and Peace*.
It is even difficult to write a long, truthful, and interesting
novel about contemporary Russian life without including in it
at least some thoughts of suicide, so common has it unfortunately become in our life.

At any rate, the great merit of *War and Peace* is the fact
that its tragedy is sober and healthy, not ugly, as in the case
of so many of our other writers. It is not what we find in
Dostoevsky—the tragedy of flophouses, brothels, and what

almost amounts to the Preobrazhensky Hospital.[1] The tragedy
in *War and Peace* is wholesome: it inspires one to military
heroism for one's homeland. But Dostoevsky's tragedy can
probably only inspire some sort of psychopaths living about in
poorly furnished rooms.

And even in *Anna Karenina* Vronsky's attempted suicide
and Anna's real one drown in such an abundance of health,
strength, physical beauty, luster, peace, and mirth that they
cannot too deeply offend the heart and taste of the normal
reader.

In both novels, the incredible subtlety of Tolstoy's mind
could not kill his sense of the healthy, or, let us say, his
"flair."

The author's historical service, or more precisely his direct
political service in *War and Peace*, is enormous. Did many
people in our country think about the year 1812 before he
so splendidly and unforgettably reminded them of it? Very
few! And although the Count rather "tendentiously" and theo-
philanthropically condemns war—now in his own person, now
through the mouth of the good but eternally distracted
Pierre—he is so truthful an artist that it is very easy for the
reader not to listen either to him or to Pierre and to go on
regarding war as one of the highest, one of the ideal manifestations of life on earth, despite all the personal misfortunes
it brings. (These misfortunes, let us note incidentally, are
accompanied for many by special joys that peace never provides!)

And in our age, when the craze for "universal utilitarian
bliss" is far from cured, that is a great political service!

Now I shall say why I preferred above to say a "political"
service instead of an "historical" one. By the expression "a
writer's historical service" is understood a service having to
do with precision and accuracy of depiction rather than with

---

[1] A poorhouse in Moscow sponsored by the Fedoseyevtsy, a splinter
group of the Old Believers. [Tr.]

a strong and useful influence. That is why. How accurate the depiction of the period is in *War and Peace* is not easy to decide; but it is easy to acknowledge that this depiction leaves a deep patriotic imprint on the reader's soul. Given our tendency always to suspect something wrong in ourselves and to see the poor and weak, rather than the good and strong, in all that we have, Count Tolstoy's outermost devices—at one time subtle and captious to the point of artificiality, at another to the point of crudeness—are very useful. Had all this been written in a somewhat more ideal, simple, and general style, we probably would not believe it. But when the Russian reader sees that Count Tolstoy is even more attentive and captious than himself, when this disciple of the "Gogolian" and "semi-Gogolian" period sees that with Lev Nikolayevich, one hero (a real hero) begins to snuffle, another breaks out sobbing, another sets up a squeal; that one hero becomes frightened, a second intrigues, a third is an out-and-out scoundrel (he does, however, die for his country—young Kuragin, for example)—when this eternally wavering Russian reader notices that Count Tolstoy ridicules almost all his characters a little (all of them, I believe, except Tsar Alexander Pavlovich, Andrey Bolkonsky, and, for some reason or other, the malicious Dolokhov), then he, too, this reader is more inclined to believe everything that is good, lofty, and ideal.

The Russian reader of our time (particularly if he is from the middle of the social scale) wants more than the kind of realism that says: this person is weak, that one, insidious; one person is cruel, another, ridiculous, tactless, pitiful, et cetera. That, too, I suppose, is temperate and truthful realism; we are all weak and sinful; but, as I say, that is not enough for us. We must have someone snuffle, et cetera. It doesn't matter if the reader himself by no means so frequently notices people in real life spitting in anger, snuffling, et cetera. But his "coryphaei" have trained him so that on mention of a wart, he is more inclined to believe in nobility, on mention of snuffling, he is more inclined to sympathize with a character's love, et cetera; and if at the same time, someone "pours himself a glass of vodka with a nervous movement of the hand," and then instead of smiling, "grins," his confidence will be complete!

In my eyes—I am ready to confess—all this is a great shortcoming more or less common to all Russian novels and stories, beginning with *Dead Souls* (where it still answers the purpose), almost down to Count Tolstoy's "What Men Live By" (where, thank heaven, it does not exist at all). Perhaps only our talented female writers such as Eugenia Tur, Marko Vovchok, and "Kokhanovskaya"[1] have rid themselves of it. I remember what a sign of relief I gave as far back as 1860 when I first heard the pleasant, musical, and fragrant (although tendentiously liberal) language of Marko Vovchok. It was about the same thing, but somehow it was different!

"I am so depraved, Felitsa, in my aesthetics"—but unlike Derzhavin,[2] I cannot go on and say: "But the whole world is like me." On the contrary! Who is at fault, I or our best writers and the public? I don't know. Even if my "ladylike" tastes on this score are wrong, I have not renounced them over a period of thirty years,[3] and, of course, I am not going to renounce them now.

But Count Tolstoy is right all the same; I realize it. He is right in two respects: first, because for a long time he felt an indominitable need to observe in this way and no other and to express himself in this way and no other; he could not shift to the simple and pure style of his late tales for the people without first having had his fill of all those bumps and prickles

---

[1] Pseudonym of Nadezhda Stepanovna Sokhanskaya (1825–1884). Her stories and plays mainly depict the life of the petty nobility. [Tr.]

[2] G. R. Derzhavin (1743–1816), the greatest Russian poet of the eighteenth century. The line is from his well-known ode to Catherine the Great. [Tr.]

[3] See *Notes of the Fatherland* (March, 1861) for my early article on the works of Marko Vovchok; it is in the same spirit.

of the Natural School, without having far outdone the others (Turgenev, for example), even in this sphere of rather crude excess. Without having served one style to satiety, an artist finds it difficult, and perhaps even impossible, to set out on a new path.

Second, Count Tolstoy is also right, because, and I repeat, he has consciously or unconsciously done his readers a patriotic service with all those little outward debasements of life; they like that, and because of it, are more ready to believe in what is lofty and are more deeply impressed by what is elegant in his work.

I V

When, according to P. Boborykin, Turgenev so nobly and judiciously said that his own talent could not be compared to Tolstoy's, and that "Lyovushka Tolstoy is an elephant," it seems to me that he was at that moment thinking particularly of *War and Peace*. It is indeed an elephant! Or, if you wish something more monstrous, it is an excavated Sivatherium in the flesh—the Sivatherium, whose huge skulls are kept in India in temples of the god Siva. The trunk, the huge body, the tusks (besides tusks, there are also horns) all run contrary to every zoological rule of propriety.

Or one might also liken *War and Peace* to an Indian idol: three heads, or four faces, and six arms! The proportions are enormous, the material is precious, and the eyes are of rubies and diamonds, not only below the brow, but on it as well! !

The general plan is sustained, and there is an inexhaustible supply of details, even to the point of ponderosity; there are four heroines of almost equal importance (in the eyes of both the author and the reader) and three heroes (Natasha, Marya, Sonya, Yelena, Bezukhov, Bolkonsky, and Rostov). In the majority of instances, the psychological analysis is striking, precisely because the most diverse people are subjected to it: Napoleon, when sick at Borodino; the peasant girl who witnesses the council meeting at Fili; Natasha and Kutuzov; Pierre and Prince Andrey; Princess Marya and the modest Captain Tushin; Nikolay Bolkonsky and both of the Rostov brothers. Let us note here in passing that there is a marked difference between these two brothers, Nikolay and Petya, in their first encounter with combat danger: Nikolay, who later proves to be a brave and trustworthy officer, is timid and frightened in his first battle; the sixteen-year-old Petya, not in the least. I noticed this difference in my first reading of the novel and wondered if it was merely because the author did not want to repeat himself or if there was a physiological reason for it in the characters themselves. And I found that there is. Petya is more imaginative and enthusiastic—Nikolay, more obtuse and far more staid; if the young man is not a complete coward by nature, it is because his vivid imagination, which is militarily inclined, can so possess him that he does not even think of his own safety. His heroic imagination stifles his natural sense of fear. But Nikolay's imagination is weak and cannot take the place of habit; he must first come under fire. One can make a great many such observations.

Which of our writers has described small but bloody battles so well, so excitingly, so fearfully, so Homerically, and at the same time, so modernly? Gogol in *Taras Bul 'ba*? Yes, but that is only Homeric, not modern. We cannot live the thoughts and emotions of those crude and distant people as we can live the thoughts and emotions of the civilian Pierre, the energetic idealist Andrey, and the ordinary but good Russian officer Nikolay Rostov.

And on the other hand, who in our time has so beautifully, so subtly, and, as it were, so fragrantly depicted scenes from the life of high society? For example, the ball in the presence of the Tsar, where the rejuvenated widower Bolkonsky, dressed in a white uniform, dances with Natasha, who is mad with success, and where at every turn of the waltz, Yelena Bezukhov's velvet dress spreads out and seems to flash as she whirls around?

In which other writer can we find this? Only in Markevich[1]—in his *Quarter of a Century* and *Crisis*. But even here the way was first paved by Tolstoy (without a hint of negation).

Both in the depiction of this ball in St. Petersburg and later in the description of the one in Moscow in *Anna Karenina* (the ball at which Anna unexpectedly takes Vronsky away from Kitty), as well as in the scene of the courtiers' steeplechase (again in the second novel), we see only the poetry of truth, and are unable to find even a hint of negation, derision, or malevolence, as we always see in Turgenev when he crosses the threshold of a true drawing room; he never even dared enter a large ballroom with complete freedom and impartiality, as Tolstoy or Markevich did. Or, as a third example of the unusual breadth and wealth of content of *War and Peace*, let us take the author's treatment of religious feeling. Of the leading characters in the novel, there are, strictly speaking, but three genuinely religious Orthodox people from the upper classes: old Kutuzov; Nikolay Rostov, at times, and Princess Marya, always. For the time being, I shall leave both Nikolay and the Tsar aside and compare in this connection Princess Marya with Liza Kalitina from *A Nest of Gentlefolk*. Liza is, of course, the most charming and noble of Turgenev's heroines; her pure and saintly image will remain an everlasting adornment of our literature; but, nevertheless, even in this connection, we must again give Tolstoy preference in the matter of creativity, and once again render Turgenev moral honor for the impartiality of his opinion: "Tolstoy is an elephant." (It is well known that an elephant's trunk can easily lift a large log and cast it aside, as well as carefully remove a butterfly from a flower.)

We know that Liza Kalitina believes in and fears God. She

---

[1] Boleslav Markevich (1822–1884), a reactionary novelist. [Tr.]

says to Lavretsky: "We shall all die." We know her nurse's
stories about martyrs in whose blood flowers bloomed. We
remember with tender emotion little Liza's question about that
holy blood and those miraculous flowers: "Were they wall-
flowers?" We feel exactly what the noble Lavretsky feels
when she, now a nun, walks past him from one choir loft to
another with bowed head. We are grateful to Turgenev that
in this instance he did not analyze anything, but only said that
there are situations in life where one should not go into detail;
one should "merely point them out and pass on." I have not
forgotten those words, and I am writing them now from
memory; but when I think of them, even now, after twenty-
eight years, I feel like crying. But—(again this "but," always
in Tolstoy's favor—what can one do?) we see everything about
Liza from the outside only. We see her as Lavretsky saw her,
for Turgenev almost always analyzes the soul of only one of
his leading characters, the one whose psychological make-up
most clearly resembles his own. But Tolstoy's analysis knows
no obstacles—neither in a person's temperament, age, nor
sex—not even in zoological differences; for a moment he even
shows us the feelings of a bull, the thoughts of a dog, the
pondering of a horse. One perhaps notices only that nationality
can resist him more than anything else, for he analyzes the
French in *War and Peace* much less successfully than his
compatriots. For example, we see nothing human in Napoleon—only pride, cruelty, and vanity. Is that really the way
it was?

We see Liza Kalitina through Lavretsky's eyes, but we are
better acquainted with the piety of Princess Marya, because,
together with the author, we frequently penetrate the very
depths of her soul. We not only see the purity of her Orthodox principles, but are sometimes present even during the
inner struggle of her thoughts and feelings. When the young
Kuragin comes to Bleak Hills to seek her hand in marriage,
her sister-in-law, Princess Liza, and her companion, Mlle.
Bourienne, dress her up in all her finery, but they do not suc-

ceed in making her any more beautiful; on the contrary, she looks even worse:

> Princess Marya was left alone. She did not comply with Liza's wish. She not only left her hair as it was, but did not even glance at herself in the mirror. She let her arms fall helplessly, lowered her eyes, and sat silently and thought. She imagined a husband, a man who was a strong, dominant, and strangely attractive being, who suddenly transferred her into a completely different world of his own. . . .
> [They call her to tea.]
> She roused herself and was horrified at what she had been thinking. And before going downstairs, she got up, went into the room where the icons were, and turned her eyes to the dark face of the Savior on a large icon illuminated by an icon-lamp; she stood in front of it for several minutes with folded hands. In Princess Marya's heart, there was tormenting doubt. Was the joy of love, an earthly love for a man, possible for her? In her thoughts of marriage, Princess Marya had dreamed of domestic happiness and children, but her strongest, most deeply hidden longing was for an earthly love. The more she tried to conceal this feeling from others and even from herself, the stronger it became. "My God," she said, "how am I to renounce forever these evil thoughts in order calmly to do Thy will?" She had scarcely asked this question when God answered her in her own heart. "Desire nothing for yourself, seek nothing, be not anxious or envious. The future of mankind and your own fate must be unknown to you; but live so you are ready for anything. If it be God's will to test you with the obligations of marriage, be ready to do His will." With this comforting thought (but yet with a hope for the realization of her forbidden earthly longing), Princess Marya sighed, crossed herself, and went downstairs, not thinking of her dress, of how she would enter, or of what she would say. What could all this matter in comparison with the predetermination of God, without Whose will not a hair can fall from a person's head?

Count Tolstoy can depict with equal success not only different kinds of passionate feelings, but also the thought processes in people of different religious beliefs. Let us recall, merely for comparison with the Princess's train of genuine Orthodox thought, those poetic and nebulous visions of a sort of philanthropic pantheism which her gifted and unfortunate brother sees as he is dying.

And that is by no means all! What contrasts there are: the conflagration of Moscow and the children's games—the charming inventions of the children of the good Rostov family; the couples—so dissimilar, but of equal interest to us; the frosts in the fields and balls in the palaces; emperors and bast-shoe-clad peasants; hunts in the country; carousals in the army; the chitchat of soldiers! Chastity and sensuality are expressed with equal truth. The stout and decrepit warrior Kutuzov is seen praying at one time, using cunning at another, crying at another, and on the eve of Borodino calmly reading a French novel to himself and joking with the priest's wife. And by doing practically nothing, he achieves all. It is amazing!

And still another of the author's original habits: he stops both the course of the action and the working of his outward observation, sometimes for a long stretch, and then, as it were, suddenly throws the doors of the human soul wide open before the reader; thereupon, he places before the reader's eyes (at times almost forcibly) a sort of psychological microscope of his own making and plunges him into a world of fantasy—at one time in a full state of wakefulness, at another in a semisleep, at another in a deep sleep; at one time in the heat of battle, and at another on the bed of a person dying a slow and gently pacifying death.

Even this philosophy of fatalism is inserted in the story in large, whole pieces, contrary to all accepted practice. And finally there is the patently philanthropic tendency which reveals itself ever more and more clearly as we approach the end of this strange, unique, and great epic.

It is possible not to sympathize with this tendency; it is necessary even to be able to distinguish it sharply from true Christianity, but it is impossible not to marvel at the originality

The Novels of Count L. N. Tolstoy 251

and daring of an author who was not afraid of the customary reproaches for irrelevant philosophizing.

v

Somewhat earlier, I spoke of the choice of period and said that it is an equally laudable achievement to depict so splendidly the year 1812, a time of national triumph, or to depict with unprecedented impartiality, subtlety, and depth the life of the people of the upper class, our contemporaries. Now I want to speak not of the choice of period, but of the extent to which the general atmosphere of these two depictions is true and appropriate to the spirit of the periods themselves.

A sense of this "spirit" and this "atmosphere" is one of the most difficult to express in words and at the same time it is one of our strongest feelings. Facts and major events can be conveyed quite truthfully and accurately. The people of a certain period and a certain locale will in the majority of cases act in a book exactly as they did in real life; but with one writer, the general air, so to say, will be true to the time and place, and with another, false or less true. This difference can sometimes be found in two different works of one and the same author.

This difference sometimes occurs, for example, because of the kind of language with which the various events and the adventure of the characters are told, because of the kind of expressions used to convey the characters' emotions, et cetera. It sometimes even seems to me that precisely on this completely external device also depends that subtle, but striking, "color" or "aroma" of the time, place, and milieu about which I am speaking, that psychological music common to the entire work, which I am pointing out. For complete illusion, for complete satisfaction, I need more than what is told me: also important to me is how this has been narrated and even by whom—by the author himself, for example, or a person of the period, place, nation, faith, and class that the author is depicting. In the latter case, given a felicitous device, it is much easier to preserve the illusion than in the former, where the author tells in his own name of an environment other than his own. However, some writers are so successful in capturing the spirit of an alien environment that even a story told directly in their own name remains true to this spirit, true not only in theme and content, not only in the main trend of thought, but also in style, language, and, in general, those external devices that correspond perfectly to the inner psychological make-up of the person being depicted.

Two people have told us about the Pugachov Rebellion: Pushkin, through the character Grinyov,[1] a man of the period, and Count Salias[2] in his own name. It is quite possible that Count Salias had in his hands many more documents and other sources than Pushkin had. (I do not know if he did, but I can assume so.) Perhaps he had also heard more stories about it than Pushkin. Count Salias's imagination, well experienced from three whole decades of fastidious and insatiable observation, ponderous in its subleties—for that is the way it was in all his principal and best predecessors—this imagination could not content itself with the lofty and pure "water-color" method preferred by Pushkin's sober genius. Thus, the author of *The Pugachov Rebels* gave us a great many details, which are perhaps accurate (I do not know) and perhaps only very picturesque and vivid, both about the daily life of the eighteenth-century nobility and about the brutal atrocities that our Russian "God-bearing people"[3] can give way to when the government's scourge is not raised over its head! All this is most picturesque and most detailed; all of it is plausible, and perhaps even very true and precise. As for the last phrase, as I said before, I do not know.

---

[1] In *The Captain's Daughter*. [Tr.]

[2] Count Evgeny Salias de Turnemir (1840–1908), a second-rate writer of historical novels. [Tr.]

[3] According to the Slavophiles, the Russian people bore God in their hearts and were carrying out His mission. [Tr.]

For example, I recall something like this: After deciding
to raise the rebellion, Pugachov gallops with a comrade at
breakneck speed across the steppe and shouts with savage
joy: "Watch out, Moscow! I'll get you in the guts!" [*Derzhis',
Moskva! Vdaryu pod zhilki!*] I believe it was something like
that—I do not have the book with me now. . . . But here is
the trouble: this mimicry and sound imitation, which have
bored us to death for so many years, convey less of the eighteenth-century atmosphere than does the pure, simple, and
brief story of the early landed nobility in *The Captain's Daughter*. In reading Pushkin, you sincerely believe that this was
written by Grinyov, a man who had personally witnessed it
all; in reading Count Salias, you simply feel like closing the
book and saying: "I know all that!" (*"Vashe skorodie!"*[1]
"Tp-rru"[2]—said to a horse—and so on.) We have long been
familiar with the rather awkward details in Turgenev (especially in his early works) and in so very many other writers,
unfortunately, not excluding even Count Tolstoy himself! (For
example, *"Vasyaso,"* for *"Vashe siyatel'stvo"*[3] in "A Young
Landowner's Morning," or *"Ozhig-zhig-zhig,"* to indicate a
sword being sharpened in *War and Peace*.)

Grinyov's story conveys the atmosphere of the eighteenth
century, but Count Salias's *Pugachov Rebels* smacks of the
sixties and seventies of our time.

From excessive detail, captiousness, and even subtlety of
observation, it turns out crude.

One can experience the very same feeling in comparing
two short tales of folk life by Count Tolstoy himself: one
old, the other new. His new stories—those written after *Anna
Karenina*—are, in this sense (in the sense of conveying folk
spirit), incomparably superior and more truthful, not to mention the fact that they are much more elegant. I beg you not

[1] "Your Worship." The correct Russian form is *"Vashe vysoko-
blagorodie."* [Tr.]
[2] "Whoa!" The regular form is *"Tpru."* [Tr.]
[3] "Your Excellency." [Tr.]

take my word for it, but to go to the trouble of glancing over at least the beginning of the brightly colored, highly ornamented, and wooden "Polikushka" and the beginning of the pale, noble, and porcelain "A Spark Neglected Burns the House," "What Men Live By," or the Arabian story "The Devil Is Pliable, but God Stands Strong."

Of course, in the latter stories, there is incomparably more folk atmosphere than in "Polikushka." If one were to imagine a kind and intelligent peasant of the time setting out to tell the touching (in content) story of Polikushka, one would, of course, expect him to tell it more as Count Tolstoy told of the angel appearing to the shoemaker ("Where Love Is, God Is") or of the inextinguishable candle ("The Little Candle") than as follows:

> The carriage was harnessed, but the driver tarried—he had gone into the coachmen's hut. In the hut, it was hot, stuffy, dark, and oppressive, and it smelled strongly of freshly baked bread, cabbage, and sheepskin. Several coachmen were in the room; the cook was busy at the stove. On the bed over the stove, a sick man was lying on some sheepskins.
>
> "Uncle Khvyodor! Hey, Uncle Khvyodor!" said the young coachman . . . (et cetera).
>
> "Whatcha want Fed'ka for, you windbag?" asked one of the drivers. (From "Three Deaths" by Count Tolstoy.)

("Vdaryu pod zhilki," "ozhig-zhig-zhig," "Vashe skorodie," and "Vasyaso," et cetera.) The distance between all this and "Tolda-kolda"[1] is far less than the distance between the sublime and the ridiculous!

In this connection, I recall a superb critical article on Nekrasov's poetry by Eugene Markov.[2] The article, by virtue of the sum total of its merits, and by virtue of the inimitable

---

[1] A dialectal pronunciation of the Russian words "togda-kogda" ("when"). [Tr.]

[2] E. L. Markov (1835–1903), a writer of rural novels somewhat in the style of Turgenev. [Tr.]

accuracy of its critical comments (highly unfavorable to Nekrasov), is in its way just such an accomplishment as Belinsky's article on Pushkin. In my opinion, after Belinsky's article on Pushkin there is little new or important that one can say about the nature of Pushkin's genius (as a matter of fact, nothing new was said at the celebration in 1880).[1] And after Eugene Markov's article there is almost nothing strictly truthful that can be said about Nekrasov's bungling and insincere talent. After speaking contemptuously of Nekrasov's trivial satire and contrasting the truly great satirists with him, Eugene Markov goes on to contrast genuine folk poems and songs with his pseudofolk poetastering and to point out that the former are always tender and pleasant, and that a ray of conciliation shines through their affection.

And it is true that if instead of this St. Petersburg editor, corrupted by fashionable spite and the bad habits of the "Natural School," the cattle dealer Koltsov[2] had taken it into his head to write a touching poem about "Frost, the Red Nose," and had written his "Daryushka"[3] differently from Nekrasov's, people *with straightforward feeling and unspoiled taste* would have regretted it. And there would have been a world of genuine poetry in Koltsov's work.

Or if some common girl, a bourgeoise or a housemaid—one who does not as yet say *"obyazatel'no"* ("definitely") or *"bezrazlichno"* ("it's all the same to me")—if such an intelligent, but not as yet "cultured," girl wanted to tell us something about herself or her friend—her story would remind us more of Marko Vovchok's charming early stories than of Turgenev's *Huntsman's Sketches*; more of Count Tolstoy's late stories than his early ones. She would be more likely to begin:

[1] In connection with the dedication of the Pushkin monument in Moscow. [Tr.]

[2] A. V. Koltsov (1809–1842), a self-taught poet whose simple poems deal with the life of the peasants. [Tr.]

[3] The leading character in Nekrasov's poem "Frost, the Red Nose." [Tr.]

"I come from far away; I hardly remember my birthplace—
they took me away from there when I was six. All I remember
is a long street and a row of smoky huts. There were two
birch trees at the end of the street, in the pasture." (M. Vovchok, "The Little Toy.")

She would be less likely to begin:

"In a rich village, very important for its holdings of land
and serfs, a daughter was born to a cowherd. This event,
which, as a matter of fact, was quite insignificant, did, however, have . . ., et cetera. ("The Village," one of Grigorovich's[1]
stories from the forties.)

That is what I shall permit myself to call the "atmosphere"
of the period or milieu, or the lack of it.

Not only *what* was told, but also *how* it was told. By what
outer devices was it communicated to me? That is the question.

And if I turn with similar demands to both of Tolstoy's
outstanding novels, I shall find, despite the great merits of
War and Peace, that *Anna Karenina* has its advantages, precisely from the standpoint of good and healthy realism.

If I ask myself: "Is the outer work in *War and Peace* as
pure as that in *Anna Karenina?*"

I want to say: "No, it is not as pure."

"Is the psychological analysis as precise and mature in the
semiepic, semichronicle *War and Peace* as it is in the contemporary novel?"

"No, it is not as precise and mature."

"Is the general atmosphere of *War and Peace* as true to
the style and spirit of the life of 1812 as the atmosphere of
Anna Karenina is true to the style and spirit of our time?"

"It seems to me that it isn't."

And finally:

---

[1] D. V. Grigorovich (1822–1900), a sentimental realist who took his
subjects from peasant life. It was he who introduced the young Dostoevsky to Belinsky. [Tr.]

"Can one say of *War and Peace* what the Russian connoisseur, whose words I quoted above, said of *Anna Karenina*: namely, that from the second novel, 'One can study life itself'?" I think not.

V I

First about analysis.

When it was necessary in *Anna Karenina* to make Vronsky—that proud, stable, and calmly self-assured man, who is endowed with all the blessings of this world—suddenly attempt suicide, Count Tolstoy realized that Vronsky's passion for Anna and certain external obstacles were not enough. First it was necessary to humiliate him in his own eyes, at least slightly. But how to achieve this? Another man would not be able to humiliate him deliberately; Vronsky would kill him, or would himself be killed in the fight, but he would never let himself be humiliated in his own eyes by an adversary, as almost all Turgenev's weak-willed heroes are humiliated, or as Tolstoy's energetic and brave, but tactless, shy, and socially awkward Levin is frequently, if not humiliated, at least thrown into confusion. Vronsky is not like that. How then to overcome him? Into what unusual, but at the same time natural, circumstances could he be placed so as to lose his "moral balance"? Count Tolstoy found those circumstances. Vronsky's loved one, as she is supposedly dying, humiliates him before the ugly, old, and prosaic Karenin. Let us also recall that a short time earlier, as if on purpose, Vronsky had misgivings about himself for the first time in his life. He felt a dislike for himself as a result of his acquaintance with a foreign prince. The prince had annoyed him with his subtle and profound arrogance, and in the unpleasant features of this high-ranking foreigner, Vronsky saw, as if through a magnifying glass, his own features, and exclaimed: "The stupid ox! Is it possible that I'm like that?"

And then when Anna subsequently makes him ask Karenin's forgiveness, he shoots himself with no great struggle. "For about two minutes he stood motionless with the revolver in his hands, with lowered head and an expression of a strained effort of thought. 'Of course,' he said to himself," et cetera.

What truth! Vronsky was so unaccustomed to humiliation and self-criticism that even this was enough for him.

Everyone knows that people who are accustomed to insults and sorrow do not attempt suicide as readily as those who are unaccustomed to such things. For example, the young (at least in our time) decide on suicide more often than the old. Even in newspaper accounts, one frequently finds great surprise expressed over the fact that "as it was, the suicide was old."

This particular kind of psychological preparation for Vronsky's attempt at suicide is so astonishingly true, and at the same time it is original. It is such a true tour de force of talent that one can perhaps regard it as being of purely scientific value.

I can provide still another example here, equal to this one, but by no means similar. It has to do with the mushroom that prevents Sergey Ivanovich Koznyshov from asking Varenka to marry him. Just as he is about to declare his love for her, she finds a large mushroom and disrupts not so much his thoughts as his emotions. Also, the children come running up at the wrong moment. It is precisely his emotions that are disrupted, for the thoughts of a man accustomed to public debate could not be disrupted by such nonsense. But the mushroom and the children's shouting are enough to dampen the new and comparatively weak rational love in this sedate, bookish man, who had long ago become settled in his excellent social position. In an instant, the drop of fervent emotion ready to emerge from the vessel of his soul, now filled to overflowing with the poetry of village life and with this charming encounter with a "suitable" girl, grows cold. It grows cold, this drop, and immediately his experienced reason says to itself: "What is the purpose of this? Of course, it is all very attractive, but . . . wouldn't it be more sensible to live out my life as a bachelor?"

And not another word.

This touch of psychological analysis is enough to prepare Vronsky for a pistol shot in the chest! It is a touch that is also original, and at the same time completely individual and precise. The mushroom would not have deterred Vronsky, who despite all his apparent reserve is passionate and decisive; nor Prince Oblonsky, a frivolous and amorous epicurean; nor Levin, who it is true wavers, but who at the same time is highly impetuous. It just might disrupt Levin's *thoughts* for a whole day, but under no circumstances would it disrupt his *feelings* for good.

To the number of such surprisingly beautiful, subtle, and true observations, by the way, also belongs the passage where Vronsky, as he pensively and distractedly gets into his carriage to go to the races, momentarily admires some "whirling columns of gnats."

Let us recall that at this time he is both happy and agitated. Anna has just told him that she is carrying his child. For the first time, a much more serious, perhaps even tragic element, or at any rate a vague fear of something severe and dangerous, has been added to their love and passion, which hitherto was only pleasant.

Eneregtic people, when carried away by passion, if they are not yet wearied by the life struggle, are not frightened by such a serious tinge in their emotions or by such hints by life at the possibility of tragedy; they are only more greatly aroused and are inclined to even greater firmness and determination. But no matter how firm and calm a person may outwardly be (that is, in his meetings and dealings with other people), this agitation does not appear in him for nothing; in such moments, every person inwardly, when alone with himself, is not exactly the same as he usually is. Vronsky is by no means a dreamer; he is not in the least inclined to ponder over anything for very long, to let himself be distracted, et cetera. Moreover, he is hurrying to the races. And suddenly, instead of simply getting into the carriage, he stares at "gnats swarming in the sun." I must admit that on reading this for the first time I thought it was one of Tolstoy's descriptive remarks that lead to nothing—analysis for analysis' sake, an observation for observation's sake. "It sometimes happens that a person suddenly stares in wonderment at gnats." But on reading farther, I soon repented and honored the author with the sincerest enthusiasm possible. I shan't dwell here on the superb description of the officers' races; I hope that everyone very well remembers how many factors converged at that one time to destroy in Vronsky's soul precisely the composure which, according to the English trainer, he needed to defeat Makhotin: the news of Anna's pregnancy, the presence of the Sovereign and the entire court, the presence of Anna and her husband, the unpleasant remarks of his brother, his sportsman's feelings in themselves, and, at the very bottom of his heart, a certain tendency to unaccustomed contemplation, to fanciful distraction, a tendency at not quite an opportune moment to stare at gnats. And then Vronsky, again in a moment of distraction, through a false and clumsy movement, breaks the back of his favorite horse!

When I reached the point where Frou-Frou falls, I understood the full significance of those "gnats in the sun." Precisely for Vronsky. I might also note in connection with these same gnats, another profound touch, another subtle but very strong connection: Vronsky is something of a painter by nature, and when in Italy, he even tries, although unsuccessfully, to engage in serious painting.

In Anna's preparations for suicide, which, on the whole, are superbly depicted, there are also two particularly significant details that determine everything that happens later. One is the opinion loudly expressed in the railway carriage, in

Anna's presence, by an unknown lady (a lady whose person, let us note, Anna found very unpleasant): "Man has been given reason to rid himself of what bothers him." The other is the fact that Anna quickly and irrevocably decides on suicide only when a peasant working near the tracks reminds her momentarily of the entire past, beginning with the workman who was crushed on the rails during her first meeting with Vronsky.

Prior to the unpleasant lady's remark and prior to the moment she saw the workman, Anna herself probably did not know what she would do.

Of course, Anna had often heard the opinion that "reason will provide a way out"; but it is a common psychological law that a most infallible and ancient idea, or, on the contrary, a most clever and recent idea, has a strong effect on us and influences our actions only when we are prepared by our emotions for its perception.

Our emotions are prepared; another person's idea has a strong effect on us, and our will carries this idea out.

The hackneyed idea expressed by chance, but at an opportune moment, by the unpleasant lady had an intellectual or rational, so to say, influence on Anna's decision, which was prepared by her emotions. The sight of the worker later on acted instantaneously, almost like something mystical, on her imagination and will.

It is amazing!

In Anna's preliminary deliberations, there is still another very touching and true observation: She sees a sign: "*Tyut'kin coiffeur. Je me fais coiffer par Tyut'kin.*"

"'I'll tell him about that,' and she smiled; but at that very moment she recalled that now she had no one to whom she could tell something funny."

A momentary flash of something funny, cheerful, and good-natured in the midst of all the horrors of mental confusion. That often happens, particularly with people of a lively disposition. In the most brutal moments of life, there comes to mind some amusing and cheerful bit of nonsense. But this true and subtle observation has no connection with any future action. And I intentionally introduced it here for contrast only, in order better to explain my views on the different kinds of analysis in Tolstoy and their relative merit.

It is also interesting to compare both preparations for suicide: those of Vronsky and those of Anna.

Both these people have, of course, been led to this act by a whole series of inner processes and outer stimuli. But, nevertheless, there is a great difference. Vronsky is stronger of will and firmer. He knows in advance what he wants. Anna is more impressionable, active, and timid; up to the last minute before her encounter with the workman, she does not yet know what she will do. Vronsky's decision depends primarily on his own careful and ponderous reasoning; he thinks his decision over alone in his room. There are no outer stimuli, no outside opinions, no chance or decisive meetings. He thinks it over; he says to himself: "Of course!"—and he fires the shot.

Anna leaves the house without any plan or decision; her decision is made almost instinctively, under the influence of chance impressions. "And suddenly, as she recalled the man who was crushed on the day of her first meeting with Vronsky, she realized what she must do."

I do not know in which other writer or where else we can find personal variations on one and the same psychological theme which are so strikingly true to life.

It seems in no other writer in the world.

VII

To the sphere of psychological analysis also belong all those passages in Tolstoy's novels where his characters see and hear something during sleep or the semisleep of dozing and awakening, or where they think something during a state of semiconsciousness resulting from sickness or premortal exhaustion. Or finally, when they are fully awake and fully conscious and imagine something semifantastic.

All the author's chief instances of a physically sick and premortal psychology fall to the lot of Prince Andrey Bolkonsky.

When first wounded in the head at Austerlitz, Prince Andrey lies on the battlefield and looks at the sky—"distant, lofty, and infinite." Napoleon rides up, notices him lying on his back with the broken flagstaff at his side, and says: "That is a splendid way to die!"

Bolkonsky knows this is Napoleon, whom he had previously esteemed very highly. "But at that moment, Napoleon seemed a small, insignificant man, compared to what was now taking place between his soul and that lofty, infinite sky, with clouds hurrying across it," et cetera. "He only wanted these people [who had ridden up] to help him and to bring him back to life, which seemed so splendid to him: because now he had a completely different understanding of it," et cetera.

Excellent! But I shall take the liberty here merely to note in passing: first of all, isn't all this too clear and conscious for just such a head wound? And, in general, doesn't Count Tolstoy sometimes destroy a certain perspective when depicting our inner processes? Isn't he too bold (from the standpoint of realistic precision) in presenting to our mind's eye strong and well-defined feelings on one and the same level and to one and the same extent as short-lived and barely perceptible ones? Sharp, clear thoughts as well as those that are vague and which hardly deserve even to be called thoughts? When I read descriptions like the one just cited (where a man with an injured head, a man who is barely alive and who cannot say a single word properly, begins, while lying on his back and looking off into the infinite sky, to renounce military heroism and to construct a new theory of a splendid and humane life, when all this could no more than have flashed across his mind in the vaguest possible way, in such a way that he would never even recall it afterwards)—when I read that passage, I immediately think of a draftsman in a dissecting room who, while drawing from a specimen of some body tissue or other visible to the naked eye (for example, skin on the arm), takes it into his head to show the skin sliced away in several places, and in these openings or little wounds, he shows, on the very same scale and on the very same plane as all the rest, the tiniest cells and finest fibers visible only with the most powerful microscope.

Therefore, despite all the sublime poetry of this passage, its entire psychology seems to me not so much the condition of the wounded Prince Bolkonsky himself as the condition of the author trying to imagine himself in Bolkonsky's situation and using this occasion once again to condemn that great and superhuman institution, war. Had Prince Andrey thought all this at a much later date, after his wound had already begun to heal, I believe it would have been more accurate.

A little later, but on that same day, Bolkonsky again regains consciousness, this time in the French hospital. He looks at a small holy image which had been blessed by his sister, and thinks of the nature of God.

He says to himself: "How happy and peaceful I would be if I could now say: 'Lord, have mercy on me!' But to whom am I to say it? Either this is a force, indefinite and incomprehensible, with which I am unable to speak, which I cannot express in words—the great all or nothing—or it is that God Whom Princess Marya sewed up here in this amulet. Nothing, nothing is certain but the insignificance of all that is comprehensible to me, and the grandeur of something incomprehensible, but most important."

Still later, Prince Andrey is wounded a second time, this time mortally, at Borodino. Weak and worn out from suffering, he becomes delirious—at one time, as he falls asleep; at another, as he awakens; and at another, as he is on the point of falling asleep at night in the hut. He sees a "white sphinx"— it is Captain Timokhin, also wounded, lying there with one knee raised and covered with a white sheet. Then, beside this motionless, reclining sphinx, there appears in the door "another white sphinx in an upright position"—it is Natasha in her nightgown and bed jacket.

This depiction of semisleep and semiwakefulness, the alternate transition from feverish delirium to consciousness, is so splendid, so profound, and so true that I cannot find the proper words to express my amazement! From this entire wonderful page, I would discard but one thing—again the unnatural and strained attempt at sound imitation: "And piti, piti-piti, and titi, and piti-piti-boom, the fly hit against the ceiling."

I must confess that I cannot even understand what is going on here. Is a large fly actually hitting against the ceiling of the hut, or is it the need on the part of the patient himself to repeat one and the same meaningless word? The latter case is frequently met with. I myself remember from my early medical practice an impressionable fourteen-year-old boy who, although he was not even delirious, just feverish, felt the need continuously to repeat nonexistent words; it comforted him very much. This incomprehensible and aesthetically tactless "piti-piti, and titi" is unrelated to what precedes or follows, and in my opinion, it is simply terrible.

I once had occasion to read *War and Peace* aloud to a very young but intelligent and well-developed peasant couple, and I omitted this passage (and all others like it). In such places, I felt ill at ease and ashamed of the author and his work, which interested and delighted them both so much that at the end of the reading they were just as anxious about Pierre's fate as they would have been about that of a real person. The young wife said: "Well, thank heaven, Pierre finally married; if only he doesn't ruin himself, what with his spineless character." And the husband retorted: "No, Natasha won't let him ruin himself now." Both of them had forgotten serfdom, even though they themselves were children of serfs—so well had Count Tolstoy succeeded in making them love the gentry. As the reader, I enjoyed myself along with them and grew young myself under the influence of their sincere freshness. As I had read this marvelous, but uneven, book several times before, I knew in advance when an unpleasant stumbling stone was about to appear, and, almost without hesitation, I would cast it from the splendid flowering path. With great joy, I noticed that in *Anna Karenina* there are none of these ugly sound imitations. Of course, the author himself realized that they were unpleasant and completely out of place. I say he realized it himself, because our best critics (as far as I recall) did not take the liberty to reproach Count Tolstoy for this and everything like it.

But the height of perfection in this sphere of psychological analysis must be considered the story of Prince Andrey's quiet death in Yaroslavl. Here, both poetry and truth have been combined to such a splendid extent that improvement is impossible. In my opinion, Andrey's last days and his death itself immeasurably surpass everything of this sort in Tolstoy's work. These pages are better than those describing his delirium during the night's lodging in the village for the mere fact that there is no nonsense here as "piti-piti"—there is no intolerable fly intruding to tear the splendid lace fabric of emotions, which we so admire.

The description of Prince Bolkonsky's death is far superior to the descriptions of the slow death of Ivan Ilyich and the sudden death of the officer Proskukhin at Sevastopol ("Sevastopol in May, 1855"). In both these depictions there is much less poetry and truth than in the depiction of Prince Andrey's last days and minutes. For greater clarity, I shall quote all three examples almost in their entirety and ask that they be carefully read and compared.

1. Proskukhin's Death

At that instant, a red light penetrated his still closed eyelids, and something hit him in the middle of the chest with a terrible crash. He set off at a run, stumbled over his sword which got between his legs, and fell on his side.

"Thank God, I'm only bruised," was his first thought, and he wanted to touch his chest with his hands, but his arms seemed tied to his body, and his head felt as if it were being squeezed in a vise. Some soldiers rushed quickly past him, and he counted them unconsciously: "One, two, three soldiers, and there, the one in the tucked-up overcoat is an officer," he thought. Then lightning flashed before his eyes, and he wondered what the shot came from: "A mortar or a cannon? Probably from a cannon. And there's another shot, and some more soldiers are coming: five, six, seven soldiers; they are all passing by." Suddenly he became terrified that they would crush him. He wanted to shout that he was hurt, but his mouth was so dry that his tongue stuck to the roof, and a terrible thirst tormented him. He felt that there was a wetness around his chest: this sensation of wetness reminded him of water, and he felt like drinking even whatever it was that had made him wet. "I probably hit myself in falling and made the blood come," he thought. Beginning to give way more and more to the fear that the soldiers who continued to rush past would crush him, he mustered all his strength and tried to shout: "Take me with you!" But instead, he began to groan so horribly that the sound terrified him.

Then some red lights began to dance before his eyes, and it seemed that the soldiers were piling stones on him; the lights danced less and less, but the stones they were piling on him pressed down on him more and more heavily. He made an effort to push away the stones, stretched out, and saw, heard, thought, and felt no more. He had been killed on the spot by a shell splinter in the middle of the chest.

2. The Entire Final Chapter From
The Death of Ivan Ilyich

From that moment, the screaming began which lasted three days, and which was so horrible that one could not hear it even through two closed doors without becoming terror-stricken. The moment he answered his wife, he realized that he was done for, that there was no return, that the end had come, the very end, and his doubts were still unsolved and still remained doubts.

"Oh! Oh! Oh!" he cried in different intonations. He had begun by shouting: "I won't have it! I won't!" And continued to scream on the last vowel sound.

Three whole days, during which time did not exist for him, he wallowed about in the black sack into which an invisible, insuperable force kept pushing him. He struggled as a man condemned to death struggles in the hands of his executioner, although he knows that he cannot be saved; every moment he felt that despite all his efforts to struggle, he was coming nearer and nearer to what terrified him. He felt that his torment came from being sucked into that black hole and even more from his inability to make his way into it. He was prevented from entering it by the conviction that his life had been a good one. This justification of his life caught hold of him and kept him from moving forward, and tormented him more than anything else.

Suddenly some force struck him in the chest and the side, making it more difficult to breathe, and he fell into the hole; there at the bottom, a light began to shine. It was the feeling you often have in a railroad coach—you feel you are going forward, but in reality you are going backward, and suddenly you realize the true direction!

"Yes, it was all the wrong thing," he said to himself, "but that doesn't matter. It is possible, it is possible to do the right thing. But what *is* the right thing?" he asked himself and suddenly calmed down.

That was at the end of the third day, two hours before his death. Just then, his schoolboy son came quietly in and went up to his father's bed. The dying man was screaming desperately and throwing his arms about. His hand fell on the schoolboy's head; the boy caught it, pressed it to his lips, and began to cry.

At that same time, Ivan Ilyich fell through and caught sight of the light. It was revealed to him that his life was not what it should have been, but that this could still be corrected. He asked himself: "What then is the right thing?"—and he quieted down while listening for an answer. At that point, he felt someone kissing his hand. He opened his eyes and glanced at his son. He felt sorry for him. His wife came up. He glanced at her. With open mouth and undried tears on her nose and cheeks, and with an expression of despair, she was looking at him. He felt sorry for her.

"Yes, I'm tormenting them," he thought. "They feel sorry, but they will be better off when I'm dead." He wanted to say that, but did not have the strength to get it out. "But why speak? I must act," he thought. With a glance at his wife, he indicated his son and said: "Take him away—I feel sorry for him—and you—" He wanted to add: "Forgive me," but said "Forego—" and lacking the strength to correct himself, he made a gesture with his hand, knowing that it would be understood by the one who really mattered.

And suddenly it became clear to him that what had been oppressing him and would not leave was all at once withdrawing from two sides, from ten sides, from all sides.

He pitied them; he had to act so as not to hurt them. To free them and to free himself from this suffering. "How good and how simple," he thought. "And the pain?" he asked himself. "Where has it gone? Now then, where are you pain?"

He began to listen.

"Yes, there it is. Well, so what? Let the pain be."

"And death? Where is it?"

He looked for his former customary fear of death, but could not find it. "Where is it? What death?" There was no fear, because there was no death.

Instead of death, there was light.

"So that's the way it is!" he suddenly said aloud. "What joy!"

For him, all this happened in an instant, and the meaning of that instant did not change. But for those present, his agony went on for two hours more. In his chest, something kept rattling, his exhausted body twitched. Then the rattling and wheezing became less and less frequent.

"It's finished," said someone over him.

He heard these words and repeated them in his heart. "Death is finished," he said to himself. "It is no more."

He drew in a breath, stopped in the middle of a sigh, stretched out and died.

3. Prince Andrey's Last Days and Hours
(With minor omissions)

Prince Andrey not only knew he would die, but felt that he was dying, that he was already half-dead. He was experiencing a sense of estrangement from everything earthly, and a strange, joyful lightness of existence. Patiently and untroubled, he waited for what lay before him. That inexorable, eternal, distant, and unknown thing—the presence of which he had never ceased to feel throughout his life—was now close to him, and, because of the strange lightness that he was now experiencing, it was almost comprehensible and perceptible.

Formerly he had feared the end. Twice he had experienced that horrible, agonizing fear of death, of the end, but now he no longer understood that fear . . . .

. . . .

As he fell asleep, he still continued to think of what always occupied his mind—life and death. But mostly death. He felt himself nearer to it.

"Love? What is love?" he thought.

"Love hinders death. Love is life. Everything, everything that I understand, I understand only because I love. Everything is bound by it alone. Love is God, and to die means that I, a particle of love, am returning to its universal and eternal source." These thoughts seemed comforting to him. But they were mere thoughts. Something was lacking in them, something was one-sidedly personal and intellectual—they were not self-evident. And there was the same anxiety and uncertainty as before. He fell asleep.

He dreamed he was lying in the room in which he actually was, but that he was well and unwounded. Many different people—unimportant and indifferent—appeared before him. He spoke with them and argued about some trivial matter. They were getting ready to go off somewhere. Prince Andrey had a vague feeling that all this was trivial, and that he had other cares of much greater importance; but he continued to surprise them by saying empty and witty words. Gradually, imperceptibly, all these people began to disappear, and a single question, that of the closed door, replaced everything else. He rose and went to the door to bolt and lock it. Everything depended on whether he would or would not manage to lock it. He went, he tried to hurry, but his legs would not move, and he knew that he would not be in time to lock the door, but still he painfully strained every nerve to do so. An agonizing fear seized him. And that fear was the fear of death. Behind the door, IT was standing. But just as he was weakly and clumsily creeping up to the door, this horrible something was already pressing on the other side of it, trying to force its way in. Something inhuman—death— was forcing its way through the door, and he had to stop it. He grasped the door, straining every muscle to hold it—to lock it was impossible—but his efforts were weak and clumsy, and the door, pushed from behind by that terrible thing, opened and closed again.

Once again IT was pressing from outside. His last superhuman efforts were futile, and both halves of the door opened silently. It entered, and It was death. And Prince Andrey died.

But at the same instant he died, Prince Andrey remembered that he was asleep, and at the same instant that he died, he made a great effort and awoke. "Yes, that was death. I died—I awoke. Yes, death is an awakening," suddenly flashed through his mind, and the curtain that had previously concealed the unknown was lifted from his spiritual vision. He felt as if powers until then confined within him had been freed, and this strange lightness did not leave him again. . . . .

. . . .

With his awakening from sleep that day, there came to Prince Andrey an awakening from life. And compared to the duration of life, it did not seem to him any slower than the awakening from sleep as compared to the duration of a dream.

Nothing was horrible or violent about this comparatively slow awakening.

His last days and hours passed in an ordinary and simple way. Both Princess Marya and Natasha, who stayed at his side, sensed this. They did not cry or shudder, and during these last days they themselves felt they were no longer looking after him (he was no longer there, he had left them), but after what reminded them most closely of him—his body. They both sensed this so strongly that the external and horrible side of death did not affect them, and they did not find it necessary to exacerbate their grief. They cried neither when with him nor when away from him, and they never spoke with each other about him. They felt that they could not express in words what they understood.

They both saw that he was sinking slowly and quietly, farther and farther from them, and both of them knew that this must be, and that it was right.

He confessed, and received communion; everyone came to take leave of him. When they brought his son, he pressed his lips to the boy's and turned away, not because it was distressing and sad for him (Princess Marya and Natasha understood that), but simply because he thought that it was all that was required of him; but when they told him to bless the boy, he did what was expected, and looked around as if asking whether there was anything more to do.

When the body, abandoned by the spirit, gave its final convulsive movements, Princess Marya and Natasha were present.

"Is it finished?" said Princess Marya several minutes after his body lay there motionless and growing cold before them. Natasha went up, glanced into his dead eyes, and hastened to close them. She closed them, but did not kiss them; instead she kissed in her mind what was the dearest memory of him.

"Where has he gone? Where is he now?" . . . .
. . . .

And nothing more . . .

VIII

In these three depictions of death the author observes excellently and with all possible precision available to the human mind those nuances and differences, some of which depend on the nature of the illness or on injury to the organism in general, and others on the nature of the dying man himself and the ideals by which he lived.

Proskukhin is not sick. His death is sudden, in the tumult and confusion of battle. Of course, the thought of death is constantly in his mind, because men are being killed all around him, but there is no preparation whatsoever of his emotions for separation from life. Moreover, Proskukhin is by no means ideal—not in any sense; he is not even religious, not Orthodox in his feelings, as in the case of Mikhailov, the other officer whom Count Tolstoy describes in the same sketch. When Mikhailov suffers a bloody gash in the head from a rock, he thinks he has been killed and exclaims mentally: "Lord, receive my spirit!" Proskukhin, on the contrary, imagines that he is merely contused, and gives no thought whatsoever to God or his soul.

One can more or less successfully imagine the confusion of thought and emotion during combat in an ordinary man, who, while no coward, is not particularly brave either, and who cherishes no lofty ideal in his heart. It is possible to experience this in time of combat danger, quite independently of how the battle may end for one: in death, a wound, or no harm whatsoever.

But we definitely do not know what a person thinks or feels upon crossing that elusive boundary called death. To depict the change of thoughts and emotions in a contused or wounded man is artistic courage; but to depict the postmortal state of the soul is no longer courage—it is feeble pretense, and nothing more.

I find, for example, that the depiction of Prince Andrey's last days and minutes contains not only more poetry, but also more truth than the death of Proskukhin or Ivan Ilyich, because in these latter two deaths Count Tolstoy permits himself to look more boldly behind that fearful and mysterious veil which separates earthly life from the life beyond the grave; in the description of Prince Andrey's death, he very skillfully avoids this.

Proskukhin is killed: "He saw, heard, thought, and felt no more," et cetera.

Ivan Ilyich, on the contrary, experiences no fear whatsoever in his very last minutes, because there is no death.

"In place of death, there was light. . . . 'Death is finished,' he said to himself. 'It is no more.' He drew in a breath, stopped in the middle of a sigh, stretched out, and died."

Of course, such an expedient is incomparably more clever,

profound, and subtle in an artistic sense than the flat assertion that Proskukhin thought or saw no more.

Here, in the depiction of Ivan Ilyich's last minutes, the artist cleverly leaves the reader in doubt: what is this light, et cetera? Perhaps it is darkened consciousness, something on the order of semidelirium. Or perhaps it is a presentiment of another personal life, incomparably clearer than this life of the spirit, which is still shackled by the earthly flesh known to us.

In this discussion, we must not forget that between *Stories of Sevastopol* and *The Death of Ivan Ilyich* there passed for Count Tolstoy thirty whole years of intellectual work and varied life experience; it will then be clear why in the latter work he tried to avoid his earlier crude decisiveness. Ivan Ilyich simply "died," and that is all. This is also better from the standpoint of scientific accuracy. We have no rational right to assert that the soul is not immortal, and that after the numbing, stiffening, and cooling of the body, which we call death, the soul also feels nothing. And we might even add that the stricter we are in regard to scientific accuracy, the less of a rational right we have to reject what we do not know from experience. Here, precisely here, on this question of a person's postmortal condition, both our faith and metaphysical inclinations come into their own. By lack of knowledge on the part of exact science in this case, the field is cleared not only for sincere beliefs, but also philosophical preferences. The anguish of our heart and its yearning for immortality acquire rational rights on this field, which has been cleared and yielded by scrupulous phenomenology. As our reason does not clash with phenomenology anywhere on this field, it has, so to say, a rational right to follow the dictates of feeling, which are so often nothing but a true presentiment of a future rational truth.

Therefore, from the standpoint of semiscientific, or even of completely scientific, accuracy, Ivan Ilyich's death is better and truer than Proskukhin's.

He died, and that is all. But still, the "black sack" and the "light" that he sees when fully conscious are again something of a feeble attempt.

Count Tolstoy tackled this matter in a far better way in his description of Prince Andrey's slow and almost painless death. I said earlier that there is both more truth and more poetry here than in the deaths of Ivan Ilyich and Proskukhin.

First, I shall speak of truth or accuracy. I said it was good that in depicting Ivan Ilyich's last minutes the author leaves us in doubt as to what sort of light Ivan momentarily sees, and in what state the dying man is in these moments—one of semiconsciousness or semidelirium. I said this is better than the categorical and crude definition of Proskukhin's postmortal state. But still, my bewilderment is much worse for me than is the incomparably clearer impression left in me by the scene of Prince Andrey's last hours and minutes. Here, the narration is also simple, brief, and clear: "When the body gave its final convulsive movements as it was being abandoned by the spirit. Princess Marya and Natasha were present. 'Is it finished?' said Princess Marya. . . . 'Where has he gone? Where is he now?' "

Splendid! We need nothing more. Prepared by the premortal details and the splendid picture of Andrey's gradual exhaustion and spiritual enlightenment, we are completely satisfied that the author limits himself in this final moment to a most natural device: he puts himself at this moment in the place of Natasha and Princess Marya, and not in that of the dying or dead man himself. And it is so much truer!

As for Prince Andrey's condition immediately preceding those final moments, it must also be said that Count Tolstoy, in depicting his own fearful thoughts of death (it forces its way through the door) in the form of a dream that Prince Andrey has while semiconscious, is more direct than in his depiction of some sort of light, and he satisfies the demands of psychological realism. Prince Andrey is asleep or half asleep and half delirious; he dreams that he dies and awakens. This is plausible and, at the same time, it contains a remote but profound hint of something mystical, of an awakening of the eternal soul after physical death.

In the unusual poetry of the depiction of Andrey Bolkonsky's last days of life and his quiet, touching death, there is also a vast amount of truth, both psychological and medical. Both these kinds of truth will be even clearer if we again compare this death with that of Ivan Ilyich. However, in comparing these two deaths here, I do not want to give preference merely to the work and creative genius of the one book over the work and creative genius of the other, but to Prince Andrey himself over Ivan Ilyich. The work and the creative genius (except for the "sack" and the "light," which were pointed out earlier) are equally splendid; but Ivan Ilyich himself is one of Count Tolstoy's insignificant heroes, whereas Andrey Bolkonsky is the most poetic of all heroes. The author himself pities Ivan Ilyich only as a sufferer; he despises his character, his life, and his ideals. He likes Prince Bolkonsky; he obviously admires him without trying to conceal his faults.

Prince Andrey dies quietly in the arms of the two women he loves and by whom he is loved; he dies slowly from a deep and extensive wound received in the celebrated battle of great and glorious Borodino.

Ivan Ilyich also dies a fairly slow death, but it is brutal and horrible in every respect. Here, too, as I said before, the author has strictly observed both medical and psychological truth. Many chronic diseases of the abdominal organs are excruciatingly painful. It seems to me that Count Tolstoy wants to show the formation of an internal abcess when he mentions the terrible shooting and spiraling pain that suddenly commences near the end. It is not the external festering of an open gun wound, but an entirely different process, a truly horrible one! I myself have seen such dying men. The moral condition of Ivan Ilyich also derives from both the nature of the disease and his own character. His animosity towards other people, his implacability, his frenzied grumbling at God, of Whom he evidently never even gives a thought except momentarily, and then only to reproach Him for his suffering—all this is natural. This man never sought anything lofty or ideal—neither in religion, the love for a woman, the realm of pure thought, nor even in politics. He was content on this earth with that which is comparatively small and average in everything. He was content not as a result of the victory of humility and the fear of God over a proud mind, a passionate heart, or a powerful imagination, as a person richly endowed by nature is frequently content with that which is both average and small, and even wretched and low, under the prolonged pressure of ascetic ideals and religious feeling. No! Like many people, Ivan Ilyich is simply content with his bourgeois nature! He never thinks of anything lofty, fearful, vast, monstrous, or ideal, and then an event that is in its way fearful, lofty and monstrous—a death that is senseless, unexpected, inevitable and (considering its cause: a slight bump) deeply humiliating—takes him by surprise. Evidently he does not believe in the life beyond the grave, although at the suggestion of his wife, he does perfunctorily take communion; for whoever believes in that life thinks of it often, even when healthy; he forces himself to think of it frequently, and is very glad to take communion, even when well. Unfortunately, the sick Ivan Ilyich is in no way sympathetic. There is but one thing about him with which everyone can (and probably even should) sympathize—his annoyance with the hypocrisy and lies of the people around him, not one of whom (except the peasant Gerasim) can come right out and say to him: "Yes, you are dying. Prepare yourself."

I do not know when it was or who it was who introduced into our customs this disgusting "tact," which to the greatest possible degree degrades our dignity by imagining that the bitter truth will definitely poison a sick person's last days and hours. One thing is certain: this cowardly practice shows the depth of disbelief in our stupidly enlightened majority. A person who is himself a believer will, on the contrary, not be afraid to tell a dying person that the end is near. He remembers the aphorism: "As I find you, so shall I judge you," and no matter how sorrowful and painful it may be to distress a suffering friend, he will suppress this pity in himself; he will consider it his duty, even by increasing this person's fear, to move him to penitence and serious thought of God. In monasteries, those salutary repositories of Christian tradition, they never hesitate to come right out and tell people in good time that they are dying.

But in that bourgeois-commercial and spiritually bankrupt environment in which Ivan Ilyich moved (an environment with which we are, alas, far too familiar), one is not allowed to prepare people for death with Christian courage.

Ivan Ilyich was right for being exasperated with this practice, even though his justifiable exasperation resulted not from the possession of some lofty ideal or other (which even the peasant Gerasim possesses: "We're all going to die"), but simply from his annoyance with everyone and everything.

The death of Ivan Ilyich is the disgusting and truthfully depicted prose of the death of a prosaic and ordinary man. The death of Prince Andrey is depicted with no less truth, but it is the poetic death of a man who, even when healthy, was in an ideal frame of mind.

I said that Count Tolstoy likes Prince Andrey and even seems to admire him. He never depicted anyone more lofty, more complete, or more ideal than Prince Andrey. I am not saying that he idealized him, not in the least. I am saying that Bolkonsky himself turned out to be ideal in Tolstoy's hands. He is an idealist of firm, energetic character, and he is portrayed with truth, profundity, and unusual subtlety. He is superior to all the other principal young heroes of both *War and Peace* and *Anna Karenina*. Nikolay Rostov is simply a good man; he is not intelligent; he has strong convictions of heart, but absolutely no aspirations of mind. The noble and intellectual Pierre is ugly with his stoutness and clumsiness; he is comical; he is weak-willed, and even his intrepidity derives partly from his pensiveness and distraction. Levin is intellectually the same sort of idealist and "seeker" as Prince Andrey, but he is much more fatuous; moreover, he lacks Andrey's outward finesse, adroitness, handsomeness, and physical grace; in general, he is somewhat more coarse and awkward, less poetic in his totality.

Vronsky is poetic in appearance. He even has one advantage over Prince Andrey (and in our time a very important one): he is much sounder both in body and in spirit; he is calmer, more resolute, and more even-tempered; but he is more obtuse than Andrey. He is incomparably more *terre à terre* than he. Vronsky is poetic in one respect only; he is objectively poetic. Subjectively, in his own mind, he is not too ideal. If he is an idealist at heart, it is not so much from his nature as from his refined upbringing and chivalrous spirit, something that has not yet died out among our military elite. By having in this respect limited Vronsky's good points, which are admirable as it is, the author displayed great artistic tact and an astonishing sense of measure with this device of his. Had he decided to add the intelligence of Levin or Prince Andrey to the strong character of Vronsky, it would have been necessary to write the whole novel in an entirely different way. It would have been necessary to write a novel about the youth of a great and brilliant man who overwhelmed everything around him with his mental abilities. And it would have been awkward to conduct the modest and moral story of the country squire Levin on the same level as his story. (As it is, Levin and Kitty's half of the book is somewhat more boring than Anna and Vronsky's.)

Thus, even Vronsky, with all his traits, adventures, inclinations, and aspirations taken together, is less poetic than Prince Andrey. Adhering to our earlier terminology, we can say that

Bolkonsky's ideality and poetic nature are both objective and subjective—that is, to the reader, to Natasha, and to Pierre, he seems a very brave, very intelligent, refined, well-educated, businesslike, and noble man who loves everything that is beautiful. His pride, ambition, certain of his whims, and even his coldness towards his wife (who is so dull)—all this pleases us. Even his own inner world is filled with ideal and lofty aspirations such as true friendship, romantic love, patriotism, honorable and well-deserved glory, and even religious mysticism, which, unfortunately, does not have time to assume a more definite and clear (dogmatic) form.

Such is Tolstoy's Prince Andrey.

In running over in one's mind all the best heroes of our literature from the time of Onegin down to Markevich's Troyekurov inclusive, recalling Pechorin, Rudin, et cetera, one cannot help concluding that Prince Andrey, on the strength of both his refined and noble qualities, if considered as a real live person (and without regard to the period), is the most noble and complete of them all! With the possible exception of physical strength and a sound mind, as I already mentioned, for in this respect, Vronsky and Troyekurov surpass him.

And then this man, filled with hope and talent, is mortally wounded in a horrible battle for his native land. And he dies slowly and meekly in the arms of his devoted sister and of Natasha, with whom he had been so passionately in love a short time before.

One cannot imagine anything more poetic than this death. And all this poetry is nothing more than the real truth of life. There is not one false note, not one strained interpretation, not a hint of exaggeration or affectation.

Prince Andrey had to die in such an ideal way!

But Count Tolstoy is a realist: he bears in mind that no matter how ideal a man is in his premortal thoughts, the clarity and continuity of such thoughts depend largely on the nature of the disease from which he is dying. Prince Andrey dies, slowly exhausted by external suppuration; it may be that there is also a slight intestinal injury. While serving as a medical officer in the Crimean War, I myself saw that, for the most part, people died quietly and peacefully both from extensive suppuration and from chronic intestinal injury. They had an air of indifference about them, a sort of aloofness from everything around them. And that is how Prince Andrey passes away, while think of universal love, of death, and of God (at least in so far as he could understand God, what with his philanthropic pantheism).

True, one would like, would very much like, to draw the firm, clear contours of dogmatic Christianity on that light-blue, heavenly, and infinite background of Andrey's too general dreams. It is painful that they are missing from the excessively pale and boundless azure of his inner world! It is very painful that we no longer have the possibility to help transform this humane and nebulous pantheism into that firm and architectonic spiritualism which is the distinguishing feature of true (ecclesiastical) Christianity! It is pleasant that we can apply to this "death of a life" almost all the touching epithets of ecclesiastical prayer: "peaceful," "painless," and, of course, "not shameful," but "honorable and glorious." But it is very annoying that we cannot apply the most important of these epithets—"the death of a Christian life." This is, of course, a pity; it is both painful and annoying.

But even regret of this sort merely shows how Tolstoy can sometimes become the "master of our thoughts" and how realistic (in the good sense) are his most ideal characters.

Because of our Orthodox feelings, we cannot sympathize with Prince Andrey's arbitrary and amorphous beliefs, no matter how much we would like to; but at the same time, we cannot help liking him as a person. Also we cannot help delighting in the author's genius, "devoutly venerating the sanctity of beauty."

Neither in *Anna Karenina* nor in any other of Count Tolstoy's works can we find anything in this same vein, similar to or equal to the description of Bolkonsky's death. There is no other description of death in his works equal to this one in depth of poetry.

In *Anna Karenina*, there are two deaths: Nikolay Levin's death from tuberculosis, and Anna's suicide.

Vronsky's unsuccessful attempt at suicide is limited to a mere fainting spell from the bleeding, and therefore does not even need to be mentioned here.

The account of Nikolay Levin's death can be considered an irreproachably accurate example of the purely external observation of a certain type of dying man. It all very much resembles the death of consumptives. The observation is done entirely by Konstantin Levin, and this time the author does not penetrate the soul of Nikolay Levin himself. As an artistic device, this is very commendable in the given instance. Tolstoy had already engaged in a good deal of inner analysis on other occasions, and this could finally have wearied the reader—all the more so as Nikolay Levin himself, no matter how much we pity his brother, who has loved him from childhood on, is not particularly interesting to us. He is one of those intolerable, incorrigible, and bewildered (mostly through their own fault) Russians who so abound in our times and with whom we can be patient (and even then, only to a certain degree) only out of the deepest feeling of Christian love. But who can really like them?

The story of Nikolay Levin's death is irreproachably accurate, but there is no poetry whatsoever either in Nikolay himself or in the scene of his death.

As for Anna's sudden and violent death, there can, of course, be no question of the actual process of dying. There can only be a long and detailed discussion of those thoughts and emotions, the succession of which finally led the heroine to her ultimate decision. And this succession, as I already said, is sustained to a surprising degree of perfection.

But, in my opinion, all this precision is spoiled by the closing words, after Anna has already been pulled down by the wheel of the coach: "And the candle by which she had been reading the book filled with anxiety, deceit, and evil flared up much more brightly than ever before, illuminated for her everything that had previously been in darkness, flickered, and began to grow dim, and then went out forever."

What are these words? This candle, et cetera? A beautiful allegory, and nothing more! A clever way of concealing our total ignorance and incomprehension of reality at such a moment. What candle? How is it that it flares up more brightly and then flickers? And in what sense does it die out forever? Upon looking, even briefly, into this matter and removing the poetic veil of beautiful words, we find that it is impossible to imagine anything here at all.

The "deceit" of these last words cannot even be said to "uplift" us. After all, in the words "the candle died out forever" there is a direct hint at the denial of personal immortality. For not only the person who believes with all his heart in the immortality of the soul, but even the one who merely grants in his mind the possibility of this immortality can not possibly imagine that after Anna's death it became darker, that nothing could be seen. On the contrary—independently even of unconditional submission to the dogmatic instructions of Christianity, such a person, who acknowledges the immortality of the soul, must by reason alone inevitably arrive at the conclusion that after death we see and comprehend everything incomparably more clearly, immeasurably more broadly, than before. It must be one of two things: either there is no immortality, and then, of course, all is darkness and "nirvana," or there is immortality, in which case the soul is freed from the constraining bonds of its earthly flesh; in other words, it sees, hears, and comprehends everything better and more clearly.

To what extent it sees more clearly, or in what respect it comprehends better, we do not know; but at any rate, we can by no means assume that the soul sees less clearly and comprehends less well after death. Such an assumption on the part of reason that postmortal comprehension is clearer in no way contradicts the teachings of the church concerning rewards and punishments beyond the grave, eternal bliss and eternal torment, for it is impossible even to reach the highest degree of blissful happiness without the highest degree of self-consciousness, and in order for torment to reach its highest degree, it must be completely conscious.

And if this is so, then what "elevation of spirit" can we find in the "deceit" of these superfluous, although seemingly poetic words (candle, et cetera) with which the author cleverly and beautifully conceals something from us—either his unbelief or the inconsistency of his thinking—I don't know.

As it is, "everything is so vile" in life, not only in the opinion of Anna, who has been led by her passion to despair, but evidently in the far too strict opinion of the author as well. And suddenly we find here that either there is nothing at all, or there is something, but that it is much darker.

Therefore, in those words "candle" and "darkness" there is neither strict accuracy nor true poetry. True poetry cannot be torn from a phenomenon as clothing or a mask: it is the essence of a beautiful phenomenon.

When Count Tolstoy in his own name depicted for us Prince Andrey's frightful dream, in which "IT" (death) breaks through a closed door, he created a touching and fearful poetry that cannot be forcibly, so to say, torn from the incident itself. This "IT" is as terrifying and mysterious as death itself, and as fantastic as a dream. Here we have poetry, accuracy, reality, and elevation!

Anna's "candle" is the equivalent of Ivan Ilyich's "sack" and "light"; it is something in the nature of an obscure and not particularly successful allegory. And the words "died out forever" are the equivalent of those accompanying Proskukhin's death: "He saw, heard, thought, and felt no more," et cetera.

How does Count Tolstoy know this? He did not rise from the dead and visit us after his resurrection. One can, for example, believe him in the same way that one believes the Pope or the Ecumenical Council, or a spiritual elder—after all, we are not in the least bound either by our reason or by our heart.

That is also why, by the way, when I spoke of Prince Andrey's death, I said that even in *Anna Karenina* there is nothing to equal these pages.

In the description of Nikolay Levin's death there is much truth, but little poetry. In the depiction of Anna's last moments there is no solid truth, and the poetry of the concluding words is deceptive; it is precisely what is known as rhetoric—a beautiful phrase without definite or vital content.

But in the depiction of Prince Andrey's death there is everything.

In my introductory chapters I said that, on the whole, there is much more poetry and grandeur in *War and Peace* than in *Anna Karenina*. This thought of mine can best of all be applied to this particular question: Where and how is death best depicted in Tolstoy's novels? All the depictions of death and the minutes immediately preceding it in *War and Peace* are in their way superb and true to reality in general (particularly in so far as their external features are concerned). Such is the instantaneous death of Petya Rostov in a fit of combat enthusiasm. Such is the simple, honorable, Orthodox, and gentle (although fairly ordinary) death of the kind old man Count Rostov. The death of the old Prince Bolkonsky, stricken with apoplexy because Napoleon had dared set foot in Russia, would also have been very good, had the author not striven once again for that intolerable sound imitation, which he completely abandoned, thank heaven, in *Anna Karenina*. For example, the dying old man says: "*Go-go boi.*" This, would you believe it, means, "My soul is in pain," and his daughter understands!

This "*go-go*" is, of course, just as inappropriate and pretentious as the attempt to convince us that after death, all is darkness; but, in addition, it is terribly awkward and unnecessarily cacophonous. In itself, the apoplexy of this proud patriot of the time of Catherine the Great, caused by consternation and anger over the fact that some of the French had even dared set foot in Smolensk Province, is both noble and true.

The author even depicts the death of Prince Andrey's young wife in childbirth with a special kind of high tragedy, not at all infrequent in real life. This young lady does not of her own accord win the reader's heart. Her husband, on the contrary, becomes our favorite almost from his first appearance, and our sympathy for him grows continuously. But Princess Liza arouses a certain antipathy in us for her from the mere fact that she fails to understand her husband and seems a hindrance to him in all that he does. Her character is somewhat ordinary and insignificant; she is inferior to all the other young women in *War and Peace*. Even the false, wanton, and inwardly coarse Yelena Bezukhov is more outstanding in every respect than Liza. She constantly troubles the reader's moral sense. But Princess Liza does not even make that sort of strong impression. We only put up with her out of sympathy for her talented husband. And then this ordinary, but pretty—by no means malicious, merely empty—woman unexpectedly dies. She disappears instantaneously from the life scene while giving birth to a child by that very husband whom she had so annoyed. No one, of course, blames Prince Andrey; but everyone understands how painful and even awkward it is for him when he sees that little mouth, opened plaintively, just as if wanting to say: "Why did you do this to me?" Then, too, there is the unexpected arrival of her husband from the front—her husband, who himself was so long on the point of death from a wound! That fateful winter evening on the wealthy Prince's estate! Yes, this is real tragedy. It is the poetry of the truth of life!

I cannot keep from also mentioning Anatoly Kuragin here.

His death is not described. We only know that he died, probably as a result of his amputation. But, along with Bolkonsky, we see this rather stupid, handsome man and shameless rake sobbing like a child on the operating table after the Battle of Borodino, where he fought for his native land no worse than all the rest. And along with Prince Andrey, we not only forgive him at this moment, but even love and pity him with all our heart.

Yes, there are many deaths in *War and Peace*, and they are all depicted differently and superbly. There is much less of this sort of loftiness in *Anna Karenina*.

As for the other question—that of a greater (in my opinion) organic bond between the psychological analysis and the development of the action itself in *Anna Karenina*—I shall have to speak about this matter separately and in greater detail than before.

IX

I have finished with the psychological analysis of states of sickness and premortality, and shall now turn to descriptions of dreams, drowsiness, and semisleep when the character is in a state of health, and of various flights of imagination when he is fully awake. There are several such depictions in *War and Peace*, and they are all good, but to a varying degree.

As an example of the latter state (unbridled imagination in a full state of wakefulness), let us take the scene where Captain Tushin is with his battery at Schöngraben. Completely oblivious of the danger, and fascinated by the artillery fire, he imagines that "over there, where the smoke is rising from the enemy's cannons, an invisible man is smoking a pipe," et cetera. He calls one of his cannons "Matveyevna," and exclaims mentally: "Well, Matveyevna, old girl, don't fail us!"

Or another example: "You see, it's taken another breath, another one" (in reference to the alternately diminishing and increasing sound of gunfire, which reminds him of a person breathing). "The French seemed like ants beside their guns." "In his dreamworld, the handsome and drunken soldier, the number-one gunner of the second cannon, was 'uncle.'" "He imagined himself a mighty man of immense stature, hurling cannon balls at the French with both hands."

As an example of splendidly depicted, pure, and true dreaming, let us take Nikolenka Bolkonsky's dream at the end of *War and Peace*:

> Nikolenka had just awakened in a cold sweat and was sitting on his bed, staring with wide-open eyes in front of him. He had been awakened by a terrible dream. He had dreamt that he and Pierre were wearing helmets like those depicted in his edition of Plutarch and were marching in front of a huge army. The army was composed of white, slanting lines that filled the air like those cobwebs that float about in autumn and which Desalles [his tutor] called '*le fil de la Vierge*.' Up in front was Glory, just like the rest of the threads, but somewhat thicker. They, Pierre and he, were carried along lightly and joyfully nearer and nearer to their goal. Suddenly the threads that were moving them began to grow weak and tangled; it became difficult to move. And Uncle Nikolay Ilyich stood in front of them in a stern severe attitude.
>
> "Was it you who did this?" he said, pointing to the broken pieces of sealing wax and pens. "I loved you, but Arakcheyev has ordered me, and I will kill the first man who moves forward."
>
> Nikolenka turned around, looking for Pierre, but Pierre was no longer there. In Pierre's place was his father—Prince Andrey—and his father had no shape or form, but he was there; upon seeing him, Nikolenka grew faint with love: he felt himself helpless, as if he were without bones, like liquid. His father was caressing and pitying him. But Uncle Nikolay Ilyich was drawing closer and closer to them. Terror seized Nikolenka, and he awoke.

The drowsiness that immediately precedes sleep overcomes Petya the evening before the partisan attack on the French and before his unexpected death.

The semidrowsiness that accompanies the morning awakening—when a person, still seeing and even thinking things in a dream, is awakened by other people, and their words are confused with this person's own thoughts—this strange state of body and mind is very truthfully depicted in the scene where Pierre Bezukhov falls asleep in the tavern yard after Borodino and is later awakened by his groom with the words: "We must harness the horses." Half-asleep, only vaguely hearing, and still pondering over his theophilanthropy in his unfinished dream, Pierre almost exclaims: "Yes, yes, we must not unite our thoughts, but harness them."

All three of these examples are purely physiological. Captain Tushin with his battery, Petya falling asleep on the cart, and Count Bezukhov at the inn—all three of these people are healthy; they are not wounded, not sick, not dying. In my opinion, Nikolenka's dream is the best of it all. "The army is a cobweb; Glory is also a cobweb, but somewhat thicker." Children, particularly those who are impressionable and intelligent, are often in a state of semidelirium and fanciful creativity, not only when asleep, but when fully awake. This is a state into which adults lapse when fully awake only in the exceptional circumstances of sickness, temporary insanity, poetic inspiration (partly even premeditated) during the writing of verse, et cetera. Furthermore, in these moments common sense fails to function in children; nothing restrains the unconscious creativity of their minds. At these times they are not shy or ashamed. Each of us has seen children like this, who invent amazing things while at play, things that are often incredibly witty and original.

Therefore, the dream of the delicate and well-read Nikolenka Bolkonsky is understandable and truthful. In it, side by side with unusually creative fantasy, are reflected impressions from as recent as yesterday: the pieces of sealing wax and the argument of his elders about Arakcheyev. And at the same time, this dream conveys the atmosphere of the period—Plutarch, ancient helmets, military glory. In those days, one did not forcibly "cram" the classics in the original in order to strengthen the memory and will, but read them for pleasure and the development of feeling and intellect, even if it was done in French translation. Those Plutarchian helmets as well as the imaginary "sphinxes" which the wounded Prince Andrey sees when semidelirious convey the atmosphere of the period. All this is more realistic (in the good sense of the word) than that intolerable, ultranaturalistic, but unnatural, "*piti-piti-boom*," which I have already pointed out. Moreover, Nikolenka's dream is just as ethereal in its poetry as is the remarkable delirium of his splendid father.

Petya Rostov's drowsiness is good, but it is marred by that "*ozhig-zhig-zhig*," about which I have already complained bitterly. After all, it is not characteristic.

Pierre's awakening ("unite" and "harness") is real. It is possible at all times and with all people partly to hear and partly not to hear someone else's words and to answer them when half-asleep with something that is sometimes even nonsensical.

With Pierre, by chance, as a result of the preceding stream of thought in his dream, something comes out that makes sense. But do thoughts flow so regularly in a dream? And are the thoughts of a dream remembered as well as its fragmentary images? Here, I am obliged to doubt.

There remains Captain Tushin with his "puffs of smoke," his "pipe," and "Matveyevna." Tushin is, of course, the son of poor—or perhaps not poor, but not very refined—members of the nobility of the time. His upbringing is rather crude; however, for an artillery officer, he is "learned" and even something of an admirer of Voltaire. In appearance, he is of slender and impressive build; by nature, he is probably not without imagination. He is brave, and, at the same time, evidently something of a dreamer. I said earlier that a militarily oriented imagination always triples one's innate courage. The play of his imagination (which, by the way, is fairly simple: the pipe and Matveyevna) helps keep his mind off death and brings him to a state of total and heroic self-oblivion. All this is possible, and all of it is excellent, for the simple reason that is shows character. But the "unite" and "harness" shows nothing whatsoever of Pierre's character; it is nothing but a fairly accurate depiction of a chance physiological fact. But, as you know, the long-standing rules of aesthetics tell us to discard all that is fortuitous and all that is superfluous. And I would gladly discard this superfluous physiological observation.

All these inner mental processes enumerated above are depicted excellently in *War and Peace*; but I still insist that upon strict analysis we shall find that descriptions of this kind in *War and Peace* have less of an organic bond with the characters' future—a bond that is striking when one carefully reads similar passages in *Anna Karenina*.

Moreover, it is questionable to me whether Count Tolstoy could imagine the inner processes of the people of 1812 as correctly and precisely as he could imagine these same processes in his contemporaries. I ask: Was it in this manner that the people of 1812 dreamed, daydreamed, and even raved when delirious? I really do not know if it was. Isn't this manner in many instances similar to the psychological manner of Count Tolstoy himself, our exceptional contemporary, a man whose individuality and genius verge on ugliness?

I do not know if I am correct in my instinctive doubt. I only know that in my first reading of the novel in 1868 I sensed this failure, in general, to convey the atmosphere of 1812; even then, I sensed it so strongly that at first I was very displeased with *War and Peace* for many reasons, among them, its excess of psychological analysis. I thought then: "There is too much of our time and of our contemporary insight about it all." I had read with enthusiasm, but when I finished I had doubts and was dissatisfied for a long time afterward. Somewhat later, when I read N. N. Strakhov's[1] article in *Dawn*, I came to my senses, and even thanked him for it

[1] N. N. Strakhov (1828–1895), a Slavophile friend and biographer of Dostoevsky. [Tr.]

when we met; I thanked him for having corrected my one-sided opinion. Strakhov had paid more attention to the great content, and I to the too modern form: to the sum total of all those petty details and nuances that constitute the style or the atmosphere. Since then (since my good lesson from Mr. Strakhov), I have read *War and Peace* several times, and each time Tolstoy's powerful spirit wins me more and more; but still, it is *his* spirit, and not the spirit of the period. I am like stubborn Galileo; I keep repeating to myself: "Excellent, but somehow it conveys the wrong atmosphere!" I can repeat Buffon's words here: "*Le style—c'est l'homme!*" But I cannot say: "*Le style—c'est l'époque.*" And if one carefully considers both these ideas, one will probably find that my altered version: "*Le style—c'est l'époque*" is more precise and clear than Buffon's original statement. . . .

X

In *Anna Karenina*, as I said before, there are neither detailed descriptions of delirium nor depictions of inner mental processes during a slow death from disease. Nor are there flights of imagination in a full state of wakefulness (such as, for example, with Captain Tushin). But there are daydreams, there is momentary and deeply significant self-oblivion and musing, there are dreams and the processes of falling asleep.

I shall try to be specific. The chief passages of a suitable nature in *Anna Karenina* are as follows: (1) the one where Anna falls asleep in the railway carriage; (2) the one where Anna and Vronsky simultaneously have frightening dreams; and (3) the one where Levin sees a cloud upon meeting Kitty on the highway.

Let us carefully analyze all this and compare these passages with each other as well as with appropriate passages in *War and Peace*. I think this comparison will show what I indicated at the very beginning: that in *Anna Karenina* there is less of the author's personal fantasy; that the observation is more restrained, but that the psychological analysis is more precise, true, and real, almost more scientific; that the flow of poetry is more restrained, but that there are many less of all those intolerable obstacles and rough spots; and that there is none whatsoever of that forced mimicry.

But, above all, this comparison will convince us that all these passages in *Anna Karenina* are more organically connected with the course of the action than are similar scenes in *War and Peace*. And not only do they not give rise to even a shadow of doubt, they positively delight us with the almost scientific precision of Tolstoy's "psychomechanics." These "psychomechanics" are, of course, good in *War and Peace* also, but in *Anna Karenina*, they are made strikingly clear.

And so, Anna falls asleep in the railway carriage:

She felt that her nerves were like strings being stretched tighter and tighter on some sort of turning pegs. She felt that her eyes were opening wider and wider, that her fingers and toes were twitching nervously, that something inside her was making it difficult to breathe, and that all the images and sounds in this quivering semidarkness were striking her with extraordinary clarity. She was continuously being assailed by moments of doubt as to whether the coach was moving forward or backward or standing completely still; whether it was Annushka beside her or a stranger. "What's that on the arm of the seat— a fur coat or a wild animal? And am I here myself? Is it I, or someone else?" She was afraid to surrender herself to this oblivion. But something kept drawing her into it, and she was able to surrender herself to it or hold back at will. She got up in order to come to her senses; she pushed aside the traveling rug, and took off the cape of her warm dress. For a moment, she recovered her senses, and realized that the thin peasant who had come in, wearing a long nankeen coat with one button missing, was the stovetender, that he was looking at the thermometer, that the wind and the snow had burst through the door with him; but then everything became mixed up again. . . . The long-

waisted peasant started gnawing at something in the wall; the
old woman stretched out her legs the entire length of the coach
and filled it like a black cloud; then something began to creak
and knock in a terrifying way, as if someone were being torn to
pieces; then a red light blinded her eyes, and then everything
was hidden by the wall. Anna felt as if she had fallen into an
abyss. But all this was not terrible, it was fun. The voice of the
bundled-up, snow-covered man shouted something in her ear.
She stood up and came to her senses; she realized that they had
come to a station, and that it was the conductor.
And nothing more . . .

Now Vronsky's dream:

Vronsky fell asleep. He awoke in the darkness, trembling from
fear, and quickly lit a candle. "What was that? What? What was
that terrible thing I was dreaming about? Yes, yes. The peasant
bear-baiter, so it seems—that dirty, little man with a disheveled
beard was bending over, doing something, and suddenly, he
began to say some strange words in French. No, there was
nothing more to the dream," he said to himself. "But why, then,
was it so terrible?" He again vividly recalled the peasant and
those incomprehensible French words that the peasant had
uttered, and the terror sent a chill up and down his spine.

Anna tells Vronsky that she had a terrible dream:

"A dream," repeated Vronsky, immediately recalling the
peasant in his dream.
"Yes, a dream," she said. "I first dreamed it a long time ago.
I dreamed that I ran into my bedroom, that I had to get something there, to find out something: you know how it is in a
dream," she said, opening her eyes wide in terror, "and in a corner
of the bedroom, there was something standing."
"Oh, what nonsense! How can you believe . . ."
But she did not let him interrupt her. What she was saying
was too important to her.
"And that something turned around, and I saw that it was a
peasant with a disheveled beard, a horrible little man. I wanted
to run, but he bent down over a sack and rummaged in it with
his hands . . ."

She showed him how he rummaged in the bag. There was an expression of terror on her face. And Vronsky recalled his own dream, and felt the very same terror filling his heart.

"He was rummaging and speaking very, very fast in French, and do you know, he was burring his r's, *'Il faut battre le fer, le broyer, le pétrir.'* And from fear, I wanted to awaken, and I did awaken—but I awakened in my dream. And I began to ask myself: what does this mean? And Korney said to me: 'You're going to die in childbirth, in childbirth, my dear.' And I awakened."

"What nonsense, what nonsense!" said Vronsky, but he himself felt there was no conviction in his voice.

Let us compare these passages with each other. Their comparison will also be of use in weighing the relative merits of similar passages in *War and Peace*.

The similar dreams of Anna and Vronsky are, in my opinion, the high point of the psychological analysis about which I have been speaking; Anna's falling asleep in the railway carriage is its low point. Without the scene where Anna falls asleep, the inner bond between the heroine's future feelings and actions and her past and indelible impressions would not in the least be destroyed. The scene where she falls asleep is detailed description for description's sake, depiction for depiction's sake, a series of feelings in the present only; perhaps it could also be linked with the past, but not without straining matters—by the thought that Anna, already practically in love and agitated, is on her way home to her husband. But all this is much better reflected in her state of mind as she reads the English novel than as she falls asleep. She reads the novel, but she herself wants to live, to experience everything for herself. But, for her to doze and to see things around her differently from the way they are, to fail to recognize her maid, to take the old lady for a wild animal, et cetera—all this is possible even without her love for Vronsky. And Anna's subsequent behavior is, of course, also possible without this scene. This is precisely what I call redundancy, a ponderosity of petty details. After all, even feathers weigh a lot when there are a lot of them. And there are many more such ponderous details in *War and Peace* than in *Anna Karenina*.

The artistic and psychological significance of Anna's and Vronsky's similar dreams is not at all like this. Anna's drowsiness could be omitted without detriment to either the beauty of the work or the bond with the subsequent action. But to discard from the novel these two similar dreams would mean not only to deprive it of one of its most poetic adornments, but also cruelly to destroy the strikingly close psychological bond between the heroine's past and her future. Recall that a worker is crushed by the locomotive during Anna and Vronsky's first meeting; Vronsky sees his mutilated corpse, and Anna hears of it. Later in St. Petersburg, they have similar dreams. After as much time again, Anna throws herself on the tracks and is killed. At almost the last moment, she sees the worker, et cetera.

This is great profundity and truth. There is neither redundancy nor idle, so to say, description. The psychological bond between the immutable past, the momentary present, and the unknown future is preserved and is evident almost to the point of mathematical precision. And in addition to this realistic psychological coherence, there is in all this also a certain suggestion of something mysterious and prophetic: the worker crushed on the railroad during the first encounter of these two people who are practically lovers; the peasant working at the rails in their common, simultaneous dreams; and again, the worker just before Anna's death on the tracks. One glance at this man decides her fate. Before that glance, she had not yet decided what to do with herself.

Wasn't it such moments that the late Katkov[1] had in mind when, according to N. A. Lyubimov,[2] he said: "It is not we who control life, but life which controls us"?

---

[1] M. N. Katkov (1818–1887), a reactionary political journalist. [Tr.]
[2] N. A. Lyubimov (1830–1897), a physicist and publicist. [Tr.]

Now about Levin's "cloud" and the "oak" in the forest through which the widowed Andrey Bolkonsky rides twice, before and after his meeting with Natasha. These two scenes are almost identical from a psychological point of view. If in Anna's and Vronsky's simultaneous dreams there is something objective, something totally independent of these people's consciousness, then in Prince Andrey's "forest" and Levin's "cloud" there is charmingly depicted another feature of our mental life: the acknowledged allegoric bond between nature and our hearts and minds. In Anna's and Vronsky's dreams, nature (or more precisely the spirit invisibly governing nature) forces them to see what they were not looking for. But here, both of Tolstoy's heroes see in nature what their hearts are seeking: symbols of their own inner condition. Andrey, morose and lonesome, but by no means old at heart, rides through the forest in early spring and sees that all is green, that just one large oak stands there sad and bare. Upon returning in summer (after his first meeting with Natasha), he sees that this oak, too, has finally covered itself with foliage and become beautiful. This is supposedly said in the name of the author, but we understand that a trace of this allegory, not yet fully applied to life, remains in Andrey's imagination. Levin's "cloud" is somewhat more conscious and subtle, but not in the personal sense that Levin himself is more conscious or subtle than Andrey— no, in this respect, they are, I think, equal—but in the general life sense, whereby there cannot be two completely identical states of mind in life, only homogeneous and similar ones.

Both scenes are excellent, both are true, and both are filled with poetry. But still the "cloud" has one point in its favor: the bond between it and the hero's future is closer and more evident. Andrey's "oak" has, as yet, a very remote and vague connection with his love for Natasha (it is not the ball in St. Petersburg, where "the wine of her youth went to his head"); but the change in the "cloud" is a phenomenon occurring simultaneously with the sudden change taking place in Levin himself. This symbolic simultaneity surprises both him and the reader.

If, after having examined all these dreams, daydreams, and states of sleep and semisleep in *Anna Karenina*, we now turn once again to the instances I cited from *War and Peace*, it will, I think, be clear to us that what I said before is true: that in the latter instances there is more fantasy and poetry, but less of an organic bond between them and the subsequent action.

Nikolenka's dream, for example, is delightful: it is the height of poetry and truth in the present, but it has no connection with the future; the epic ends with this dream. What happens later to Nikolenka, we do not know.

Captain Tushin's flights of imagination during the Battle of Schöngraben are quite possible; they are highly original and can serve to complete the portrayal of his character. But he could have performed all his heroic feats that day without these fantasies. These fantasies, or this almost childish delirium while in a full state of wakefulness, are in no way connected with the main action. They can be of great value only in themselves, and not in relation to anything later on.

Nor does the description of Petya Rostov's drowsiness on the cart the night before the raid on the French involve anything more. Even if this drowsiness had not been described, Petya could have displayed his courage in the morning just as he did, and have ended up being killed, or, on the contrary, in remaining alive. There is physiological truth in the description of the drowsiness itself, but there is no connection between it or anything else.

Even the superb depiction of Andrey Bolkonsky's semidelirium and the noble scene of his quiet death are excellent only in themselves. These states of his mind do not cause any of his later actions, for he dies immediately afterward. They— these inner states—cannot even have an effect on the other people present, for they are inaccessible and unknown to them. Everything of importance that later happens to Natasha,

Pierre, and Princess Marya could happen even if Prince Andrey had simply been killed outright, as in the case of Petya Rostov. Pierre could marry Natasha; Princess Marya could marry Nikolay Rostov; and all three of them, Pierre, Princess Marya, and Natasha, could cherish their sacred memory of Prince Andrey just as they now do. True, Natasha would not have to ask forgiveness or to look after him, and, above all, we, the readers, would be deprived of several exemplary pages and a great aesthetic pleasure; but still, we do not see why Natasha should not marry Pierre as it is. Her repentance would have remained in her heart, and would then have grown cold. Even here the connection between the emotions and future action is not particularly strong. . . .

There is still another special kind of psychological analysis that became fashionable with us as early as the forties and fifties. Count Tolstoy in his time also engaged in it frequently. It can be called analysis of suspiciousness or of unnecessary eavesdropping.

For example: "A certain lady-in-waiting, when mentioning the name of the Empress Marya Fyodorovna, or in speaking of the royal family in general, would make a sad face," or Kutuzov, while speaking eloquently and subtly with the Austrian general, evidently "listened to his own voice with pleasure" (Part II, Chapter 3). Or another example: "It was evident that the regimental commander was pleased at his own display of anger," et cetera (Part II, Chapter 1). Fault-finding and supposition of this sort, what with their affectation and, as it were, subtlety, can often be quite unfounded and lead to nothing in particular in the character development; not to mention the fact that this habit of our writers has become so very boring.

There is even one place in *War and Peace* where this analysis of suspiciousness is completely irrelevant and unjust. It is where Count Tolstoy suspects all mothers of envying their daughters' marital happiness.

In Part III, Chapter 2 of *War and Peace*, he describes the

evening party and supper at the Kuragins', where the rich
Pierre Bezukhov is almost unexpectedly betrothed to Yelena.
Anna Mikhailovna Drubetskoy congratulates Madame Kuragin
on this engagement, but the latter remains silent, so "tormented is she with envy at her daughter's happiness."

But we can allow this passage. The Kuragin family is, in
general, devoid of moral principles and moral feelings and
can be given to the author to tear to pieces. But the person I
am ready to defend passionately and for whom I am ready
to attack the author in connection with such fault-finding is
the kind and philoprogenitive Countess Rostov, who, from all
indications, the author himself likes. She shows her son Nikolay
the letter from Andrey Bolkonsky, who is already engaged to
Natasha, "with that repressed feeling of grudge which mothers
always have in regard to their daughter's future marital happiness."

Why this unwarranted assumption? What is admissible in
Princess Kuragin is completely unnatural in the kind and
honorable Countess Rostov! Had a woman written this, one
might sadly ponder the matter and ask oneself: "Is it possible
she knows this for certain?" Moreover, if I were going to be
suspicious and find fault, I would in such a case, rather suspect
this female novelist herself of some personal grudge against
her own mother or the mothers of some of her friends than to
accuse each and every elderly mother of such a not only
wicked but stupid feeling.

At this point, I, for my part, want to quibble with Count
Tolstoy. I ask insistently: Why did he need this almost ugly
and completely unfounded sally? Perhaps this vicious mental
impulse of the old Countess is connected with something later
on? Perhaps this barely visible seed of spite will later grow
into a large tree? Perhaps Madame Rostov, by some words
and deeds or other, will break up her daughter's marriage
to Bolkonsky? No, there will be no mention of this at all. The
old Countess will behave irreproachably in this whole mat-

ter up to the end, and her feelings toward her daughter, who is indeed blameworthy, will remain cordial. She will even without demur allow Prince Andrey to die in her house in Natasha's arms. Consequently, there will be no connection with anything that follows.

Or perhaps the author had to invent this vicious and unclean impulse of a mother's heart merely to keep the Countess Rostov from turning into too perfect a character. The author esteems and loves people who are ideal in real life, but wants no idealization in art; he wants all the best characters in his novels to have weaknesses and flaws and not to be without extremely vicious, although transitory, feelings.

After all, Countess Rostov is not perfect as it is: she is a good wife, a kind woman, and a tender, loving mother; but, in the first place, she is not distinguished by any particular intelligence; she is sometimes rather capricious and is far less kind and generous than her husband (for example, in the matter of the carts for the wounded after Borodino); she treats poor Sonya, who is completely dependent on her, cruelly and ignobly, calling her an intriguer to her face for her quite natural desire to become the wife of Nikolay, whom she unalterably loves. Isn't all this enough, when the shadows are mixed within reasonable limits with the light traits, to make her character quite prominent?

Of course, it is. Moreover, this invention of an unclean feeling is by no means meant by the author to apply specifically to the soul of Countess Rostov, but to all mothers who succeed in arranging a good marriage for their daughters. They should indeed arrange a good marriage for their daughters, but not envy or bear a secret grudge against them. Good heavens! What an unwarranted assumption, and what inordinate psychological pretension! Who could prove the universality and inevitability of such an absurd impulse? No one.

The point of the matter is not even in this, but in the fact that Count Tolstoy, when he wrote these lines, had not yet entirely rid himself of precisely those bad habits of the Russian school about which I spoke above. There is analysis and analysis. Analysis is nothing more than sound analysis: a person experiences such and such feelings; the impression that remains in his heart and mind is, let us assume, a strong one; later, as a result of all this, he performs such and such actions. Or it is the dull analysis of captious objection and of suspicion, not at all true to real life. A person suddenly, without rhyme or reason, experiences a feeling that is bound to be wicked, petty, base, spiteful, or cowardly. Isn't there also a sort of negative exaggeration in this? Or is it perhaps that all our writers who were reared on the spirit of the forties themselves experienced in such cases a petty feeling such as great shame, a certain feeling of literary cowardice before the practices of negation? I think that this was the case, and that Leo Tolstoy himself, despite all his strength and originality, paid generous tribute to this weakness from youth on.

And who indeed has not paid this tribute? We are now accustomed to praise almost indiscriminately the literature of the forties and fifties with the purpose of opposing it to the coarse, frankly revolutionary, truculent, and, on top of all this, extremely boorish and clumsy literature of the sixties and seventies. But even in this much-praised literature of the forties and fifties, one must differentiate between two of its aspects—the theoretical, so to say, and the practical. On the one hand, its aesthetic views, aesthetic theories, and aesthetic world view in general, its critique of the philosophy of life and of the beautiful. On the other, its artistic execution or artistic practice, its poems, stories, novels, and plays. In making this differentiation, one can find an exceedingly important fulcrum for judging certain aspects of our literature.

In those days, our aesthetic theories were very noble and profound in ideals, for they were under the influence of German idealist criticism and philosophy, higher than which one can scarcely rise on this same soil.

But our artistic practice very soon assumed more or less of a negative, derisive, biting, and somber character.

This practice fell under the overwhelming influence of Gogol. Or more precisely, under the influence of his late and most mature, but precisely biting, somber, and narrowly satirical works, which depict nothing but vulgarity, and particularly the vulgarity of our life.

After all, it was not the sublime pathos of *Taras Bul'ba*, "Rome," or "The Terrible Vengeance," it was not the powerful fantasy of the story "Viy," or the charming gaiety of *Evenings on a Farm Near Dikan'ka*, that left a strong, deep, and to this day almost ineffaceable imprint on the literature that followed, but either the satire of *Dead Souls*, *The Inspector General*, et cetera, or the depiction of the bitter, pathetic, and morbid aspects of our life, the ugly tragedy of our humdrum existence (particularly urban), in "The Overcoat," "Nevsky Prospect," and "Notes of a Madman."

One might even permit himself to say outright that from the spirit of these latter three Petersburg tales of Gogol there sprang and developed almost the entire morbid and one-sided talent of Dostoevsky, just as almost all of Saltykov-Shchedrin sprang from *The Inspector General* and *Dead Souls*.

Turgenev and Tolstoy can, of course, be linked more closely with Pushkin and Lermontov, for in their works we also find many elegant images from Russian life, but in Dostoevsky and Saltykov-Shchedrin, there is not a vestige of elegance; they did not even know how to portray it.

However, everyone knows that both Turgenev and Tolstoy accustomed themselves—not suddenly, but very gradually—to see in the life of educated Russian society features that were more positive, characters that were stronger, and types that were more refined. With the years, both of them grew bolder and bolder in this respect.

With the years, both of them, to a different degree and in different circumstances, lost the habit of everywhere seeing only the poverty and insignificance of our spirit and life. Unfortunately, Turgenev often yielded anew to foreign revolutionary tendencies, and as a result, deprived his talent of originality. But Tolstoy cannot be accused of anything like that: he was always independent, and if he was not right, at least he did things in his own way. His tendency everywhere to see only the poverty of spirit and only the insignificance of life grew weaker of its own accord. Having begun with *Childhood and Adolescence*, where there is so much of the captiousness and petty suspiciousness about which we have been speaking, he finished with *Anna Karenina*, where there is very little of it, and with the tales for the people, where, thank heaven, there is not even a trace of all these pranks and tricks.

It will do no harm here also to recall the Sevastopol stories about military life.

In the same sketch from which I took the death of Proskukhin ("Sevastopol in May, 1855"), this urge to search for vanity in all people and on all occasions expresses itself with unusual strength. . . . People fight, they die; each of them can at any moment expect death or mutilation. Yet each officer constantly worries about how he will be treated by those officers who are superior to him in social standing, wealth, elegance, eminence, et cetera.

This sketch is characterized almost from the beginning by the question: "Why did Homer and Shakespeare write about this and that (about glory, love, et cetera), but not about vanity, whereas everyone now writes about vanity?"

I shall speak, just briefly, about two aspects of this matter.

First, in the times of Homer and Shakespeare, people probably found nothing contemptible or wrong with a person's thinking about how he is looked upon by those who are superior, stronger, more eminent, more lustrous, et cetera. It seemed so natural and so simple that there was no reason here to be disturbed.

Second, the desire to please and to make a favorable impression on others appears in people at the sight of more than just their superiors. For example, in our "democratic" times, the desire to ingratiate oneself with the lower classes, the mob, the common man, has grown stronger and more harmful than the ancient, everlasting, and natural desire to equal one's superiors in at least something or other (even while remaining in one's own place), to be liked by them, to obtain access to their society, et cetera.

Let us further note that it is by no means pride alone that is at work here. Often it is simply good taste; a person finds that in high society, things are better, more pleasant, merrier. And in many cases, he is right.

Why such morbid and strained fault-finding of an egalitarian nature?

It is again those microscopic nerve fibers which the artist depicted in the form of large, true nerves and placed in the foreground in false perspective.

If some petty impulse of pride were to make a person betray his duty, his love, a true feeling, or some other noble matter, one could censure him for it. But if people do their work, do their duty, as more or less all the Russian officers in Tolstoy's stories do, what harm is there if they amuse themselves a little, even by aspiring to that which is superior, a practice which the young (at the time) author called especially vain?

It is special, and it is incorrect, for one can be vain about anything at all—about the most diverse things: a luxurious and a spartan way of life; tidiness and slovenliness; an illustrious and a base origin; pride and humility, et cetera.

Moreover, we might ask how Count Tolstoy knew for certain in 1855 what the various officers felt?

Of course, this is nothing more than suspicious conjecture by a mind still immature and driven in one direction by the morbid negation characteristic of the fifties. Finally—and forgive me for being personal—if Count Tolstoy was inwardly unsettled in youth and like this himself, we are not obliged to believe that through it, he thoroughly and accurately knew the soul of everyone else. I might furthermore add, by the way, that at that time Count Tolstoy found all these proud and vain impulses in people of the educated class only. He is silent everywhere about the pride and vanity of soldiers and peasants.

Why is this? Is it because he is completely unable to analyze their inner processes? Is it because the psychological analysis both of Levin's dog, Laska, (during the hunt) and even of Napoleon I seemed simpler to him than the analysis of the thoughts and feelings of Karatayev and other "common" Russian people?

Or is it because he thinks that peasants and soldiers do not experience the very same pride and vanity as we? Can it be that Count Tolstoy really thinks this, after having studied them for so long? I, too, know them rather well and find that in many respects these Russian commoners are more proud and vain than we.

The frequent application of these universal feelings can be different with them, and the forms of their manifestation unlike ours—and nothing more; the essence is always the same.

Even the peasant scullery boy Gerasim in *The Death of Ivan Ilyich*, when at home in the village or in his own society in general, could be bound by its customs, rules of propriety, and vanity in the very same way as Ivan Ilyich was bound throughout his life by the customs and rules of propriety of his circle, and by the vanity resulting from this dependence.

I shall even go further: Russian commoners, when in their own circle, are, for reasons of pride, much more afraid than we to violate the rules of propriety. I shall cite just one example (although there are a great many of them). In our cities, people from both the middle and upper classes visit each other, chat for hours on end, sit, and then leave without expecting any refreshments at all. They want to see each other, to have a chat, and nothing more. But just let a Moscow chambermaid or yardman try to invite friends in as we do. They would be laughed at, criticized, and their pride would be hurt. I know this from experience. While living in Moscow quite recently, I often asked my servants: "Why don't you ever invite some guests in? Doesn't anyone come to see you? It's boring for you." And they would answer me: "We can't do as you; your friends come, have some tea, and then leave, or they drop in for no particular reason. But with us, it would cost a lot of money; we would have to treat them to this, that, and the other thing. Otherwise, they would laugh at us."

Is it possible that Count Tolstoy does not know about this? Moreover, there are people among us who even see their pride in doing everything in public in their own way, but it would never even occur to the common folk to ignore the public opinion of their environment. They take the opinion of that environment to heart much more so than our people do.

The point is that in the days of Homer and Shakespeare there prevailed a world outlook that was religious and aristocratic, or heroic and consequently more aesthetic than today's. But today, there prevails a world outlook that is utilitarian and moral, with a tendency toward egalitarianism. Therefore, all these suspicions and captious objections have also multiplied so awkwardly in our literature since the forties.

It is extremely pleasant to see that as early as in *War and Peace* Count Tolstoy's psychological analysis had abandoned its narrow and false path and assumed a healthier, kinder, and, so to say, more diverse and organic character.

As for *Anna Karenina*, it contains even less of this sort of analysis. There is, of course, vanity—how could there not be? And in places, it is even very strongly expressed in the behavior of the characters, but the author himself obviously searches for it less and grieves over it less than before.

It seems to me that in *Anna Karenina*, even the author's scoffing, which in places is very subtle, witty, and charming, takes on that benevolent and conciliatory nature which permeates Goncharov's humor and scoffing. There is neither spleen, spite, nor captious objection—simply life itself, in all its fullness and with that balance of good and evil which is readily understandable to any person of common sense.

This Goncharovian, almost gentle, subtle, and kind type of comedy, humor, or mockery as applied to the life of the upper and rich circles is a complete novelty in our literature. And, moreover, this novelty attests to a certain extremely honest and respectable feeling, under the influence of which the author found himself during the maturation of this latter novel of his.

We do not exactly know what he had in mind. But if, contrary to expectations, he intended to write a "negative" novel, he made a mistake.

By force, one can find negation in everything. Dobrolyubov was even able to represent Ostrovsky as a negative writer, and the younger Gromeka[1] found that Vronsky was empty because he did not rush hither and thither in those damned quests, the way such a large number of our untalented and spineless people do now. . . .

The life depicted in *Anna Karenina* can be severely criticized from one standpoint only: it is insufficiently religious, insufficiently Orthodox, but this is the fault of Russian society, not of Count Tolstoy. . . . In order to describe true Russian Orthodox life, which is also not devoid either of vices and weaknesses or drama and poetry, one must have a particular type of experience that Count Tolstoy lacked. And in order to depict such a life, which he does not know and clearly does not understand, Count Tolstoy is too much of a realist and too conscientious from an artistic standpoint.

Dostoevsky, due to his lyric and subjective nature, could imagine that he was showing us true Orthodoxy and Russian

---

[1] M. S. Gromeka (1852–1883), the son of the noted publicist; a teacher of the Russian language and of history, and author of the book *The Late Works of Count L. Tolstoy.* [Tr.]

monasticism in *The Brothers Karamazov*. For Dostoevsky, his own dreams of a heavenly Jerusalem on this earth were dearer to him than either the truth of life or true church customs, but for Count Tolstoy, his philanthropic tendency could never of its own accord spoil the poetry of life or the truth of life.

No matter what the author himself thought of the life he depicted in *Anna Karenina*, we love it, that life; and although we may regret that a more ecclesiastical and ascetic ideal is not linked to it and raised above it (for then it would be even better in many respects), we can nevertheless be satisfied to a certain extent with its pithiness and completeness—particularly if we are firmly convinced that there will never be a "heavenly Jerusalem" on this earth which is known to us.

XI

Now about coarseness, untidiness, and purely physical observation in general. There is coarseness and coarseness. I am by no means unconditionally opposed to coarseness. I even like it when it is apropos. What I am mainly opposed to is the awkwardness of our present-day language, which is distorted and twisted this way and that by those "bumps," "prickles," and "cavities" of naturalism, which I have already frequently mentioned. I am opposed to the cacophony and caco-psychics of our almost universal style that lead to nothing. I am opposed to the whipping up of dirty suds to the very ceiling—a whipping-up process equal to the one that produced the sweet rhetorical foam of the last century (equal in excess, but by no means in quality); for it is a hundred times better to have foam that is fragrant and even somewhat cloying and strong, if the rhetorician is talented enough to uplift our thoughts, than to have a whole pile of rubbish and trash covered with useless slops. When Tolstoy's Ivan Ilyich uses the bedpan— this is not bad. But when Gogol's Tentetnikov awakens in the morning and lies there "rubbing his eyes," and his eyes are "little"—this is both very disgusting and unnecessary. One feels like going immediately to General Betrishchev's and saying to the ideal Ulinka: "Listen, don't marry Tentetnikov; in the morning, as attested by N. V. Gogol himself, he is awfully repulsive!" What is the reason for this? Ivan Ilyich's trait is a vital one; we pity him. But when a young man who is loved by a heroine whom the author deeply respects "rubs his little eyes," it is no longer a trait, but a sort of cudgel, a sort of aesthetic stumbling block. He would not have to rub his eyes each time. Or his eyes could be a bit larger. There is nothing organic here; it is merely disgusting.

Both in *War and Peace* and even in *Anna Karenina* (although much less in the latter), we can find examples similar to the two just mentioned.

As Andrey Bolkonsky is riding in a carriage with Kutuzov, and Kutuzov is arguing that it will be necessary to put many men in the future battles, Andrey looks at an old scar on the general's temple and thinks with deep respect: "Kutuzov himself has already experienced all the personal dangers of war, and therefore has the right to speak this way." This is excellent as psychological analysis of Andrey's mind and satisfactory as physical observation. That is, it would have been satisfactory, had the author simply said: "the scar" or "the deep scar." But precisely what I call the bad practices of naturalism made Count Tolstoy add: "the carefully washed seams of the scar." I very much like the physical cleanliness of this illustrious and well-bred soldier, but in this instance I cannot praise the also illustrious and also well-bred author for this unnecessary detail of the toilet. Later on, I shall, in passing, again comment on this same page on which the "washed scar" is mentioned.

Somewhat before this passage, as Kutuzov is taking leave of Bagration before the Battle of Schöngraben, he blesses him with tears in his eyes. This is excellent. But—"with his left arm he drew Bagration to him, and with his right hand, on which he wore a ring, he made the sign of the cross over him, evidently an habitual gesture, and then offered him his plump cheek . . ." et cetera. Now I ask you, why should I know with precisely which arm he drew Bagration to him? And why is the ring mentioned here? The fact that Kutuzov is fat, that he has plump cheeks, a plump neck, and probably plump hands as well, we have known for a long time as it is. We have already heard it more than once, and we shall hear it again. This nuance "evidently an habitual gesture" is also an expression or an observation that is not simple, not inevitable, but one of those that have somehow multiplied in our literature since the forties. And there is a great deal of this in *War and Peace*.

Let us go back a page. Prince Bolkonsky has quarreled with a convoy officer and is about to strike him. "The officer made a gesture of resignation and hastily rode off." Two lines later: "Prince Andrey rode hastily from the doctor's wife." In itself, this word "hastily" is neither good nor bad. But everyone in our country has become so accustomed to use it automatically, thinking it his duty to imitate the "coryphaci," that it is high time the "coryphaei" themselves took a dislike to it. Still another example on the same page (Part II, Chapter 13)— "Nesvitsky, munching something in his moist mouth," calls Andrey Bolkonsky over to him. Of course, he could call him over without munching anything. After all, this is still that same "excess of observation" about which I spoke at the beginning.

("'No, Masha, I don't love you any more,' Eugene said through his teeth, as he cut his meat, raising his elbows high.")

As everyone's mouth is moist when he is healthy, it was not necessary to mention Nesvitsky's mouth. Well, all right, so be it, suppose his mouth was especially moist; but, after all, we knew this already—ever since the time our men burned the bridge over the River Enns. This same staff officer, Nesvitsky, was there, too—and there, too, he was joking with the other officers and "chewing a meat roll in his handsome, moist mouth." (Part II, Chapter 6).

In all that has been cited here, there is, of course, nothing improper, coarse, or untidy. But it is awkward and unnecessary—there is the trouble. Better if it were improper.

Let us take another more striking example. At the end of the book, Natasha, now married, brings the baby's diapers into the living room to show that the stains are no longer green, but yellow. Although this is very coarse and ugly, it is relevant here, and of great significance. It shows the extent to which Natasha, like many Russian women, grows slovenly after marriage and the extent to which her maternal instinct makes her forget that other people, even those who love her family, are not at all interested in such medical observations. After all, it would have been enough for even the closest friend of the family to hear from her that the child is better. Count Tolstoy, in his own name, praises Natasha for totally neglecting her appearance after marriage. But the reader is not obliged to agree with him about this; the reader must only acknowledge on this occasion as well the extent to which the power of talent was able to make our favorite heroine attractive and interesting even in this final and slovenly phase of her development. Therefore, I consider these diapers not only admissible, but even very necessary in realistic art.

But when Pierre dandles this same child on his huge right palm (those hands!), and the baby suddenly makes a mess in his hands, this is not at all necessary; it shows nothing. It is dirt for dirt's sake, art for art's sake, naturalism for its own sake. Or, in this same scene, when Pierre smiles "with his toothless mouth," it is even worse. What is the purpose of this? It is ugliness for ugliness's sake. A baby does not make a mess all over its parents every minute, and Pierre Bezukhov's age (even at the end of the book) is not yet such that he would definitely be toothless. He might be, and he might not. This is no longer sound realism; it is "bad habit," like the Russian common people's habit of taking hold of a white door not by the handle, but of grasping it without fail where they shouldn't.

I shall take the liberty of repeating once again: I am speak-

ing here not only of strictly coarse or strictly slovenly observation, but of excessive physical observation in general, just
as I spoke earlier of Russian novelists' excessive psychological
captiousness. For example, Natasha, upon returning to the devastated city of Moscow, for no reason whatsoever bumps her
head against the door as she is leaving the room in a state of
agitation after her first meeting with Pierre. It seems to me
that if she had bumped against the door just before declaring
her love for Pierre, or, in general, before some conversation
or other, and not after, something very important psychologically could have been connected with this physical act—just
as in the case of Koznyshov's mushroom, or the "piece of paper
on a plate" given to Pierre at Bagration's dinner (Dolokhov
snatches it up before he does, and for this, Pierre, already
exasperated, immediately challenges him to a duel). Had
Natasha struck her head beforehand, she would have sat down
and begun to cry. Pierre would have taken her by the hand,
et cetera. Both of them, mollified and deeply moved (she
from physical pain, he from compassion), would little by little
have declared their love for each other. But afterward, upon
leaving the room—this is pointless! It is not Sergey Ivanovich's
mushroom, nor Dolokhov's and Pierre's piece of paper; it is not
even the diapers—it is happenstance for happenstance's sake;
it is one of those strained interpretations typical of realism.
Even if we were to assume that one of Count Tolstoy's older
relatives or acquaintances told him that in 1813 a certain aunt
of his, very much like Natasha, in an exactly similar situation,
also on leaving a room, bumped her head against a door, or
that a certain Count Bezborodka, at a time when he was still
fathering children, was already toothless—even so, we should
omit all this, as neither of these instances is organically connected with anything internal, and as they are both very ugly
in themselves.

If we again recall Gogol in this connection, we shall find
that Gogol is both better and worse. He is worse, he is weaker

than Tolstoy, because in the very same work, five or ten pages later, he is completely unable to reward us as Tolstoy rewards us for all those well-washed scars, those diapers, the wheezing, and the toothlessness—now with a description of a lady's ball attire so subtle that it could be the envy of any female writer, now with an elegant depiction of Tsar Alexander, now with other features of nineteenth-century life so poetic they would not be out of place on the most fragrant pages of George Sand. In Gogol's late novels and stories (from the life of the Russian petty nobility), we, of course, find nothing like that. Tolstoy's devices are more diverse, more complete; and they more closely resemble the diversity and completeness of real life. But precisely for this reason, that is, because Gogol was so one-sidedly intensive, he needed "Petrushka's odor," "Nozdryov's puppy's navel," and the "hiccuping" that begins "A Lawsuit," and "*Obmokni*," instead of "Yevdokiya."[1]

"Gogol—*c'est un genre*, but with the rest of your writers, all this is out of place." That is what a very intelligent Moscow lady, a friend of Khomyakov,[2] told me in the fifties. She said this in reference to "The District Doctor" from *A Huntsman's Sketches*, which she did not at all like, but with which I was so delighted as a youth that I rated them higher than *Dead Souls*. Later, to my surprise, I realized that this lady was in many respects more correct than I. "Gogol, *c'est un genre!*" With him, there is almost no middle ground between the poetry and pathos of "Rome," *Taras Bul'ba*, and "Viy," and the abomination of desolation of *Dead Souls* and *The Inspector General*. But why the extensive, almost inexhaustible Tolstoy needed these excesses, I do not know. It would have been enough to include the major, organic, Shakespearian crudities; it would have been enough to include the diapers and Pierre's dirty

---

[1] A female Christian name, also from "A Lawsuit." In this dramatic fragment, a nephew suspects forgery, as his aunt's will is signed "*Obmokni*" (dip), instead of "Yevdokiya" (the aunt's given name). [Tr.]

[2] A. S. Khomyakov (1804–1860), a poet and theologian, the author of several outstanding studies on Greek Orthodox dogma. [Tr.]

toes when he was in captivity. Why do we or the author need these little nuisances? They are bad habit, nothing more. . . .

In oral reading, this complexity of language is particularly noticeable; for example, all the repetitions: "hastily," "hastily," "involuntarily," "involuntarily," "alien," "alien," "nervously," "nervously," "nervously," "plump," "plump," et cetera, "a moist mouth," "a toothless mouth." This frequent psychological eavesdropping and unnecessary physical observation, not only in Tolstoy, but even in the majority of our best writers—in Turgenev, in Pisemsky, and in Dostoevsky—is sometimes simply unbearable when read aloud! And in Tolstoy, these flaws, or more accurately, excesses, are far more noticeable, glaring, and frequent than in the rest.

Perhaps it is because with him, everything—all the outstanding features of our school, both good and bad—is ten times larger than with the rest. Both the light and the shadow are more prominent. As I said earlier: He is a Sivatherium of the category of pachyderms.

XII

Can we find all these not entirely praiseworthy things: the coarseness, the slight crudities, the unnecessary observation, and all those obstructive "bumps" in the very language, in the very speech, which I have been lamenting so sincerely and for so long—can we find all this, I ask myself, in *Anna Karenina*? Of course, we can, but to a lesser extent than in *War and Peace*.

One would have expected the author to tolerate more of all this in a contemporary novel than in an epic-chronicle set in 1812, for all of it—the captious mental analysis, ever ready to spy something out, the "carefully washed seams of the scar," the completely unnecessary "toothless mouth," the "raising his elbows high," the "lisping" [see Dostoevsky almost everywhere], and everything like it—is a Russian literary peculiarity of recent times, and not at all characteristic of the Consulate and the First Empire. I have already said that an exacting connoisseur, for the greatest degree of his aesthetic pleasure, holds dear not only the events, but also the general psychological music accompanying them; he holds dear the atmosphere of the period. At the time of Austerlitz and Berezina, people did not delve very deeply into another man's mind (perhaps for practical purposes, so that someone would not turn out contrary to their expectations). If they noticed a pimple on someone, they probably did not find it the duty of the present to immerse themselves in this person's contemplation. They had not yet read Gogol, and Gogol himself (i.e., a Ukrainian nobleman of quite average means) would not even have begun at that time to write about an "overcoat" or "dead souls," but would probably have written odes about some sort of "erupting volcanoes of popular passion," and upon making the acquaintance of General Betrishchev, he would not have described in fine detail how the General washes himself, but would have celebrated his valor in verse. Something like this: "Arise, intrepid chief, Betrishchev, grand and stately!"

At that time, everything in our life was simpler (i.e., less complex). Observation was much more superficial, the tastes of the upper circles were more refined and at the same time more "foreign," so to say, and more uniform than now. In fact, there was perhaps also more selflessness than now (I don't know), but there was incomparably less needless self-criticism for the mere love of it or from imitative intellectual habit.

Therefore, I say that one might have expected much less of all this (both the Gogolian and Turgenevian aspects) in a novel from the life of 1812, and very much of it in *Anna Karenina*. However, it turned out the other way around. It happened because Count Tolstoy wrote *War and Peace* first, and *Anna Karenina* later. Artists who are very rich in spirit and who have successfully employed one style to satiety hasten to shift to another. They seek new paths, new forms, and frequently they find them. Thus it happened in the case of these two novels of Count Tolstoy. In the first book, he rid his heart of a vast and diverse supply of personal material; he rid himself of it and set out on a new path with a lighter, but by no means exhausted burden. Enough of this personal artistic supply was still left to give us the splendid content of *Anna Karenina*. And at the same time, the weight of this supply was so diminished that he found it easier to cope with the order, purity, and truthfulness of the work. The very language, even when read aloud, became smoother and more pleasant. The mirror of artistic reflection became cleaner and truer. Not a bit of either the poetry or the clarity was lost. All that was obliterated were the "specks" made by those unbearable flies of the Natural School.

It would seem that a novel about a distant period would have to be more objective and one about a recent period more subjective; but it turned out just the reverse. Adhering to the terminology popular when Herzen,[1] Katkov,[2] Bakunin,[3] and Belinsky were young, we might say that *War and Peace* is a work that is more objective in intent, but that its objectivity is highly subjective; whereas *Anna Karenina* is a work that is more subjective, because of the proximity of both the period and the milieu to the author, and because of the nature of the leading character (Levin), but that its subjectivity is objectified to the highest possible degree of perfection.

The question now is: Were all those disgusting flyspecks of our Natural School obliterated from *Anna Karenina*?

Of course, not all. Tolstoy completely obliterated them only in the little stories for the people ("What Men Live By," "The

---

[1] A. I. Herzen (1812–1870), a revolutionary publicist, mainly remembered for his excellently written memoirs. [Tr.]

[2] M. N. Katkov (1818–1887), a reactionary journalist. [Tr.]

[3] M. A. Bakunin (1814–1876), an anarchist and revolutionary. [Tr.]

Little Candle," et cetera). By the way, they were considerably obliterated even much earlier: in "A Prisoner of the Caucasus," in the superb story "God Sees the Truth but Waits," and, in general, in the little stories for children and the common folk. (The lucky children! The lucky common folk! Literally speaking, they are better educated than we: they have no need of those flyspecks on the artistic mirror! On this score, *The Lives of the Saints,* "Bova Koralevich," and "The Battle of the Russians with the Kabardians"[1] are, of course, more edifying than *Dead Souls, A Huntsman's Sketches,* or the mad stratagems of morbid and impotent pride in the works of Dostoevsky!)

Where then are these unnecessary "flyspecks" in *Anna Karenina?* I shall pick on the unnecessary ones only. Let us see.

The newly wed Kitty Levin sits and looks at the "back of the head and the red neck of her husband," who is busy at the table. She looks at him "with a feeling of possession." Clear, clever, decent, and necessary.

Anna arrives in Petersburg from Moscow after her acquaintance with Vronsky, and for the first time notices that her elderly husband's "ears were hideously protruding from under his top hat." Also clear, subtle, true, and tidy. But when Karenin falls asleep beside his wife, who is already in love with another man, and begins to "make a whistling sound through his nose"—it goes against the grain. It is repulsive, awkward, and unnecessary. Or again, when Vronsky washes his neck (also red) in the presence of his comrades. This, let us assume, cannot be called physically offensive. There is nothing offensive about a strong man's sunburned neck. Even this, like some strange force, can be pleasing to us, just as the perspiration of a healthy soldier or peasant in the fresh air was always pleasing to Count Tolstoy himself. But as Vronsky's comrades are not Kitty or Anna, it is completely unnecessary. It is burdensome, like Nesvitsky's "moist mouth" and Kutuzov's "plump cheek" and "plump hand."

[1] Three works from very early Russian literature. [Tr.]

Then, at the very end of this excellent and carefully planned book, we come across one such spot, where it would seem that not one but ten flies had sat for a long time and made such a mess that it cannot even be scraped clean.

It is Vronsky's toothache before his departure for Serbia.

After Anna's tragic death, Vronsky goes to fight for the Slavs. He equips an entire detachment at his own expense. Morose, inconsolable, and depressed, but always the same firm and decisive man, he walks up and down the platform.

As Vronsky walks, he chats with S. I. Koznyshov, who in this instance plays the same active role that I. S. Aksakov[1] played at the time of Chernyayev's[2] heroic deeds in Serbia.

In order to make the reserved and proud Vronsky express his innermost feelings so simply and frankly to Koznyshov, who was by no means close to him, and who did not even like him up to this moment—this is indeed brilliant invention! Precisely to him! To whom else could it have been? Not, of course, to Vronsky's brother or mother, who were always opposed to his love for Anna. Not to some comrade; all his military comrades must have been unbearably irksome by then: they reminded him of irretrievable days of rapture, struggle, and happiness. Besides, many of them were too frivolous in matters of the heart and did not measure up to Vronsky's profound nature. Certainly it was not possible to bring him together on that platform with Levin (who was awkward and also ill-disposed to Vronsky) and make him pour out his heart with a frankness not at all customary of him. With whom, then, could it be? The appearance of Koznyshov was a perfect solution to this artistic problem of the author. It enabled him to draw the young Count's character to ideal per-

[1] I. S. Aksakov (1823–1886), a poet, political publicist, and leader of the Slavophiles. During the Serbo-Turkish war referred to here, he was in charge of fund-raising for the Serbs and of sending volunteers to fight on their side. [Tr.]

[2] M. G. Chernyayev (1828–1898), a Russian general, Commander-in-Chief of the Serbian Army in 1876. [Tr.]

fection—a character which is complex and wholehearted, reserved, and, when necessary, straightforward; and on all of life's occasions, strong.

Vronsky and Koznyshov are drawn together by a mutual interest: the Serbian War. True, with Koznyshov, the Serbian affair is his main purpose; he is moved by a political idea. But Vronsky is under the influence of personal grief; for him, Serbia is not an end, but a means, an outlet worthy of his energy and practical mind. But, nevertheless, his immediate interest is one and the same as Koznyshov's. Koznyshov fervently wants the Serbs and the Russian volunteers to win. But, after all, Vronsky, who had probably not even thought of Serbia up to then, of course wants the same thing now. Moreover, Koznyshov is well along in years. He is noble, intelligent, serious, and he inspires confidence. Like everyone else, he, too, of course, knows about Vronsky's affair with Anna, but the chief thing (for Vronsky) is that despite all Koznyshov's qualities, he is a person completely alien to this whole affair, and therefore he does not read anything between the lines with Vronsky. And so with this stranger, who is perhaps going off "to the slaughter," Vronsky speaks more willingly and more frankly of his great sorrow than he would have with Petritsky, with his brother, with Serpukhovsky, or even with Yashvin. Wonderful! But once again there is a fly in the ointment.

Vronsky has a toothache, and his mouth fills with saliva.

Come now, isn't it possible for a young, distinguished, handsome, and healthy hero to go off to war without a cold, without salivation, or without stomach cramps? I think it is. And this toothache is not related to anything psychological, to anything organic, either in the present or the future. Vronsky is upset enough as it is, and in Koznyshov, according to the tacit attestation of the author himself, no particular inner process occurs as a result of this toothache of his fellow conversationalist. It is neither Natasha's "diapers," "the back of Levin's neck" as perceived by Kitty, nor Karenin's "ears" as seen through Anna's mind and heart.

It only proves that when Count Tolstoy completed the sublime and thoroughly real character of his noble hero with this last poetic touch (the departure for Serbia), he apparently became frightened by what he thought was excess poetry (although it is quite possible in life) and quickly placed about half a dozen of those natural "flies" on his excellent portrait all at once.

This aching tooth is not a requirement of life. It is the personal requirement of an author not yet completely satiated with naturalism. This ugly and needless pain does not relate to the life psychology of the character, but to the literary psychology of the novelist himself. . . .

As is evident from the examples quoted above, all the faults about which I have been speaking occur in *Anna Karenina* as well, but less frequently than in *War and Peace*. The work is cleaner. The psychological analysis is truer; it is more organically connected with the characters' actions, et cetera. The language, even when read aloud, is more pleasant. And there is somewhat less of all sorts of those "flies." Even great talents have their mental limitations. The personally brilliant Tolstoy nevertheless grew up on a triple Russian negation—first, on a political negation, i.e., a negation of everything at the top of the social structure. Result: excessive idolization of the peasant, soldier, and simple army officer such as Maksim Maksimych,[1] et cetera. Second, on a moral negation: in his early works, particularly in *Childhood* and *Stories of Sevastopol*, all is vanity, vanity! The analysis is one-sided and captious; there is an artificial and unnatural magnification of microscopic fibers and cells to the size of tissues visible to the naked eye. And finally, on an aesthetic negation: on the overpowering examples of the great Gogol and partly on the weaknesses of Turgenev, who, under the influence of the

[1] In Lermontov's *Hero of Our Times*. [Tr.]

times, spoiled his delicate, elegant, and fragrant talent, now by pretensions to a sort of humor, of which he possessed very little, now by pretensions to spleen. I say "pretensions," for if you really want to have your fill of frenzied spleen, you should not read Turgenev, but Saltykov-Shchedrin, or Dostoevsky's *Notes from the Underground.* Saltykov-Shchedrin's spleen is dry, gloating, and rather base, but it is powerful in its baseness. Dostoevsky's spleen is morbid and mixed with bitter and often deeply moving tears. Tolstoy grew up on this entire negative school of ours, and although he splendidly outgrew it in his two great novels, even in them the scars from those natural nets in which his mighty talent long struggled in youth are still too noticeable.

The only place these scars, these flies, these rough spots, and these bumps are not evident is in his stories for the common folk. These small stories are like fine vessels of pure, white, translucent, expensive porcelain. The clever draftsman has tenderly and discreetly drawn on them little pink and blue flowers, little golden lines, and some ladybirds with little black spots on their red and straw-colored backs.

Ars longa, vita brevis! Alas, even for genius!

XIII

I shall continue with this same thing.

Language, or to put it in a more general way as they did in the old days, style (or I can express it in still another way— the manner of narration), is an outward thing, but this outward thing in literature is just like the face and manners of a person: it is the most visible outward expression of the innermost and sacred life of the spirit. The face and manners of people express incomparably more of the unconscious than the conscious; more of their nature or developed character than their intelligence. From this outward appearance, many of us learn to guess the differences in character, but scarcely a person can be found who, from the manners and faces of two different people, could determine the differences in their minds without knowing their thoughts or without having heard their conversation. Similarly, in works of fiction, there is something almost unconscious, or completely unconscious and profound, which is expressed with striking clarity in precisely the external devices, the general flow of speech, its rhythm, the very choice of words, sometimes even in the involuntary choice. The author cannot find other words; he has forgotten them, or he dislikes them, owing to some sort of unpleasant associations in his mind. He is accustomed to other words that do not jar on him. . . .

Of course, "table" will be "table" with everyone, and "chair," "chair"; but "person" with one writer will simply be "person," whereas with another nowadays it will be "gentleman," or even "individual," or "fellow." "A well-developed gentleman," "an amazing fellow." Try to get a person with good taste to use the expression "an intellectual" without derision; try to get him to write this word simply and seriously without quotation marks—he will never agree to it. I would rather use some obscene word than let myself say a "well-developed gentleman" instead of "an intelligent man." And so on. People of different periods, different sex, and different aesthetic upbringing express themselves differently about one and the same thing. In a broader context, this difference is even noticeable in whole nations. The French prefer to make everything somewhat more lofty than life; this was particularly true in the past. The Russians of the most recent semi-Gogolian period (not yet finished) prefer to make everything as base as possible. The English take a middle course. Suppose, for example, it is necessary to say that one of the male characters was frightened. An Englishman would more than likely simply say, without exaggerating either one way or the other, either positively or negatively: "Intensely frightened, James stood motionless," et cetera. A Frenchman: "Alfred began to tremble!

A deathly pallor covered his handsome face. He withdrew, but with dignity."

The Russian writer would prefer to express himself thus: "My hero, like a blackguard, got cold feet and trudged off home." Perhaps even better: "dashed off home."

This all relates to the choice of individual words and whole phrases.

Now something also about the manner of speech and manner of exposition. Earlier writers, very early ones, generally preferred in their narrative works to tell the story for several pages in their own name, inserting only from time to time bits of the characters' conversation, or even just their most characteristic words and phrases. Nowadays, the author tries to shorten his own account, perhaps intentionally, in order to please the reader, who is too impatient, active, and spoiled by the speed of present-day life; or perhaps unintentionally, because he is accustomed to write this way himself, and no other way pleases him. Today, narration in the name of the author is generally shorter, and all the space is taken up by the conversation, movement, and little pranks of the characters themselves, frequently to the point of needless and tiresome nonsense. This is called "action," or "verve."

Suppose, for example, one must say that the heroine's meditation was interrupted when she was called to tea. A much earlier writer, even if disposed to realism, would have preferred to tell us of this, I suppose, as follows:

"But her deep meditation did not last long. They called her to tea, and she went, thinking sadly and apprehensively of the difficult explanation facing her with her father."

But today he would write:

" 'It's terrible! It's terrible. What am I to do?' she kept repeating, while shaking her head and looking at her clean, pink fingernails. [This, too, is absolutely necessary for some reason or other.]

" 'Miss, please come to tea,' said the servant in a bass voice, upon entering the room."

And it is good if it is only "in a bass voice." Sometimes it is in greater detail. For example: "The door opened with a creak. The flies that had just settled down on it to rest, flew up in a thick swarm. Bending sideways and slightly thrusting himself through the half-open door, Arkhip showed his grinning face . . ." (or perhaps even his ugly pock-marked mug), et cetera.

I do not understand—what is the point of this? In my opinion, it greatly mars the style. Students and young people in general must be kept from these models. One should allow this style only as an exception, and not set it as an example, as the supreme model, or as an inevitable form. One can tolerate this style in such writers as Tolstoy, Pisemsky,[1] and Turgenev. We can and even must (although with a wry face) forgive them for it, either because of other merits, or because, with Tolstoy, for example, even these essentially useless things frequently turn out more cleverly than with all the rest. He sometimes uses these bad habits of our universal school quite deftly and resourcefully in order to present us with some very amusing or profound psychological observation. But at this point, it is once again appropriate to recall the old saying: "*Quod licet bovi, non licet Iovi.*" That is, on the one hand: "What comes off well with Tolstoy, is very disgusting in an average talent"; and on the other, just the reverse: "What is right for Mr. X should not be met with in Tolstoy."

I might furthermore note here that the majority today finds it more real and truthful to write: "Miss, please come and have your tea," rather than "They called her to tea."

Is that really the way it happens? One might have doubts. In life itself, in material life, let us assume, it actually happens that way. People enter, they speak, et cetera. Perhaps flies even swarm up from the door, leaving specks behind. But is that the way all this is imprinted in our spiritual life? In

---

[1] A. F. Pisemsky (1820–1881), a novelist and playwright, one of the great realists of Russian literature. Unlike so many of his compatriots, he had little use for ideas and theories. [Tr.]

our memory there remain only certain images, certain words and sounds, certain of our own and other people's movements and utterances, even from yesterday. They—these images, colors, sounds, movements, and words—are scattered here and there over a general background of sadness or joy, distress or happiness; or they shine like occasional lights in the general and dark gulf of indifferent oblivion. No one exactly remembers a conversation in its entirety and development, not even from yesterday. All one remembers is the general spirit and certain individual words and ideas. Therefore, I find that the ancient manner of narration (somewhat more from the author and in a general way, and somewhat less in the form of conversation and description of all the characters' movements) is more *real*, in the best sense of the word, i.e., more truthful and natural according to the basic laws of our spirit.

Of course, and I repeat, it is not easy to rid oneself of the practices of the time and the school, not even for genius. In order to do this, one must first satiate himself almost to revulsion with the given school, both as reader and writer, and then consciously seek new paths—drive out the old nail with a new one; or sometimes even the reverse: drive out yesterday's nail with a very old and forgotten one, often one that is intentionally alien and different, foreign, or ancient. Or one must have in his own nature something special, something physiological, something that automatically turns away from the extremes and routine of the prevailing style. Genius is not absolutely necessary here. What is necessary, I say, is a physiological, or some other, peculiarity of sex, age, environment, et cetera.

In our country, for example, from the end of the forties to the present, our female talents, as a direct result of their natural tendencies, have yielded less to the influence of the Gogolian style and the Natural School in general. The most talented of our female writers—Eugenia Tur, Marko Vovchok, and Kokhanovskaya—have, in form, style, and manner, avoided this pressure to belittle everything more so than have the richer and more interesting male talents, their contemporaries. *The Niece, Three Stages of Life,* and other novellas of Eugenia Tur are written in a language that is pure and simple—that of the old nobility, so to say—a language more reminiscent of the thirties than the forties. I have already spoken of the delicate, lacelike, and harmonious speech of Marko Vovchok. Kokhanovskaya is heavier than they, and in places even much coarser. In this respect, she comes closer to the contemporary male writers than the other two. On the other hand, her poetry is so powerful and distinctive, her language so picturesquely original and in places impassioned that she compensates a hundredfold for certain blunders in her style. Sometimes she even reminds one of something Gogolian—but what? She reminds one of the *positive* aspects of the great Gogolian muse: his strong pathos, his expressive, lyric, and impassioned regard for nature, et cetera. In passing, I should also like to remark about the content, the choice of heroes, and the method of presenting these heroes' outward appearance and their character. The men, particularly those whom the heroines more or less like, are presented by all these women in a much more favorable light than is done even by Turgenev, that is, by the most elegant—in this respect and for this time—male author (I am, of course, speaking of the time before Bolkonsky, Oblonsky, Troyekurov, Vronsky, et cetera). Prince Chelsky in Eugenia Tur's *The Niece* is much worse from a moral standpoint than Lavretsky. But the aesthetic ray of feminine sympathy presents him in a more favorable light than the sincere respect felt by Lavretsky's male creator could do for him. In the novel *Three Stages of Life*, Eugenia Tur grieves over the fate of her weak, but interesting, hero. She does not despise or humiliate him as almost all the writers of the time more or less despised and humiliated their weak heroes: as Pisemsky did with Tyufak,[1] Goncharov with Alexander Aduyev,[2] and Turgenev with so many of his heroes. (Later on, Tolstoy

[1] In the novel of the same name. [Tr.]
[2] In the novel *A Common Story.* [Tr.]

somewhat despised his Olenin in *The Cossacks*.) Marko Vovchok's female narrators, for the most part young peasants, servants, et cetera, owing to the emancipatory tendency of the author, often blame their "masters" for a good many things, but it never occurs to these amiable narrators to degrade and vilify these same masters (for example, their seducers) by unnecessary fault-finding or in some way having to do with their appearance. Her servant and peasant girls are tidier in this respect than our better artists of the gentry: *Elles sont plus comme il faut* in their style. As for Kokhanovskaya, there is no need even to mention her in this regard: the negative and revolutionary critics of the sixties reproached her precisely for speaking with pathos even about people she did not like (for example, those with too much of a European upbringing).

Thus, it was not some sort of genius, superior to the extremely great talents of Turgenev, Dostoevsky, Pisemsky, and Goncharov, which gave these female talents their particular originality—that was not what created the relative positiveness of their world view. It was not genius that cleansed, with each in her own way, the language and the entire external style of all those "bumps, growths, prickles, and flies," which I myself am sick of mentioning. It was not genius, of course, but the natural inclination of woman toward a more poetic, tidy, and "positive" view of life, of literature and of real, live men, the models for their creations.

The same thing that was given these three women in literature by their sex was given Sergey Timofeyevich Aksakov by his years, when he created his wonderful and irreproachable *Family Chronicle* at, I believe, almost the age of seventy.

That is a thing that really conveys the atmosphere of the time, place, and milieu!

This old man was no genius himself. But *A Family Chronicle* is a work of genius, in the sense that it is truly "classic." It contains nothing at all—not one false feature—that would spoil either the taste, language, or observational practices of anyone who falls under its influence. It can only improve them and lead to a cleaner, straighter, and more judicious path. And, moreover, no matter what one's frame of mind, it will in no way offend the most discriminating, stringent, or whimsical taste. A *Family Chronicle* cannot offend this taste, just as the whole of Pushkin cannot offend it, just as Zhukovsky's "Ondine" or Tolstoy's late tales for the common folk do not offend it.

Everything can bore, even perfection. One does not have to read this completely inoffensive and perfect work again, but if one does ever read it, even for the tenth time, the aesthetic impression will always be the same—a rather pure one—and the verdict also will always be the same: it is irreproachable!

XIV

I am not comparing Aksakov with Tolstoy; that would never do. I am merely comparing A *Family Chronicle* and *Anna Karenina* with *War and Peace*—one work with another, and even then, in one respect only.

I am comparing atmosphere with lack of atmosphere. There are some works that are striking in their isolation. They are brilliant, classic, and exemplary works of nonbrilliant people. These isolated works, in their perfection and artistic charm, not only equal but sometimes even surpass the works of first-rate artists. Such is our *Woe from Wit*. Griboyedov[1] not only was not brilliant himself, he was not even particularly talented in anything else that he wrote, both before and after this comedy. But *Woe from Wit* is brilliant. The very fact that it does not stage well is, in my opinion, a merit rather than a fault. (Theatrical effectiveness is nothing but banality: theatrical effectiveness is really nothing more than the subordi-

---

[1] A. S. Griboyedov (1795–1829), a playwright, poet, musician, linguist, and diplomat. He was killed by a mob while on an official mission in Persia. [Tr.]

nation of the intellect and the higher senses to acoustical and optical conditions, to the nervousness of the audience, et cetera.) *Woe from Wit* is truly inimitable, and in this sense, it is far superior to the more universally intelligible and theatrically effective *Inspector General*. In *Woe from Wit*, there is even warmth; there is poetry. Through the reproachfulness and vexation of Chatsky (or of the author himself), there nevertheless shines a certain ray of love for this reproachable but dear city of Moscow. But what love, what poetry is there in the gray *Inspector General?* None at all. There is much more of it in "After the Play,"[1] which was written after *The Inspector General*. One also finds in other literatures such isolated and classic works which are brilliant creations of nonbrilliant authors. In French literature, there are two such works that were dashed off by their authors in a felicitous and unique moment of complete inner illumination. They are: *Paul and Virginia* of Bernardin de Saint-Pierre and *Manon Lescaut* of Abbé Provost. In English literature, one must include in this category *The Vicar of Wakefield* and perhaps *Jane Eyre*. Had *Werther* been written not by Goethe, but someone else, it, too, could be included here.

In our literature, I cannot think of anything other than *Woe from Wit* and *A Family Chronicle* that would be appropriate here—perhaps only the superb *Story About the Holy Land* by the monk Parfeny, of which Apollon Grigoriev[2] was first to make such a correct appraisal.

A Family Chronicle—there is a wonderful example of the atmosphere corresponding to the spirit of the time, about which we have been speaking. "The idea acquired a simple language and the voice of noble passion!" The degree of delving "into the soul" of the characters, the choice of expressions, the coherence and flow of the Russian language, the general

---

[1] A dialogue written by Gogol in defense of *The Inspector General*. [Tr.]

[2] A. A. Grigoriev (1822–1864), a critic and poet. [Tr.]

nature of the world outlook—everything breathes the period being depicted. If, in addition, we recall still another, also truthful but incomparably weaker work by this same Aksakov—*Childhood Years of Bagrov's Grandson*—then the naturalness and even to a certain extent the physiological inevitability of this "general breathing" corresponding to the period will be even more comprehensible. S. T. Aksakov had seen all the characters in *A Family Chronicle* himself; he had lived with them, had grown up under their influence, had learned how to speak and reason from them. His inner world was filled with the images, the speech, the tone, and even the physical movements of those people, who had long since passed into eternity. The indelible stock of these impressions was preserved in the "Elysium" of his kind and loving heart until the moment he took it into his head to share his riches with us and to incarnate so faultlessly and splendidly for all time those shadows of the past so dear to his heart.

Of course, there is a certain moderation in all this (or to be more precise, there is a slightly perceptible moderation); there is moderation in the psychological withdrawal and moderation in its proximity, which is conducive to the fullness of the result. If Sergey Timofeyevich had been a man of that time and milieu only, if he had not been Timofey Stepanovich's son, but, let us say, his younger brother, who did not live to the time of Zhukovsky, Pushkin, Gogol, Khomyakov, or Belinsky, if he had not even survived many (almost all) of the writers just named, he would not have been able to write *A Family Chronicle* as he did write it: he would have written it worse, less colorfully. Or more likely, he would not even have begun at the time to write about this subject; he would not have found all this sufficiently interesting.

It goes without saying that the influence not only of eminent contemporaries, but also of younger talents and even of his own so fortunately gifted and broadly educated sons played its role. All these influences only helped this splendid old man to present more clearly everything that had existed in him so deeply, so immutably, so semiconsciously, and for so long, but no one could bend him his way—not even Gogol, whom, it is said, he very much respected. He was both too old and too radiant for sad, coarse negation.

At the proper time he brought forth his fragrant, healthy fruit and then passed away. Tyutchev's line fits him: "His light shone forth and then died out."

Yes, one can believe, one cannot help feeling that the poetry of *A Family Chronicle* is the poetry of precisely its period. Its general spirit is the spirit of the time and the milieu—a spirit which was only waiting for the stimulating influences of the most recent period to embody it in sounds and images. Not only the words and actions of the main characters, but also the words of the author himself convey the atmosphere of a simpler and calmer period, just as everything in *Anna Karenina* breathes its time—a time that is incomparably more complex and mentally disturbed. But I cannot bring myself to say the same thing so sincerely about *War and Peace*. I doubt, I distrust, I waver.

For greater clarification of my critical idea, I shall permit myself here to imagine something else—something quite impossible as actual fact, but most natural, I think, as retrospective fancy. I shall permit myself to imagine that D'Anthès missed his mark, and that Pushkin, in the forties, wrote a long novel about the year 1812. Would he have written it as Tolstoy did? No, he would not! Perhaps worse, but not in that way. Pushkin's novel would probably be less original, less subjective, less overburdened, perhaps even less pithy, than *War and Peace*, but on the other hand, it would contain absolutely none of those unnecessary "flies" on the characters or those "stumbling blocks" in the language. The psychological analysis would be less "burrowing" and captious in some instances, and less magnificent in others. The fantasy of all those dreams, semidreams, waking dreams, and those instances of dying and death would be less individual than with Tolstoy. It would probably be less delicate or ethereal, less powerful than with him, but on the other hand, it would give rise to fewer doubts. The philosophy of war and of life would be different with Pushkin and would not be inserted in the story in large, whole pieces as with Tolstoy. The patriotic lyricism would be diffused more evenly throughout, and would not be constantly dampened by theophilanthropic reservations. "Our every step" would be "marked by the grace of the god of war."[1] Pushkin's *Year 1812* would also (to judge from his final, premortal turn of mind) be a much more Orthodox work than *War and Peace*. Pushkin would most likely portray the events in his work more as an excellent article in the magazine *Faith and Reason* recently portrayed this same struggle of Napoleon against Alexander and Kutuzov than as Tolstoy did. With Tolstoy, God is a sort of blind and cruel fate, whom Whose hands I do not know how one even can save himself by means of the free choice of love alone. In the *Faith and Reason* article, God is a living and personal God, Whose ways only are inscrutable for a certain time. Pushkin, in his own name, would probably not even call the French marshals and generals fleeing in carriages and fur coats "wicked and insignificant men who had done a great deal of evil," just as those same Russian heroes who drove them from Moscow in 1812 and cursed them from passion and not from a dull, moral philosophy probably did not call them "in their hearts." At that time, bellicosity was fashionable, and educated people were more direct and frank in their chivalrous world view than today. Today even those who for some reason or other crave war will fib right up until its declaration, saying they do not want it: "War is disaster," they say, and that is all. No one dares speak otherwise now. But after its declaration, the very next day, they all suddenly draw and rattle their "intellectual" swords (at long last sincerely!) and continue to do so until the day peace is signed. In those days, so glorious

[1] From Pushkin's poem "Poltava." [Tr.]

for the poetry of life, man's ideal was the soldier, not the village teacher or office worker!

The religion in Pushkin's book would more closely resemble the universally national one. Perhaps it would also be highly subjective in sincerity, but it would be less individual in manner and less cosmopolitan in spirit than with Tolstoy. Both Pushkin's heroes, and especially he himself where he spoke in his own name would, where necessary, speak almost the same language spoken at the time, i.e., one that was simpler, lighter, more pellucid, not dense, not overburdened, not too highly colored in one way or another—at one time too coarse and black, at another, too refined and purple, as with Tolstoy.

And precisely because of this "general atmosphere," Pushkin's general psychological music of the time and place would be more precise and true. His work would inspire greater historical confidence and at the same time would create a more perfect artistic illusion for us than does *War and Peace*. Pushkin would write of 1812 in the way he wrote his *Dubrovsky, Captain's Daughter,* and *Blackamoor of Peter the Great.* Wasn't it Tolstoy's false "general spirit," wasn't it his manner, too highly ornamented and ponderous in details for the period, which provoked the late Norov,[1] an eyewitness, to protest to him so sharply—and at the same time so feebly? The Russian people of that time could not think as clearly, imagine as vividly, or observe as closely as we. In will-power, intensity of passion, intensity of feeling, intensity of faith—in all this, they probably surpassed us, but how could they compare and contend with us in the field of thought and observation! But Norov's protest was so feeble and pale that I, for example, with my rather good memory, do not remember anything from his remarks except the fact that "a horse ran by with its face shot away" and that "our soldiers wanted to finish off a

---

[1] A. S. Norov (1795–1869), a statesman and minor writer. His travel sketches were perhaps his best work. [Tr.]

wounded comrade who was writhing in agony." Norov's feeling, his "hunch," was probably true; his thinking was poor, his imagination weak, and he was unable to defend in his own way the period he loved and which, in his opinion, Tolstoy had not quite accurately depicted.

Returning once again for a moment to this imaginary novel of Pushkin, I should like also to say that in admiring this nonexistent novel we would probably be submitting equally to the genius of the author and to the spirit of the period. In reading *War and Peace*, also with the greatest of pleasure, we very clearly sense that we are captivated not so much by the spirit of the period as by the personal genius of the author; that we are satisfied not with the "atmosphere" of the time and place, but with the original, unique (in its totality), and creative work of our contemporary. In admiring *War and Peace*, we nevertheless have a certain right to shake our heads skeptically. The characters of *A Family Chronicle* and the characters of *Anna Karenina* are true not only to themselves from beginning to end, true in a universally human and a psychological way, but also to their time and place. In this very same way, the characters of this imaginary novel by Pushkin would be true to themselves and to the period, if we are to judge by *The Blackamoor of Peter the Great* and *Dubrovsky*. Neither the characters, the atmosphere, the actual people depicted, nor the personal music of their author-narrator would breathe our time.

In *War and Peace*, the characters are completely true and verisimilar only to themselves, psychologically—and I shall even go further: the accuracy, detail, and truth of their general psychological treatment is so profound that they could not even be equaled by Pushkin himself, who, because of the nature of his talent, liked more to look at life *à vol d'oiseau* than to rummage around in its depths, digging from there, along with precious gems, the vile worms of the "naturalistic breeding farm." As for these same characters in *War and Peace* (particularly the two main heroes—Andrey and Pierre), if they are considered from the standpoint of their fidelity to the period, then one might doubt. In general, I cannot speak as decisively about these characters as I did about the excess of observation, the captiousness of the analysis, the awkwardness of the language, and the certain triteness of the universally Russian and universally naturalistic style.

When I am told for the tenth time: "a brawny arm," "a pudgy hand," "a dry hand," I haven't the slightest doubt that I am right in being displeased with this.

When I am assured that Kutuzov "liked to hear himself speak," I exclaim with disgust (not physical, but mental and moral): "That's old! That's old! We've heard so much of that from Turgenev, Dostoevsky, and from Count Tolstoy himself as far back as *Childhood and Adolescence* that we're sated to the point of disgust. It is not the healthy, almost scientific analysis that everyone must admire in Tolstoy, examples of which I have already cited. It is analysis that is broken and useless, analysis that makes an elephant out of a fly!"

I am disgusted when a writer (any writer at all, Pisemsky, Turgenev, or Tolstoy himself, it makes no difference) tells me as follows: "'Miss, please come to tea,' he said in a bass voice, while stupidly grinning . . ." et cetera, instead of "She was sitting by the window deep in thought when they called her to tea."

I can admit that by repudiating the first method I am an aesthetic monomaniac, an artistic psychopath, if it turns out that absolutely no one sympathizes with me in this almost acoustic demand. But even so, I do not waver, but sense the difference—I sense it very strongly.

I can waver in determining the value or the correctness of this strange feeling of mine. But I cannot help realizing its strength, and I do not want to part with it, even if it is found to be abnormal. And I shall always say: a straightforward, simple account in the author's name, even if it is somewhat drawn out and sluggish, or, on the contrary, too concise, is better than this everlasting exposition that we have today.

" 'Yes,' said so and so, giving a sidelong glance at his boot, which had been excellently polished that morning."

" 'Oh,' exclaimed so and so, sipping his tea, which had long since grown cold and which had been served him an hour ago by Anfisa Sergeyevna, a middle-aged cook in a checkered dress that had been made for two silver rubles by the dressmaker Tolstikova."

No, gentlemen, we've had enough. Enough! It is intolerable, even in Tolstoy.

In the first two cases—that is, in my condemnation of the excess, the unevenness, and the eavesdropping—I am definitely right.

In the third matter ("They called her to tea" and "Miss, please come . . ."), it may be that I still want to travel along the highway in a coach and four, while everyone else is more than content to go by railroad, not in the least annoyed by its inconvenience, bondage, crowdedness, and frequent jolting. In the first two cases, I am convinced of my intellectual integrity, but here, I do not even pretend to be right. I am merely content with my strange taste. (However, I am not unhopeful that at least a few other people will understand me when they recall certain of their own feelings similar to mine.)

But when it is a question of whether the characters of *War and Peace* are true to the spirit of the period or to its "aroma," so to say, I can only waver and doubt. I ask searching questions, now of myself, now of the author, and after a long, a very long, period of hesitation and mental struggle, I finally tend to think that some of the characters are indisputably authentic (for example, Nikolay Rostov, Denisov, Dolokhov), but that others (for example, Pierre Bezukhov and Andrey Bolkonsky) . . . well, I don't know.

If someone will convince me that the depiction of Pierre

Bezukhov's character is as true to its period as the depiction
of Levin, Vronsky, and Karenin's characters are true to ours,
I shall be very glad.

But I do not know if this is easy to decide.

XV

I still insist on asking: "To what extent are Pierre Bezukhov
and Andrey Bolkonsky true to their period; to what extent are
Levin and Vronsky true to their own time?" Like all the
characters in *War and Peace*, they may be psychologically
true, in a general sense, without respect to the period, but
I do not know if they are historically true in all the shades of
their depiction. One might first of all doubt whether actual
people of that time—a Pierre Bezborodka (let's say) or an
Andrey Volkhonsky—were really so subtle and complex in
their thinking. That they did not speak the same language
that Bezukhov and Bolkonsky speak—of this there is almost
no doubt. Otherwise, some traces of it would have remained in
Russian literature of the beginning of this century, in memoirs,
and in other written records. Let us assume that many of our
people even now are more complex, more profound, and much
bolder in their thinking and speaking than in their writing and
publishing. Let us assume that between the time a person has
a clear and clever thought and the time he is able or decides
to transmit it in writing to others, much time passes—even
with experienced writers, and not just with intelligent people
who write very little; however, we must, nevertheless, assume
such a disproportion: Russian prose writers, poets, and thinkers
of the first quarter of our century were simpler, less complex,
more superficial, and more pallid in their thinking and writing
than those two well-bred men of that same time, one of whom
(Pierre) tries to think about everything without restraint, but
cannot settle on anything at all, and cannot write anything
except his Masonic diary; the other (Andrey) also thinks a
great deal, although with restraint, but he is so unaccustomed

to coherent and consistent thought that upon meeting the seminarian Speransky he is astounded at the scholarly, Western coherency of his thinking. Of course, Gromeka was right in his epilogue when he said to Levin[1] (this time as if directly to Count Tolstoy): "It is as if I am in a dream and cannot make all this out very well, but I remember that when awake, I knew that both Bolkonsky and Bezukhov were you: Bolkonsky, the dry you, and Bezukhov, you also, but when you are kind and open to the whole world." To call Prince Andrey dry is as much an error and untruth as to call Vronsky inane (as this same Gromeka did call him), but Gromeka is right in saying that Count Tolstoy made his two chief heroes of 1812 think almost his own thoughts in the manner of the sixties; he made both these well-bred men—who grew up partly on Russian literature of that time, either poor or imitative, and partly on French literature, rich but bombastic—think the thoughts, first, of a man of genius, and second, of a man who was highly original personally and moreover who had already survived (more or less) Goethe, Pushkin, Schopenhauer, Herzen, the Slavophiles, and, above all, two of his predecessors, who were also very clever in the use of psychological analysis—Turgenev and Dostoevsky.

Here, however, it is necessary to pause and say that I do not sympathize with the rash habit of our critics who continually place these three names on a par with each other. And always just these names. It is unfair: "Turgenev, Tolstoy, and Dostoevsky; Dostoevsky, Turgenev, and Tolstoy; Tolstoy, Dostoevsky, and Turgenev." True, Tolstoy must be mentioned: he is the crowning achievement of the realist school. He is its supreme and most complete manifestation. But why, for example, not sometimes say: "Tolstoy, Markevich, and Pisemsky"? Or: "Tolstoy, Kokhanovskaya, and Markevich"? Equal glory and equal success are by no means guaranteed to equal merit. . . .

In just mentioning Dostoevsky and Turgenev in connection

[1] See M. S. Gromeka's book *The Late Works of Count L. N. Tolstoy.*

with analysis, I did not in the least want to equate them with Tolstoy. I merely mean that, although Count Tolstoy has left them both far behind on this path, they, of course, set out on it before he did. Particularly important here is Turgenev, who more closely resembles him in the choice of milieu and in the nature of his talent (but not, of course, in its magnitude). It goes without saying that Turgenev's analysis is much more one-sided and homogeneous than Tolstoy's. With few exceptions, it is always one and the same thing: the proud remorse, the annoyance with himself, and the indecision of an intelligent and sensitive, but weak man; the hero's self-condemnation or his melancholy. Dostoevsky's analysis is fairly uniform in its morbid, ardent, and frenzied corruption.

As an example, let us recall the beginning of *Notes from the Underground*:

> I'm a sick man. I'm a malicious man, I'm an unattractive man. I think my liver is diseased. By the way, I don't understand a damned thing [how much spite there is in that phrase "a damned thing!"] about my sickness, and I don't know for sure just what is wrong with me. I don't go to a doctor—I never have—although I respect medicine and doctors. Besides, I'm extremely superstitious; well, at least enough to respect medicine. (I'm well-enough educated not to be superstitious, but I *am* superstitious.) No, sir, I don't want to go to a doctor out of spite . . . et cetera.

His impotent irritation continues to grow and grow. And to a greater or lesser extent, this monotonous motif can even be heard in those works of Dostoevsky where he tries to be more objective.

But Tolstoy's analysis is healthy, calm, heterogeneous, and sober. The two cannot even be compared in this regard. I said that Tolstoy himself had read Turgenev and Dostoevsky from the time of his youth; however, Pierre Bezukhov and Prince Bolkonsky, at the beginning of this century, had not yet read "The Diary of a Superfluous Man," *Poor Folk*, or *The*

Humiliated and Insulted; they did not yet know Onegin,
Pechorin, Hegel, Schopenhauer, George Sand, or Gogol.

Well, then, is it plausible that these people of the time of
the Consulate and the Empire thought in almost the same style
as we do now—we who are sometimes burdened to the break-
ing point with all the words and thoughts of our precursors; we
who have had all their diseases and have experienced all their
enthusiasms?

Somehow, I do not believe it!

I want to resort here again (for greater clarity) to the
expedient to which I resorted once before when I imagined
that Pushkin had written a novel on the life of 1812. I want
to explain something that actually exists by something that
does not and which is impossible. Let us imagine that Count
Tolstoy wrote *War and Peace* not about the time of Alexander I, but about a period closer to us—the time of the Siege
of Sevastopol and the Danube campaign against the Turks. At
the time of those battles, Count Tolstoy was already well over
twenty years old himself: and in those same years (the fifties),
he was, on the one hand, already a very well-known writer; on
the other hand, he had personally participated in the war.
He knew perfectly well what many people thought at the
time and how they expressed themselves; he knew the extent
to which fault-finding and the morbid refinement of psychological analysis went at that precise time in real life, even
among friends. (See in *Childhood, Adolescence, and Youth*
Nikolay Irtenyev's relations with Prince Neklyudov, and also
many other works of the time.) He could personally attest that
in the fifties rifts and quarrels, for example, between highly cultured friends occurred much less seldom over political views
than today, and much more frequently over what Turgenev's
Hamlet of the Shchigrov District complained of when he
said that a coterie is a terrible thing, that in a coterie, "everyone considers it his right to thrust his dirty hands into someone else's vitals." (Forgive me if I do not remember it word for

word.) Count Tolstoy knows from experience that whereas the political unrest in Russia since the beginning of the sixties has greatly disorganized our society, it has also brought about, on that score, a significant "recovery" in us, as Aksakov liked to express it. Since then, we have begun to spend incomparably less time finding fault with the "nature" of our neighbor and have become stricter about the shades of his "tendency." Educated, intelligent, and refined people of the post-Reform years have become, so to say, more "tendentious" than the people of the pre-Reform years; but, on the other hand, they have become more sober in their personal relations.

On the boundary of this sudden personal and social change, there looms in our memory the bloody tragedy of our three-year struggle on the banks of the Danube and in the Crimea. I myself served as a medical officer at the time, and experienced all this as a youth. I am sure that Count Tolstoy remembers what a disproportionate difference there was then between the proud "Hamlet-like" subtlety and vacillation of some people and the simplicity and lack of complexity of others, from both the highest and the lowest levels of society—between the Rudins,[1] the Olenins,[2] the "superfluous men,"[3] on the one hand, and the Volyntsevs,[4] the Prince N.'s (that man of the world and rival of the intelligent but unfortunate Chulkaturin in "A Superfluous Man"[5]), and the Vronskys of the time, who led the Russian common people in the Crimea and perished along with them for our native land. The people of the upper class indeed learned to humble themselves before the "Karatayevs"[6] of the time, but the Volyntsevs did not (see *Rudin*); nor did the Nikolay Rostovs or the Vronskys of the fifties who, although

---

[1] Turgenev's impractical hero in the novel of the same name. [Tr.]

[2] The hero of Tolstoy's *The Cossacks*. [Tr.]

[3] The weak, ineffective male characters who predominate in the fiction of Turgenev and other nineteenth-century Russian writers. [Tr.]

[4] A character in *Rudin*. [Tr.]

[5] Turgenev's "Diary of a Superfluous Man." [Tr.]

[6] The simple-hearted peasant soldier in *War and Peace* who accepts with resignation all that comes his way. [Tr.]

they liked the Karatayevs, would on occasion readily whip them, and at times call them "beasts." However, the Lavretsky's,[1] the Aksakovs,[2] and sometimes even the more Western Rudins and Beltovs[3] during the time of the Count's youth and my own did humble themselves before the "people."

It is highly doubtful to me, for instance, whether Count Bezukhov in 1812 could idolize Karatayev and the soldiers in general exactly as he does idolize them. Here is what he thinks after Borodino:

> "Oh, what a terrible thing fear is," thought Pierre, "and how disgracefully I yielded to it! But they . . . *they* were firm and calm all the time up to the end. . . ."
>
> They in Pierre's mind, were the soldiers—those who had been with the battery, those who had fed him, and those who prayed to the icon. *They*—these strange people, previously unknown to him—*they* stood out clearly and sharply in his mind, apart from all the other people.
>
> "To be a soldier, just a soldier. To enter with all one's being into that common life, to be imbued with what makes them as they are! But how can you throw off everything that is unnecessary and diabolical, all the burden of the outer man? At one time, I could be like that. I could run away from father as I wanted. After my duel with Dolokhov, I could have been sent off as an ordinary soldier." And there flashed across Pierre's mind the dinner at the club, at which he had challenged Dolokhov to a duel, and afterward the memory of his benefactor in Torzhok. And then Pierre imagined the solemn lodge meeting. It was being held at the English Club. And someone he knew, someone close and dear to him, was sitting at the end of the table.
>
> "Yes, it's he! It's my benefactor. But surely he died," thought Pierre. "Yes, he died, but I didn't know he was alive. How sorry I was that he died, and how happy I am that he's alive again!"

[1] The submissive hero of Turgenev's *A Nest of Gentlefolk*. [Tr.]
[2] Konstantin and Ivan Aksakov, leading Slavophiles, the sons of Sergey Aksakov (*A Family Chronicle*). [Tr.]
[3] Another superfluous man, the hero of Herzen's *Whose Fault?* [Tr.]

On one side of the table were sitting Anatoly, Dolokhov, Nesvitsky, Denisov and other such men (in Pierre's dream, this group of people was just as clearly defined as was the group of people he called "they"), and those men, Anatoly and Dolokhov, were shouting and singing loudly; but above their noise, the voice of his benefactor could be heard speaking unceasingly, and the sound of his words was significant and as unbroken as the rumble on the battlefield, but it was pleasant and consoling. Pierre did not understand what his benefactor was saying, but he knew (the category of these thoughts was also clear in his dream) that his benefactor was speaking about goodness, about the possibility of being like them. And *they*, with their simple, kind, resolute faces were surrounding his benefactor on all sides. But although they were kind, they did not look at Pierre; they did not know him. Pierre suddenly wanted to attract their attention and say something to them. He raised himself slightly, but at that same moment, he realized that his legs had become uncovered and were cold. . . .

"The most difficult thing is the subjection of man's freedom to the laws of God," said the voice. "Simplicity is submission to God; you cannot escape Him. And *they* are simple. *They* do not speak, but act."

This is by no means Count Bezukhov of 1812; it is Count L. N. Tolstoy of the fifties and sixties himself. It is the author of the stories of Sevastopol and the Caucasus from the early period.

I do not believe that Count Bezukhov thought of the people in precisely this way. Kind and educated people of the time could, of course, pity the people and deeply sympathize with their needs and misfortunes, particularly if, at the same time, they had liberal tendencies of the Western type. But to admire the common people in precisely this way, with such an obvious touch of Slavophilism, as Pierre does—this, he could hardly have done at the time.

It seems to me that if one of our most refined, most intelligent, and best educated people had been moved at the sight of folk simplicity and unpretentiousness, his emotion would probably have assumed a sort of pastoral or semiclassical character, in the French manner. Even at that time, of course, something resembling the future Slavophile type of love for the common folk could have appeared for a moment, but only for a moment. But in Pierre's mind, all this is so clear, definite, and distinct that it much more closely resembles the words of the author himself, or those of Dostoevsky about the "God-bearing people" than the thoughts of a liberal of the time of Alexander I. Only toward the end of the sixties, and after the Slavophiles, did Count Tolstoy himself hit upon this clear and excellent expression of his "populist" feelings and reach the point where he could create the almost saintly character of Karatayev. Yet, we are to believe that his hero (without even being the brilliant artist that his creator was) could understand all this so clearly half a century earlier. (Half a century, counting back from the sixties, when Count Tolstoy wrote and published *War and Peace*.)

I cannot believe it!

In 1812, everything in the life of Russian society with the exception of national patriotism was expressed somewhat more pallidly, weakly, simply, and flatly (not poorly, but flatly), in bas-relief, so to say, than it was in the period of the Crimean War. By the fifties, the intensity of national patriotism had greatly diminished, but all other psychological and intellectual resources of society had grown to the utmost. I find that since then nothing of quality has been added to our life. Everything was already in reserve, theoretically, even nihilism—of the contemporary, not the early French, type.

Everything was in reserve, everything was already diverse and in high relief: subtlety of mind, a distinctively mature imagination (Fet's early poems, Gogol's lofty, fantastic, and deeply moving pages: "A Terrible Vengeance," "Rome," "Russia, the Troika," et cetera), bitter disbelief, and an abhorrence of things Russian, which verged on joy upon our defeat in the Crimea.

All that was needed was will and dissemination. We needed the opportunity more freely to draw on these vast and diverse psychological stores.

The will was provided. And now we are harvesting the wheat and the tares which we sowed so thickly in the forties and fifties.

In the days of Kutuzov and Arakcheyev everything in our life was already quite variegated, but pale in appearance; everything was still in bas-relief. By the time of the Crimean War, much—practically everything—stood out in greater relief and more statuesquely against the general national background. In the sixties and seventies, everything jumped down from its pedestal or broke away from the ancient walls to which it had been attached and dashed off somewhere, having become confused in the struggle and commotion!

The complex and accelerated movement of community life could not help being reflected in the life of the personal spirit as well. Our thoughts and feelings became complicated by new problems and nuances, and their interchange became much faster than before.

This accelerated, contemporary complexity of our spiritual life is conveyed equally well in both *War and Peace* and *Anna Karenina*. In the latter it is appropriate. I do not know if it is in the former.

XVI

Thus, having imagined something highly imaginable, but in fact impossible—an epic-chronicle of the forties and fifties written by Count Tolstoy—I have come to the following conclusions: this nonexistent epic-chronicle would be more authentic than *War and Peace*; its characters and their conversation would be truer to their time; the degree of their subtlety—

no longer imitative as in 1812, but original and for the most part negative, or even caviling at trifles—would be in keeping with the period. The narration on the part of the author (remaining exactly as we see it in the *War and Peace* of 1812) would resemble the way almost all our people (both Turgenev and the rest, even Tolstoy himself) thought, spoke, and wrote at that precise time.

The character or style of the author's narration is always in some way or other reflected in both the characters and the events. Just as one and the same landscape is illuminated differently by the dawn, the noonday sun, the moon, and a Bengal light, so are the very same events and the very same people illuminated differently by different devices of the author, even his subsidiary ones.

The period of the Crimean War was much more conscious and psychologically complex than that of 1812; therefore, it is clear that a writer's speech that is more vivid and "dense" would be in harmony with the period.

Even here (i.e., in a novel from the life of the fifties), I would probably dislike this much-too-familiar complexity; but I would say to myself: that is the way the best talents write today—that is the way they write, they are successful, and their fame has grown before my very eyes. I myself at one time (in the fifties) always submitted unconditionally to it. And it was not only I who submitted, nor was it just a handful of other people with unusual tastes, but the overwhelming majority of writers, critics, and readers. Before my very eyes, the number of people has decreased who, like that Moscow lady, would say: "Gogol, *c'est un genre*, but in the rest of your writers [i.e., mine at the time], all this is out of place." Their number has dwindled and dwindled, and for a long time now, whenever it is a question of unevenness of style, impedimenta in the language, and nonessentials in the thinking, the most "loquacious orators from among our critics are like mute fish" (N. N. Strakhov, for example).

So great is the force of habit, even in thinking people!

After considering all this, I would admit that this imaginary epic-novel about the forties and fifties would, in form, be completely in keeping with its period. I would feel that it would impart the life that the artist is depicting. On the other hand, the portrayal that Count Tolstoy gives of the period of Napoleon and Kutuzov is at times too bright and at times too negative in manner. Moreover, it is too personal, subjective, and individual, in the Tolstoyan manner, for the reflection to seem true. It should be simpler—more like a watercolor.

An inexperienced photographer in the backwoods, without the necessary conveniences, once took a picture of a forty-year-old acquaintance of mine. The facial features and the expression of the eyes were very true; but instead of looking forty years old in the portrait, my friend looked sixty. Why was that? As in the case of a man who had lived a life of thought and passion, he had fine lines on his face, but in order to see them, one had to stand very close. In the evening, he seemed even younger than forty. The photograph was taken on a bright day in bright sunshine, and all the tiny wrinkles came out very deep and very dark, and all the light spots too prominent and white. That is why.

Count Tolstoy, with the too bright sun of his present-day development, has illuminated a life that was much less developed than ours today—in almost all respects: in respect to mental subtlety and the captious analysis of both one's own heart and that of others; in respect to fantasy[1] and philosophical consciousness, in respect to the coarseness, excess, and uselessness of external or fleshly, so to say, observation; and finally, in respect to a most clear and conscious understanding of such folk types as Platon Karatayev.

The basic design is true; the colors are too rich and bright. The skeleton is characteristic; the flesh, I think, is not quite

[1] Fantasy in our literature was only imitative at the time. For example, Zhukovsky. Highly original fantasy first appeared with Gogol.

characteristic. The rhythm and type of blood circulation
are questionable; the cells and microscopic fibers are too numerous and diverse. At one time, they are too large and gran-
ular, at another, too small and delicate.

A word or two more about subtleties, profundities, and
complexities.

During the time of Alexander I, the subtlety in our life
was worldly, and of the highest standard. There was also
a diplomatic subtlety; there was an imitative subtlety in literary tastes, and there was a natural subtlety in tastes of the
heart, particularly in the uppermost circle—among the fine
nobility. (It did not as yet extend below the nobility.)

These aspects are correctly depicted in Count Tolstoy. I
do not know if the scoffing, and even negative, letters of the
diplomat Bilibin were thought up by the author, or if they are
documentary; but, as you know, these letters are written, first,
by a diplomat, and second, in French. Here, the type of subtlety and the type of negation breathe the spirit of their time.
It is not the subtlety of the purely Russian psychological captiousness of a later date; is is not the subtlety of the lacy and
highly developed fantasy of our best Russian artists of the
fifties and seventies; it is not the subtlety of—let's put it
this way—the realistic coarseness, common to us all since
the time of Gogol, Turgenev, Grigorovich, et cetera.

It is a different subtlety: a bitingly mundane, French
subtlety. These letters could have been written by an actual
diplomat of the time, by some B*a*l*a*bin, for example. Here the
negation even smells differently from that peculiarly Russian
negation to which our literature of the last forty years has
so accustomed us that the majority of readers do not, as I
have already said, even notice it.

Bilibin's negation is the sharp and subtle venom of straightforward and large-scale condemnation; it is a spiteful but
calm criticism of our strategic operations of the time; it is
a mockery of the mistakes and the unconscientiousness of our

generals. It is not the realistic slops of our time, not personal psychological fault-finding, not useless and burdensome observation.

These letters are either "documentary" or superbly fabricated.

Also good are the semiecclesiastical spiritual profundities and subtleties of the Masonic diary kept by Pierre. Many touches here are quite natural, even for the beginning of the nineteenth century, precisely because their style is close to the Old Church Slavic, or purely Orthodox, one. Even at that time, these subtle touches had long been no novelty with us. They are also characteristic of the ancient ascetic writers.

Also, I do not know if the answers given Napoleon by our captive Russian officers after Austerlitz are documentary or superbly invented. But they are certainly characteristic of the time. Napoleon says to Prince Repnin:

"Your regiment did its duty honorably!"
"The praise of a great general is a soldier's best reward," answered Repnin.

Napoleon smiles as he looks at the nineteen-year-old Lieutenant Sukhtelen and says:

"He's rather young to come to meddle with us."
"Youth is no hindrance to bravery," answers Sukhtelen.

This rings true.

At that time, educated people liked to consider themselves heroes, and once they tried their valor, they no longer pondered over the question of whether military heroism is necessary, et cetera, as Olenin, for example, does in The Cossacks, and as many other of Tolstoy's characters do. In this sense, both Andrey Bolkonsky and Denisov are, I think, truer to their time than Pierre, who, it always seems to me, philosophizes and vacillates too much the way people do today, too much the way the author himself and other people of a much later date might have vacillated.

He not only seems to me too well developed and too self-conscious, he is almost a man of genius, despite his sometimes intolerable spinelessness. If such people already existed in real life, why is it that nothing of the sort is reflected in the literature of the time? Aren't the wrinkles in his portrait too deep and dark, and the light protruding spots too bright?

True, we all love, and we all personally know this Pierre Bezukhov in almost the same way we love and intimately know an actual living, or even deceased, friend or acquaintance of ours. Genuine talent (of an objective nature) has the power of creating, as it were, living people. Whether we want to or not, we are obliged to remember them as real people. One cannot forget them, one cannot help recognizing them. It is impossible to forget Pechorin, Chichikov, Oblomov, Rudin, Bazarov, Platon Karatayev, or Vronsky; Natasha Rostova, Darya Alexandrovna Oblonskaya, or her husband; or Pisemsky's Kalinovich, Pitershchik, or his ardent, old Freemason; or Markevich's Troyekurov, Olga Rantsova, Kira, Rantsova's father, or Ashanin. It must be said that from the standpoint of an abundance of irreproachably lifelike and artistically sustained characters, this same Russian literature of the last forty years (almost half a century!) is exceedingly rich and distinguished. I must agree with that, and, moreover, must admit that only English literature can perhaps compete with ours in this respect. But even that is doubtful! In attacking the things I dislike about our literature, I do not have the right to forget its merits. I shall even go further: my strictness with our realist school partly derives from a respect for its strong points. That these strong points are great is demonstrated by the mere fact that in the person of its chief representatives, we gained for the first time the upper hand in the field of literature over our former teachers, the Europeans. Western writers did not study us before the time of Turgenev and Tolstoy.

They can now study our literature, not only as a particular type of school, but as the true reflection of a particular life.

From the sum of our novels and stories, one can get a very clear idea of the life of nineteenth-century Russian society. Accuracy, fidelity to real life—that is the particular strength of our literature. Everyone knows it. . . .

I love, I even adore, *War and Peace*: for its gigantic creative work, for the author's bold insertion in the novel of whole pieces of philosophy and strategy, despite the rules of artistic restraint and tidiness which have also prevailed for so long with us; for the patriotic fervor, which at times glows so brightly on its pages; for its stunning battle scenes; for its equally charming depictions of both the temptations of the world and the joys of family life; for the staggering diversity of its characters and their general psychological sustainment; for the all-inspiring image of Natasha, so true and so attractive; for the astonishing poetry of all its dreams, semidreams, states of delirium, and premortality. And finally, for the fact that the best and noblest of the poem's heroes, Prince Andrey, is not a professor or an orator, but an elegant and brave soldier and a staunch idealist. I revere Count Tolstoy even for the force he used on me personally in making me know and love as close, living friends people who seem to me almost my contemporaries, dressed merely at the will of the author in the clothes of "Borodino" and transferred merely by the power of his genius half a century back in history. But after recalling, along with this, the sum of all that I have said, I feel I am justified in thinking that this is precisely what I was speaking of earlier: "A huge, precious, golden idol with three heads, a great number of arms, and eyes of rubies and diamonds—only not below the brow, but *on it* as well."

Of course, this means nothing so far as the over-all merit is concerned, as I have already said several times; but it means a great deal when it is a question of accuracy and strict realism.

The magnificent and colossal image of the Hindu Brahma is in its way as worthy as the Olympian Zeus. And there are not only moments, but even years and centuries, when the marvelous Brahma will please our hearts and minds much more than Zeus, who is, let us say, properly handsome, but who is, nevertheless, a person like everyone else. But here is the difference: one can admire an image of Brahma or Buddha, one can determine from it the world view of Hindu artists and priests, but one cannot also judge from this majestic piece of sculpture the actual appearance of the inhabitants of India. But from Zeus, the Laocoön, and the Gladiator, one can imagine, if only approximately, the appearance of the handsome people of ancient Greece and Rome. There is the difference, and a very important one it is for my primary objectives! Tolstoy's strength, remarkable even in its weaknesses, has carried me too far from these objectives. Unexpectedly even to myself, I put aside the questions of our community life and felt the irrepressible need to render a clear account (first and foremost to myself) of my aesthetic views on the works of our celebrated realist. I could not help realizing that in considering them also from this aspect, I think and feel something that I have not heard from others.

I repeat: with regard to the character depiction in *War and Peace*, this is not certainty, but merely question and doubt.

It is quite possible that if we were to undertake to pass the characters of Andrey Bolkonsky and especially of Pierre Bezukhov through a special type of intellectual filter, which I want to propose, they would turn out to be authentic and quite conceivable in their main contours, not only for the time of the Count's youth and my own, but also for the beginning of the nineteenth century. . . .

This filter would consist of:

(1) simplifying (mentally, in one's own mind) Tolstoy's language in general; making it more like the language of Pushkin's prose or the language of Tolstoy himself in the short tale "The Prisoner of the Caucasus" and other stories of his that are cleansed of naturalism.

(2) completely doing away with unnecessary peeping into the characters' souls.

(3) discarding from the narrative all those expressions, turns of speech, and epithets that smack too much of the post-Push-kin school, as well as all those peculiar repetitions character-istic of Tolstoy himself. . . .

(4) especially rejecting the possibility of idolizing Kara-tayev and the common people in general too much the way the Slavophiles idolized them in the forties and sixties.

If, as I say, we thus filter the very essence of the narrative, the very course of both the patriotic and domestic aspects of the drama; if on the bottom of our mental vessel, we retain the entire plot, all the events, and even a fairly large part of the characters' thoughts, words, and feelings—that is, how they fell in love, erred, rejoiced, raged, feared, et cetera; and if, on the filter, we leave all the sediment belonging to the Russian Natural School in general, as well as all those very fine hairs or little threads and those large, useless cobblestones that belong personally to Tolstoy—then it is quite possible in such a purification that not only Andrey Bolkonsky, but all the others—even the highly questionable Pierre Bezukhov—will turn out to be people as plausible for their time as Vronsky and Levin are for theirs.

Nevertheless, except for the too Slavophile regard for Karatayev, Karatayev himself is quite real. He could have ex-isted even in 1812. But Pierre's regard for him smacks of anach-ronism.

In this regard, I am even ready with joy to suspect my-self of a complex and false mental process such as this: I am listening to an opera on Turkish or French life. The libretto is taken from reality. The characters act in a way that is, in general, historically plausible and correct. But the music of this opera is neither in the Turkish nor the French style, but based entirely, let us say, on Russian melodies. And this confuses me. . . .

The general psychological music of this great novelist is

so much like the psychological music of our time in general and so unlike the accompaniments familiar to us from the time of the Consulate and the Empire that it automatically makes us also question the complete authenticity of the singers and actors.

Therein is my unresolved doubt. Doubt as to Lev Tolstoy's accuracy, and doubt also as to the critical legitimacy of my own demands.

Still another example.

Shakespeare's tragedies from ancient classical life (*Coriolanus* and *Julius Caesar*) can have a much stronger effect on contemporary readers and audiences than Sophocles' *Oedipus Rex* or *Antigone*. The feelings, passions, brilliance of the images, degree of psychological depth—all this in Shakespeare (the son of a more complex time) is perhaps much closer to our psychological make-up than it is in Sophocles. We can admire Shakespeare much more sincerely and understand him much more keenly in the depths of our soul. However, we still have the right to feel, think, and say that Sophocles imparts more of the true spirit of antiquity than Shakespeare does in *Coriolanus* and *Julius Caesar*.

I beg you to permit me one more comparison. It will be the last.

Let us assume that Count Alexey Tolstoy[1] constructed his trilogy (*Ivan, Fyodor,* and *Boris*) on more accurate historical and everyday-life facts than Pushkin did in *Boris Godunov*. I say, let's just assume; I do not know if this was so. Let's assume that it was. Moreover, there is no question that the trilogy stages better than *Boris Godunov*. Even when read aloud, it has a stronger effect on our feelings than Pushkin's simple and rather shallow tragedy.

But doesn't the very simplicity, shallowness, and bas-relief

---

[1] A. K. Tolstoy (1817–1875), a distant cousin of Lev Tolstoy. The dramatic trilogy referred to here (*The Death of Ivan the Terrible, Tsar Theodore,* and *Tsar Boris*) is his best-known work. [Tr.]

of *Godunov* convey incomparably more of Muscovite antiquity—which, in fact, was not very expressive—than does the bright relief of Alexey Tolstoy? Surely this, too, must be clear.

That is all I wanted to say.

I know that this work of mine has many repetitions and omissions (and in places perhaps even stupidities). I suspect that my indecision is, in some cases, very dull and my self-confidence, in others, too capricious. But I beg my readers and judges to forgive me these shortcomings in return for my sincerity and frankness.

PUSHKIN AND GOGOL[1]

VASILY ROZANOV

(1894)

⚱

I N the early chapters of my essay on Dostoevsky's *Legend of the Grand Inquisitor*, I had occasion to touch on Gogol's creative work, and in particular on his attitude toward reality, which, instead of repeating itself in our later writers, aroused their opposition. This thought encountered in our respected critic Mr. Nikolayev[2] several objections specifically intended to determine more accurately the significance of Gogol's personality and also of his creative work. Despite all that has been said on both sides, much still remains unclear and debatable about the subject itself; therefore, it seemed to me proper and not without interest to draw the reader's attention to it once again.

First of all, I consider it my duty to specify that I did not have Pushkin in mind when I said that not until the literature of a much later period (Turgenev, Count Tolstoy, et cetera) did living people make their appearance for the first time. I said this only in connection with Gogol himself, and not with what lay behind him. But about Pushkin, below; let us now return to the point of the matter.

[1] Apropos of Govorukha-Otrok's article, written under the pseudonym Yu. Nikolayev: "Something about Gogol and Dostoevsky."

[2] Later, apropos of the opinion I had expressed about Gogol, there appeared in our periodicals several more articles, part of which are of value. However, their general shortcoming lies in the fact that they do not at all examine either the nature of Gogol's creative work or my remarks about it.

I

Gogol is the progenitor of the ironic mood in our society and literature. He created the form and the type into which all our thoughts and feelings already have been flowing for several decades, while forgetting their original and natural direction. Ideas that he never expressed and feelings that he never aroused, but which sprang up long after his death, were all, however, formed according to one definite type, the source of which is in his works. Ever since we have had these works before us, everything that is not in Gogol's spirit has had no strength; and vice versa, everything that is in harmony with it, no matter how weak it inherently is, has been growing and acquiring strength. The spiritual life of an historically developing society took a sharp turn in his personality, after which, it went irresistibly in one path downhill, destroying some concepts and forming others, but all of them always of the same type. What was the significance of that turn? This question is answered, in particular, in Gogol's relation to Pushkin.

My critic compares them and finds them "equal." But, above all, they are heterogeneous. They cannot even be compared, and by generalizing under the single concept of "beauty" and "art," we completely lose sight of their inner relationship, which later developed in life as well as in literature, once they became an inseparable part of it. The versatile, many-sided Pushkin is the antithesis of Gogol, who moves in two directions only: one of intense and aimless lyricism, which withdraws upward to the realm of fancy; the other of irony, which is directed toward all that lies below. But in addition to this antithesis of form, or of outer contours, their creative work is also antithetical in its very essence.

Pushkin is, as it were, the symbol of life: he is all movement, and because of this, his creative work is so diverse. Everything that lives attracts him, and in approaching everything, he loves and incarnates it. His words are never unrelated to reality; they cover it, and by means of it become images and contours. It is he who is the *real founder of the Natural School*,[1] for he is always true to man's nature and true to his fate as well. There is nothing intense about him, no morbid imagination, no false emotion whatsoever.

Thence the individualism of his characters, which can never be reduced to general types. A type in literature is already a defect; it is a generalization—that is, a certain alteration of reality, albeit a very subtle one. People do not form types; they simply live in reality, each one his own particular life, each one bearing within himself his own purpose and significance. It is precisely this—man's inability to merge his person with that of another—which distinguishes him from all else in nature, where everything is grouped into genera and species, with only the local population being indivisible. Art should not touch this principal treasure in man—and in Pushkin, it does not touch it. Of our recent writers, only Count Lev Tolstoy was able to achieve this, and then only to an imperfect degree: as a result, he is considered the greatest representative of naturalism in our literature. But we must not forget that all this was already inherent in Pushkin, but for some reason or other, it went unnoticed.

At any rate, it is the surest sign in works of art that the life that has been transferred from reality has been preserved. But it is not only as an "incarnator" that Pushkin sets the norm for a correct attitude toward reality: his poetry contains directions as to how art itself, once it has embodied life, must act in reverse on it. In this action, there must be nothing accelerative or formative: poetry merely clarifies reality and warms it; it does not alter, distort, or deflect it from the tendency already embedded in the vital nature of man himself. It *does not hinder* life—and this, too, is due to the fact that it has none of that morbid imagination which often creates a second world

[1] All the italics in this essay are Rozanov's. [Tr.]

above the real one and then tries to adapt the first world to the second. Pushkin teaches us how to experience purer and nobler emotions; he cleans away all the "scale" that has accumulated on the spirit, but he does not impose any stifling form on us. And in loving his poetry, each person remains *himself*.

All this also makes his poetry the ideal for a normal, healthy development. In it are placed directions, which, if followed, will never divert life from its course, no matter how complex it becomes; it will become fuller, more diverse, and finally more profound: but from this, it will not lose either its former unity and integrity or its composure and serenity. Something different will be understood by it, and something different will be accomplished by it from what was understood and accomplished by it in Pushkin's time; but nothing that is understood by it will trouble the soul, and nothing that is accomplished by it will be ugly in its movements.

II

But then Gogol appeared. Although we do not distinguish types in the psychological development of people, we group everything of genius in creative art into a whole. And, in general, we think that it is not disassociated, but that it is inwardly harmonious, and that one part strengthens the other. But this is not so: only a genius can be harmful to another genius, especially a genius of a different or an opposite type. We know very well how Gogol began to grieve after Pushkin's premature death. At that time, *Dead Souls* was already taking shape in him, but it had not yet appeared, and the person who could have counterbalanced it with his later works was no longer alive. Without a doubt, the full mystery of genius is unknown even to its possessor: but the fact that he senses its power and knows its limits is clear. If we, after opening *Dead Souls* at random, do not hurry off to take care of some necessary business, but continue to turn page after page, it is obvious that the wonderful author of this book himself knew what a force was coming into the world with him. And he, the bearer of this force, was now alone. He knew—he could not help knowing—that he would expel Pushkin from the consciousness of the people, and along with him, everything that his poetry bore within itself. This was the origin of his anxiety, and it increased as the chapters of *Dead Souls* began to appear. In letters to friends, he tried to learn the impression that had been made on them. He asked what sort it was, but he himself remained stubbornly silent about the meaning of his poem. His rapidly spreading fame was of no interest to him. He withdrew deeper and deeper into himself, and the tone of his letters became more and more troubled and strange. One can say of genius more than of anything else that its center and direction lie in "other worlds"; but the person who is its personal bearer, nevertheless, sees and knows this direction, although he is helpless to interfere with it. Gogol burned the final chapters of *Dead Souls*, but even those that managed to come out distorted the spiritual countenance of our society by depicting it in an entirely different way from the one in which Pushkin had begun to depict it.

Why is it that one genius of equal merit is supplanted by another?[1] The explanation for this lies in the very essence of their heterogeneous creative work and in the particular effect each has on the soul. If we simultaneously open *Dead Souls* and *The Captain's Daughter* or "The Queen of Spades" and begin to compare them and to study the impression they make on us, we immediately notice that the impression made by Pushkin is not as stable. His words and scenes enter the soul like a wave, and, after refreshing and agitating it, they recede,

[1] The idea that Pushkin was ousted from the living consciousness of our society by the criticism of the sixties is completely unjust and degrading to his memory: *he was no longer being read* when this criticism appeared, and precisely for this reason, it was comprehensible to everyone. Just when did he *cease* to be read?

again like a wave: the mark made by them on our soul closes
and heals. On the contrary, the mark made by Gogol remains
fixed; it neither grows nor diminishes. As it was originally,
so it remains forever. How Sobakevich deliberately errs in
drawing up his list of dead souls, or how Korobochka fails
to understand Chichikov—all this we remember in detail, even
though we have read it only once, and a very long time ago
at that; but what actually happens to Herman in the card
game—in order to recall that, we must once again open "The
Queen of Spades." And this is even more surprising if we
take into account the continual sameness of *Dead Souls* and,
on the contrary, the originality and romantic nature of Pushkin's scenes. Where then is the secret of this peculiar power
of Gogol's creative work, and at the same time, of course, its
essence? Let us turn to the first page of *Dead Souls*:

> His arrival caused no commotion in the town whatsoever, and
> was not accompanied by anything in particular; only two Rus-
> sian peasants standing at the door of the tavern, opposite the
> hotel, made several remarks, which related, however, more to
> the carriage than to the person in it. "Look at that," said the
> one to the other. "What a wheel! What do you think, would that
> wheel make it to Moscow if it had to, or wouldn't it?" "Sure it
> would," answered the other. "Well, I don't think it would make
> it to Kazan." "No, it wouldn't make it to Kazan," answered the
> other. With that, the conversation ended. Furthermore, when the
> carriage drove up to the hotel, it passed a young man in white
> duck trousers, exceptionally tight and short, and a frock coat
> with claims to fashion, beneath which was visible a shirt front
> fastened with a Tula pin in the shape of a bronze pistol. The
> young man turned around, looked at the carriage, caught hold
> of his cap, which the wind had almost blown off, and then went
> his way.

If we closely examine the flow of this speech, we see that it
is lifeless. It is a waxen language in which nothing stirs, in
which not one word pushes forward or wants to say more

than is said by any of the rest. And no matter where we open the book, no matter which humorous scene we hit upon, we everywhere see this same dead tissue of language in which all the figures being portrayed are wrapped as if in their common shroud. And from this it follows that the thoughts of all these figures do not continue, that their impressions do not connect with each other. The figures all stand motionless, with the features they had when the author left them; they do not continue to grow—neither within themselves, nor in the soul of the reader on whom the impression is made. Hence the indelibility of this impression: it does not close, it does not heal, because there is nothing there that can grow. It is dead tissue, which will always remain in the reader's soul in the same form in which it was originally introduced there.

None of this was understood about Gogol, and he was considered the founder of "The Natural School," that is, a school whose writers supposedly *reproduce* reality in their works. It is only to this naïve assertion that my negative remarks apply, and their corroboration can be found in all the reminiscences of Gogol recorded by his friends: "In January, 1850," writes S. T. Aksakov, "Gogol once again read us the first chapter of *Dead Souls*. We were struck with amazement: the chapter seemed even better, as if it had been written anew. Gogol was very pleased with this impression and said: 'That's what it means when a painter has given the final touch to his picture. The corrections, apparently, are most insignificant: *a word cut here, one added there, one shifted in still another place*, [my italics], and everything turns out differently. Then one should publish, when all the chapters have been given the finishing touch.'"

The word "picture," that is, something *painted*, was evidently placed here by mistake: it is not a painter's brush or paints, filled with variety and life, which reproduce the variety of another reality; it is rather a *mosaic of words*, the one attached to the other, the secret of which was known to Gogol alone. Not only in our literature, but in world literature as well, he stands the lonely genius, and his world is unlike any other. He alone inhabited it. And for us to enter that world, to connect it with our life, or even to judge our life by the huge wax picture molded by this wonderful craftsman, would mean to attempt suicide.

In this picture, there are absolutely no live people: they are tiny wax figures, but they all make their grimaces so cleverly that we have long suspected them of actually moving. But they are motionless. Examine once again the excerpt quoted above: the cap is the only living person there who wants to live, and even it is restrained just in time. It is the author who moves their feet forward, turns them around, asks, and answers for them: they are incapable of doing it for themselves. And this is not at all because they are stupid; stupidity is the second thing here, it goes without saying, that results from the lifelessness. Recall Plyushkin: he is indeed an amazing character; but certainly not because of the original way in which he was conceived, but because of the original way in which he was executed. Right beside him stands the Avaricious Knight,[1] a living person from head to foot; a man who knows both what art is and what crime is, and this alone does he dominate with his passion. You can fear him, you can hate him, but you cannot help respecting him: he is a person. But is Plyushkin really a person? Can this word be applied to anyone with whom Chichikov had his talks and dealings? Like Plyushkin, they all came into this world in a special way having nothing in common with a natural birth. They were made from a waxen mass of words, and the secret of this artistic method of production was known only to Gogol. We laugh at them: but, remarkably enough, it is not the spirited laughter with which we respond to something we encounter in life and then reject or struggle against. Gogol's world is a world that has oddly withdrawn

[1] In Pushkin's little tragedy by the same name. [Tr.]

from us into the distance, a world which we observe through a magnifying glass. We are amazed at much that is in it, we laugh at it all, and what we have seen we never forget; but we never have anything in common with it, or anything that connects us with anyone we have seen in it, and not only in a positive sense, but in a negative one as well.

My critic points to the lofty, moral side of Gogol. Indeed, it cannot be valued too highly: what he decided to do had never been done by anyone else in history. We said earlier that the direction and source of genius least of all lie in the will of its individual possessor. But this person *can be fully aware of* his genius; he can *appraise it* for other people and for the future. Gogol *stifled his genius.* Is that not evidence enough of what it was?

III

Thanks to Pushkin's characters and thanks to recent literature, all of which has been trying to rehabilitate Pushkin while struggling against Gogol, this genius will die out sooner or later in our life as well. And, indeed, his irony for all living things has repeatedly caused the most ardent enthusiasm to grow cold. Recall Dostoevsky's speech at the Pushkin Celebration: at a moment of such ecstasy, of such enchantment on the part of everyone, he fell as if mowed down, when Gogol's corpses were flung at his feet. Hence the painful vexation with which he answered Professor Gradovsky.[1] He

---

[1] A. D. Gradovsky (1841–1889), a professor of law. He attacked Dostoevsky for ignoring the political reasons for the Russians' desire to "wander" and their lack of roots, two things Dostoevsky had stressed in his Pushkin Speech. Although Pushkin had indeed depicted the first Russian wanderer in Aleko, he had not, Gradovsky said, reproduced the gloomy world that these wanderers had rejected. That was done by Gogol—the great reverse side of Pushkin. Gogol had told the world why Aleko fled to the gypsies, why Onegin was bored, why the superfluous people immortalized by Turgenev came into this world. This, Gradovsky said, was a social problem, and it could not be solved by individual self-education, as Dostoevsky had preached. [Tr.]

realized that no matter how much more he might say, that no matter what dialectics he might resort to, none of this would be clear, but that those everlasting corpses were clear to everyone, and along with them, the truth that man can only despise his fellow man. And indeed everything in his polemic has been forgotten; no one remembers the details of the argument, but very likely everyone remembers the idea that in the old days, people of noble spirit had nowhere to go except to gypsy camps in order to escape the living corpses that inhabit the city. But the same thing could be said about every period: Gogol's unforgettable characters have separated people with an insurmountable barrier which forces them not to seek each other out, but to flee from each other; not to seek shelter, the one near the other, but to withdraw from each and every one. His rapturous lyricism, the fruit of an overtaxed imagination,[1] has caused everyone to love and respect only one's own dreams, and at the same time to feel a revulsion for all that is real, particular, and individual. All that lives no longer attracts us, and for that very reason, the whole of our life, our characters, and plans have become so filled with the fantastic. Read "Nevsky Prospect," that amazing combination of the coarsest realism and the most morbid

---

[1] In his early works, the nature descriptions are a complete analogy to this lyricism ("How entrancing, how splendid is a summer's day in the Ukraine," et cetera); they are always intense and always abstract; they present only the general panorama, not a collection of details, of which each is dear and attractive. If we were to compare them with the nature descriptions of Turgenev, for example, we would immediately note that Turgenev saw, knew, and loved nature: a multitude of details had evidently been *imprinted in his mind,* and he *reproduced* them, although perhaps unconsciously. In Gogol's descriptions, one senses a man who has *never even looked with curiosity at nature* (see also various reminiscences of him). In general, the remarkable thing about Gogol is that he viewed all phenomena and objects not in their reality, but *in their extreme:* thence the poetry of his Ukrainian stories, which is not at all like the simple reality of the Ukraine; thence his Petersburg tales, *Dead Souls,* and *The Inspector General,* which raise dull, ordinary life to the height of vulgarity. It was precisely with Gogol that our society began *to lose its sense of reality,* and it was from him that we *got our aversion to it.*

idealism, and you will understand that it was the prologue inaugurating a chain of events that made a very sad story. Great people live according to their psychological make-up, which disintegrates into the psychological make-up of millions of other people, from which tangible facts are then, of necessity, born.

Tranquillity—that is what we need most of all. There is no serenity in our consciousness, no naturalness in the expression of our emotions, no simplicity in our attitude toward reality. We are excited and alarmed, and this excitement and alarm reveal themselves in the convulsiveness of our actions and in the confusion of our thoughts. Given such a state, further development can reach great heights; but at the same time, it will never be a normal, healthy development.

Gogol indeed stands on the path to this natural development, which is not so accelerated, but which will definitely rise to greater heights. He stands on the path to it, not so much by virtue of his irony and lack of confidence in and respect for man as by virtue of the complete cast of his genius, which has become the cast of our soul and our history. His imagination, with its wrong attitude toward reality, and its wrong attitude toward fancy as well, has *corrupted* our hearts and *disrupted* our lives, after having filled both of them with the deepest of suffering. Surely we must admit this. Surely we are not so depraved already that we have begun to love real life less than the play of shadows in a mirror?

Fortunately, there are features in Gogol's creative work itself from which we can finally determine its essence. We shall return to specific fact to clarify all that has been said and to strengthen it to the point where it will apparently be invincible. By a certain inverse irony that ridicules the wisest of people, two child characters have been included in Gogol's skillfully executed poem. They are the famous Themistoklius and Alcides, unlike anything in the child's world, either real or poeticized. Surely we can imagine that *they* are pure and fine, and that they as yet have none of that "carnalization" of the spirit, about which Mr. Nikolayev speaks. And yet they are dolls, pitiful and ludicrous, like all the other figures in *Dead Souls*. Doesn't that plainly reveal to us the nature of the rest of the poem as well? "Suffer the little children to come to Me," said the Savior. Even He did not look on them with a condemning eye, but held out his arms and drew them to Him; just as He rebuked and instructed, but never ridiculed, the "carnal" in spirit. How, then, can we speak of a "religious height" in the light of which the famous satirist judged people? If it is a height, then it has nothing in common with the one from which Christ looked on man, where his Gospel and cross lie, and toward which, of course, nations must head in fleeing from all that delusively glitters at them from the opposite side—fortunately always from very different points.

HOW THE CHARACTER AKAKY
AKAKIYEVICH ORIGINATED

VASILY ROZANOV

(1894)

$

WHILE looking through Gogol's collected works in their classic edition prepared by our recently deceased scholar, N. S. Tikhonravov,[1] I happened to learn how and in what precise relation to reality the character Akaky Akakiyevich (in the story "The Overcoat") originated. (This character is so very typical of all Gogol's creative work, and one that, to a certain extent, combines in its features, if not all, at least the main characters created by him.) To my surprise, this information in Tikhonravov's edition unexpectedly and strikingly confirmed, and indeed by fact, all that I was trying to say earlier, while vaguely searching and perhaps falling into incidental error. Here is that fact, which needs almost no commentary: "In telling of a small circle of writers," says N. S. Tikhonravov, "that used to meet at Gogol's, mainly to discuss artistic events, P. V. Annenkov[2] notes that never, not even in the midst of lively and heated debate, did a continual look of observation leave Gogol's face; indeed, it seemed to have grown fast to it. Both here and in other spheres of Gogol's life, nothing went to waste. He would listen attentively to the remarks, descriptions, anecdotes, and observations of his circle, and it sometimes happened that he would use them. In this, and also in the free expression of its thoughts and opinions,

---

[1] N. S. Tikhonravov (1832–1893), a literary historian and professor of Moscow University. [Tr.]

[2] P. V. Annenkov (1812–1887), a literary critic and memoirist. He knew Gogol personally for many years, was on friendly terms with him, and, incidentally, sometimes copied certain of his works from their rough drafts (*Dead Souls*, for example). [Tr.]

the circle worked for him. Once, in Gogol's presence, someone told an office joke about *a poor government clerk, an ardent bird hunter, who, by extraordinary economizing and untiring, increased efforts over and above those required by his job, had accumulated enough money to buy a good Le Page rifle for about two hundred rubles. The first time he went out in his little boat on the Bay of Finland to hunt, he put his precious rifle in front of him on the bow, and then, according to his own assertion, found himself in a state of oblivion. He came to his senses only upon glancing at the bow and failing to see his new acquisition.*[1] The rifle had been pushed into the water somewhere along the way, as he passed through a thick patch of reeds, and all efforts to find it were futile. The clerk returned home, went to bed, and had to stay there: he had come down with a fever. *Only by a joint subscription on the part of his comrades, who had learned of the incident and bought him a new rifle, was he restored to life;* but he could never recall that terrible incident without a deathly pallor covering his face."

We can almost see this clerk, who, of course, received a tiny salary, toiling away over papers needed by people far more spiritually impoverished than he—a man who, in the stupid reality that had been created for him, was able, as if by hiding from it, to create for himself a new, sensible, and, to a certain extent, poetic reality: after all, a passion for hunting is, first and foremost, a passion for nature—something of a thoughtful regard for it, a keen perception of it. And none of his comrades around him blamed him for this *useless* attachment of his, undoubtedly because of their thoughtful consideration of him, and of his desire to get away from the city and out into nature: they did not criticize him irritably; they did not laugh at him, as they would have laughed at some ill-judged venture. Nor would they have remunerated him for the loss of some useless object. From their equally tiny

---

[1] All the italics in this essay are Rozanov's. [Tr.]

savings, and, of course, by denying themselves of necessities, they bought him another gun! Here, in this "collection," we sense their common pity for themselves and an awareness of the situation created for them and for thousands of similar persons by the genius of Speransky,[1] which has been described, summed up, and crowned by history—a genius, like a gigantic skeleton without muscles and without nerves, which lay down on living Russia around the beginning of the century and continues to this day to crush everything in it.

At any rate, in the spirit of the incident recounted in this circle of friends, there was not even the slightest indication *of lifelessness, of a dead inertia of the surroundings* in which it occurred. Nor did anything indicate *a spiritual "narrowness"* in the chief person mentioned in it.

"Everyone," continues Annenkov, "laughed at this anecdote, *which was based on actual fact*, with the exception of Gogol, who listened to it pensively and then lowered his head. The anecdote was the first idea for his wonderful story 'The Overcoat,' and it imprinted itself on his mind *that very evening*." Not in the least realizing the importance of the fact lying right in front of him and shedding light on all of Gogol's creative work, the learned editor concludes: "The meetings of the circle about which Annenkov speaks took place in Gogol's apartment on Malaya Morskaya, in Lepen's house. And Gogol lived in that apartment in 1834. Thus, the first idea for the story 'The Overcoat' embedded itself in Gogol's mind in 1834."

While examining Gogol's manuscripts in the minutest detail,

---

[1] M. M. Speransky (1772–1839), an adviser to Alexander I who planned numerous governmental reforms, among them the abolition of serfdom. Of the reforms realized, perhaps the most important was the establishment of the Council of State, a consultative body whose duties were to discuss the laws, principal measures of administration, and certain judicial cases.

Speransky was mainly opposed by the aristocracy for his determination to tax their class more effectively and to require examinations for the civil service. [Tr.]

Professor Tikhonravov discovered in the Moscow Public Museum all the successive drafts of the famous story, and among them, the first one, which had been copied by Pogodin,[1] and which the editor quotes in his annotations on the story's final text, along with all its corrections and words that are incomplete or, finally, crossed out, letter for letter. From this rough draft with its corrections, which is so short that one can see in it the work of no more than an evening or two, we can, as if being present in Gogol's very study, follow the working of his imagination on an incident provided by reality, and determine its full intrinsic meaning. Noting that the first manuscript (written on three pages of letter paper 8 vo) does not even include Akaky Akakiyevich's name, but merely contains a kind of artistic sketch of a nameless person who later on, in the episode of his christening finally does acquire a name for himself, we quote it in its entirety, indicating in brackets the words inserted in Gogol's own hand (above Pogodin's text):

A Story of a Clerk Who Stole Overcoats[2]

In the Tax Collection Department, which, by the way, is sometimes called the Department of Dirty Tricks and Nonsense, not because any dirty tricks were actually played there, but because clerks, like army officers, like to have a little joke now and then—and so, in this department, there served a clerk who *was not very good-looking—quite short, balding, pock-marked, with a reddish complexion, and even somewhat weaksighted.* [His work was irreproachable.] At that time, the decree that buttoned clerks up in uniforms had not yet been issued. He went around in a frock coat the color of gingerbread. He was [very] pleased with his job and the rank of titular councillor. He had no intentions of trying for collegiate assessor, and no hopes for an increase in salary. [He was what is known as an eternal titular

---

[1] M. P. Pogodin (1800–1875), a historian, publicist, and writer. [Tr.]

[2] It is curious that already in the very title, i.e., *in the theme* of the story that flashed through Gogol's pensive and lowered head, doubtless at the very moment the story was being told, or very soon thereafter, there is revealed the swift action of Gogol's creative imagination *to belittle and distort reality.*

councillor—a rank that, as is well known, has been made the
butt of many a joke by various writers whose works still amuse
various naïve readers who like to read a little from boredom or
just to pass away the time.] *Basically, this was a very kind creature, and what is known as a man of good intentions, for, indeed,
one almost never heard either a good or bad word from him. He
lived entirely for and enjoyed his official work,* and therefore
almost never paid any attention to his appearance; he even
*shaved without a mirror. There were feathers perpetually cling-
ing to his frock coat,* and when he walked down the street, he had
the peculiar knack *of being under a window at the very moment
when some rubbish was being thrown out; therefore, he always
carried away watermelon and cantaloupe rinds and other such
nonsense on his hat.* On the other hand, one really had to see
him *sitting at his desk in the office, copying.* One really had *to
see the pleasure that was expressed on his face. Certain letters
were his favorites,* and when he came to them, *his face simply
beamed with delight.* [Then he would experience such delight
as cannot be described: he would *give a little laugh, blink, and
bend his head completely to one side,* so that at times anyone
who felt like it could read each letter on his face—z, m, s, t. *His
lips would involuntarily press themselves together and then
slightly relax*; it seemed as if they even helped to a certain extent.
At those times, he would look at nothing else and listen to
nothing that was said: not even if one clerk were to tell another
that he had ordered a new coat, and even the price of the
material, or to arguments about who is the best tailor, about
Peterhof, about the theater, or even to that anecdote which is
extremely interesting, because it is fairly old and well known,
about how a certain commandant was told that the tail had been
cut off the statue of Peter the Great.] *He always came to the
office earlier than* the others. If there was nothing to copy, he
would file papers or sharpen quills. [Of course, that was very
little, but it was difficult to give him anything more important,
because *once when they tried to use him for a fairly important
job, namely [he was given] he was charged with taking a previously prepared document and making reference to a certain
government office—the whole job consisted in changing only the*

title and shifting all that was in the first person to the third, but
it gave him so much trouble that he perspired all over: he wiped
his brow, and finally asked them to give him something to copy.]
In brief, he served his country most zealously, but [all] he
obtained for his services [—it seems very little—] was a decoration for his lapel and hemorrhoids in his backside [—and that's
the extent of it]. Despite all that, very little respect was shown
him: *the other clerks made fun of him and scattered his head*
with bits of paper which they called snow; the older ones flung
documents at him, saying: "Here, copy these." The guards would
not even rise from their places when he passed by. His salary was
four hundred rubles a year. On that salary, he ate [had himself a
great deal of pleasure] something on the order of [cabbage soup
or gruel—God only knows what] and some dish made of beef,
[which smelled awful], and which was unmercifully seasoned
with onions; *he would lie on his bed to his heart's content* [would
loll about in his narrow little room] in his room over a shed in
Svechnoy Lane; he paid to have his trousers patched, almost
always [eternally] in one and the same spot—and all this was
done on those four hundred rubles, and he even had enough left
to have his boots soled once a year [for soles for his boots, *which*
he took very good care of, and therefore, when he was at home,
on his days off, he always went around in his apartment
in his stocking feet]. I really do not remember his name.
The fact is he would have been the first man on earth to
be satisfied with his lot, had it not been for a small, but very
unpleasant, occurrence. At the time when Petersburg shivers
from the cold, and when the twenty-degree frost sharply nips
the noses of even privy councillors of the first and second class,
the poor titular councillors are absolutely without any protection.
The clerk in question would somehow or other, as best he knew
how, cover his *nose*, which, by the way, was not a very remarkable one, but *rather flat* and *somewhat like the pastry called*
puffs, which Petersburg cooks make [for certain clerks]. He
would cover it with something that was more like a dressing
gown than an overcoat, something very difficult to classify and
very shabby. Long ago, he noticed that as time went on, the
overcoat seemed to keep him less and less warm. When it got

to the point where he could see right through it, even without
holding it up to the light, he decided to take it to a tailor [who
was just as well acquainted with this overcoat as with his own;
he knew perfectly the location of all the places that were weak
and worn through], who, despite his being *blind* in one eye [and
having *pockmarks* all over his body], did a fairly good job of
repairing the trousers and frock coats of officials and all others.

The first draft ends here. In examining it, as well as the
subsequent changes made in the story, and the final redaction,
we note that the essence of Gogol's method of depiction consists in selecting to go with an already-chosen feature—apparently the *thematic* one of the character being created—other
features that *are always similar*, and that only continue and
intensify it, strictly observing that *not even one disharmonious
or simply unrelated feature becomes mixed in* with them (in
Akaky Akakiyevich's face and body, everything is ugly; in his
character, everything is downtrodden). The combination of
these selected traits is like a pencil of similarly directed rays,
well focused by a concave mirror, and it strikes the reader's
memory brightly and unforgettably; but, of course, it is not
the natural, diffused light that we know in nature, but light
that is produced artificially in the laboratory. And to see a
figure, or more precisely one of its features, under a ray of
this light, when all its other features are left in total darkness,
means that we learn less about it than if we were to see the
complete figure, with all its features combined, under ordinary
light (our recent art). It is well known that the task of the
subsequent volumes of *Dead Souls* was to portray positive
characters; but, given the method of depiction characteristic of
Gogol, they would nevertheless have been a constriction of
reality, a simplification and watering-down of it (after all,
such are the characters Ulinka and Kostanzhoglo, which were
already begun). But we know that in the first volume of this
work, Gogol carried out only the negative half of the task
in which he was interested. Isn't it clear that we find here

not a constriction of man, but his *mutilation*, as against the way he is in reality?

From the alterations, we can note one general tendency in this process of character depiction: as soon as Gogol's imagination begins to work, he tries to capture in the picture the greatest possible number of objects; later, the unnecessary ones are discarded, and the action of the concave mirror is, as it were, concentrated, but what it does to the object standing before it is intensified. This can be partly seen from the additions included above in brackets, which were added in Gogol's own hand in the story's first text; but it is even more noticeable when compared with the final redaction. Thus, in the latter, the story's beginning is *simplified*:

> "In the Department of . . . , but perhaps it is better not to say in which department. . . ."

That is, the unnecessary phrases "dirty tricks and nonsense" and also "the clerks and army officers" have been discarded. On the other hand, there have been added to the pitiful figure of Akaky Akakiyevich in these same first lines a trait or two that further magnifies his ugliness.

> And so, in a certain department, there served a certain clerk— a clerk whom one could hardly call very remarkable; he was rather short, somewhat pock-marked, with rather reddish hair, rather poor eyes, and a small bald patch over his forehead, and *wrinkles along both cheeks and a complexion known as hemorrhoidal.*

Several lines later, the colors depicting both his physical appearance and his inner content are intensified as against those of the original draft and are brought to an unsurpassable degree of brilliance:

> His uniform was not green, but a sort of rusty-flour color. *The collar was rather tight and low,* so that his *neck,* even though it was not a long one, seemed unusually long when it stuck out of

the collar, *as with those plaster kittens* with nodding heads which foreigners carry about by the dozen on their heads and peddle in Russia. And there was *always something sticking to his uniform: either a bit of straw, or a thread.* . . .

But even when he did *look at something, he saw all over it nothing but his clear, evenly written lines,* and it was only when a horse pushed its nose, from heaven knows where, over his shoulders and from its nostrils blew a whole gust of wind on his cheek that he would notice that he was not in the middle of a line he was copying, but rather in the middle of the street. On coming home, he would quickly gulp down some cabbage soup . . . *without noticing its taste, but ate it all, flies and whatever else God may have sent him at the time.* When he noticed that his stomach was beginning to swell, he would get up from the table, *take out his bottle of ink and copy documents which he had brought home with him.* But if there was no homework, *he would deliberately, for his own pleasure, copy something for himself*—particularly, if he had a document which was remarkable, not for the beauty of its style, but because it was *addressed to some new or important person.* . . .

Having written *his fill, he would go to bed, smiling at the thought of the next day—wondering what God would send him to copy.*

Thus slipped by the peaceful life of a man who knew how to be content with his lot on a salary of four hundred rubles, et cetera.

There follows the transition to the "formidable enemy" of all such clerks—the northern frost—which is already included at the end of the story's first redaction; consequently, all these insertions were made on precisely the first draft of the story's beginning, which was quoted above.

Let us turn from the methods of this depiction to the artist doing the depicting himself. The words of the *first* draft which were *omitted* in later ones: *"Basically this was a very kind creature"* show us the point of view from which the portrait was drawn. One glance at it, and we understand precisely why a disparaging trait was chosen in the portrait being painted: a creature, devoid of principles and ideals, insensate—such was his theme. And yet it flashed through the artist's mind during a story showing precisely a man who was inspired, who was filled with thought and a feeling of joy over God's world. It is enough to recall the *self-oblivion* of the hunter, who had gone out on the smooth waters of the Bay of Finland after perhaps a long period of anticipation, and compare it with the *insensibility* of the chancery clerk (who, when crossing the street, notices that he is not in the middle of a line of writing only when a horse nuzzles his shoulder from behind) to understand *what relation Gogol's creative work had to reality, to understand the way it depicted reality.* Gogol not only did not reproduce reality in his works, but like a man who encounters its phenomena or hears of them, he was astonished by it; he recoiled and withdrew from it, as his clerks withdrew from the cold "into their shabby dressing gowns," into the strange world of morbid imagination, where, side by side with radiant characters such as his Annunziata in "Rome," there are emasculated characters such as Akaky Akakiyevich and others like him with their balding heads and wrinkled cheeks: but both these and the "radiant" characters are without life,[1] without natural light on themselves, without

---

[1] And indeed it is almost impossible to understand the character Akaky Akakiyevich without setting him off in your mind with this character Annunziata: "Try to look at lightning when it breaks through clouds black as coal and begins unbearably to flash a whole flood of bright light. Such are the *eyes* of the Albanian girl Annunziata. Everything about her reminds one of those ancient times when marble came to life, and chisels glistened in the sculptors' hands. A heavy braid of thick, pitch-black hair is wound in two rings on top of her head and spills down about her neck. No matter how she turns the radiant snow of her *face*, its image imprints itself completely on one's heart. If she stands in *profile*, an air of glorious nobility exudes from it, and the beautiful play of line surpasses anything ever created by a painter's brush. If she turns completely around, revealing the *back of her head*, with its lovely upswept hair, her gleaming *neck*, her *shoulders*, more beautiful than the world has ever seen before, then, too, is she a marvel. But she is most wonderful of all when she *looks* you straight in the eyes and sends cold pangs of anxiety through your heart. Her full *voice* resounds like brass. No lithe panther can

movement, without the capability of prolonged thought or of developing feeling.[1] He alone lived with these strange characters; he was burdened with them, and he expressed them. And in doing so, he himself believed, and by the power of his craftsmanship he made several generations of other people believe, that he was depicting not the fantastic and lonely world of his own soul, but the bright life playing before him, but which he never *saw, heard,* or *felt.*

However, if Gogol had left us only *Dead Souls* and *The Inspector General,* he would still be amazing as an artist, but he would not be great as a person as well. Over and above the chief characteristic which we have already noted in him— his *constriction and debasement* of man—there is another one, as result of which he became so incomprehensible and mysterious to everyone, and by which he attracts our hearts and invites the future to himself. Like the first characteristic, it enchants our minds and repels the past. This characteristic— and it, too, will now be explained by his rough drafts—is his endless *lyricism,* torn like all else from any connection with reality. To what does it relate? Only to the irony; it is linked

---

compare with her in strength, swiftness, or majesty of *movement.* Everything about her is the crowning achievement of creation—*from her shoulders* to her classically beautiful *feet,* and on down to the last *toes of these feet.* No matter where she goes, she always makes a picture in the eye of the beholder: whether she hurries at evening to the fountain with a hammered brass vase on her head," et cetera.

This is a description that moves in anatomical sequence, and at the same time, one that tries to become impassioned; it is a strict and merely inversely directed parallel to the character of Akaky Akakiyevich: the features of the one rise infinitely upward, those of the other downward— but they both *withdraw from reality* and are equally *devoid* of movement, *life,* and spirituality.

[1] It is remarkable that not one of Gogol's works shows a person in whom there is a development of passion, of character, et cetera. In his work, we know only *portraits,* a person *in statu,* not moving, not changing, not growing, not diminishing. And it seems that he regarded nature in the same way: he never described *a storm, the wind,* or even the *rustling* of leaves or grass. In all the vast panorama of his painting, nothing moves—and this, of course, is not without relation to the nature of his genius.

with the irony and without it would not have appeared. Gogol's lyricism is always nothing but pity, sorrow, and "invisible tears through visible laughter," which are somehow mixed in with this laughter: but it is remarkable that they do not precede, but always *follow* it. It is a feeling of deep pity for the person who has thus been depicted—the artist's sorrow for the law of his creative work, his lament for an amazing picture, which he could not draw otherwise (recall his *attempts* to write the second volume of *Dead Souls*), and having drawn it in this way he admires it, but at the same time he hates and despises it. We find an early glimmer of this lyricism in the story now under discussion. From the contents of the rough drafts, we are convinced that it did not exist at all in the original text— it appeared only as an *insertion* in the final one, i.e., after the actual work of *drawing* was already completed. We shall quote it in context with the insertion, so that the lack of any connection between the two is evident:

> The young clerks laughed at him and made jokes at his expense, to the best of their civil-service wit; they would even tell to his face various stories they had made up about him—about his landlady, an old woman of seventy, who, they said, beat him, and would ask when the wedding was to be; they would scatter bits of paper on his head, calling them snow.

And then, as if interrupting this torrent of ridicule, and striking the hand irresistibly depicting it, there is added in the side margin a sort of postscript, which was later pasted in the text:

> . . . but Akaky Akakiyevich never answered a word, as if there were no one there. It did not even affect his work: in the midst of all these annoyances, he never made a single error in his copying. It was only when the joke became too unbearable, when they bumped his arm and kept him from doing his work, that he would say: "Leave me alone! Why do you insult me?" *And there was a strange ring in these words and in the voice in which they*

were said. In that voice could be heard something that moved one to compassion—so much so that one young man, recently appointed, who followed the example set by the rest and permitted himself to ridicule him, suddenly stopped as though pierced to the quick, and from that time on, everything seemed to change and to appear in a different light; some unknown force seemed to repel him from the comrades with whom he had become acquainted because he thought they were decent, well-bred men. And for a long time afterward, during his happiest moments, he could visualize the little clerk with the bald spot on his forehead, and hear his heart-rending words: "Leave me alone! Why do you insult me?" And in these heart-rending words, he caught the ringing sound of others: "I am your brother." And the poor young man would bury his face in his hands, and many times later in life would shudder, seeing how much inhumanity there is in man, how much savage coarseness is hidden behind education and good breeding, and—Oh, God!—is even found in that very man society considers noble and honorable!

It would be hard to find a man who lived so much for his work. It is not enough to say that he worked with zeal—no, he worked with devotion. There, in that copying, he found a varied and pleasant world of his own. His face expressed delight; certain letters were his favorites, and when he came to them, he was beside himself with joy: he would smile, wink, and help with his lips so that it seemed as though every letter his pen was forming could be read in his face. If he had been rewarded according to his zeal . . . et cetera.

The same bits of paper continue to be scattered on the head of this "basically kind creature" as before. Beyond all doubt, the lyrical excerpt quoted above is an outburst of deep sorrow on the part of the author at the sight of what he has created; it is he who "shudders" upon completing a work of "savage coarseness," it is he who "buries his face in his hands" and repeats the words: "I am your brother," which ring in his ears, and which resound ever louder and louder in his soul as his creative genius rises to greater and greater creations in its maturity. We shall hear it, this lament of the artist for his soul, in the lyrical digressions of *Dead Souls*, in the speech of the first comic actor in "After the Play," in *The Inspector General*, and in the concluding line of "The Story of How Ivan Ivanovich Quarreled with Ivan Nikiforovich."[1] It rings out to us from numerous of his personal letters which are of the deepest significance, and finally, it muffles everything else, and drives out the remnants of any "laughter" from "An Author's Confession," "My Testament," and *Selected Passages from Correspondence with Friends*. And—there he is, the complete Gogol, in the totality of his image, with none of its features eliminated: a great man, in whom a mind of genius divorced itself from a simple heart and for a long time mastered him and stifled a natural tendency to protest against it. But in the end, Gogol managed to overcome it, to fetter and reject it, after a struggle that, however, cost him his life.

And if all this was incomprehensible about him, we should not be surprised: after all, to struggle with oneself is so alien to us, so incomprehensible. Could we understand and appreciate it in someone else? It always seemed to us that, like ourselves, he was "struggling against sad reality." With such a view, a good half of his activities were inexplicable about him. He is completely inexplicable as a person, what with his agonizing wandering from country to country, with his eagerness to flee his native land, with his prayers, his asceticism, his trip to Jerusalem, and his burning of the second volume of *Dead Souls*. Why should we be concerned about him? After

---

[1] It is curious that everywhere in his work where he is able to create characters that are not negative (in *Evenings on a Farm Near Dikan'ka*, *Mirgorod*, et cetera), these lyrical digressions are absent; yet, from the flow of speech, one would have expected him to rise to lyricism particularly here. And when he depicts something negative, it is only where the picture reaches the highest degree of vividness, the highest degree of tension (as in the case of Akaky Akakiyevich), that sorrow seizes the author's heart and expresses itself in a lyrical digression, addressed, according to the law of artistic objectivization, to the person being depicted, but which, in truth, refers *to the portrayal itself and the person doing the portraying*.

all, because of all this, he was beginning to be of assistance to *us*. But a great man is worthy of being considered as an individual. In the history of his soul, although it is unique, he is perhaps more important than a whole society in the history of its petty cares, troubles, expectations, and spite. And if, after having crowned his grave with stone and praise, and being ready to crown misunderstanding and vanity with bronze in spite of this changed view of him, we retract our opinion, then only those features that were imposed on him will disappear from his image, and he will remain for us in precisely that special grandeur which actually existed in him, and which he pointed out to us. But we never listened to what he said.

INDEX

[385]